W9-ARJ-219

Contemporary Higher Education

International Issues for the Twenty-First Century

Series Editor

Philip G. Altbach
Boston College

A GARLAND SERIES

Contents of the Series

The Academic Profession
The Professoriate in Crisis

Edited with an introduction by

Philip G. Altbach
Boston College

Martin J. Finkelstein
Seton Hall University

GARLAND PUBLISHING, INC.
A MEMBER OF THE TAYLOR & FRANCIS GROUP
New York & London
1997

Library of Congress Cataloging-in-Publication Data

The academic profession : the professoriate in crisis / edited with an
introduction by Philip G. Altbach and Martin J. Finkelstein.
     p.   cm. — (Contemporary higher education ; 1)
    Includes bibliographical references.
    ISBN 0-8153-2666-1 (alk. paper)
    1. College teaching—United States. 2. College teachers—United
States—Social conditions. 3. Universities and colleges—United
States—Sociological aspects. I. Altbach, Philip G.
II. Finkelstein, Martin J., 1949–   . III. Series.
LB2331.A286 1997
378.1'2'0973—dc21   97-26205
                                         CIP

Printed on acid-free, 250-year-life paper
Manufactured in the United States of America

Contents

Volume Introduction

by Philip G. Altbach and Martin J. Finkelstein

The Academic Profession Approaches the Turn of the Century

The story of the American academic profession in the post–World War II period has been one of dramatic growth and moderate diversification—largely paralleling the growth and diversification of the higher education enterprise in the United States. This was the period when most states established large public systems of higher education, upgraded normal schools to comprehensive colleges and regional universities, and created a system of two-year community colleges to meet the rising tide of student enrollments. A measure of this growth can be seen in the five-year period between 1965 and 1970, when the academic profession expanded by 150,000—more than the total professoriate in 1940 (Lipset and Ladd, 1979). By 1993, the National Center for Education Statistics counted over half a million full-time faculty, now joined by a growing cadre of some 350,000 part-time faculty (NCES, 1995).

Not only did the profession grow, but it diversified as well. Many faculty were hired in the professional and career fields (health sciences, business, education, and others) so that today a majority of the American faculty (some 53%) have disciplinary affiliations outside the traditional arts and sciences. Many more women and members of racial and ethnic minority groups were hired, especially in the decade of the 1980s and early 1990s, to address affirmative action imperatives. Many faculty were hired by institutions *outside* the research university sector (including comprehensive institutions and community colleges) to the point now where not much more than a quarter of the American professoriate functions in the traditional scholarly role of the professor at a research university. Finally, many faculty, largely in response to financial pressures, have been hired into a variety of nonregular (or, non-tenure-eligible) appointments as well as part-time appointments (Gappa and Leslie, 1993). Indeed, the most recent data from the National Center for Education Statistics suggest that over one-third of the headcount faculty are part-timers and that about one-fifth are in non-tenure-track positions—and that latter figure increases to about one-third among those entering the profession in the last seven years (Finkelstein, Seal, and Schuster, 1996).

In the face of such diversification, the American academic profession has so far maintained a basic cultural and social cohesion. It is embedded in a complex historical, organizational, and disciplinary tradition that significantly shapes the conditions of work and the norms of the professoriate. Change in the basic orientation of the profession is slow. The professoriate is the historical embodiment of the idea of the university, and has protected its traditions and prerogatives. It has been pointed out that academics may be more liberal in their political attitudes than the rest of society, but at the same time they tend to be conservative when it comes to issues relating to university reform or change.

The academic profession is also shaped by what is perceived as the dominant academic model. David Riesman has written of the "meandering academic procession," in which the research universities dominate the rest of academe in a hierarchical fashion (Riesman, 1958). This, he argues, has limited the diversity of American higher education and has meant that the professoriate tends to value research as the highest goal, even in institutions without a research mission. The traditional arts and sciences disciplines are perceived at the top of the hierarchy—with scholars who identify more with their disciplines than with their institutions seen as the most prestigious. Alvin Gouldner (1957, pp. 281–303) analyzed the differences between the discipline-oriented and more mobile "cosmopolitans" and the institution-specific and often more teaching-focused "locals." It is clear from these and other analyses that the academic profession is differentiated, varied, and difficult to change. Its innate conservatism has protected the universities from fads and fashions, but at the same time has made it quite difficult for academic institutions to adapt to changing circumstances.

This basic cohesion is, however, under increasing pressure. The wave of faculty hired in the late 1960s and early 1970s to support growth will by the year 2000 be reaching their sixties—what has until the recent uncapping been the traditional retirement age. It seems likely that with the possible exception of those at the research universities, most will either retire or substantially cut back their institutional commitments. That means that most of those who brought with them the individualistic, research-oriented ethos that has defined American higher education over the past two generations will be exiting and a new academic generation will be entering. While it is still too early to predict what kind of influence this new generation will exert on the system (see Finkelstein, Seal, Schuster for a preliminary assessment), it is nonetheless clear that their overall influence is likely to be substantially lower in light of the powerfully determinative *external forces* that have already begun to operate on the system. These include:

Economic shifts. The United States is moving from an industrial to an information-based economy and finds itself now competing in global markets. This has placed a premium on the preparation of a competitive work force, and colleges, universities and their faculties will find it increasingly necessary to orient their work, especially their teaching, to these objectives.

Technological shifts. The past five years in particular have witnessed a revolution in the dominant technology of academic work. Scholars increasingly rely on digital technology for accessing information and for communicating with colleagues and students. Teaching practices have historically proven extremely resistant to change, but indications are that new technologies are gaining acceptance in the classroom as well. For example, in the early 1990s, barely 10 percent of the professoriate used digital technology in their teaching; by 1995 that figure had jumped to 30 percent (Green, 1996).

In the last quarter century, then, the vast majority of the American faculty faced a bewildering mix of external forces that is already beginning to change the rules governing academic careers and the expectations for academic work. Thus, while American academics continue by and large to be satisfied with their careers and the intrinsic qualities of academic work, factors such as a move to regulate workloads, tenure reviews, static salary growth, and a declining job market have all affected morale, and have generated a growing list of complaints.

Current Challenges and Future Trends

Unquestionably, the post–World War II "golden age" of the professoriate is at an end, and general conditions for the profession are changing in ways we do not yet fully understand (Altbach, 1995). The following elements are part of the equation.

• Accountability will inevitably increase. Professors, once used to considerable autonomy in shaping their research, teaching, and their career options, will be increasingly constrained by the needs of employing institutions and subject to the measurement of output. Academic labor will be more carefully monitored and controlled.

• There will be a greater emphasis on teaching, although research productivity will remain the "gold standard." There has been a strong demand to reconfigure the system of academic rewards and to "open up" the system. The quality of teaching will be emphasized more, and it is likely that most faculty will do more teaching. Average teaching loads will increase.

• While the tenure system will not be abolished, it may be circumvented for many entering the profession. It is interesting that as the demands for the abolition of tenure that were common in the 1970 have abated, and a significant proportion of the full-time professoriate is tenured—an artifact of the aging of the profession—"tenure-track" positions are becoming less of the norm. There has been a rapid expansion of part-time faculty who have no possibility of regular appointments. Alternative career paths are being proposed and even implemented. Renewable contracts and long-term non-tenure-track positions are increasingly common. It is likely that these trends will increase as institutions strive for greater flexibility in resource allocation in the face of continued financial difficulties. The proportion of full-time tenure-track and tenured faculty will drop.

• Pressures to generate external funding will continue to increase, mainly in the research university sector. Academics have been asked to obtain funds through consulting, service to local industry and commerce, research, and other revenue-generating schemes. As academic institutions, especially in the public sector, find their budgets constrained, they seek other funding sources—and this will inevitably involve the professoriate. The demand for "university-industry linkages," common in higher education, is a part of this trend.

• The environment of research funding is not only indicative of other changes in the fiscal reality for higher education, but of other factors as well. Basic research is less emphasized as government funding diminishes and as the quest for "results" and immediate payoff takes precedent. For a half-century or more, universities were seen as the home of basic research—scientific research that would yield results in the long term but might have little immediate benefit. Funders are now less willing to support this kind of research. Accountability for research results is an increasing part of the pattern.

    • The academic profession will increasingly lose power in the context of accountability and budgetary difficulties. In a difficult job market with limited mobility at the upper levels of the profession, academics are simply at a disadvantage. Those who have control over the budget will gain the upper hand—senior administrators will inevitably wield more authority, and the faculty will have less control over the university. One of the implications of this trend will be a lessening of autonomy for individual faculty.

    • The differentiation between the "haves" and the "have nots" among institutions and in the academic profession will continue, and perhaps even become exacerbated. The "research cadre"—those senior professors located mainly at the top fifty to seventy-five American universities, with a strong commitment to research, access to external funding, and low teaching loads—will find that their working conditions may deteriorate modestly, but that they will be able to continue functioning with minimal alteration. The significant declines will occur at the second-tier institutions. It is likely that the system will be further segmented by the expansion in the number of "non-tenure-track" full-time contract faculty hired mainly to teach, and of the continued growth of part-time faculty, creating a "three-class" professoriate.

    • The sense of community, on the decline since the 1950s, will further deteriorate as the professoriate is divided demographically and by competing interests, increasingly differentiated institutions, and other forces.

    These factors do not constitute a revolution in the academic profession, and we foresee academic life in the American university continuing on largely as before. Yet, the pressures on the academic profession will be unprecedented and significant change will inevitably take place. The new realities will affect different segments of the profession in different ways—but there is no doubt that we are in a period of challenge.

The Nature and Purpose of the Current Volume

In the context of the ascendance of the academic profession during the post–World War II period, it is not surprising that academics have come to command increasing research attention. Indeed, the literature on the academic profession has dramatically expanded in recent years. A decade ago, one of us was able to synthesize much of the research on the American professoriate up to that time in a single volume (Finkelstein, 1984). It would now be considerably more difficult to coherently summarize the available research. The social science literature on the profession began in earnest following the Second World War, with Logan Wilson's pioneering study, *The Academic Man* (Wilson, 1995, originally published in 1942). There are, of course, a few pioneering studies, such as Thorstein Veblen's *The Higher Learning in America*, originally published in 1918, but the literature is remarkably limited prior to the 1950s.

    This dramatic growth has taken place for a number of reasons. The most significant among these is that the academic enterprise has itself become a major force in society, accounting for considerable resources and playing central roles not only in educating more than half of the relevant age group, but also conducting much of the research on which the postindustrial economy is based. The development of the field of higher education studies and of institutional research has also contributed to the expansion of the literature in the field of higher education, and on the academic profession specifically. There is now a considerable literature dealing with most aspects of the professoriate. We know the general configurations of the attitudes of professors over a period of more than three decades. There have been a number of studies of academic work and work styles. There is a growing literature concerning teaching and learning, although it is perhaps significant that research on this topic has been slower to develop, perhaps reflecting the emphasis on research that has dominated academic thinking from the 1950s until quite recently.

This volume includes a collection of essays that have been selected to illuminate the most critical aspects of the professoriate's growth and diversification from a variety of theoretical and disciplinary perspectives. Section I includes a more detailed overview of the historical development and current status of the academic profession by each of the editors. Section II examines the structure of academic careers, including chapters on the strands, and stages of the career, job mobility, the case of nonregular appointments and part-time faculty roles. Section III focuses on the norms that constitute academic culture and the socialization into academic careers. It includes discussions on academic culture and socialization, the experience of women academics, faculty in community college settings, and analyses of academic freedom and tenure issues. Section IV examines the reward structure of the academic career and the operation of the academic marketplace. Finally, Section V includes several treatments of substantive aspects of academic work, that is, teaching and research activities.

Understanding the contemporary academic profession is not an easy task. It is hoped that this volume will provide a compact guide to the best of what we know.

References

Altbach, Philip G. 1995. "Problems and Possibilities: The U.S. Academic Profession," *Studies in Higher Education* 20, no. 1: 27–44.

Boyer, Ernest L. 1990. *Scholarship Reconsidered*. Princeton, N.J.: Carnegie Foundation for the Advancement of Teaching.

Finkelstein, Martin, Robert Seal, and Jack Schuster. 1996. "The American Faculty in Transition: A First Look at the New Academic Generation." Preliminary Report to the National Center for Education Statistics.

Finkelstein, Martin J. 1984. *The American Academic Profession: A Synthesis of Social Scientific Inquiry Since World War II*. Columbus: Ohio State University Press.

Gappa, Judith M. and David W. Leslie. 1993. *The Invisible Faculty: Improving the Status of Part-Timers in Higher Education*. San Francisco: Jossey-Bass.

Gouldner, Alvin. 1957. "Cosmopolitans and Locals: Toward an Analysis of Latent Social Roles–I" *Administrative Science Quarterly* 2 (December): 281–303.

Green, Kenneth C. 1996. "Technology Use Jumps on College Campuses." (Claremont, Calif.: The Campus Computing Project, Claremont Graduate School (January).

Haas, Gene. 1996. "The American Academic Profession," in *The International Academic Profession: Portraits from 14 Countries*, ed. Philip G. Altbach. Princeton, N.J.: Carnegie Foundation for the Advancement of Teaching.

Lipset, Seymour M. and Everett C. Ladd. 1979. The Changing Social Origin of American Academics. In

Qualitative and Quantitive Social Research, edited by Robert Merton, James Coleman, and Peter Rossi. New York: Free Press.

National Center for Education Statistics. 1995. *Faculty and Instructional Staff: Who Are They and What Do They Do?* Washington, D.C.: U.S. Department of Education.

Reisman, David. 1958. *Constraint and Variety in American Education.* Garden City, N.Y.: Doubleday.

Shils, Edward. 1983. *The Academic Ethic.* Chicago: University of Chicago Press.

Veblen, Thorstein. 1993. *The Higher Learning in America.* New Brunswick, N.J.: Transaction. Originally published in 1918.

Wilson, Logan. 1995. *The Academic Man.* New Brunswick, N.J.: Transaction. Originally published in 1942.

Historical Context

Problems and Possibilities: the US academic profession

PHILIP G. ALTBACH

School of Education, Boston College, MA

ABSTRACT   *The US professoriate is a large and differentiated group, numbering some 600,000 in more than 3000 colleges and universities. The profession is organized hierarchically, with scholars at the top 100 research-oriented universities wielding the most influence. Yet, faculty members at liberal arts college, comprehensive universities and the more than 25% of the profession who teach in the 2-year community college sector also constitute important segments of US academia. The academic profession faces difficult and, in some ways, unprecedented challenges in the final years of the century. Cutbacks in resources have been combined with steady or increasing enrollments. Research funds are more difficult to obtain. There are efforts to redefine the role of the professor and to place more emphasis on teaching and less on research. Despite these pressures, however, the US academic profession remains quite stable. The tenure system is firmly established and academic freedom is not in jeopardy. Yet, around the edges change is taking place. For example, the number of part-time faculty has dramatically increased and there has been a significant move from basic to applied research funding. The future of the US professoriate is not bright, nor is it disastrous.*

Introduction

US higher education is in a period of unprecedented decline. Financial cutbacks, enrollment uncertainties, economic recession, pressures for accountability, and confusion about academic goals are among the challenges facing US colleges and universities at the end of the twentieth century. The situation is in many ways quite paradoxical. The US academic model is the most successful in the world—it is admired internationally because it has permitted wide access to higher education while maintaining some of the best universities in the world. Yet, higher education has come under widespread criticism. Some have argued that the academic system is wasteful and inefficient and that the professoriate is at the heart of the problem [l]. Others have urged that higher education reconsider its priorities and place more emphasis on teaching, arguing that the core function of the university has been underemphasized as the professoriate has focused on research [2]. Again, the professoriate is central to this criticism.

A combination of economic recession, the restructuring of the US economy, and a popular revolt against paying for public services, including education, have contributed to the pervasive fiscal problems that colleges and universities face. While the economic recession has eased, most observers believe that higher education will not fully recover financially in the foreseeable future. It has been argued that higher education's 'golden age'—the period of strong enrollment growth, increasing research budgets and general public support-is over [3]. This will mean that the academic profession, as well as higher education in general, must

0307-5079/95/010027–18 © 1995 Society for Research into Higher Education adjust to new circumstances. This adjustment, which has already begun, is difficult under any circumstances, but it is all the more troubling to the professoriate because it comes directly following the greatest period of growth and prosperity in the history of US higher education.

The US professoriate has been profoundly influenced by the social, political and economic context of higher education. While academia has relatively strong internal autonomy and, with some exceptions, a considerable degree of academic freedom, societal trends and public policy have played a major role in shaping institutions of higher education as well as national and state policies concerning academia. There are many examples. The Land Grant Acts in the 1860s stimulated the expansion of public higher education and an emphasis on both service and research, while the G.I. Bill following World War II stimulated the greatest and most sustained period of growth in the history of US higher education. Court decisions regarding the role of government in private higher education, race relations, affirmative action, the scope of unions on campus, and other issues have had an impact on higher education policy. Because education is a basic responsibility of the states, the actions of the various state governments have been primary, ranging from governmental support for the Wisconsin Idea in the nineteenth century in that state to the promulgation of the California Master Plan in the 1960s. In New York and Massachusetts, and elsewhere, state policies in the post-war period had a profound influence on the shape of post-secondary education and on the professoriate [4]. A recurring theme in this essay is the tension between the autonomy and 'internal life' of the academic profession, on one hand, and the many external forces for accountability that have shaped the direction of US higher education, on the other.

Precisely because the university is one of the central institutions of post-modern society, the professoriate finds itself subject to pressures from many directions. Increasingly complicated accounting procedures attempt to measure professorial 'productivity'—as part of the effort to increase accountability. But there is so far no way to measure accurately the educational outcomes of teaching. Calls for the professoriate to provide 'social relevance' in the 1960s were replaced in the 1980s by student demands for vocationally oriented courses. A deteriorating academic job market raised the standards for the award of tenure and increased the emphasis on research and publication. At the same time, there were demands to devote more time and attention to teaching.

A constant tension exists between the traditional autonomy of the academic profession and external pressures. The processes of academic promotion and hiring remain in professorial hands, but with significant changes, including affirmative action requirements, tenure quotas in some institutions, and the occasional intrusion of the courts into promotion and tenure decisions. The curriculum is still largely a responsibility of the faculty, but the debates over, for example, multicultural courses and vocational courses affect curricular decisions. Governmental agencies influence the curriculum through grants and awards. The states engage in programme reviews and approvals and through these procedures have gained some power in areas traditionally in the hands of the faculty.

The academic profession has been largely ineffective in explaining its centrality to society and in making the case for traditional academic values. Entrenched power, a complicated governance structure, and the weight of tradition have helped to protect academic perquisites in a difficult period. But the professoriate itself has not articulated its own ethos [5]. The rise of academic unions helped to increase salaries during the 1970s, but has contributed to an increasingly adversarial relationship between the faculty and administrators in some universities [6].

The unions, with the partial exception of the American Association of University Professors, have not effectively defended or articulated the traditional professorial role. Few have effectively argued that the traditional autonomy of the faculty and of faculty control over many key aspects of academic governance should be maintained. We are in a period of profound change in US higher education, and it is likely that these changes will result in further weakening of the power and autonomy of the professoriate. This essay focuses on the interplay of forces that have influenced the changing role of the US academic profession.

A Diverse Profession

The US professoriate is large and highly differentiated, making generalizations difficult. There are more than 370,000 full-time faculty members in 3535 institutions of post-secondary education. Almost 1400 of these institutions grant baccalaureate or higher degrees and 213 give the doctoral degree. More than a quarter of the total number of institutions are community colleges. A growing number of faculty are part-time academic staff, numbering at least 200,000 nationwide. They have little or no job security and only tenuous ties with their employing institutions. The proportion of part-time staff has been growing in recent years, reflecting fiscal constraints. Faculty are further divided by discipline and department. While it is possible to speak broadly of the US professoriate, the working life and culture of most academics is encapsulated in a disciplinary and institutional framework. Variations among the different sectors within the academic system—research universities, community colleges, liberal arts institutions, and others—also shape the academic profession [7]. The differences in working styles, outlooks, remuneration, and responsibilities of a senior professor at Harvard and a beginning assistant professor in a community college are enormous. Further distinctions reflect field and discipline: the outlooks of medical school professors, on the one hand, and scholars of medieval philosophy, on the other, are quite dissimilar.

A half-century ago, the academic profession was largely white, male and Protestant. It has grown increasingly diverse. In recent years, the proportion of women in academia has grown steadily and is now 29% of the total, although women tend to be concentrated at lower academic ranks and suffer some salary discrimination [8]. Yet, it is a fact that the proportion of women in the academic profession has increased by only a few per cent since the 1930s, despite the existence of affirmative action programs. Racial and ethnic minority participation has also grown, and while Asian Americans well represented in the academic profession, African Americans and Hispanics remain proportionately few. African Americans constitute only around 3% of the total professoriate, and they are concentrated in the historically black colleges and universities [9]. Racial minorities number about 9% of the total academic profession. The substantial discrimination that once existed against Catholics and Jews has been largely overcome, and there has been a modest decline in the middle- and upper middle-class domination of the academic profession [10]. Despite these demographic changes and expansion in higher education, the academic profession retains considerable continuity in terms of its overall composition.

Without question, any consideration of the role of the professoriate must take into account the demographic, cultural, disciplinary and other variations in the academic profession. If there ever was a sense of community among professors in the United States, it has long since disappeared. Some elements are common to the academic profession, but these grow weaker as numbers increase and the profession becomes more diverse.

5

The Historical Context

The academic profession is conditioned by a complex historical development. Universities have a long historical tradition, dating to medieval Europe, and the professoriate is the most visible repository of this tradition [11]. It should be noted that while national academic systems differ, all stem from common roots in Europe. The vision of professorial power that characterized the medieval University of Paris, the power of the dons at Oxford and Cambridge, and the centrality of the 'chairs' in the nineteenth-century German universities are all part of the history of US higher education. The medieval origins were instrumental for the recognition of the self-governing nature of the professorial community and the idea that universities are 'communities of scholars'. Much later, the reforms in German higher education in the nineteenth century greatly increased the power and prestige of the professoriate, while at the same time linking both the universities and the academic profession to the state [12]. Professors were civil servants and the universities were expected to contribute to the development of Germany as a modern industrial nation. Research, for the first time, became a key responsibility for universities. The role and status of the academic profession at Oxford and Cambridge in England also had an impact on the US professoriate, since the early US colleges were patterned on the British model and the USA, for many years, was greatly influenced by intellectual trends from Britain [13].

These models, plus academic realities in the USA, helped to shape the US academic profession. To understand the contemporary academic profession, the most crucial period of development begins with the rise of land-grant colleges following the Civil War and the establishment of the innovative, research-oriented private universities in the last decade of the nineteenth century [14]. Several aspects of the development of the modern US university are critical to the growth of the academic profession. The commitment of the university to public service and to 'relevance' meant that many academics became involved with societal issues, with applied aspects of scholarship, and with training for the emerging professions and for skilled occupations involving technology. The contribution of the land-grant colleges to US agriculture was the first and best known example. Following the German lead, the new innovative private universities (Johns Hopkins, Chicago, Stanford and Cornell), followed a little later by such public universities as Michigan, Wisconsin and California, emphasized research and graduate training. The doctorate soon became a requirement for entry into at least the upper reaches of the academic profession—earlier, top US professors obtained their doctorates in Germany. The prestige of élite universities gradually came to dominate the academic system, and the ethos of research, graduate training, and professionalism spread throughout much of academia. As these norms and values gradually permeated the US academic enterprise, they have come to form the base of professional values in the late twentieth century.

The hallmark of the post-World War II period has been massive growth in all sectors of US higher education. The profession tripled in numbers, and student numbers expanded just as rapidly. The number of institutions also grew, and many universities added graduate programs. Expansion characterized every sector from the community colleges to the research universities. Expansion was especially rapid in the decade of the 1960s, a fact that has special relevance for the 1990s, for many academics hired at that time will soon be retiring, creating an unprecedented generational shift in the academic profession. Expansion became the norm, and departments, academic institutions, and individuals based their plans on continued expansion.

But expansion ended in the early 1970s, and a combination of circumstances, including broader population shifts, inflation, and government fiscal deficits, all brought the expansion to an end. Part of the problem in adjusting to the current period of diminished resources is the very fact that the previous period was one of unusual expansion and was a temporary condition. Indeed, it can be argued that the period of post-war growth was an aberration and that the *current* situation is more 'normal [15]. The legacy of the period of expansion is quite significant for understanding contemporary realities.

Expansion shaped the vision of the academic profession for several decades, just as prolonged stagnation now affects perceptions. Post-war growth introduced other changes, factors that came to be seen as permanent, when in fact they were not. The academic job market became a 'sellers market' in which individual professors were able to sell their services at a premium. Almost every field had a shortage of teachers and researchers [16]. Average academic salaries improved significantly and the US professor moved from a state of semi-penury into the increasingly affluent middle class [17]. The image of Mr Chips was replaced by the jet-set professor. University budgets increased and research-oriented institutions at the top of the academic hierarchy had unprecedented access to research funds. The space program, the Cold War, rapid advances in technology, and a fear in 1958 (after Sputnik) that the USA was 'falling behind' in education contributed to greater spending by the federal government for higher education. Expanding enrollments meant that the states also invested more in higher education and that private institutions also prospered.

The academic profession benefited substantially. Those obtaining their doctorates found ready employment. Rapid career advancement could be expected, and inter-institutional mobility was fairly easy. This contributed to diminished institutional loyalty and commitment. In order to retain faculty, colleges and universities lowered teaching loads. The average time spent in the classroom declined during the 1960s. Salaries and fringe benefits increased. Access to research funds from external sources increased substantially, not only in the sciences but also to a lesser extent in the social sciences and humanities. The availability of external research funds made academics with such access less dependent on their institutions. Those few professors able to obtain significant funds were able to build institutes, centers, and in general to develop 'empires' within their institutions.

Rapid expansion also meant unprecedented growth in the profession itself, and this has had lasting implications. An abnormally large cohort of young academics entered professorial ranks in the 1960s. This extraordinarily large academic generation is now causing a variety of problems relating to its size, training and experiences. With the end of expansion, this large group has, in effect, limited entry to new scholars and has created a 'bulge' of tenured faculty members who will retire in massive numbers in the 1990s. Many in this cohort participated in the campus turmoil of the 1960s and were affected by it. Some graduated from universities of lower prestige which began to offer doctoral degrees during this period and may not have been fully socialized into the traditional academic values and norms. But this generation expected a continuing improvement in the working conditions of higher education. When these expectations were dashed with the changing circumstances of the 1970s, morale plummeted and adjustment has been difficult.

A final influence of the recent past is the turmoil of the 1960s. A number of factors converged in the turbulent 1960s that contributed to emerging problems for higher education. The very success of the universities in moving to the center of society meant that they were taken more seriously. In the heady days of expansion, many in the academic community thought that higher education could solve the nation's social problems, from providing mobility to minorities to suggesting solutions to urban blight and deteriorating standards in the public schools. It is not surprising, in this context, that the colleges and universities became involved in the most traumatic social crises of the period, that is the civil rights struggle and the Vietnam War. The anti-war movement emerged from the campuses and was

7

most powerful there [18]. Student activism came to be seen by many, including government officials, as a social problem for which the universities were to be blamed. Many saw the professors as contributing to student militancy.

The campus crisis of the 1960s went deeper than the anti-war movement. A new and much larger generation of students, from more diverse backgrounds, seemed less committed to traditional academic values. The faculty turned its attention from undergraduate education, abandoned in *loco parentis*, and allowed the undergraduate curriculum to fall into disarray. Overcrowded facilities were common. The overwhelming malaise caused by the Vietnam War, racial unrest, and related social problems produced a powerful combination of discontent. Many faculty, unable to deal constructively with the crisis and feeling under attack from students, the public, and government authority, quickly became demoralized. Faculty governance structures proved unable to bring the diverse interests of the academic community together. This period was one of considerable debate and intellectual liveliness on campus, with faculty taking part in teach-ins, and a small number becoming involved in the anti-war movement. However, the lasting legacy of the 1960s for the professoriate was largely one of divisiveness, and the politicization of the campus.

The Sociological and Organizational Context

Academics are at the same time both professionals and employees of large bureaucratic organizations. Their self-image as independent scholars with considerable control over their working environment is increasingly at odds with the realities of the modern US university [19]. Indeed, the conflict between the traditional autonomy of the scholar and demands for accountability to a variety of internal and external constituencies is one of the central issues of contemporary US higher education. The rules of academic institutions, from stipulations concerning teaching loads to policies concerning the granting of tenure, govern the working lives of the professoriate. Despite the existence, in most institutions, of the infrastructures of collegial self-government, academics feel themselves increasingly alienated from their institutions and somewhat demoralized. For example, two-thirds in a recent poll described faculty morale as fair or poor, and 60% had negative feelings about the 'sense of community' at their institution [20].

Academics continue to exercise considerable autonomy over their basic working conditions, although even here pressures are evident. The classroom remains virtually sacrosanct and beyond bureaucratic controls. Professors have considerable say over the use of their time outside of the classroom. They choose their own research topics and largely determine what and how much they publish, although research in some fields and on some topics requires substantial funding and therefore depends on external support. There are considerable variations based on institutional type, with faculty at community colleges and at unselective teaching-oriented institutions subject to more restraints on autonomy than professors at prestigious research universities.

As colleges and universities have become increasingly bureaucratized and as demands for 'accountability' have extended to professors, this sense of autonomy has come under attack. The trend toward decreased teaching loads for academics during the 1960s has been reversed, and now more emphasis is placed on teaching and, to some extent, on the quality of teaching. Without question, there is now considerable tension between the norm (some would say the myth) of professional autonomy and the pressures for accountability. There is little doubt that the academic profession will be subjected to increased controls as academic institutions seek to survive in an environment of financial difficulties. Professorial myths—of collegial decision-making, individual autonomy, and of the disinterested pursuit of knowledge—have come into conflict with the realities of complex organizational structures and bureaucracies. Important academic decisions are reviewed by a bewildering assortment of committees and administrators. These levels of authority have become more powerful as arbiters of academic decision-making.

The US academic system is enmeshed in a series of complex hierarchies. These hierarchies, framed by discipline, institution, rank, and specialty, help to determine working conditions, prestige, and, in many ways, one's orientation to the profession. As David Riesman pointed out three decades ago, US higher education is a 'meandering procession' dominated by the prestigious graduate schools and ebbing downward through other universities, 4-year colleges, and finally to the community college system [21]. Most of the profession attempts to follow the norms, and the fads, of the prestigious research-oriented universities. Notable exceptions are the community colleges, which employ one-quarter of US academics, and some of the non-selective 4-year schools. Generally, prestige is defined by how close an institution, or an individual professor's working life, comes to the norm of publication and research, of participation in the 'cosmopolitan' orientation to the discipline and the national profession, rather than to 'local' teaching and institutionally focused norms [22]. Even in periods of fiscal constraint, the hold of the traditional academic models remains very strong indeed. Current efforts to emphasize teaching and to ensure greater 'productivity' from the faculty face considerable challenges from the traditional academic hierarchy.

Within institutions, academics are also part of a hierarchical system, with the distinctions between tenured and untenured staff a key to this hierarchy. The dramatic growth of part-time teachers has added another layer at the bottom of the institutional hierarchy [23]. Disciplines and departments are also ranked into hierarchies, with the traditional academic specialties in the arts and sciences along with medicine and, to some extent, law at the top. The 'hard' sciences tend to have more prestige than the social sciences or humanities. Other applied fields, such as education and agriculture, are considerably lower on the scale. These hierarchies are very much part of the realities and perceptions of the academic profession.

Just as the realities of post-war expansion shaped academic organizations and affected salaries, prestige, and working conditions, and gave more power to the professoriate over the governance of colleges and universities, current diminished circumstances also bring change. While it is unlikely that the basic structural or organizational realities of US higher education will profoundly change, there has been an increase in the authority of administrators and increased bureaucratic control over working conditions on campus. In general, the professors have lost a significant part of their bargaining power, power that was rooted in moral authority. As academic institutions adjust to a period of declining resources, there will be ongoing, subtle organizational shifts that will inevitably work against the perquisites, and the authority, of the academic profession. Universities, as organizations, adjust to changing realities, and these adjustments will work against the professoriate.

Legislation, Regulations, Guidelines and the Courts

In a number of areas the academic profession has been directly affected by the decisions of external authorities. US higher education has always been subject to external decisions, from the Dartmouth College case in the period immediately following the American Revolution to the Land Grant Act in the mid-nineteenth century. The actions by the courts or by legislative authority, have profoundly affected higher education and the professoriate. In the contemporary period, governmental decisions continue to have an impact on US higher education and the academic profession. It is not possible in this context to discuss all of the government policies that have shaped the profession. It is my intention to indicate how decisions create a context for academic life. The fiscal crisis of higher education has already been discussed. However, academia's problems stem not only from a downturn in the US economy, but also from quite deliberate policies by government at both the federal and state levels to de-emphasize higher education and research. Other pressing social needs combined with public reluctance to pay higher taxes worked to restrict higher education budget allocations, which especially affected public colleges and universities. Cuts in research funding have been felt by both public and private institutions and by faculty.

Specific governmental policies have also had an impact on the profession. One area of considerable controversy has been affirmative action—the effort to ensure that college and university faculties include larger numbers of women and members of underrepresented minorities to reflect the national population [24]. A variety of specific regulations has been mandated by federal and state governments relating to hiring, promotion and other aspects of faculty life to ensure that women and minorities have opportunities in the academic profession. Many professors have opposed these regulations, viewing them as an unwarranted intrusion on academic autonomy. These policies have, nonetheless, had an impact on academic life. Special admissions and remedial programs for underrepresented students have also aroused considerable controversy on campus and have also been opposed by many faculty, they too have been implemented by governmental intervention.

The legal system has had a profound influence on the academic profession in the past several decades. The courts have ruled on university hiring and promotion policies, as well as on specific personnel cases. While the courts are generally reluctant to interfere in the internal workings of academic institutions, they have reviewed cases of gender or other discrimination, sometimes reversing academic decisions. Recently, the US Supreme Court ruled that compulsory retirement regulations were unconstitutional. This ruling is having a profound impact on the academic profession and on institutions since mandatory retirement is no longer legal.

These examples illustrate the significance and pervasiveness of governmental policies on the academic profession. Legislation concerning faculty workloads as well as policies on affirmative action affect the profession. Shifts in public opinion are often reflected in governmental policies concerning higher education and the professoriate. The courts, through the cases they are called on to decide, also play a role. The cumulative impact of governmental policies, laws and decisions of all kinds have profoundly influenced the professoriate [25]. In the post-World War II era, as higher education has become more central to the society, government has involved itself to a greater extent with higher education, and this trend is likely to continue.

The Realities at the End of the Century

The academic profession faces an uncertain future in the decade of the 1990s. The past decade has been, without question, one of the low points in the post-war history of the US professoriate. The immediate coming period does not offer the promise of significant improvement. However, demographic changes and the possibility that the profession itself will be able to adjust successfully to new circumstances may provide a somewhat more optimistic future. The basic configuration of US higher education is unlikely to change dramatically. There has been deterioration but all within the context of the established system. This section examines some of the realities of the decade of the 1990s, with a particular stress on the relationship of the academic profession to the structure of the higher education system and the impact of society on the profession.

Teaching, Research and Service

One of the main debates of the decade concerns the appropriate balance between teaching and research in academia, a debate that goes to the role of the university as an institution and is critical for the academic profession. Many outside academia, and quite a few within the universities, have argued that there should be more emphasis on teaching in the US higher education system. It is agreed that research is overvalued and that, especially considering fiscal constraints and demands for accountability, professors should be more 'productive' [26]. The reward system in academia has produced this imbalance. Critics charge that, outside the 100 or so major research universities, the quality and relevance of much academic research is questionable. Some have gone further to say that much academic research is a 'scam' [27].

The issue of faculty productivity has produced action in several states and on a few campuses. Massachusetts, Nevada, New York, Arizona and Wisconsin are among the states that have been involved in workload studies. The California State University has compared teaching loads of its faculty members with professors in other institutions. A few states require annual reports on workloads, and some have mandated minimum teaching loads. Hawaii and Florida, for example, require 12 hours of classroom instruction or the equivalent for faculty in 4-year institutions [28]. Academic institutions are also studying workloads.

US professors seem to be working longer, not shorter hours, and classroom hours have not declined in recent years. In 1992, according to a study by the Carnegie Foundation for the Advancement of Teaching, US professors spent a median 18.7 hours in activities relating to teaching (including preparation, student advice, etc.) [29]. On average, professors spend 13.1 hours per week in direct instructional activity, with those in research universities spending 11.4 hours and those in other 4-year institutions teaching 13.8 hours per week [30]. Not surprisingly, professors in research universities produce more publications than their colleagues in other institutions. For example, 61% of faculty in research universities report publishing six or more journal articles in the past 3 years as compared to 31% of faculty working elsewhere [31].

With the pressure for the professoriate to focus more on teaching, and, probably, to spend more time in the classroom, there is likely to be more differentiation among sectors within the academic system, so that academics at the top research universities will teach significantly less than their compeers in comprehensive colleges and universities. Greater stratification between the academic sectors and perhaps less mobility among them are probable outcomes. A shift in thinking has taken place about research and its role. External funding for research has declined and competition for resources is in most fields intense. There is also an orientation toward more applied research, closer links between industry and the universities, and more service to the private sector. These changes will affect the kind of research that is conducted. There may well be less basic research and more small-scale research linked to products.

So far, the professoriate has not fully responded to these externally induced debates and changes. The profession has sought to adapt to changing patterns in funding and to the more competitive research climate. In the long run, however, these structural changes will transform the research culture and the organization of research. In some ways, academics have moved closer to their clientele through the emphasis on service to external constituencies. The debate about Total Quality Management (TQM) in higher education is, in part, an effort to convince academic institutions, and the professoriate, to think more directly about student needs, using a model designed to focus attention on the 'customer' [32].

11

Demographic Changes and the Decline of Community

The 'age bulge,' discussed earlier, means that the large cohort of academics who entered the profession in the 1960s and 1970s take up a disproportionate share of jobs, especially when openings are restricted. Part-time faculty make up an increasing segment of the profession, further altering the nature and orientation of the profession [33]. It is much harder for a mid-career academic to find another position if he or she becomes dissatisfied or desires a change in location. The 'safety valve' of job mobility no longer functions as well. While the number of retirements is rising rapidly and many institutions have used early retirement incentives to meet mandated budget cuts, this has not produced significant numbers of full-time academic jobs. This is still a time of diminished expectations.

Prospects for new entrants into the profession also declined. Few young PhDs were hired and, as it became clear that the academic job market had dried up, enrollments in many fields at the graduate level fell, especially in the traditional arts and sciences disciplines. Bright undergraduates gravitated to law school or management studies. Perhaps the greatest long-term implication is a 'missing generation' of younger scholars. The combination of the enlarged academic cohort of the 1960s and the decline of new positions in the 1970s and 1980s meant that very few younger scholars were being hired, with reverberations on the age structure of the profession. Further, a generation of fresh ideas has been lost. According to some demographic projections, there will be another shortage of trained doctorates around the turn of the century, causing different but nonetheless serious strains on the profession and on the universities [34].

The size and increased diversity of the academic profession have made a sense of community more difficult [35]. As institutions have grown to include well over 1000 academic staff, with elected senates and other, more bureaucratic, governance arrangements in place of the traditional general faculty meeting, a sense of shared academic purpose has become more elusive. Even academic departments in larger US universities can number up to 50. Committees have become ubiquitous and the sense of participation in a common academic enterprise has declined. Increasing specialization in the disciplines contributed to this trend. Two-thirds of the US professoriate in the Carnegie study judged morale to be fair or poor on campus and 60% felt similarly about the 'sense of community' at their institution [36].

Tenure, Retrenchment and Unions

The profession has seen its economic status eroded after a decade of significant gains in 'real income' during the 1960s. Academic salaries began to decline in terms of actual purchasing power in the 1970s, and the slide has continued unabated. Indeed, many faculty members in such states as Massachusetts and California have faced actual salary cuts while many states, including New York and Maryland, froze salaries, sometimes for more than one year. Professional prerogatives seemed less secure, and autonomy was threatened.

The tenure system came under attack in the 1970s. Some argued that the permanent appointments offered to professors once they had been evaluated and promoted from assistant to associate professor bred sloth among those with tenure, although there was little evidence to back up this claim [37]. Tenure was also criticized because it interfered with the institution's ability to respond to fiscal problems or changes in program needs. Professors could not easily be replaced or dismissed. Originally intended to protect academic freedom, the tenure system grew into a means of evaluating assistant professors as well as offering lifetime appointments. As fiscal problems grew and the job market

12

deteriorated, it became somewhat harder for young assistant professors to be promoted. Tenure 'quotas' were imposed at some institutions, and many simply raised the standards for awarding tenure. These measures added to the pressures felt by junior staff. The system that was put into place to protect professors was increasingly seen as a problem.

It is significant that the intense debate about the tenure system that characterized the 1970s has, for the most part, ended. Tenure remains one of the keystones of US higher education and, as a concept, is not now under threat. The professoriate sees tenure as one of its most important perquisites and has defended it vigorously. Administrators and policy-makers have recognized the centrality of tenure to the self-concept of the profession.

Retrenchment—the dismissal of academic staff without regard to tenure—has always been one of the major fears of the professoriate [38]. During the first wave of fiscal crises in the 1970s, a number of universities attempted to solve their financial problems by dismissing professors, including some with tenure, following programmatic reviews and analyses of enrollment trends. The American Association of University Professors (AAUP), several academic unions, and a number of individual professors sued the universities in the courts, claiming that such retrenchment was against the implied lifetime employment arrangement offered through the tenure system. The courts consistently ruled against the professors, arguing that tenure protects academic freedom but does not prevent dismissals due to fiscal crisis. Universities that were especially hard hit, such as the City University of New York and the State University of New York, declared fiscal emergencies and dismissed academic staff—including some tenured professors—and closed departments and programs. Many institutions found that the legal challenges, decline in morale, and bad national publicity were not worth the financial savings, and in later crises fewer tenured faculty were dismissed. The fact is that tenure in US higher education does not fully protect lifetime employment, although, in general, commitments are honored by colleges and universities [39]. The retrenchments, and discussions and debates about retrenchment, have left a significant imprint on the thinking of the academic profession, contributing to low morale and feelings of alienation.

The growth of academic unions in the 1970s was a direct reaction to the difficulties faced by the professoriate in this period. Most professors turned to unions with some reluctance, and despite accelerating difficulties in the universities, the union movement has not become dominant. Indeed, the growth of unions slowed and even stopped in the late 1980s. In 1980, 682 campuses were represented by academic unions. Of this number, 254 were 4-year institutions—unions are most entrenched in the community college sector. Very few research universities are unionized, only one of the members of the prestigious Association of American Universities, for example. Unions are concentrated in the community college sector and in the public lower and middle tiers of the system [40]. Relatively few private colleges and universities are unionized, in part because the US Supreme Court, in the *Yeshiva* case, made unionization in private institutions quite difficult. The Court ruled that faculty members in private institutions were, by definition, part of 'management' and could not be seen as 'workers' in the traditional sense.

The growth of academic unions has essentially stopped in the past decade. Legal challenges such as the *Yeshiva* decision and a realization that academic unions were not able to solve the basic problems of higher education have been contributing factors. In addition, while unions brought significant increases in salaries in the first years of contractual arrange-ments, this advantage ended in later contract periods. In normal periods, many faculty see unions as somehow opposed to the traditional values, such as meritocratic evaluation, of academia; often, unions are voted in following severe campus conflict between faculty and administration. Further, unions have been unable to save faculty from retrenchment or a deterioration in working conditions. Both public university systems in New York are unionized, and both have been hard hit by fiscal problems, faculty unions have not shielded staff from retrenchment, salary freezes and the like. Neither the rhetoric of the AAUP nor the trade union tactics of the American Federation of Teachers has kept academic institutions, and sometimes state legislatures, from cutting budgets, increasing workloads, or, in some cases, dismissing professors. Unions, however, were part of an effort to stop the erosion of faculty advantages in the 1970s. Unions were also an expression of the attempt on the part of professors in institutions with only limited autonomy and weak faculty governance structures to assert faculty power. In both of these areas, unions had only limited success.

Accountability and Autonomy

The academic profession has traditionally enjoyed a high degree of autonomy, particularly in the classroom and in research. While most academics are only dimly aware of it, the thrust toward accountability has begun to affect their professional lives. This trend will intensify not only due to fiscal constraints but because all public institutions have come under greater scrutiny. Institutions, often impelled (in the case of public universities) by state budget offices, require an increasingly large amount of data concerning faculty work, research productivity, the expenditure of funds for ancillary support, and other aspects of academic life. What is more, criteria for student–faculty ratios and levels of financial support for different kinds of post-secondary education and for productivity of academic staff have been established. The new sources of data permit fiscal authorities to monitor closely how institutions meet established criteria so that adjustments in budgets can be quickly implemented. While most of these measures of accountability are only indirectly perceived by most academics, they nonetheless have a considerable impact on the operation of universities and colleges, since resources are allocated on the basis of formulae that are more closely measured. It is worth noting that the basic 'outputs' of academic institutions—the quality of teaching and the quality and impact of research—cannot be calculated through these efforts at accountability. Indeed, even the definitions of teaching quality and research productivity remain elusive.

If autonomy is the opposite side of the accountability coin, then one would expect academic autonomy to have declined significantly. But, at least on the surface, this has not yet occurred. Basic decisions concerning the curriculum, course and degree requirements, the process of teaching and learning, and indeed all of the matters traditionally the domain of the faculty have remained in the hands of departments and other parts of the faculty governance structure. Most academics retain the sense of autonomy that has characterized higher education for a century. This is especially the case in the top-tier institutions. There have been few efforts to dismantle the basic structure of academic work in ways that would destroy the traditional arrangements.

Yet, there is change taking place at the margins that will continue to shift the balance increasingly from autonomy to accountability and erode the base of faculty power. Decisions concerning class size, the future of low-enrollment fields, the overall academic direction of the institution, and other issues have been shifted from the faculty to the administration or even to system-wide agencies. Academic planning, traditionally far removed from the individual professor and seldom impinging on the academic career, has become more of a reality as institutions seek to streamline their operations and worry more about external measures of productivity.

14

Academic Freedom

US professors at present enjoy a fairly high degree of academic freedom, although just half of the professoriate agrees that there are 'no political or ideological restrictions on what a scholar may publish' [41]. There are few public pressures aimed at ensuring political or intellectual conformity from professors and the concept of academic freedom seems well entrenched. The AAUP noted very few cases in which institutions have sought to violate the academic freedom of their staff. There has been virtually no governmental pressure to limit academic freedom. The tensions of the McCarthy era, when government investigators were searching for campus 'communists', seem far removed from the current period. The fact that the past decade or more has been without the major ideological and political unrest and activism that characterized some earlier periods, such as the Vietnam War era, certainly contributed to the calm on campus; however, even during the Vietnam period, academic freedom remained relatively secure. That record was, however, not entirely spotless. A number of junior faculty were denied tenure during this period because of their political views [42].

However, academic freedom remains a contentious issue. Perhaps the most visible academic debate of the current period relates to 'political correctness', an unfortunate shorthand term for a variety of disputes concerning the nature and organization of the undergraduate curriculum, the interpretation of US culture, and the perspectives of some disciplines in the humanities and social sciences, and what some conservatives have claimed is the infusion of ideology into academia. Dinesh D'Souza, a conservative writer, argued in his 1991 book, *Illiberal Education*, that US higher education was being taken over by left-wing ideologists seeking to transform the curriculum through the infusion of multicultural approaches and the destruction of the traditional focus on Western values and civilization [43]. Conservative critics, including then US Secretary of Education William Bennett, took up the call and a major national discussion ensued [44]. Some conservatives claim that the academic freedom of some conservative faculty is being violated, although there is no evidence that this is the case. The debate, however, has made an impression on thinking about the curriculum and the role of multiculturalism on campus. While it has not affected academic freedom directly, the politics of race, gender and ethnicity have had a significant effect on academic life [45]. These social issues have entered into discussions of the curriculum and some faculty have claimed that they have inappropriately influenced decision-making. There have also been incidents of racial or gender-based intolerance on some campuses.

Most would say that academic freedom is quite free from structural restraints and that external authorities, including both government and college and university trustees, have been overwhelmingly supportive of academic freedom during the past several decades. Contemporary concerns come from public debate about 'political correctness' and from the resulting campus acrimony. Recently outlawed restrictions on student 'hate speech' may also have added to professorial concern.

Students

The two basic elements of academia are students and faculty. These two central groups within the college and university are not often linked in analyses of higher education. Students have profoundly affected the academic profession throughout the history of US higher education. Prior to the rise of the research university at the end of the nineteenth century, US higher education was student-oriented and the interaction between faculty and students was substantial. Even in the post-war period, most colleges remained oriented to teaching, although with the decline of *in loco parentis* in the 1960s, faculty became less

15

centrally involved in the lives of students [46]. Students affect faculty in many ways. Increases in student numbers had the result of expanding the professoriate and changes in patterns of enrollments also affected the academic profession. Student demands for 'relevance' in the 1960s had implications for the faculty, as did the later vocationalism of student interests. US higher education has traditionally responded to changing student curricular interests by expanding fields and departments, or by cutting offerings in unpopular areas. Student 'consumerism' is a central part of the ethos of US higher education [47].

Student interests have also had a limited impact on academic policy and governance. In the 1960s, students demanded participation in academic governance, and many colleges and universities opened committees and other structures to them. The lasting impact of these changes was minimal, but the student demands aroused considerable debate and tension on campus [48]. Recently, students have shown little interest in participating in governance and have been only minimally involved in any political activism, on campus or off, although there has been a recent increase in student voluntarism for social causes. Student interests and attitudes affect the classroom and enrollments in different fields of study. Students are themselves influenced by societal trends, government policies concerning the financial aspects of higher education, perceptions of the employment market, and many other factors. These impressions are brought to the campus and are translated into attitudes, choices and orientations to higher education. Student opinions of the faculty and of the academic enterprise have a significant influence on institutional culture and morale [49].

Conclusion

The analysis presented in this essay is not terribly optimistic. The academic profession has been under considerable pressure, and the basic conditions of academic work in the USA have deteriorated. Some, but by no means all, of the gains made during the period of post-war expansion have been lost. The 'golden age' of the US university is probably over, but it is likely that the medium-term future will be somewhat more favorable than the immediate past, just because of changing demographic realities, although even here, the imposition of larger classes and the increased use of instructional technology as well as the continued use of part-time faculty has meant that conditions will not dramatically improve. The basic fact is, however, that the essential structure of US higher education remains unaltered and it is unlikely to change fundamentally. There will, thus, be a considerable degree of continuity amidst change.

The professoriate stands at the center of any academic institution and is, in a way, buffered from direct interaction with many of higher education's external constituencies. Academics do not generally deal with trustees, legislators, or parents. Their concerns are with their own teaching and research, and with their direct academic surroundings, such as the department. Yet, external constituencies and realities increasingly affect academic life.

It is possible to summarize some of the basic trends that have been discussed in this analysis-realities that are likely to continue to affect the academic profession in the coming period.

- Reallocations and increased competition for federal research funds made research funds in most fields more difficult to obtain [50]. Governmental commitment to basic research declined as well, and funds for the social sciences and humanities have declined. With the end of the Cold War, the emphasis on military research has diminished, but there are few signs of other fields benefiting from the 'peace dividend'.
- Financial difficulties for scholarly publishers and cutbacks in budgets for academic

libraries reduced opportunities for publishing scholarly work, thereby placing added stress on younger scholars, in particular, and on the entire knowledge system in academia. Library cutbacks also place restrictions on access to knowledge.

- Changes in student curricular choices have been significant in the past two decades—from the social sciences in the 1960s to business, engineering and law in the 1980s and currently back to a limited extent, to the social sciences. Declines in enrollments in the traditional arts and sciences at the graduate level were also notable.
- Demands for budgetary and programmatic accountability from government have affected higher education at every level.
- In this climate of increased accountability, academic administrators have gained power over their institutions, and inevitably, over the lives of the professoriate.
- Economic problems in society have caused major financial problems for higher education, affecting the faculty directly in terms of salaries, perquisites, and sometimes higher teaching loads. The financial future of higher education, regardless of broader economic trends, is not favorable in the medium term.
- A decline in public esteem and support for higher education, triggered first by the unrest of the 1960s and enhanced by widespread questioning of the academic benefits of a college degree, has caused additional stress for the professoriate. There is a tendency to see an academic degree as a 'private good' rather than a 'public good': individuals and families rather than the state should pay for higher education.
- The shrinking academic employment market has meant that few younger scholars have been able to enter the profession, and has limited the mobility of those currently in the profession. The increased use of part-time faculty has further restricted growth.

Given these factors, it is surprising that the basic working conditions of the US professoriate have remained relatively stable. The structure of post-secondary education remains essentially unchanged, but there have been important qualitative changes, generally in a negative direction from the perspective of the professoriate. Academic freedom and the tenure system remain largely intact, but there have been increased demands for accountability. Academics retain basic control over the curriculum, and most institutions continue to be based on the department, which remains strongly influenced by the professoriate. Institutional governance, although increasingly influenced by administrators, remains unchanged.

The period of expansion and professorial power of the middle years of the century will not return. How, then, can academics face the challenges of the coming period? At one level, the academic profession needs to represent itself more effectively to external constituencies. If academic unions could more effectively assimilate traditional academic norms, they might have the potential of representing the academic profession. The traditional academic governance structures are the most logical agency to take responsibility for presenting the case for the academic profession to a wider audience, both to the public and to political leaders, probably in co-operation with university administrators.

The professoriate reacted to the challenges of the post-war period. It was glad to accept more responsibilities, move into research, and seek funding from external agencies. It relinquished much of its responsibility to students (at least in the research-oriented universities) as research became the dominating academic value. The curriculum lost its coherence in the rush toward specialization. Now, it is necessary to re-establish a sense of academic mission that emphasizes teaching and the curriculum. To an extent, this has been done on many campuses with the rebuilding of the undergraduate general education curriculum and the re-establishment of liberal education as a key curricular goal. The current emphasis on teaching is another important trend that may restore the credibility of the profession.

17

It is always more difficult to induce changes as a result of conscious planning and concern than it is to react to external circumstances. For much of this century, the professoriate has reacted. Now, there are signs that the crisis has stimulated the academic profession to implement positive solutions to difficult problems.

Acknowledgement

I am indebted to Lionel S. Lewis, Patricia Gumport, Robert Berdahl and Edith S. Hoshino for comments on this essay.

Correspondence: Professor Philip G. Altbach, School of Education, Boston College, Chestnut Hill, MA 02167, USA.

NOTES

An earlier version of this article appeared in PHILIP G. ALTBACH, ROBERT O. BERDAHL & PATRICIA GUMPORT (Eds) *Higher Education in American Society* (Amherst, NY, Prometheus, 1994).

[1] See ALLAN BLOOM, *The Closing of the American Mind: how higher education has failed democracy and impoverished the souls of today's students* (New York, Simon & Schuster, 1987); CHARLES J. SYKES, *Profscam: professors and the demise of higher education* (Washington, DC, Regenery, 1988); and MARTIN ANDERSON, *Imposters in the Temple* (New York, Simon & Schuster, 1992).

[2] ERNEST L. BOYER, *Scholarship Reconsidered: priorities of the professoriate* (Princeton, NJ, Carnegie Foundation for the Advancement of Teaching, 1990).

[3] HAROLD T. SHAPIRO, The functions and resources of the American university of the twenty-first century, *Minerva*, 30 (Summer, 1992), pp. 163–174.

[4] RICHARD M. FREELAND, *Academia's Golden Age: universities in Massachusetts, 1945–1970* (New York, Oxford University Press, 1992).

[5] EDWARD SHILS, The academic ethos under strain, *Minerva*, 13 (Spring, 1975), pp. 1–37. See also HENRY ROSOVSKY, *The University: an owner's manual* (New York, Norton, 1990).

[6] ROBERT BIRNBAUM, Unionization and faculty compensation, Part II, *Educational Record*, 57 (Spring, 1976) pp. 116–118.

[7] KENNETH P. RUSCIO, Many sectors, many professions, in: BURTON, R. CLARK (Ed.) *The Academic Profession: national, disciplinary and institutional settings* (Berkeley, University of California Press, 1987), pp. 331–368.

[8] MARY M. DWYER, ARLENE A. FLYNN & PATRICIA S. INMAN, Differential progress of women faculty: status 1980–1990, in: JOHN SMART (Ed.) *Higher Education: handbook of theory and research, Volume 7* (New York, Agathon, 1991), pp. 173–222.

[9] MARTIN J. FINKELSTEIN, *The American Academic Profession* (Columbus, OH, Ohio State University Press, 1984), pp. 187–189.

[10] JAKE RYAN & CHARLES SACKREY, *Strangers in Paradise: academics from the working class* (Boston, MA, South End Press, 1984).

[11] CHARLES HOMER HASKINS, *The Rise of Universities* (Ithaca, NY: Cornell University Press, 1965).

[12] JOSEPH BEN-DAVID & AWRAHAM ZLOCZOWER, Universities and academic systems in modern societies, *European Journal of Sociology*, 3, (1962), pp. 45–84.

[13] FREDERICK RUDOLPH, *The American College and University: a history* (New York, Vintage, 1965).

[14] LAURENCE VEYSEY, *The Emergence of the American University* (Chicago, IL, University of Chicago Press, 1965).

[15] This theme is developed at greater length in DAVID HENRY, *Challenges Past, Challenges Present* (San Francisco, CA: Jossey-Bass, 1975).

[16] The academic job market of this period is captured well in THEODORE CAPLOW & REECE J. MCGEE, *The Academic Marketplace* (New York, Basic Books, 1958). Current realities are reflected in DOLORES L. BURKE, *A New Academic Marketplace* (Westport, CT, Greenwood, 1988), a replication of the earlier CAPLOW & MCGEE study.

[17] See LOGAN WILSON, *American Academics: then and now* (New York, Oxford University Press, 1979).

[18] SEYMOUR MARTIN LIPSET, *Rebellion in the University* (New Brunswick, NJ, Transaction, 1993).

[19] BURTON R. CLARK, *The Academic Life* (Princeton, NJ, Carnegie Foundation for the Advancement of

Teaching, 1987). For a structural discussion of US higher education, see TALCOTT PARSONS & GERALD PLATT, *The American University* (Cambridge, Harvard University Press, 1973).

[20] These figures come from a survey of the views of the American academic profession undertaken by the Carnegie Foundation for the Advancement of Teaching in 1992. See ERNEST L. BOYES, PHILIP G. ALTBACH & MARY JEAN WHITELAW, The Academic Profession: an international perspective (Princeton, NJ: Carnegie Foundation for the Advancement of Teaching, 1994).

[21] DAVID RIESMAN, *The Academic Procession, in Constraint and Variety in American Education* (Garden City, NY, Doubleday, 1958), pp. 25–65.

[22] ALVIN GOULDNER, Cosmopolitans and locals: toward an analysis of latent social roles, 1 and 2, *Administrative Science Quarterly*, 2 (December 1957 and March 1958), pp. 281–303 and 445–467.

[23] JUDITH M. GAPPA & DAVID W. LESLIE, *The Invisible Faculty: improving the status of part-timers in higher education* (San Francisco, CA, Jossey–Bass, 1993).

[24] See, for example, VALORA WASHINGTON & WILLIAM HARVEY, *Affirmative Rhetoric, Negative Action: African–American and Hispanic faculty at predominantly white institutions* (Washington, DC, School of Education, George Washington University, 1989).

[25] EDWARD R. HINES & L. S. HARTMARK, *The Politics of Higher Education* (Washington, DC, American Association for Higher Education, 1980).

[26] The most influential consideration of this topic is E. L. BOYER, *Scholarship Reconsidered: priorities of the professoriate* (Princeton, NJ, Carnegie Foundation for the Advancement of Teaching, 1990). See also WILLIAM F. MASSY & ROBERT ZEMSKY, *Faculty Discretionary Time: departments and the academic ratchet* (Philadelphia, PA, Pew Higher Education Research Program, 1992) and The lattice and the ratchet, *Policy Perspectives*, 2(4) (1990).

[27] C. J. SYKES, *Profscam: professors and the demise of higher education* (Washington, DC, Regenery, 1988). See also PAGE SMITH, *Killing the Spirit: higher education in America* (New York: Viking, 1990). Both of these volumes received widespread attention in the popular media and sold well.

[28] ARTHUR LEVINE & JANA NIDIFFER, Faculty Productivity: a re-examination of current attitudes and actions (unpublished paper, Institute of Educational Management, Harvard Graduate School of Education, 1993).

[29] 1992 Carnegie Survey of the International Academic Profession. It is worth noting that academics in other countries report that they teach similar amounts: Germany, 16.4 hours per week; Japan, 19.4; Sweden, 15.9; England, 21.3.

[30] BOYES *et al.* op. cit.

[31] Ibid.

[32] D. SEYMOUR, TQM: focus on performance, not resources, *Educational Record*, 74 (Spring, 1993), pp. 6–14.

[33] ELAINE EL-KHAWAS, *Campus Trends, 1991* (Washington, DC, American Council on Education, 1991), p. 7.

[34] WILLIAM G. BOWEN & JULIE ANN SOSA, *Prospects for Faculty in the Arts and Sciences* (Princeton, NJ, Princeton University Press, 1989). Demographic projections, however, must be carefully evaluated because they have frequently been wrong.

[35] Carnegie Foundation for the Advancement of Teaching, *Campus Life: in search of community* (Princeton, NJ: Carnegie Foundation for the Advancement of Teaching, 1990). See also IRVING J. SPITZBERG, JR. & VIRGINIA V. THORNDIKE, *Creating Community on College Campuses* (Albany, NJ: State University of New York Press, 1992).

[36] BOYES *et al.* op. cit.

[37] BARDWELL SMITH *et al.* (Eds), *The Tenure Debate* (San Francisco, CA, Jossey–Bass, 1973). For a more recent attack on tenure, see M. ANDERSON, *Imposters in the Temple* (New York, Simon & Schuster, 1992).

[38] See MARJORIE C. MIX, *Tenure and Termination in Financial Exigency* (Washington, DC, American Association for Higher Education, 1978).

[39] SHEILA SLAUGHTER, Retrenchment in the 1980s: the politics of prestige and gender, *Journal of Higher Education*, 64 (May/June, 1993), pp. 250–282. See also PATRICIA GUMPORT, The contested terrain of academic program reduction, *Journal of Higher Education*, 64 (May/June, 1993), pp. 283–311.

[40] For example, in the 64 campus State University of New York system, which is unionized, there is a bifurcation between the four research-oriented university centers, which have been reluctant to unionize, and the 14 4-year colleges, which favor the union. Since the 4-year college faculty are in the majority, the union has prevailed.

[41] 1992 Carnegie Survey of the Academic Profession. It may be worth noting that the USA falls at the lower end on this question, with scholars in Russia, Sweden, Mexico, Germany, Japan and other countries feeling more positive about the freedom to publish.

[42] JOSEPH FASHING & STEPHEN F. DEUTSCH, *Academics in Retreat* (Albuquerque, NM, University of New Mexico Press, 1971).

[43] DINESH D'SOUZA, *Illiberal Education: the politics of race and sex on campus* (New York, Free Press, 1991).

[44] Among the numerous books on the topic, see PAUL BERMAN (Ed.). *Debating PC: the controversy over political correctness on college campuses* (New York, Dell, 1992); PATRICIA AUFDERHEIDE (Ed.) *Beyond PC: towards a politics of understanding* (Saint Paul, MN, Graywolf Press, 1992); and FRANCIS J. BECKWITH & MICHAEL E. BAUMAN (Eds) *Are You Politically Correct?: debating America's cultural standards* (Buffalo, NY, Prometheus, 1993).

[45] PHILIP G. ALTBACH & KOFI LOMOTEY (Eds) *The Racial Crisis in American Higher Education* (Albany, NY, State University of New York Press, 1991).

[46] HELEN LEFLOWITZ HOROWITZ, *Campus Life: undergraduate cultures from the end of the eighteenth century to the present* (Chicago, IL, University of Chicago Press, 1987).

[47] ARTHUR LEVINE, *When Dreams and Heroes Died: a portrait of today's college student* (San Francisco, CA, Jossey–Bass, 1980).

[48] ALEXANDER W. ASTIN, *et al.*, *The Power of Protest* (San Francisco, CA, Jossey–Bass, 1975).

[49] ALEXANDER W. ASTIN, *What Matters in College: four critical years revisited* (San Francisco, CA, Jossey–Bass, 1993).

[50] See ROGER L. GEIGER, *Research and Relevant Knowledge: American research universities since World War II* (New York, Oxford University Press, 1993).

The Emergence of the Modern Academic Role

By World War II nearly one hundred and fifty thousand faculty were instructing some one and a half million students—about 15 percent of the eighteen to twenty-one age cohort. American higher education, generally, and the academic profession, in particular, were about to undergo their most explosive growth surge. During the next thirty years, the ranks of the American professoriate were to nearly quadruple. Between 1965 and 1970 alone, they swelled by one hundred and fifty thousand with the number of *new* positions exceeding the entire number of positions in 1940 (Lipset and Ladd, 1979). Now six hundred thousand strong, college and university professors were instructing nearly 50 percent of the college-age population.

This chapter seeks to chronicle the critical stages of that ascent in order to provide the historical context within which subsequent discussion of contemporary academics must be understood. In so doing, it focuses primarily on the early development of the professorial role during the latter half of the eighteenth century, the progressive professionalization of the faculty during the nineteenth century, and the subsequent consolidation of the modern academic role during the post–World War I period.

The generalizations presented here are drawn from a variety of secondary sources, including institutional and general histories of American higher education, several recent statistical studies of college faculties during the nineteenth century by McCaughey (1974) on Harvard, Creutz (1981) on Michigan, and Tobias (1982) on Dartmouth, as well as the author's own unpublished analyses of the nineteenth century faculties of Brown, Bowdoin, Yale, and Michigan.[1] Although the findings, then, cannot be viewed as representative of all of American higher education at any period, they do provide insight into developments at a half dozen or more "leading" institutions, thus avoiding the pitfalls of generalizations based on the peculiar life history of any single institution.

The findings are organized following Donald Light's (1972) conceptualization of the three analytically distinct, yet interrelated, strands of the modern academic career. The first, the disciplinary career, includes those events specifically connected with a discipline and its goals rather than with a particular job (for example, specialized training, work history prior to assumption of an academic career, involvements with disciplinary organizations and research activity). The institutional career includes those events associated with a faculty member's employment at a particular institution (for example, movement in a promotion system). Finally, the external career includes those work related activities undertaken outside the institution but rooted in a faculty member's disciplinary expertise (consulting, government service, public lecturing). Thus, we now turn to an examination of the evolutionary unfolding of these three career strands over the past two centuries.

THE EMERGENCE OF AN INSTITUTIONAL CAREER, 1750–1820

During the seventeenth century and the first half of the eighteenth century, the disciplinary career strand was, of course, virtually nonexistent, and even the institutional strand proved secondary to the external one. American colleges operated on a model not unlike the British universities after the Elizabethan Statutes of the late sixteenth century (Cowley, 1980). It was assumed that any bright graduate was ready to teach all subjects leading to the degree, and thus instructional staffs were composed entirely of *tutors,* young men, often no more than twenty, who had just received their baccalaureate degree and who were preparing for careers in the ministry (Morison, 1936). The responsibilities of tutors were both pedagogical and pastoral-custodial in nature. Ideally, a single tutor was assigned the shepherding of a single class through all four years of their baccalaureate program, both inside and outside the classroom. "Tutors were with their pupils almost every hour of the day [in the classroom recitations, study halls, and at meals], and slept in the same chamber with some of them at night. They were responsible not only for the intellectual, but for the moral and spiritual development of their charges" (Morison, 1936). In less than ideal practice, the tutorship functioned as a "revolving door"; at Harvard, prior to 1685, very seldom did a tutor see a class through all four years (only a half dozen of the forty-one tutors during this period remained at Harvard more than three years). While the next half century saw a progressive lengthening of the tutors' tenure at Harvard, and indeed the ultimate establishment of "permanent" tutorships in the latter half of the eighteenth century,[2] the "revolving door" concept of the tutorship persisted throughout this period at Yale, Brown, Dartmouth, and Bowdoin.

Development of a Small Core of "Permanent" Faculty, 1750–1800

It was not until the last half of the eighteenth century that an institution's short-term tutors were supplemented by a small core of "permanent" faculty—the professors. Carrell (1968) found only ten professors in all of American higher education in 1750, the bulk of whom were at either Harvard or William and Mary. By 1795 the professorial ranks had swelled tenfold to 105 while the number of colleges had only slightly more than doubled. All in all, some two hundred individuals had served as professors in nineteen American colleges during this period.

How did these professorships develop? At Harvard, they developed slowly and as a direct result of philanthropic bequests. During the 1720s two Hollis professorships were endowed, one in divinity, occupied by Edward Wigglesworth for forty-four years, the other in mathematics and natural philosophy, occupied initially by Isaac Greenwood for eleven years, and then by John Winthrop for forty-one years.[3] By 1750 President Holyoke was being supported in his work by three permanent faculty members—the two Hollis professors as well as Henry Flynt, permanent tutor.[4] Throughout the rest of the eighteenth century, four additional professorships were endowed, of which three were actually filled before 1800.[5] By 1800, then, permanent professors had achieved near parity with tutors on the Harvard faculty.

At Yale the first professorship was likewise established as the direct result of a philanthropic bequest. In 1746 the Livingston Professorship of Divinity was established, and nine years later, its first occupant joined President Clap and the tutors in supervising instruction. By 1800 Yale had established only one additional professorship, but two years later, with the promotion of Jeremiah Day and Benjamin Silliman from their tutorships, it counted four professors among its faculty ranks—a situation of near parity between permanent professors and transient tutors (*Historical Register,* 1939).

The pattern that developed at Harvard after over a century and at Yale after a half century was adopted early on by those colleges founded during the second half of the eighteenth century. At Brown, for example, within five years of its founding, a core permanent faculty was already emerging with Howell's promotion from tutor to professor to join forces with President and Professor Manning. By 1800 Brown's five tutors were supplemented by three permanent professors (*Historical Catalog,* 1905). At Princeton, by 1767, two decades after its founding, three permanent professors had joined the three tutors (Wertenbaker, 1946); at Dartmouth, during the administration of John Wheelock (1779–1817), several professors were appointed to supplement the single professor who together with two or three tutors constituted the faculty during the preceding administration of Eleazar Wheelock (Richardson, 1932, p. 820 as cited by Cowley, 1980, p. 80).

What were the characteristics of this early core of permanent faculty? How did they resemble or differ from their more junior colleagues, the tutors? Both professors and tutors were drawn disproportionately from the higher socioeconomic strata of colonial and postrevolutionary society: fully one-quarter came from "professional" families (with fathers engaged in the ministry, law, medicine) at a time when 1–2 percent of the labor force was "professional" and 80–90 percent were engaged in agricultural pursuits (Carrell, 1968). Moreover, both professors and tutors undertook very similar activities as part of their college responsibilities: both supervised recitations and dormitories, and assumed overall responsibility for student discipline and moral, as well as intellectual, development. There the similarity appears to end. In the first place, professors did not take charge of a class for its four years at the institution; they were appointed in a particular subject area such as natural philosophy, divinity, or ancient languages and were, for the most part, engaged in the supervision of instruction within that area. In the second place, professors were generally older and more experienced than the tutors. Professors were, on the average, at least five to ten years older than the tutors. The vast majority, unlike the tutors, had some postbaccalaureate "professional" training in theology, law, or medicine. Among the eight professors at Brown during the eighteenth century, seven had such training (*Historical Catalog,* 1905), and at Harvard all ten professors during this period had such training (Eliot, 1848).

The most fundamental respect, however, in which professors differed from tutors was in the "permanence" of their positions. Carrell's analysis of biographical sketches of 124 professors during the second half of the eighteenth century illuminates the peculiar meaning of a "permanent" faculty appointment during this period. In the first place, a professorship implied an institutional career, most often at one's alma mater. Nearly 40 percent of Carrell's sample professors taught at their alma mater, ranging from just over one-third at the College of Philadelphia (later the University of Pennsylvania) to 83 percent at Harvard. Fully 88 percent taught at only one institution during their academic careers; barely 2.5 percent taught at three or more institutions. Second, a permanent professorship remained a "nonexclusive" career. In analyzing the lifetime occupational commitment of his sample, Carrell found that less than 15 percent ($N = 23$) appeared to identify themselves exclusively as professional teachers, less than 20 percent ($N = 32$) appeared to identify themselves primarily as professional teachers (with a secondary occupation in the ministry, medicine, or law), and over half ($N = 68$) appeared to identify themselves primarily as practioners of one of the traditional professions and only secondarily as professional college teachers (often having come to a professorship following a lengthy stint as a minister or practicing physician).

If college teaching was hardly the exclusive career, or even the first-choice career, of a majority of eighteenth century professors, Carrell's (1968) subsequent analysis suggests that it became a long-term commitment for many once the move was made. In an analysis of indicators of occupational commitment of his sample professors during their teaching tenure, Carrell found strikingly different results: nearly 45 percent ($N = 56$) identified themselves exclusively as college teachers, while about one-quarter identified themselves, respectively, as *primarily* or *secondarily* college teachers. In the latter two categories, clergy were heavily represented in the first, while physicians and lawyers made up the greater portion of the second, suggesting that clergy were more likely than the other learned professions to develop a primary commitment to the professorial role once it was assumed.

That the assumption of a professorship increasingly brought with it a heightened commitment to college teaching is further supported by at least three additional pieces of evidence. (1) The average length of professors' tenures was increasing. Over the second half of the eighteenth century, the average tenure of professors at Yale increased from 21.5 years to 36.8 years, and that of professors at Brown increased from 30.7 years to 36.0 years (by 1750, Harvard's two professors had an average tenure of 42.5 years). (2) There was a negative correlation between age at first appointment and tenure in the professorial role. Carrell reported a zero order correlation of

−0.35 between these two variables, suggesting shorter tenures were, at least in part, attributable to late career entry. (3) The proportion of professors who pursued subsequent careers was relatively small. Just over half of Carrell's sample (N = 64) died in office; over 75 percent (N = 92) died within ten years of leaving teaching; less than 25 percent engaged in another occupation after leaving the professorship, and among this group several either retired because of bad health or were retired by their institutions. It would appear safe to conclude then that the professorial role, once undertaken, was pursued with a considerable degree of permanency, particularly in light of the frequency of dual occupations—medicine and agriculture, law and agriculture, religion and education—characteristic of the late eighteenth century (Carrell, 1968).

One final issue concerning the relationship of the tutor to the professor remains—the relative integration or separation of the two roles in terms of the individual career track. To what extent did the tutorship function as the first step toward a professorship? And to what extent was a professorship the reward of skillful tutoring? The evidence suggests that at least two contrasting patterns had developed by the close of the eighteenth century. The Harvard pattern was one of separate career tracks. Not a single Harvard tutor went on to a Harvard professorship during the eighteenth century. Indeed tutoring became something of a permanent career option in itself (Smith, 1966). The pattern at Yale and Brown, and it would appear at most other institutions, was one of a separate, transient career track, tempered, however, by the use of the tutorship as a very selective feeder for the professorship. Thus, at Brown, only four of eighteen tutors (22.2 percent) went on to professorial appointments at Brown; three of the eight professors appointed during that period had served as Brown tutors. At Yale, tutors were less than half as likely as their Brown counterparts to achieve professorial appointments at Yale, but all six Yale professors during the period had indeed served as Yale tutors.

The Ascent of the Institutional Career, 1800–20

The first quarter of the nineteenth century has been credited by historian Frederick Rudolph (1962) as the beginning of the "college movement"—the large-scale founding of small colleges throughout what was then the West stimulated at once by the "community building" imperative of the period and the increasing competition among religious denominations. It may also be credited as the beginning of the "professor movement." Between 1800 and 1820 the ratio of permanent professors to tutors dramatically reversed itself at many of the leading institutions: by 1820 permanent professors outnumbered tutors at both Harvard and Yale by 10 to 6 whereas but two decades earlier there was a situation of parity at Harvard (5 to 5) and a 3 to 1 majority of tutors at Yale; at Brown, professors outnumbered tutors by a ratio of 3 to 1 where only two decades earlier the tutors had been in ascendance by a 5 to 3 ratio.[6]

The momentum of the professor movement can be seen graphically in developments at Harvard during President Kirkland's administration, 1810–28. During the entire eighteenth century, six professorships were established at Harvard (Eliot, 1848). They were created when funding to support them was obtained from private donors; and indeed if the initial gift was insufficient to support an incumbent, it was allowed to accumulate over one or more decades before the professorship was filled (the Hersey and Boylston professorships, for example, remained vacant for this reason). In the decade preceding the Kirkland presidency, a subscription was launched by Harvard for the creation of a single professorship. During the eighteen years of Kirkland's presidency, the number of Harvard professorships fully doubled. Seven professors were appointed while the funds destined for their support were not always yet available. In his zeal to make appointments, Kirkland frequently had to draw upon tuition revenues to pay the newly hired incumbents (Eliot, 1848, p. 107).

How can this ascendance of the permanent faculty in a brief two decades be explained? While it is impossible to postulate strict cause and effect relationships, several developments during the period would appear to provide necessary, if not sufficient, conditions for that ascendance. The first of these is sheer growth: growth in size of some of the leading institutions—the Yale faculty doubled in size between 1800 and 1820, and those of Harvard and Brown grew by 50 percent (*Historical Register*, 1939; *Historical Catalog*, 1905; Eliot, 1848)—and growth in the number of institutions as a result of the college movement. Allied with growth was the progressive acceptance of the professorship as a long-term, if not an exclusive, career as reflected in progressively longer average tenures throughout the eighteenth century and the indicators of increasing career commitment reported by Carrell. Yet a third factor which may help to account for the rise of the professorship were changes underway during the first quarter of the nineteenth century in the ministerial career. Calhoun, in a case study of the New Hampshire clergy during the late eighteenth and early nineteenth century, reported a radical shift in clerical career patterns at about this time, which he attributes to the increasing secularization and urbanization of the populace (Calhoun, 1965, cited by Tobias, 1982). The average terms of service in local parishes, which throughout most of the eighteenth century had been measured in lifetimes, began to resemble the average tenures of modern college and university presidents. This new found job insecurity, the difficulty of obtaining even so insecure a position, together with the low salaries of clergy in rural and small town churches led many ministers to seek to enhance their careers by building organizations such as colleges and by becoming professors (Tobias, 1982). And the correlation of these developments in the clerical career with the ascent of the professorship is lent further credence by Carrell's findings that clergymen became significantly more likely than their fellow professionals in law and medicine to identify themselves *primarily* as college teachers by the end of the eighteenth century.

THE STATUS OF THE PROFESSORIATE IN 1820

By the end of the first quarter of the nineteenth century, the professor movement had produced a relatively large cohort of career academics. Although still a thoroughly homogeneous group of upper middle class, New England-born Protestants,[7] the confluence of a number of social and intellectual forces during the course of the nineteenth century wrought some fundamental changes in the group career. The progressive secularization of American society was penetrating the classical college, subjugating the demands of piety to the religion of progress and materialism, reflecting the needs of a growing industrial economy (Calhoun, 1965; Brubacher and Rudy, 1968; Hofstadter and Metzger, 1955). At the same time, the rise of science and the tremendous growth of scientific knowledge was breaking apart the classical curriculum and giving rise to the development of academic disciplines (the distinction of professional versus amateur) and of research and graduate education (Oleson and Voss, 1979; Oleson and Brown, 1976; Berelson, 1960; Wolfle, 1972; Veysey, 1965). By mid-century, increasingly large numbers of Americans were studying abroad in Germany and were importing their version of the German university and the German idea of research back to the United States (Hofstadter and Metzger, 1955). Once graduate specialization took hold in earnest in the last quarter of the nineteenth century, it was but a short step to the establishment of the major learned societies and their sponsorship of specialized, disciplinary journals: the American Chemical Society in 1876, the Modern Language Association in 1883, the American Historical Association in 1884, the American Psychological Association in 1892 (Berelson, 1960).

These developments together provided American higher education with the capability of producing graduate trained specialists and created clear career opportunities for the specialists so produced. They provided the impetus for a fundamental restructuring, toward professionalization, of the academic role. Although touted by some as a veritable "academic revolution," an examination of the evolving disciplinary, institutional, and external careers of faculty at our sample institutions suggests that the restructuring process actually proceeded by gradual steps over more than a half century as successive groups of professors were replaced by products of the latest graduate training.

Before turning to the evolution of these three career strands during the nineteenth century, let us review the status of each of them as they manifested themselves among college faculties in 1820.

The Disciplinary Career

By 1820 the outline of a disciplinary career was discernable only in the cases of a few individuals at selected campuses rather than among entire faculties. While a majority of individuals continued to come to the professorship with postbaccalaureate training in the traditional professions of divinity, medicine, and law (mostly divinity), there remained, with the exception of Harvard, a paucity of faculty with postbaccalaureate training in their teaching specialty.[8] For the most part without specialized training, the majority of faculties (50 percent at Brown and Harvard; 100 percent at Bowdoin) continued to be drawn to their initial academic appointments from nonacademic jobs, primarily in school teaching and the ministry, secondarily in law and medicine. Moreover, for a majority of faculty at some institutions, any semblance of a disciplinary career in effect ended with their institutional career. At Brown and Bowdoin, the modal pattern was for the majority of faculty to move into nonacademic careers following their stints as college teachers (50 percent of the full professors at Brown and 60 percent of those at Bowdoin; virtually all the junior faculty at both institutions). It should be noted, however, that those full professors who left teaching averaged nearly two decades in their institutional positions (21.2 years at Brown; 18.5 years at Bowdoin) so that college teaching still constituted a significant chunk of their careers.[9]

At other institutions, most notably Harvard and Yale, patterns of career commitment appeared to be differentiated along senior/ junior faculty lines. While no junior faculty at either institution persisted in an academic career beyond their tutorship or instructorship, the majority of permanent professors did (more than 80 percent at Yale and 70 percent at Harvard). Interestingly enough, this suggests that Yale, and also Brown, were shifting toward the late eighteenth century Harvard pattern of separate junior and senior faculty career tracks.

Whatever their career commitments college faculties in 1820 evidenced fairly low disciplinary commitment as measured by their associational involvements and scholarly publications. Only a single faculty member at Brown, Bowdoin, Harvard, and Yale was involved to any significant extent in the activities of the learned societies of the day, namely, Caswell at Brown, Cleaveland at Bowdoin, Peck at Harvard, and Silliman at Yale, who had the year before founded the *American Journal of Science* (*Historical Catalog*, 1905; Packard, 1882; McCaughey, 1974; *Historical Register*, 1939). And, excluding the medical faculty, it was only those same single faculty members who were at all involved in publication in their specialized field. While many professors at these institutions were indeed publishing, their work consisted chiefly in collections of sermons and addresses made at commencements and other public occasions.

The External Career

While many professors were in 1820 actively pursuing external careers, virtually none was rooted in their academic specialization. Beyond the budding careers of a few men such as Silliman and Cleaveland on the academic public lecture circuit, the vast majority of professors consumed their extra-institutional time in clerical and civic activities. Fully three-quarters of the professors at Dartmouth, two-thirds of those at Bowdoin, and half of those at Brown were engaged in itinerant preaching and work with missionary societies. Somewhat lower proportions participated actively in community life, principally by holding political office at the local and national levels, assuming leadership roles in local civic associations unrelated to education or intellectual culture (for example, tree planting societies) or, in fewer cases, holding membership in state historical societies (Tobias, 1982; Packard, 1882; *Historical Catalog*, 1905).

The Institutional Career

In 1820 the now familiar formalized institutional career track of progression through the junior ranks to a full professorship had not yet begun to take hold. Indeed, in many respects, the two-track system largely operative at the end of the eighteenth century remained intact: junior faculty in temporary, dead-end appointments and senior faculty in long-term appointments. At Harvard, fully 80 percent of the senior faculty were initially appointed to their professorships from outside the institution, with 62 percent of these claiming no previous academic experience (McCaughey, 1974).[10] While Harvard was alone in this period in having established the "instructorship" as distinguished from the tutorship and the professorship,[11] instructors almost never went on to Harvard professorships, nor did tutors move up to such instructorships.[12]

While Yale and Brown continued to reflect some departure from the Harvard pattern by promotion from within of tutors to full professorships, the departure appeared to be decreasing. Fully two-thirds of Brown and Yale arts and sciences professors had served as tutors at their employing institutions, but the portion was a significant decrement from the 100 percent who had so served on the faculties of 1800. Moreover, none of the six tutors on the Yale faculty in 1820 advanced to a Yale professorship (compared with two of six in 1800); and only two of the thirty-two tutors on the Yale faculty during the 1820s were so advanced (*Historical Register,* 1939). At Brown, even more dramatically, none of the ten tutors appointed during the decade of the 1820s advanced to a Brown professorship (*Historical Catalog,* 1905). It seems fair to conclude, then, at least on the basis of the increasing convergence of practices at Harvard, Yale, Brown, that by 1820 the dual track academic career, defined along junior-senior faculty lines, was on the ascent rather than the descent.

In sum, it may be said that there were at least two "typical" faculty members by the end of the first quarter of the nineteenth century. The first was quite young and took on a temporary assignment as either a tutor or an instructor before embarking on a non-academic career, usually the ministry. He typically came to his employing institution from the ranks of its immediate past graduates and probably undertook training in some traditional profession (usually the ministry) either during or just after his short-term appointment. The second typical faculty member, the professor, had had some postbaccalaureate training in one of the traditional professions (albeit not in his teaching specialty) and had come to a professorship at his alma mater perhaps from a tutorship at the same employing institution, or, more likely, from a nonacademic occupation (often a ministerial seat). During the course of his appointment, he was engaged in itinerant preaching and a variety of community activities that were probably noneducational and nonintellectual in nature (except perhaps for membership in the state historical society). Depending on his particular employing institution, he may have been likely to move on to a nonacademic occupation after a fairly lengthy tenure, or he may have continued his teaching activities for the rest of his life, most probably at his original employing institution. Together, these two types approached their role as a teaching/custodial function, oftentimes as an extension of an earlier or concurrent ministerial role (the college as parish).

THE EVOLUTION OF THE ACADEMIC CAREER, 1820–80

The Disciplinary Career

Well before the Civil War, the disciplinary career of the American professoriate as reflected in the incidence of specialized training, publication activity, association involvements, and career commitment was undergoing significant changes. With Harvard at the vanguard in the area of specialized training—by 1821 fully 40 percent of the faculty had received such training—isolated instances of specialty-trained faculty could be discerned during the 1830s and 1840s at Brown, Bowdoin, and Yale. These institutions, however, did not begin replicating the Harvard pattern to any significant degree until the 1850s and 1860s. In 1841 at Brown, for example, John Lincoln was sent to study in Europe prior to assuming his assistant professorship; however, it was not until the mid-1850s that nearly one-quarter of the Brown faculty were to take leaves for European study, two of them returning with European Ph.D.s (*Historical Catalog,* 1905). At Bowdoin, as early as 1835, John Goodwin was appointed professor of modern languages and dispatched to Europe for two years to prepare for his position; Goodwin, however, remained alone during his thirteen-year tenure pending several appointments in the early 1860s (Packard, 1882). At Yale in 1843 Thomas Thatcher took leave to engage in European study, but it was not until 1863 that Yale appointed its first Ph.D. to the faculty (*Historical Register,* 1939).

At Dartmouth and Williams, developments began later but proceeded more rapidly. At Dartmouth, as late as the mid-1850s, nearly all of the faculty in the academical department had received training in the traditional professions and none in a specialized academic discipline. With a half dozen appointments in the late 1860s and early 1870s, however, Dartmouth virtually reversed that trend in a single decade (Tobias, 1982). At Williams the first professionally trained faculty member was not appointed until 1858,[13] and a second did not assume professorial duties until the close of the Civil War. By 1869, however, fully five of the thirteen members of the Williams faculty could boast graduate training in their teaching specialty (Rudolph, 1956).

As the proportion of faculty with discipline-related credentials increased, so did the proportion of those embarking on an academic career immediately following their training. At Harvard, by 1869, the proportion of faculty with no previous nonacademic career had doubled since 1845, 44 percent versus 22 percent (McCaughey, 1974). Even more dramatically, at Bowdoin during the 1870s nearly two-thirds of the faculty were embarking on their academic careers immediately after their graduate training, compared with barely 20 percent during the preceding decade (Packard, 1882).

If the pattern of increased specialized training together with increased assumption of an academic career immediately following that training did not take hold until the 1850s, other aspects of the disciplinary career such as scholarly publication and participation in learned societies were developing earlier. At Bowdoin the largest jump in the faculty's "professional index"[14] during the nineteenth century occurred during the second quarter of the century. By 1845 70 percent of the faculty were publishing in their field (nearly half were publishing primarily textbooks) and some 30 percent were active in scientific associations (Packard, 1882). At Harvard the professoriate's professional index took its largest jump in the early 1840s during the Quincy presidency, nearly doubling in less than two decades (McCaughey, 1974). The most significant jump in the Brown faculty's professional index occurred between 1845 and the end of the Civil War. By 1845 fully half the Brown faculty was publishing in their field of specialization (even if in the more popular media), and by the Civil War, fully one-half were affiliated with the major disciplinary and scientific associations of the day.[15]

By the 1850s, one unmistakable sign of the ascendance of the disciplinary career was evident: institutional commitments, built on inbreeding, were breaking down in the face of professional mobility resulting from disciplinary commitments (better job opportunities at other institutions). At Bowdoin, three faculty left for positions at other institutions where only one had done so in the previous half century—Henry Wadsworth Longfellow went to Harvard (Packard, 1882). At Brown, while only one professor left during the decade preceding the Civil War, several junior faculty were beginning to pursue their career interests by moves to other institutions (*Historical Catalog*, 1905). And during the 1850s and 1860s, the University of Michigan, and to a lesser extent the University of Wisconsin, were both serving as "revolving doors," especially for senior faculty. At Michigan, for example, among forty-three professors appointed between 1845 and 1868, twenty-three left, typically after relatively short tenures. While many were clearly victims of internecine strife, at least ten left for better academic positions.[16] Thus by the eve of the Civil War, interinstitutional mobility was progressively becoming a fact of academic life.

The External Career

Beginning in the 1850s, the bare outline of an external career based more on faculty's disciplinary expertise, expertise as educators, and role as proponents of culture rather than proponents of religion was becoming discernible at some institutions. At Brown, for example, the immediate pre–Civil War period saw the first instance of a faculty member using academic expertise in the service of state government: the appointment of a professor of chemistry to head the Rhode Island board of weights and measures. By the end of the Civil War, the proportion of the Brown faculty involved in itinerant preaching and other clerical activities dropped from over a third at mid-century to only one-eighth. While a large majority (approaching 75 percent) of the faculty remained involved in civic and community affairs, a change in the nature of that involvement had taken place: only a single faculty member was directly involved in elective politics while the majority were involved in distinctively cultural, academic, and education related activities such as membership on boards of education, holding office in national honor societies, art and historical societies, and state and federal government commissions (*Historical Catalog*, 1905). At Bowdoin, by the eve of the Civil War we find a majority of faculty (four of seven) engaged in extra-institutional roles as specialists, educators, and public men of letters. Parker Cleaveland was holding public lectures on mineralogy and Alpheus Packard on education; President Woods and Professor Packard were engaging in commissioned writing for the Maine Historical Society; and Thomas Upham was producing pamphlets for the American Peace Association (Packard, 1882).

Other institutions lagged a decade or more behind in these developments of the external career. At Dartmouth, as late as 1851, three-quarters of the faculty continued to participate actively in the community as preachers, licentiates, or ordained ministers, and as civic boosters. By the late 1870s, however, the proportion of faculty engaged in clerical activities had dropped precipitously to 15 percent while over half were now significantly engaged in scientific associations in their fields of specialization (Tobias, 1982). At Wisconsin, by the early 1870s professors at the university were being called upon to head the state geological survey (Curti and Carstensen, 1949).

The Institutional Career

The disciplinary career and discipline-based external career taking shape in the immediate pre–Civil War period gave rise to two significant, interrelated changes in the institutional career during the 1860s and 1870s. First was the development of new roles (instructor, assistant professor) and the forging of these new roles into a career sequence that at once gave shape to the academic career and regulated the movement through the junior ranks to a full professorship. Concomittantly there was an expansion and professionalization of the junior faculty. Together, these developments served to integrate into a single structure the dual career track system that had characterized the early part of the nineteenth century.

The instructorship and the assistant professorship actually made their appearance quite early in the annals of some institutions. As early as 1821, fully one-third of the Harvard faculty were serving in instructorships (McCaughey, 1974). The first instructors were appointed at Yale in 1824 (during the 1830s in arts and sciences), at Michigan in 1843, and at Brown in 1844. The first assistant professors were appointed at Brown in 1835, at Yale in 1842, and at Michigan in 1857 (*Historical Catalog,* 1905; *Historical Register,* 1939; *General Catalog,* 1912). Despite the early precedents, these new roles did not take hold for several decades, even at these trend-setting institutions (with the exception of Harvard) and for an even longer period at institutions such as Dartmouth, Bowdoin, and Williams. Thus at Yale only four instructors were appointed during the two decades following the first appointment; and only four additional assistant professors were appointed during the three decades following the first appointment (*Historical Register,* 1939). Similarly, at Brown and Michigan the instructorship languished until the 1860s and the 1870s, respectively, and the assistant professorship languished until the 1890s and the 1880s, respectively (*Historical Catalog,* 1905; *General Catalog,* 1912). At some of the more insulated institutions such as Dartmouth, Bowdoin, and Williams, it was not until the 1860s that these roles first appeared and several decades later that they were firmly entrenched (Tobias, 1982; Packard, 1882; Rudolph, 1956).

These new roles represented a significant departure from the "tutorship"—their incumbents were appointed within a specific department of instruction and were likely to be the products of specialized training—and indeed significantly transformed it, leading in some institutions to the effective disappearance of tutors (at Brown in the 1840s and at Williams in the early 1860s) and in others to the effective transformation of the tutor into a junior instructor. At Yale, for example, in the 1830s tutors began to be assigned to departments of instruction (*Historical Register*, 1939). But for at least several decades they were not quite equivalent to their modern counterpart in at least one fundamental respect: they did not serve in a majority of cases as feeders to the full professorship. At both Harvard and Yale it was not until the 1860s that a substantial proportion of junior faculty advanced to a full professorship (25 percent at Harvard and just over a third at Yale), and not until the decade of the 1870s were a bare majority of the junior faculty so advanced (McCaughey, 1974; *Historical Register*, 1939). Similar patterns prevailed both at Brown and at Michigan—albeit in the latter case quite dramatically so. Between 1845 and 1868, only one of eight junior faculty at Michigan had risen to a full professorship; a single decade later fully 80 percent were so advancing (*General Catalog*, 1912).

The junior faculty role, then, had during the decade immediately following the Civil War undergone a fundamental change from a temporary, dead-end appointment to the first step in the academic career ladder. At the very same time, the ranks of the junior faculty were undergoing their most rapid expansion in terms of numbers and their largest increase in professionalization. By 1880 junior faculty outnumbered their more senior colleagues at Harvard by a ratio of 8 to 5, compared with 3 to 2 a decade earlier (McCaughey, 1974); attained full parity with senior faculty at Michigan, compared with a 2 to 8 ratio a decade earlier (*General Catalog*, 1912); and were on their way to parity at Brown, now constituting 40 percent of the faculty versus less than a third a decade earlier (*Historical Catalog*, 1905). Junior faculty were increasingly coming to their academic career directly from graduate training in their specialty or from junior appointments at other institutions. By 1880 the majority of instructors at Michigan, for example, were either working on or had just completed their doctoral degrees; and, at least at

Harvard and Brown, their professional orientation was as highly developed (as measured by McCaughey's professional index) as their senior colleagues'. The modern academic career had come of age.

Its emergence placed strong pressures on the inner life of the traditional liberal arts college still loyal to the aims of discipline and piety. These pressures were reflected in the pre–Civil War period at institutions such as Yale in the emergent, but amicable, struggles between the old and new guard concerning the relative emphasis on student discipline and moral development versus more academic concerns (Dwight, 1903). They were reflected both more dramatically and less amicably in the immediate post–Civil War period in the form of veritable faculty revolts at some of the more traditional institutions. At Williams, Mark Hopkins, the prototypical old-time college president, was faced with a faculty uprising during the later years of his administration (1868–72). While ostensibly rebelling against the president's disciplinary laxity (his attempt at discipline by precept and moral suasion), their desire for enforcing regular class attendance via a marking system was undergirded by a pervasive concern for standards of scholarship and academic performance. Two years earlier the faculty had succeeded in institutionalizing annual written exams; and in 1869, at the faculty's insistence, admissions standards were tightened and the practice initiated of sending lists of class standings to all parents—all this, despite severe enrollment difficulties. By 1872 these conflicts had led to Hopkins's resignation and the inauguration of a new president—who eight years earlier had come to Williams as only the second European-trained specialist on the faculty (Rudolph, 1956, pp. 223–24).

A decade later, at Dartmouth, fifteen of the twenty-two resident members of the faculty petitioned the Board of Trustees for the resignation of President Bartlett, also of the old guard. The petition precipitated a quasi-judicial hearing by the Board of Trustees on the conduct of President Bartlett's administration. The faculty's action came as a result of the president's attempt to secure the appointment of a new professor of Greek whose religious and moral qualifications seemed preeminent but who did not meet peer evaluation standards within the field of classics. While the faculty were not personally bitter towards Bartlett, they nonetheless viewed it as their professional responsibility to insist on the highest standards of faculty appointments, even if public controversy was necessary. While Bartlett survived the trial and lingered on for over a decade, his successor, William Jewett Tucker, recognized in his 1893 inaugural address the development of a "New Dartmouth," a new kind of college staffed by a new kind of faculty (Tobias, 1982).

CONSOLIDATION OF THE ACADEMIC CAREER
IN THE TWENTIETH CENTURY

The new academic profession in the first decade of the twentieth century, reflecting Tucker's "New Dartmouth," had clearly broken away from the traditions of the liberal arts college devoted to student discipline and piety; it had not, however, yet fully arrived at its contemporary guise. Its uneven development, the tension between the traditional and the new, was reflected in the founding of the American Association of University Professors in 1915. The coming together of eighteen academic luminaries from seven of the leading universities to charter the first national organization of professors suggests a new-found sense of collective professorial self-consciousness, a sense of colleagueship or fraternity in the service of scientific progress. As E.R.A. Seligman, one of the eighteen, proclaimed:

> Loyalty to our institution is admirable, but if our institution for some unfortunate reason stands athwart the progress of science, or even haltingly follows that path, we must use our best efforts to convince our colleagues and the authorities of the error of their ways. . . . In prosecuting this end, we need both individual and collective efforts. The leisure of the laboratory and of the study accounts for much; but almost equally important is the stimulus derived from contact with our colleagues. (cited by Hofstadter and Metzger, 1955, p. 471)

Yet, this sense of collective consciousness was highly restricted in at least two senses. In the first place, it was circumscribed by the definition of who was to be *included* in the collectivity. In the organization's initial constitution, the membership base was limited to "recognized" scholars with at least ten years of experience in the professoriate. While the base was broadened in 1920 to include faculty with three or more years of experience, nonetheless the *collectivity* that was conscious of itself constituted only a small, exclusive contingent of professionalized scholars within the professoriate. Moreover, the evidence suggests that even among those within the collectivity a sense of professional self-consciousness was not widespread. Despite the prominence of the founding team, including men such as John Dewey, J. M. Cattell, and Arthur Lovejoy, many of those initially invited refused or were wary of joining (Hofstadter and Metzger, 1955).

The initial membership invitations were accepted by 867 re-search-oriented full professors percent of the professoriate; seven years later, something less than 6 percent of the professoriate could be counted among the AAUP membership (N = 4000). And even among this select group of professors, strictly professional concerns seemed secondary to institutional ones. John Dewey had sought to direct the energies of the new organization towards developing professional standards for the university-based scholar and away from intervention into faculty-administration disputes at the institutional level. But the membership clearly saw the association's primary function as that of a grievance committee assisting individual faculty vis-à-vis institutional administrators, and during its first years, the association was overwhelmed by the grievances brought to its attention. Thus, in response to its members' needs, a new organization of professors kept strictly professional issues largely in abeyance (Hofstadter and Metzger, 1955).

It was during the period between World War I and the end of World War II that the transformation begun a century earlier was consolidated.

Consolidation of the Disciplinary Career

The two decades between the wars witnessed unprecedented growth in graduate study and research. The annual rate of production of doctorates increased five-fold, from 620 in 1920 to nearly 3,300 in 1940. More discourses and pronouncements on graduate education were published than in any previous or subsequent twenty year period, excepting the present. A cycle of intense, second-order specialization was evident in the differentiation of yet more specialized subareas within the disciplines. The social sciences, for example, spawned in quick succession the Econometric Society (1930), the American Association of Physical Anthropologists (1930), the Society for the Psychological Study of Social Issues (1936), the American Society of Criminology (1936), the Rural Sociological Society (1937), the Society for Applied Anthropology (1941), the Economic History Association (1941), and others. And these more esoteric societies sponsored, in turn, yet more specialized scholarly journals, for example, *Econometrica* (1933), *Sociometry* (1937), *Public Administration Review* (1940), *Journal of Personality* (1932). By the mid-1940s, the dominance of the graduate research model as we know it today was clearly established as was the professoriate's claim to that crucial desideratum of professionalization—specialized expertise (Berelson, 1960).

Consolidation of the External Career

This ascent of specialized expertise by World War II brought faculty into public service on a scale heretofore unknown. Although the public service role had been evolving during the pre–Civil War period and, to a larger extent, during the Progressive Era and World War I, the number of faculty remained relatively small and their national exposure limited. During the heyday of the Wisconsin Idea, (1910–11), some thirty-three individuals held official positions both with the state and with the university, mostly as agricultural experts or with the state railroad or tax commission; thirteen others were "on call" at the capital as needed, including political scientists, economists, and lawyers. Less than 10 percent of the university faculty was directly involved, and this group included representatives of only a handful of disciplines (Veysey, 1965).

During World War I, faculty served the nation primarily through two vehicles: the National Board for Historical Service and the Committee on Public Information. The former, linked to the leadership of the American Historical Association, channeled the efforts of several dozen historians into the revision of secondary schools' social studies curricula in the direction of pro-war civics. Under the latter's auspices, over a hundred social scientists were commissioned to write wartime propaganda pamphlets, and others were pressed into service to monitor foreign language newspaper editorial policies to detect disloyalty (Gruber, 1976).

The Brain Trust assembled by Franklin Roosevelt to address the economic and social havoc wrought by the Depression provided a highly visible, public showcase for faculty talent on an unprecedented scale as well as a testament to the practical utility of research and scholarship. Between 1930 and 1935, forty-one private and state-supported universities examined by Orr (1978) granted nearly three hundred leaves to full-time faculty for the express purpose of serving the federal government. A much larger number of faculty, particularly those at the larger universities with graduate departments, served state and local governments "on overload." Again, in the early 1940s, it was to academics that the federal government turned in support of the national defense effort and the prosecution of World War II.

This new found visibility and public support contributed immeasurably to the differentiation and upgrading of the faculty role. The esteem in which members of the academic profession were held increased markedly as did the prestige attached to an academic career. Bowen (1978) has documented the close association of public attitudes toward academe and levels of faculty salaries and pinpointed World War II as marking a major upturn in both the level and rate of real growth in faculty salaries. Not only did the salaries sharply increase but growing attention was focused on the economic security of faculty members. The faculty had initially been excluded from the Social Security program and only a very small group were covered by the Carnegie Corporation's faculty pension program, which was created in 1906 and was by then effectively closed. The 1930s witnessed the widespread establishment of faculty retirement plans, including incorporation of the Teacher's Insurance Annuity Association. In 1934 about 40 percent of faculty were covered, and by the beginning of World War II, the proportion had increased to nearly three-fifths (Orr, 1978).

Consolidation of the Institutional Career

On their own campuses, professors' expertise translated into the bargaining power necessary to markedly improve their lot. It was during this period that the quest for job security was satisfied. Through the nineteenth century and the first quarter of the twentieth century the modal principle of *faculty as mere employees,* though increasingly challenged, remained firmly entrenched. No provisions for job security existed, and tenure as we know it today was simply unheard of. While many full professors were on *indefinite* appointments, that simply meant that no term of appointment had been specified in their contract. Indefinite appointments were never the equivalent of *permanent* appointments, either in intent or law; and individuals on such appointments could be dismissed at any time. Practically and legally speaking, even the most senior faculty served at the pleasure of the board of trustees (Metzger, 1973). Moreover, for junior faculty, neither a recognized set of procedures nor a timetable were yet established for attaining even these *indefinite* appointments that were the reward of a full professorship. An individual faculty member might serve his institution for fifteen or twenty years and be dismissed at any time without reason given and without a hearing. And this possibility was time and again realized, even at those institutions such as Yale and Wisconsin with a tradition of faculty power (Orr, 1978). In its 1940 statement on tenure, culminating fourteen years of discussion, the American Association of University Professors articulated the judicial concept of *permanent* faculty tenure, designed a means for regularizing the flow of tenure decision-making (that is, by stipulating the six-year "probationary period"), and endorsed procedures ensuring due process on nonreappointment. By that time the AAUP had sufficient stature to gain widespread institutional acceptance of its pronouncement.

It was during this period as well that increasing recognition of faculty as professionals was being reflected in their increasing role in institutional decision-making. Cowley (1980) rightly points out that faculty governance structures had existed statutorily at several leading institutions, including Harvard, Princeton, and Pennsylvania, as early as the mid-eighteenth century when many institutions were first developing a small core of "permanent" faculty; and by the latter half of the nineteenth century, faculty bodies had developed considerable authority at institutions such as Yale, Cornell, and Wisconsin. However, although precedent may have clearly placed within their purview such areas as student discipline and admission and degree requirements (Cowley, 1980), faculty prerogatives in matters of curriculum and educational policy, and to an even greater extent in matters of faculty appointments and promotion and selection of academic administrators, were neither clearly nor consistently established. Moreover, in the early twentieth century, powerful presidents such as Nicholas Murray Butler and even William Rainey Harper (Cowley, 1980) were not unknown to ignore them with impunity.

The 1930s saw the blossoming of faculty committee structures at nearly all institutions. By 1939 Haggerty and Works found over two-fifths of their faculty sample employed at institutions accredited by the North Central Association serving on an average of two committees each. Through such committees, faculty came to share increasingly in institutional administration (two-thirds of the then extant committees were primarily administrative in function) and in a more limited way, in the formulation of educational policy (only one fifth of such committees focused on educational policy per se). These developments culminated in the report of Committee T of AAUP in November 1937, which set forth five overarching principles for faculty participation in institutional governance. Taken together, the principles mandate a role for the faculty in the selection of administrators, in the formulation and control of educational policy, and in the appointment and promotion process. While the role assigned to the faculty is largely *consultative,* the document has at its core the conviction that "faculty were not hired employees to be manipulated by president and trustees, but were academic professionals whose role involved teaching and contributing to the direction and major decisions of an institution" (Orr, 1978, pp. 347–48).

The growing recognition of faculty as professionals served not only to elevate the profession but also to broaden entry into it. Professionalization permitted (although it by no means ensured) the introduction of achievement-related criteria of success—the merit principle—and a concommitant reduction in the salience of ascriptive criteria of class origin ("gentlemanliness") and religious orthodoxy. The relaxation of barriers to entry as well as the professions' growing, though by no means great, prestige infused new blood into the academy: by World War II Catholics and Jews constituted nearly one quarter of a heretofore exclusively Protestant profession; the offspring of mid-Atlantic and upper midwestern states were supplanting New Englanders; the sons of farmers and manual laborers were increasingly joining the sons of businessmen and professionals; and *daughters* were now joining the *sons*—fully 13 percent of a sample of faculty from North Central Association accredited institutions (Kunkel, 1938; see also Lipset and Ladd, 1979).

By the end of World War II, the components of the academic role had clearly emerged and crystallized into the highly differentiated model by which we recognize the professor today—teaching, research, student advisement, administration, institutional and public service. Since its initial crystallization, the model has shown remarkable durability; over thirty-five years and enormous fluctuations in the fortunes of American higher education, it has only come to approach more closely its ideal typical expression through greater emphasis on research activity, fuller participation in academic citizenship, and fuller development of the public role.

1. In the cases of Brown, Bowdoin, and Yale, historical catalogues were employed to collect data comparable to McCaughey (1974) and Tobias (1982) on faculty at five points in time: 1800, 1820, 1845, 1869, 1880 (see *Historical Catalog,* 1905; Packard, 1882; *Historical Register,* 1939). The variables for which data were collected included: geographic origin, source of baccalaureate degree, the timing and nature of postbaccalaureate training, the nature of previous nonacademic employment, age and years of teaching experience at the time of initial appointment and at appointment to professorship, academic rank, years at focal institution, nature and timing of any subsequent occupation, nature and extent of publication activity, nature and extent of involvement with extra-institutional organizations (such as historical and literary societies and, later, disciplinary organizations and local and state government), and scores on two indices developed by McCaughey: the outsider index (assessing the relationship of the focal individual to the institution previous to initial appointment)

and the professional index (assessing the extent of professionalization as reflected in postbaccalaureate training, career pattern, publication and research activity, and associational involvements). A similar analysis was also undertaken for the University of Michigan faculty in 1845, 1869, and 1880, based on *General Catalog* (1912).

2. During the period 1685–1701, the tenure of Harvard tutors averaged 6.4 years, increasing to 9.0 years during the first half of the eighteenth century (Smith, 1966).

3. Greenwood no doubt would have stayed on if not for his abrupt dismissal on the grounds of "moral turpitude" (Eliot, 1848).

4. At Harvard, "permanence" was achieved by the appointment of "permanent" tutors as well as professors. The tutorship became institutionalized there in a way it was not at Harvard's sister institutions, largely, it would appear, as a result of the precedent set by the fifty-five year tutorship of Henry Flynt during the first half of the eighteenth century (Smith, 1966).

5. When endowment funds were insufficient for the full maintenance of a professorship, the funds were allowed to accumulate for as much as one or two decades before filling the position (Eliot, 1848).

6. Even at institutions such as Bowdoin, where the ratio of professors to tutors remained the same, appointments during the 1820s gave the permanent professors ascendance (Packard, 1882).

7. Among faculty at the "leading" institutions, over three-fourths were of old New England families; ecclesiastical and business family backgrounds continued to predominate, although the proportion of farm families had begun to increase; and protestantism continued as the professorial religion—although some of the "lower" Protestant denominations, such as Baptists and Methodists, were now rivaling the Presbyterians, the Congregationalists, and Unitarians for hegemony (Veysey, 1965).

8. Four out of ten Harvard professors had studied in Europe, but at least three of these had done so on Harvard stipends provided after their initial appointment as a means of preparation for their professorship (McCaughey, 1974).

9. These mobility patterns represent no significant change from those in 1800.

10. While we use the term "outsiders" here and subsequently to describe these appointees, it should be noted that virtually all of these outsiders at Harvard and elsewhere were in a fundamental sense "insiders" as well, that is, they were returning after a hiatus to their baccalaureate alma mater.

11. Yale did not appoint an instructor until 1824 and that in law. None were appointed in arts and sciences until the 1830s. At Brown, the first instructor was appointed in 1844.

12. Although it is true that two of Harvard's ten professors in 1820 had served as Harvard instructors, this was clearly a notable exception rather than the rule. Indeed, none of the five instructors in 1820 went on to Harvard professorships (McCaughey, 1974).

13. Thomas Clark, who had just received his doctorate in chemistry from the University of Gottingen.

14. See note 1.

15. Included in this latter group were a founder and future president of the American Philological Association; a future vice-president of the American Chemical Soci-

ety; a founder and future vice-president of the American Association for the Advancement of Science; and a founder of the National Academy of Sciences.

16. See Creutz (1981, pp. 55–64) for details on faculty–Board of Regents conflicts. For mobility data, see *General Catalog* (1912, pp. 6–9).

The Structure of
Academic Careers

Roger G. Baldwin
Robert T. Blackburn

The Academic Career as a Developmental Process

Implications for Higher Education

Since World War II, higher education has profited from a steady flow of new personnel. Young academics, fresh from graduate school, have stimulated the educational system with novel perspectives and up-to-date knowledge. It is now obvious, however, that the number of academic vacancies in colleges and universities has slowed to a trickle. Along with others, Mathis [20] fears that during the 1980s higher education may become a declining industry characterized by reduced options for maintaining quality. Assuming that knowledgeable, creative, enthusiastic faculty are essential elements of a successful higher education institution, one fundamental question requires immediate attention: How can colleges and universities most effectively capitalize on the potential of their currently employed, experienced faculty?

Higher education literature does not lack for efforts to answer this question. Most of these responses fall under the heading of "faculty development." Several books and many articles advance various techniques and policies to encourage the professional growth of college teachers. Yet many faculty development approaches seem to lack a basic understanding of individual professors. Blackburn, Behymer, and Hall [5] and Wergin, Mason, and Munson [33] show that faculty development programs often bear little relationship to the clearly defined needs of professors. Based on experience at Virginia Commonwealth University, the latter researchers conclude that "the factor most predictive of success [in faculty development is] . . . depth of knowl-

Roger G. Baldwin is project director, Academic Careers Unlimited, American Association for Higher Education. Robert T. Blackburn is professor of higher education, University of Michigan.

0022-1546/81/1181-0598$00.50/0   © 1981 Ohio State University Press
Journal of Higher Education, 1981, Vol. 52, No. 6

edge about faculty." In other words, information about major faculty characteristics—their motivations, talents, and deficiencies—is fundamental to an effective program of professional growth.

From a conceptual perspective, recent work in developmental psychology provides some useful insights on college professors. Developmental theorists hypothesize that adults, like children, proceed through a series of sequential life stages. Persons at these stages are characterized by stability in some areas and by changing interests and experiences in others.

Levinson et al. [19] describe adulthood as a series of stable and transitional periods. During stable periods the adult pursues fairly clear goals. But periodically, the individual must reorder priorities and change behavior in order to compensate for neglected dimensions of the self (e.g., unfulfilled ambitions, newly acquired interests). Gould [12] and Sheehy [27] support the developmental direction advocated by Levinson. Erikson's theory has been explored for its adult development consequences by Munley [21].

Theories of career development also support the notion that the adult years are not a static phase of life. Super [30, 31] and Hall and Nougaim [13] describe the career as an evolutionary process. First, the individual experiments with a variety of vocational options and then eventually chooses a career direction. With career ambitions firmly in place, the worker next experiences a series of successes and disappointments in pursuit of his or her goals. Later, however, with age and experience, career goals lose their driving quality and many careers become static (the maintenance stage). Last, the individual gradually begins to disengage from the vocational career in favor of other concerns.

From developmental literature, one may infer that the academic career follows an evolutionary course. Consequently, it should be possible to gain valuable information about college professors by studying them at successive ages and career stages. This assumption was the guiding principle of the present study. The research reported here, however, is not a direct test of any of these conceptual frameworks (e.g., mid-life crisis) but rather is an investigation of faculty career stages.

Research on Faculty Career Development

Studies of faculty attitudes [7, 17, 26], professional interests [11, 16, 18], and satisfaction [1, 9] reveal important distinctions among professors of different ages or career stages. For example, in a nationwide study of the professoriate, Ladd and Lipset [17] found distinct differences in the political attitudes of older and younger faculty. The researchers discovered "a neat progression (more liberal to more conservative) with movement from the youngest to the oldest cohort." Ladd and Lipset conclude that these differences cannot be ascribed to generational effects because the data show a linear progression "with none of the peaks and valleys which the generations thesis would produce" [17, p. 196].

Blackburn [4] found that faculty attitudes also vary by career stage. In a study of liberal arts college faculty, he learned that instructors had the most liberal political attitudes; associate professors had the most conservative; and assistant and full professors were in the intermediate range politically. Blackburn suggests that faculty go through a career cycle during which their liberalism periodically waxes and wanes.

Faculty role preferences also seem to evolve gradually. Fulton and Trow's [11] national study revealed that many professors' interests and values "turn away from research and toward teaching with increasing age" [11, p. 54]. Their evidence shows that the percentage of faculty who describe themselves as "exclusive teachers" doubles while the percentage of self-described "strong researchers" halves between the thirty-one to thirty-five and fifty-six to sixty age cohorts.

More concrete variables such as faculty workload [32] and productivity [3, 4, 23, 24] also seem to vary with chronological or career age. Thompson [32], for example, found that total weekly time devoted to class preparation decreases with an increase in faculty rank. Apparently there is an inverse relationship between professorial rank and percentage of time devoted to teaching.

Pelz and Andrews's [24] research has identified a saddle-shaped curve of scholarly productivity with age—a rise, fall, and another rise during the professor's fifties. Blackburn, Behymer, and Hall [5] also found the saddle-shaped curve as a function of career stage. They report that productivity decreases at about the associate professor stage but increases again at full professorship. Bayer and Dutton's [3] research reveals a more direct decline at advanced career stages. Their study shows that article publication peaks at about five to ten years of career age. Among faculty with twenty-five years of experience these researchers found only a slight decline in productivity. But they did find a substantial increase in the number of faculty who produced no scholarly work.

Four studies have limited data on mid-career phenomena of academics [10, 22, 28, 29]. However, the research on developmental trends in faculty attributes is limited. Available studies tend to focus on specific faculty characteristics or particular aspects of the professorial role. To date, the research has not been adequately synthesized to present a comprehensive picture of academic career development. Furthermore, the data come from cross-sectional, not longitudinal, studies and hence are not conclusive with respect to change over time. Therefore, it would be misleading to imply that all research on academic careers supports the basic concepts of developmental theory. Nevertheless, there is sufficient empirical evidence to warrant further investigation from the developmental perspective.

Methodology

The sample consisted of 106 male college faculty members (75 percent response rate) from twelve liberal arts colleges in the Midwest. Despite the individual distinctiveness of each institution, the set of colleges was treated as a homogeneous pool of academics. On the basis of educational preparation, the faculty are much more alike than different. In the random selection of these faculty within specified disciplines (biology, chemistry, history, philosophy, and religion)[1] and career stage, all but one happened to have the Ph.D., and most received this degree from the nation's highest ranking graduate schools. These selective colleges enjoy reputations as preferred places for academic employment.

The career stages were:

   I.   Assistant professors in the first three years of full-time college teaching
  II.   Assistant professors with more than three years of college teaching experience
 III.   Associate professors
  IV.   Full professors more than five years from retirement
   V.   Full professors within five years of formal retirement.

Faculty provided information on their careers in higher education by participating in an extensive personal interview and by completing a brief questionnaire. Data collection focused on faculty values and goals, professional strengths and weaknesses, critical career events,

[1]It turned out that career development was independent of academic discipline.

51

and problem-solving behavior. Vocational satisfaction, career reassessment, and change were also studied. (See Baldwin [2] for instruments used.)[2]

The critical life-event instrument was taken from Havighurst et al. [14]. Some of the general questions came from the Carnegie Commission national surveys of faculty. The interview schedule was pretested, revised, and then piloted on a sample of faculty in a comparable setting. Results were validated by peers. Some of the interview questions were open-ended. Responses to those items were content analyzed. (This led to data reporting percentages of respondents.) Other questions asked the subjects to rate or rank items on scales they were given. In all, the data have a high degree of reliability and validity.

The responses of the five career stage subgroups were compared on each topic of investigation. Frequencies and percentages (since Ns per category are not equal) or mean ratings (or rankings) were calculated for this purpose. Substantial differences among subgroups served to identify developmental trends and fluctuations. The data are collected in tables by topic and, hence, mix ratings, rankings, and percentages. However, because the analysis is not one using statistical techniques for testing the differences between groups, but rather an examination of academic career development, this atypical procedure is justified. Since the Ns per category are relatively small (about twenty), a shift of a few persons can change fiqures appreciably. However, it is the collection of behaviors showing a similar pattern that gives weight to the arguments, not any one item by itself.

Findings

Career development, like other developmental functions, is a very complex process. Progress in one's career is undoubtedly stimulated and qualified by the interactive effects of internal and external forces.[3] Initially, it may seem difficult to identify any common patterns in the lives of college professors. Analysis of the data, however, reveals that some faculty characteristics remain stable over time. Others evolve

[2]Due to the cross-sectional design, it is important to recognize that particular historical events may account for some of the differences found among the five subgroups. (See, e.g., Schaie [25] and Wohlwill [34].) An approaching tenure decision has different stressful consequences today than it did twenty years ago for a young assistant professor. The reader should keep this factor in mind when interpreting the study's findings.

[3]Internal forces would include such variables as the aging process and personal health. External forces would include factors such as economic recession and new employment opportunities.

consistently (steadily increase or decrease), and some fluctuate predict-
ably (e.g., increase, decrease, and then increase again) during the career. Information on critical career events also identifies important
common occurrences that help to shape and direct academic careers.
To clarify our understanding of professors' career development or evolution, the findings will be divided into four categories, viz, those that
show: (1) stable faculty characteristics; (2) evolving faculty characteristics; (3) fluctuating faculty characteristics; and (4) critical events in the
academic career.

Stable Characteristics

As Table 1 reveals, on many personal, as well as teaching and scholarly dimensions, there are only insignificant differences between fac-

TABLE 1

Important Personal, Teaching, and Scholarly Matters that are Approximately the Same at Each
Career Stage

Activities	Career Stage (N)					
	I (19)	II (22)	III (22)	IV (25)	V (18)	Average
Personal						
1. Mean *rating* of overwhelming workload as a source of pressure in the academic career	3.17*	3.24	3.17	3.24	2.75	3.13
2. Percentage who have a contribution to the development of students as a long-term goal	57.9	45.4	59.1	72.0	61.1	59.4
3. Percentage who say departmental and college affairs are the least satisfying or rewarding role	52.6	45.4	54.5	44.0	27.8	45.3
4. Percentage who mention times of new or increased responsibilities as difficult career periods	†	27.3	36.4	32.0	38.9	33.3
Teaching						
5. Mean *ranking* of the importance of teaching and interacting with students	1.05‡	1.07	1.07	1.14	1.03	1.07
6. Percentage of total professional time allotted to teaching and interacting with students	62.8	63.4	58.4	57.0	53.9	59.1
7. Percentage who mention teaching skills as one of their major professional strengths	68.4	68.2	54.4	64.0	55.5	62.3
Scholarship						
8. Mean *ranking* of the importance of traditional research and scholarship	2.31‡	2.45	2.52	2.74	2.53	2.52
9. Percentage of total professional time allotted to traditional research and scholarship	15.5	14.2	12.4	15.0	11.2	13.8
10. Percentage who mention knowledge and competence in various academic fields as one of their major professional strengths	52.6	45.4	54.5	52.0	50.0	50.9

*On scale of 4 = a great source to 1 = not a source of pressure
†Not asked of career stage 1 people
‡Ranks were on a set of five items, 1 being first or highest

53

ulty at different career stages. All five cohorts rated pressure from workload (item 1) as the greatest source of stress in their vocation. Similarly, the uniformly high ranking of the importance of teaching (item 5) not only shows infinitesimal differences between groups but also shows that variation within groups was slight.[4]

The way faculty allocate their time (items 6 and 9), the high value placed on scholarship (item 8)—a clear second to teaching, however— and other matters support the contention that many characteristics remain quite stable over the career span. (One of the five groups occasionally differs from the others—e.g., group V on items 1 and 3—but for the most part the fluctuations about the mean or percentage differences are small.)

Evolving Characteristics

The complexity of the academic career is confirmed, however, by substantial evidence of career evolution. For example, participants identified some "difficult" and some "easy" career times. The existence of difficult and easy phases suggests that the demands of the academic vocation change over the years. There was considerable agreement at all career stages on two periods of difficulty. One of these is the first few years of teaching (usually 1–3). Proportions ranging from 72 percent of experienced assistant professors (stage II) to 44 percent of retiring professors (stage V) recalled the early years as a demanding time. Fairly sizeable percentages of faculty (27 percent stage II to 39 percent, stage V) also viewed periods of new or added responsibilities as difficult. New courses covering unfamiliar material, additional committee work, and administrative responsibilities are among the tasks that sometimes increased the workload of college professors.

Table 2 shows organizational, teaching, scholarly, and personal dimensions along which faculty systematically increase or decrease over the course of the academic career. Understanding of and effective service to one's college (items 1 and 2) evolve rapidly in the early stages and continue to increase (although more slowly) in later years. The early difficulty with teaching passes and faculty increasingly become more comfortable with that role (items 3 and 4). At the same time, pleasure from teaching steadily wanes (items 6).

Scholarly matters decline on all dimensions (items 7 and 9, although group III on item 7 and group V on item 9 deviate from a linear progression), even precipitously (item 8). Similarly, pressure and stress

---

[4]Since a score of 1 was the highest rank, an average difference of only 1.07 means only about one in fourteen gave it a rank lower than 1.

TABLE 2

Organizational, Teaching, Scholarly, and Personal Matters that are Systematically Larger or Smaller at Successive Career Stages

Activities	Career Stage (N)					
	I (19)	II (22)	III (22)	IV (25)	V (18)	Average
Organizational						
1. Percentage of faculty who say they understand their institution's mode of operation	21.0	63.6	81.8	96.0	94.4	72.6
2. Percentage who mention service to one's college or department as one of their professional strengths	5.3	13.6	27.3	28.0	44.4	23.6
Teaching						
3. Mean *rating* of comfortableness with teaching	4.05*	4.39	4.41	4.56	4.57	4.40
4. Percentage who mention a teaching deficiency as one of their major professional weaknesses	52.6	50.0	27.3	24.0	11.1	33.0
5. Percentage who discuss a teaching concern with colleagues	68.4	68.2	59.1	56.0	27.8	56.6
6. Percentage who express pleasure related to teaching and its outcomes	100.0	90.9	86.4	84.0	77.8	81.7
Scholarship						
7. Mean *rating* of comfortableness with research/scholarship	3.68*	3.45	3.64	3.26	3.25	3.45
8. Percentage who mention research competence and involvement as one of their major professional strengths	26.3	22.7	13.6	12.0	0.0	15.1
9. Percentage who express pleasure with the opportunities for research, scholarship, and growth and development	47.4	36.4	22.7	12.0	22.2	27.3
Personal						
10. Mean *rating* of desire to succeed as a source of career pressure	3.17†	3.0	2.78	2.64	2.47	2.82
11. Mean rating on the amount of pressure or stress faculty experience in their occupation	3.55‡	3.29	3.39	3.36	3.13	3.35
12. Percentage who have goals concerning career advancement or change	63.2	36.4	22.7	4.0	0.0	24.5

*On scale of 5 = very comfortable to 1 = uncomfortable
†On scale of 4 = a great source to 1 = not a source
‡On scale of 5 = a great deal to 1 = very little

steadily decrease over the course of the career (item 11), but so do desires (items 10 and 12).

Fluctuating Characteristics

Most dimensions of the academic role fluctuate somewhat, at least on a short-term basis. Such variation may occur well within the larger stages established here. Even those dimensions that appear to remain relatively constant or to increase or decrease systematically most likely undergo sporadic or cyclical alterations in every academic year. Few human beings are impervious to uncontrollable environmental changes. There are, however, some characteristics that seem to follow even more complex patterns. Several of these are collected in Table 3. Some characteristics fall, but rise again (item 1). Some go up steadily to a peak and then tumble (item 2). Participation in professional development activities follows a U-shaped curve (item 4).

In the area of personal concerns there are also peak and low times. Much of the data localizes the majority of career reassessment[5] to a nebulous mid-career period. Professors in stages II, III, and IV most often stated that they had considered career changes. Likewise, these same professors most frequently acknowledged a feeling that their careers were at a "standstill." It seems, however, that reassessment experiences are most intense during the late assistant professor (II) and continuing full professor (IV) periods. Substantial proportions (II, 23 percent; IV, 48 percent) of faculty at these levels described reassess-

TABLE 3

Professional and Personal Matters that Appear to Fluctuate Over the Course of the Academic Career

	Career Stage (N)					
Activities	I (19)	II (22)	III (22)	IV (25)	V (18)	Average
Professional						
1. Mean *rating* of comfortableness with non-teaching interaction with students	4.21*	4.04	3.95	3.78	4.39	4.06
2. Percentage who state that rapport with students and colleagues is one of their major professional strengths	21.0	45.4	59.1	60.0	27.8	44.3
3. Percentage who have a contribution to one's disciplinary field as a goal	73.7	54.5	50.0	32.0	44.4	50.0
4. Percentage who have not engaged in a professional development activity in the past two years	78.9	13.6	36.4	40.0	50.0	42.4
Personal						
5. Percentage who mention personal qualities or problems that restrict their professional performance as a major professional weakness	21.0	31.8	45.4	20.0	27.8	29.2
6. Percentage who feel their career is at a standstill	21.0	40.9	50.0	28.0	11.1	31.1
7. Percentage who have considered a career change	57.9	90.9	77.3	64.0	50.0	68.9
8. Percentage who say they are very satisfied with their current professional position	42.1	13.6	50.0	52.0	72.2	45.3

*On scale of 5 = very comfortable to 1 = uncomfortable

[5]The reassessment experiences discussed here conceptually parallel the transition stages discussed by Levinson et al. [19] and other developmental theorists.

ment experiences (including mid-career crises, loss of interest, lack of recognition, and dissatisfaction) as difficult times in their careers.

These two stages are logical times to take stock of one's career. Experienced assistant professors must consider what options are available if they do not receive tenure. Continuing full professors must weigh alternatives within the academic profession. Should they remain primarily classroom teachers or should they try to diversify their responsibilities as a means to maintain their professional vitality? In contrast, only one associate professor (III) mentioned career questioning among his troublesome vocational experiences. This low percentage may reflect associate professors' recent success in the tenure process. College teachers who are advancing and receiving recognition are probably less likely to experience nagging career doubts than are those who perceive limited opportunities.

Critical Events

The faculty also listed critical events that had significantly influenced their careers. (See [6] for a related study using this technique.) For the most part, these were important occurrences that had a positive effect on professors' career development. Among these events, faculty frequently described opportunities for professional growth (e.g., sabbaticals, workshops, research projects, independent study grants). In the latter four career stages the proportion of faculty mentioning growth opportunities ranged from 59 percent of experienced assistant professors (II) to 91 percent of continuing full professors (IV). One may conclude from this finding that faculty see the beneficial effects of opportunities to expand their professional capabilities.

When listing critical career events, professors also cited various promotions and role changes as major career developments. In addition to movement up the traditional academic ladder (from assistant to full professor), faculty listed new responsibilities and new interests that influenced their career direction. Administrative duties, different research interests, and increased activity in professional organizations are some of the ways academic careers diversify. The findings indicate that professors continue to grow well beyond the time they surmount the final, formal academic hurdle—full professorship. For example, 59 percent of retiring faculty (V) listed internal administrative roles and external professional activities among their important career events. In comparison, only 45 percent of continuing full professors (IV) mentioned administrative positions and only 27 percent of this group cited outside professional activities. In general, the critical events data strongly suggest that variety, change, and a sense of progression are essential to academic careers the respondents judged successful and satisfying.

Overall Conclusions

Three overall conclusions emerge from a developmental study of the faculty career process. First, colleges and universities, as well as individual faculty, must pay greater attention to the characteristics and concerns of each phase of the academic career. Ideally, appropriate services and opportunities should be available to aid faculty at difficult career benchmarks.

Second, collegiate institutions must maintain the flexibility necessary to encourage professional growth. Kanter [15] has written convincingly of the negative impact of vocational "stuckness." By providing opportunities for meaningful career growth, colleges and universities can prevent the lowered aspirations and occupational disengagement characteristic of "stuck" professionals. Perhaps the uncreative career maintenance stage can be postponed for many academics until they are nearly ready to retire, or perhaps the stage can even be completely eliminated.

Third, by identifying important differences among faculty, developmental research emphasizes the need to treat every professor as a unique individual. Attention to individual needs should create a climate conducive to maximum faculty development and performance.

Gould [12] suggests that the static career concept must give way to a growth ideology because "the costs of ignoring the unstoppable growth processes are too great." Of course, programs to promote faculty growth require more than a change in philosophy. Colleges and universities must be willing to experiment, invest resources, accept criticism, and risk failure in order to stimulate genuine professional development. Many institutions have recently launched instructional development programs. However, this study shows that faculty needs are much broader than just assistance with teaching. In fact, except in the first year or two, teaching is a smaller concern than, say, an unfilled desire to make a contribution to one's field. Higher education institutions now need to broaden their focus to include the professional, organizational, and personal development of faculty.

Table 4 is an effort to summarize salient attributes and experiences of faculty at each of the five career stages. The descriptions consist of generalized inferences from the self-reported data. However, these inferences have not been documented systematically. The table's purpose

58

TABLE 4

Faculty Characteristics and Experiences at Five Stages of the Academic Career

I	II	III	IV	V
Assistant Professors in the First Three Years of Full-time College Teaching	Assistant Professors with More Than Three Years of College Teaching Experience	Associate Professors	Full Professors More Than Five Years from Retirement	Full Professors within Five Years of Retirement
—Idealistic (sometimes unrealistic) career ambitions	—More confident of their skills than are novice professors	—Enigmatic	—At a career turning point	—Generally content with their career achievements
—Enthusiastic about the job	—More politically sophisticated —know how their institution works and how to get things done	—Enjoy peer recognition associated with tenure and promotion	—Reduced enthusiasm for teaching and research	—Quite limited goals for the remainder of their professional career
—Adjusting to novel occupational demands	—Apprehensive about upcoming tenure evaluation	—Becoming integral part of their institution. Actively involved in college activities, especially major committees	—Sometimes question the value of the academic career	—Gradually withdrawing from various responsibilities
—Concerned about succeeding as a teacher	—Seeking recognition and advancement (confirmed by receipt of tenure)	—Generally satisfied with career progress to date	—Must decide to continue same career activities or move in different directions (choice between stagnation and diversification)	—Fear their knowledge is out-of-date
—Eager to engage in scholarship	—Experience disappointment if career does not measure up to original expectations	—Sometimes nagged by fear that career has plateaued, that there is little room left to advance professionally	—Seek to extend career (influence) beyond own campus through consultation, professional organizations	—Somewhat isolated from younger colleagues
—Unfamiliar with informal operations and governance (power) structure in their higher education institution	—Question their future in higher education and occasionally consider career alternatives		—Limited opportunities for change; advancement can lead to disillusionment at this stage	—Try to cope with problems independently
—Receptive to assistance from more experienced colleagues				—Only half will take advantage of formal professional growth opportunities
				—Particularly comfortable with service to their department or college

59

is to give some sense of the common experiences of liberal arts college professors at successive stages of the academic career. Of course, these composite descriptions do not accurately describe the career of any specific individual.

Discussion and Implications

It is important to recognize the significance of continuing faculty evolution. Many of the changes that professors experience occur in areas directly related to their performance as teachers and scholars. Hence these findings have major implications for higher education.

A developmental conception of the academic career can be very useful to college administrators and to individual professors. Developmental research helps to identify strengths and weaknesses that are prevalent at different points in the professorial career. This information permits administrators to capitalize effectively on professors' knowledge, expertise, and interests. For example, new faculty members are often restricted to introductory and service courses that are unpopular with more senior professors and that require more time and experience to teach well. Taking developmental knowledge into consideration, a department chairperson might assign a specialized upper level course to a novice teacher. This decision acknowledges the educational value of the current knowledge and up-to-date research capability possessed by a recent Ph.D.

This study indicates that experienced faculty gradually become more comfortable with the teaching role and more adept at service (e.g., governance, committee work, policy formulation) to their institution. This developmental information suggests certain roles where veteran professors may be particularly effective. Perhaps a senior, exemplary teacher in each department could act as a mentor or consultant on teaching to beginning and adjunct faculty. Likewise, experienced faculty, with their knowledge of institutional processes and personalities, should be qualified to undertake special projects for the institution. Long-range planning, studies of student attrition, and work with alumni groups are all areas where veteran faculty can use their experience to serve the institution effectively.

The knowledge that research interests decline during the career also has implications for faculty and administrators. Funding, facilities, and released time reserved for mid-career faculty could generate new enthusiasm for research and halt professional entropy.

Evidence of alternating difficult and easy periods in the academic career should also enlighten administrators and faculty. The first few years of teaching and initial periods with new or added responsibilities may be particularly stressful. This information suggests that faculty performance might be improved by easing some responsibilities (e.g., committee assignments) or providing some additional support (e.g., secretarial help, research assistance) during these periods. In contrast, during easy periods of the career, it might be beneficial for faculty to assume challenging assignments. A new administrative task or community service project may inject a sufficient dose of variety to enliven the routine of an established college teacher.

In addition, academic administrators can profit from the realization that faculty gradually change their professional development and problem-solving techniques and become more independent. Such information provides guidelines for faculty development policy by indicating who may be receptive to what types of support. Whereas younger professors may enjoy formal workshops and seminars, many senior faculty seem to prefer growth opportunities that they can design and carry out at their own pace. Logically, funds to encourage professional development should be applied where they will reap the maximum benefit. A variety of in-service development opportunities may be necessary to generate optimal faculty growth.

The mid-life experience of career doubt and reassessment likewise has implications for administrators and faculty. Once career questioning is recognized as a normal occurrence, it is possible to help faculty work through it constructively. Programs that encourage career planning can assist professors in adapting consciously and systematically to personal and institutional changes. Flexible leave policies and internship opportunities can invigorate mid-career faculty by permitting them to experiment with vocational alternatives. Early retirement programs, temporary administrative roles, and retraining for growing teaching areas are each options that may satisfy the developmental needs of some faculty. Such policies also expand institutional flexibility as they open positions for new professors.

Analysis of critical events in the academic career also affirms the importance of continued career growth and progress. Faculty described their career advancement as a series of new growth opportunities, role changes, new interests, and new responsibilities. This evidence stresses the need to maintain opportunities for ongoing career growth.

It is clear that college administrators can benefit from a developmental view of the academic career. Knowledge of developmental differences helps deans and chairpersons to identify individuals and groups deserving special attention. It helps them determine what policies and programs would provide the greatest benefit. Developmental information also helps administrators to order needs and determine where limited funds can be most effective. Likewise, it is clear that individual faculty can profit from developmental research on academic careers. In particular, the findings of the present study have implications for career and life planning. The findings suggest that a static career devoted predominantly to teaching may be less satisfying than a diversified course. Understanding the career as an evolutionary process permits a professor to anticipate and prepare for vocational changes. Planned career development should be more rational and rewarding than evolution stimulated by chance opportunities and routine periods of dissatisfaction.

This conclusion suggests that college educators should take responsibility for their career growth and advancement. They should not permit erratic events and varying conditions to dictate their career course. Instead, professors should regularly assess what they have achieved professionally, where they are headed, and how these factors match with their personal values and goals. Faculty who plan career development strategy are more likely to maintain steady professional growth and enjoy the satisfaction of regular career renewal.

References

1. Baldwin, R. G. "Adult and Career Development: What Are the Implications for Faculty." In *Current Issues in Higher Education*, edited by R. Edgerton, pp. 13–20. Washington, D.C.: American Association for Higher Education, 1979.
2. _____. "The Faculty Career Process—Continuity and Change: A Study of College Professors at Five Stages of the Academic Career." Ph.D. dissertation, University of Michigan, 1979.
3. Bayer, A. E., and J. E. Dutton. "Career Age and Research—Professional Activities of Academic Scientists." *Journal of Higher Education*, 48 (May/June 1977), 259–82.
4. Blackburn, R. T. *Tenure: Aspects of Job Security on the Changing Campus.* Research monograph 19. Atlanta: Southern Regional Education Board, 1972.
5. Blackburn, R. T., C. E. Behymer, and D. E. Hall. "Research Note: Correlates of Faculty Publications." *Sociology of Education*, 51 (April 1978), 132–41.
6. Blackburn, R. T., and R. J. Havighurst. "Career Patterns of U.S. Male Academic Social Scientists." *Higher Education*, 8 (1979), 553–72.
7. Blackburn, R. T., and J. D. Lindquist. "Faculty Behavior in the Legislative Process: Professional Attitudes vs. Behavior Concerning the Inclusion of Students in Academic Decision-Making." *Sociology of Education*, 44 (Fall 1971), 398–421.
8. Blackburn, R. T., G. R. Pellino, A. Boberg, and C. O'Connell. "Faculty Develop-

ment Programs, the Improvement of Instruction, and Faculty Goals: An Evaluation." In *Current Issues in Higher Education*, edited by R. Edgerton, pp. 32–48. Washington, D.C.: American Association for Higher Education, 1980.

9. Eckert, R. E., and H. Y. Williams. *College Faculty View Themselves and Their Jobs*. Minneapolis: College of Education, University of Minnesota, 1972.

10. Erez, M., and Z. Shneorson. "Personality Types and Motivational Characteristics of Academics Versus Professionals in Industry in the Same Occupational Discipline." *Journal of Vocational Behavior*, 17 (1980), 95–105.

11. Fulton, O., and M. Trow. "Research Activity in American Higher Education." *Sociology of Education*, 47 (Winter 1974), 29–73.

12. Gould, R. L. *Transformations*. New York: Simon and Schuster, 1978.

13. Hall, D. T., and K. Nougaim. "An Examination of Maslow's Need Hierarchy in an Organizational Setting." *Organizational Behavior and Human Performance*, 3 (1968), 12–35.

14. Havighurst, R. J., W. J. McDonald, L. Maeulen, and J. Mazel. "Male Social Scientists: Lives After 60." *The Gerontologist*, 19 (February 1979), 55–60.

15. Kanter, R. M. "Changing the Shape of Work: Reform in Academe." In *Current Issues in Higher Education*, edited by R. Edgerton. Washington, D.C.: American Association for Higher Education, 1979.

16. Klapper, H. L. "The Young College Faculty Member—A New Breed?" *Sociology of Education*, 42 (Winter 1969), 38–49.

17. Ladd, E. C., and S. M. Lipset. *The Divided Academy: Professors and Politics*. New York: McGraw-Hill, 1975.

18. _____. "What Do Professors Like Best About Their Jobs?" *Chronicle of Higher Education*, 12 (March 29, 1976), 10.

19. Levinson, D. J., C. N. Darrow, E. B. Klein, M. H. Levinson, and B. McKee. *The Seasons of a Man's Life*. New York: Alfred A. Knopf, 1978.

20. Mathis, B. C. "Academic Careers and Adult Development: A Nexus for Research." In *Current Issues in Higher Education*, edited by R. Edgerton. Washington, D.C.: American Association for Higher Education, 1979.

21. Munley, P. H. "Erickson's Theory of Psychosocial Development and Career Development." *Journal of Vocational Behavior*, 10 (1977), 261–69.

22. Neapolitan, J. "Occupational Change in Mid-Career: An Exploratory Investigation." *Journal of Vocational Behavior*, 16 (1980), 212–25.

23. Parsons, T., and G. M. Platt. *The American Academic Profession: A Pilot Study*. Cambridge, Mass.: Harvard University Press, 1968.

24. Pelz, D. C., and F. M. Andrews. *Scientists in Organizations*. Revised edition. New York: Wiley, 1976.

25. Schaie, K. W. "Cross-Sectional Methods in the Study of Psychological Aspects of Aging." *Journal of Gerontology*, 14 (April 1959), 208–15.

26. Schuman, H., and E. O. Laumann. "Do Most Professors Support the War?" *Trans-Action*, 5 (1967), 32–35.

27. Sheehy, G. M. *Passages: Predictable Crises of Adult Life*. New York: E. P. Dutton, 1976.

28. Sisson, P. J., G. L. Arthur, S. V. Fierro, and G. Gazda. "Success Variables in Outstanding Business and Industrial Leaders in America: A National Survey." *Vocational Guidance Quarterly*, 26 (1978), 197–206.

29. Snyder, R. A., A. Howard, and T. L. Hammer. "Mid-Career Change in Academia: The Decision to Become an Administrator." *Journal of Vocational Behavior*, 13 (1978), 229–41.

30. Super, D. E. *The Psychology of Careers: An Introduction to Vocational Development*. New York: Harper and Row, 1957.

31. _____. "A Life-Span, Life-Space Approach to Career Development." *Journal of Vocational Behavior*, 16 (1980), 282–98.

32. Thompson, R. K. *How Does the Faculty Spend Its Time?* Mimeographed. Seattle: University of Washington, 1971.

33. Wergin, J. F., E. J. Mason, and P. J. Munson. "The Practice of Faculty Development: An Experience-Derived Model." *Journal of Higher Education*, 47 (May/June 1976), 289–308.

34. Wohlwill, J. F. "Methodology and Research Strategy in the Study of Developmental Change. In *Life-Span Developmental Psychology: Research and Theory*, edited by L. R. Goulet and P. B. Baltes. New York: Academic Press, 1970.

Three

Employment Profiles of Part-Timers

Part-time faculty come from extraordinarily varied and interesting work lives. We interviewed corporate executives and "starving poets," medical doctors and massage therapists, chemists and coaches, musicians and politicians, entrepreneurs and entertainers. Typically, part-time faculty have other work and sources of income. The large majority spend less than half their time teaching and derive an average of 18 percent of their total income from this source (NSOPF '88).

To explore how teaching fits in with their other work and activities, we asked about professional experiences, other jobs, and other teaching assignments. We also asked whether part-time faculty experienced conflicts among their roles and what their career aspirations were. Our goal was to understand the whole person so that we could better understand why people chose to teach part-time and what this decision meant to their lives and careers.

We were able to recognize four major clusters of academic background, employment history, and motivations. These clusters are only partly consistent with the popular and widely referenced typology generated a number of years ago by Howard Tuckman's (1978) research, which we summarize for the purpose of comparison.

We can see clearly that part-timers are not a monolithic group of marginal employees. We have identified four distinct sub-populations that we describe in this chapter. We show how individuals within each of these groups need varying career options and patterns of work and compensation in order to better meet their needs and those of the institutions they serve.

Categorizing Part-Timers' Employment Experiences

The diversity of employment experience we encountered in our site visits was first recognized and documented in a path-breaking study by Howard Tuckman in 1978. From the results of a survey of 3,763 part-time faculty members, Tuckman and his associates developed a taxonomy of part-timers based on their reasons for choosing part-time employment. This taxonomy contains seven categories:

1. *Semiretireds* (2.8 percent of Tuckman's total sample) were former full-time academics or professionals who were teaching fewer hours and were less concerned about future job prospects than the part-timers in other categories.
2. *Graduate students* (21.2 percent of the total sample) were usually employed as part-timers in institutions other than the one in which they were pursuing a graduate degree. They were teaching to gain experience and to augment income.
3. *Hopeful full-timers* (16.6 percent of the sample) were those who could not find full-time academic positions but wanted them. Tuckman also included those who were working enough part-time hours at one or more institutions to constitute full-time employment but under several contracts, each of which only provided part-time status.
4. *Full-mooners* (27.6 percent of the sample) were individuals who held another primary job of at least thirty-five hours a week. Tuckman characterized these individuals as spending relatively little time preparing lectures and other teaching activities and limiting the number of hours they taught. He also included here tenured faculty teaching overload courses.
5. *Homeworkers* (6.4 percent of the sample) worked part-time because they cared for children or other relatives. Part-time employment might be the sole source of support for the homeworker's household or it might supplement the income of a spouse.
6. *Part-mooners* (13.6 percent) consisted of people working part-

66

time in one academic institution while holding a second job of fewer than thirty-five hours a week elsewhere. Reasons given for holding two jobs simultaneously were economic necessity, psychic rewards not obtainable from one job only, concern about future employment prospects, and highly specialized skills that could be used by one employer only to a limited extent.

7. *Part-unknowners* (11.8 percent) were part-time faculty whose reasons for working part-time were either unknown, transitory, or highly subjective. (See Tuckman, 1978.)

Tuckman's typology continues to provide a foundation for viewing part-time faculty employment experiences and motivations. While Tuckman and Pickerill (1988) note that no recent data permit a new test of this typology, we encountered part-timers who fit neatly into the typology among the 240 part-timers we interviewed. Our interviews indicate, however, that there are some important changes to be taken into account. For example, we found that the "full-mooners" were very dedicated to their teaching and spent a great deal of time in preparation, and we found that the label "homeworkers" now encompasses a much broader array of people with a wide variety of care-giving roles and life-style concerns. Because the interview data gave us much more information about other components of people's lives, we found the patterns of work experience and motivation too complex to fit into the narrow categories Tuckman's typology suggests.

On the basis of our interviews, we have broadened Tuckman's typology into four loose categories: career enders; specialists, experts, and professionals; aspiring academics; and freelancers. We will briefly define these four categories from the perspective of Tuckman's typology and then look at each one in turn, using our site visit interviews to draw a more comprehensive picture.

We have retained Tuckman's category of semiretireds but renamed it *career enders*. We have broadened it to include those who are already fully retired and those who are in transition from well-established careers (mostly outside of higher education) to a preretired or retired status in which part-time teaching plays a significant role. From our interviews, we would estimate that the percentage of part-timers who are retired or semiretired is now much higher than Tuckman's figure of 3 percent would suggest.

We have changed Tuckman's category of full-mooner to a designation of *specialist, expert, or professional* with a primary, usually full-time, career elsewhere. This group of people comes to higher education from a wide range of fields and careers and teaches for the love of it rather than because of a need for income. Some are hired as specialists to teach in their discipline; others are specialists in their primary occupation but teach as generalists. These specialists, experts, or professionals formed a significant portion of our total sample.

We have relabeled Tuckman's hopeful full-timers *aspiring academics* because the focus of their career aspiration is not necessarily to teach full-time but to be fully participating, recognized, and rewarded members of the faculty with a status at least similar to that currently associated with the tenure-track or tenured faculty. We include as aspiring academics only those part-timers who possess the terminal degree and want full-time academic careers and ABD doctoral students. Among the aspiring academics, we distinguish between truly part-time faculty and those who have managed to become "full-time" part-timers because they have a combination of part-time appointments at the same institution or at several institutions. (This latter group is frequently referred to as "freeway fliers.") In some cases, these full-time part-timers carry teaching loads that are greater than full-time. We also include in this group those who are fully qualified but who are "stuck," the geographically immobile who have chosen a part-time teaching career because of family or other obligations.

We have been unable to estimate how common the freeway flier phenomenon may be. We found individual part-timers at virtually every institution in our sample who held more than one part-time teaching job. Yet nowhere did it appear to be the principal mode of employment for part-timers, contrary to the standard myth we have heard repeated many times. A study conducted by the Office of the Chancellor of the California Community Colleges (1987, p. 8) estimated the number of aspiring academics in this subgroup at about one-quarter of all part-timers, a proportion that was found to be increasing. An earlier study conducted by Dykstra (1983), on the other hand, found little evidence of "crosstown teaching" in the Columbus, Ohio, metropolitan area. Anecdotal evidence from our study suggests that this form of employment, undertaken out of economic necessity, is probably more common in large metropolitan areas, and it may be more consequential for individuals and institutions in those areas. Further direct study of this phenomenon is needed, with particular attention to geography.

Our final category is a composite of Tuckman's part-unknowners, part-mooners, and homeworkers that we have broadened and relabeled *freelancers*. It is a composite of all part-timers whose current career is the *sum* of all the part-time jobs or roles they have, only one of which is part-time teaching in higher education. Freelancers are part-time faculty in higher education by choice; they are not aspiring academics.

We found a good example of the mixture of part-timers among the different groups in our interviews at one large community college. Of the forty-four part-time faculty members we interviewed, eight were otherwise unemployed (four of these by choice), six were self-employed in their own businesses, six had other full-time jobs at the same institution, five were teaching elsewhere, five were retired, three were artists, three had corporate jobs, three were graduate students, two were musicians, two were state government administrators, and one reported that he was a starving poet and massage therapist. Seventeen of the forty-four part-timers considered their part-time employment at the community college to be their primary employment.

Career Enders

Among the career enders we interviewed, one had just begun teaching international economics at a university. He had done his graduate work in the 1950s and had been a full-time faculty member for four years. He then went into the foreign service as an economic adviser in Vietnam and other Asian locations. Subsequently, he was employed by the Department of Commerce, U.S. Agency for International Development (USAID), and several major corporations. Upon his retirement from the government, he established a real estate partnership to buy inner-city property in Washington, D.C.

Continuously seeking a challenge, he had just taken up part-time teaching.

Another career ender we interviewed had been retired for a longer period of time but continued to work part-time where he had spent his career, in education:

> I taught in the public schools for twenty years and then was a principal. I spent thirty-three years in public education. I've been teaching at the local community college and at _____ for three years. I'm retired, but I currently serve on a part-time basis as the truant officer for the _____ schools and sell as much fish as I can catch in my spare time.

Others we interviewed had more prosaic reasons for teaching in retirement, such as those offered by a woman recently retired from teaching:

> I'm glad to be out of the junior high school setting. Now that I'm retired, I need a routine and a structure. This provides me with that.

Another, a man retired from a career in public administration, said,

> I've always taught, and now that I'm retired the routine is useful to keep me on track. I enjoy this because it keeps me in touch with young people and intellectually alive. I do four courses a term and love teaching.

As current faculty members reach retirement age in progressively larger numbers in the coming years, we expect that many will choose to teach part-time while phasing into full retirement. If this trend develops, it will mean that substantial numbers of experienced faculty may become available, altering the present marketplace for faculty in ways we do not yet foresee.

Specialists, Experts, and Professionals

According to NSOPF '88 data, over half of the part-time faculty in all institutions (52.5 percent) have other full-time employment.

This ranges from a low of 37 percent at liberal arts colleges and public doctorate-granting institutions to a high of 67 percent at private doctorate-granting universities. There is also variation among disciplines. Only 19 percent of those in the humanities have full-time positions elsewhere, while 59 percent of those in education, 67 percent in business, and 73 percent in engineering work full-time at other jobs.

Those who do have full-time positions elsewhere tend to have been employed at their colleges or universities as part-time faculty members for a longer period of time. About 60 percent of the part-timers who have full-time positions elsewhere have been employed more than four years as compared with an average of 48.6 percent for all part-time faculty. Similarly, the higher the terminal degree, the more likely the part-time faculty member is to have full-time employment elsewhere. Across all types of institutions, 61 percent of the part-time faculty who have doctoral or professional degrees also have full-time employment elsewhere, but only 47 percent of those with master's degrees and 52 percent of those with bachelor's degrees work full-time elsewhere (NSOPF '88).

At virtually every institution in our study, we interviewed part-timers who have full-time jobs as professionals or managers. They have advanced training in fields such as medicine, allied health, biochemistry, mathematics and statistics, public administration, business, education, social work, law, and criminal justice. Some of them teach courses closely related to their primary occupation; some of them were hired as generalists for courses such as basic mathematics. For almost all, their teaching represents a professional commitment, a community service, and a source of personal satisfaction.

Since most of the part-time faculty we interviewed who also have full-time positions elsewhere already enjoy comparatively high salaries and relative employment security, they have little economic need or motive to teach part time. They are teaching because they want to. Usually, they do not experience conflict with their full-time jobs:

> My superiors and subordinates on my full-time job are
> supportive. They don't see my teaching as competi-

tive. This job keeps me fresh and enthused. I recruit
volunteers from classes to help out at the facilities. I
can use real life examples in class.

At San Jose State University, we interviewed the dean of the
School of Engineering who talked about his proximity to Silicon
Valley and the need to graduate quality engineers:

> To make sure we graduate quality engineers, we must
> have part-timers. Industry understands this. People
> from the companies come in at all times of day. [We
> have] a partnership concept. . . . Teaching at San Jose
> State is part of the part-timers' outside work assign-
> ment with their companies.

Some fast-track professionals enjoy the intrinsic rewards of
teaching but do not always appreciate or understand the folkways
of academic life. One Ph.D. in economics had worked for a Big
Eight accounting firm and subsequently formed his own company.
He currently teaches microeconomics and would be well qualified
for a tenure-track position, but he has reservations:

> I just enjoy teaching. The rest of what [the faculty] are
> involved in is a pain in the butt. Committee work is
> redundant and a waste of time. Also, academic work
> is not as financially rewarding as work in the private
> sector. I decided to leave academe because of finances.
> But I like being in the classroom. Teaching is much
> more fulfilling than work in the private sector. Right
> now I have the best of both possible worlds.

One individual with a Ph.D. in mathematics and statistics
had originally considered an academic career. Instead he had become a statistical systems analyst for a research institute. Then he
worked at the Department of Health, Education and Welfare setting
up medical data bases and data analysis systems. He is currently
employed in a management position as a senior statistician with
another major federal agency. Despite his decision to forego an

academic career, he has been teaching evening courses since receiving his Ph.D.

> It is *fun*. I enjoy teaching, but I don't want to do it
> full-time. I had that option after I got the Ph.D. I
> looked at it as a career. I could have gotten an aca-
> demic job in 1973, but [the job market] was discourag-
> ing. I've learned a lot about myself. I'm not much of
> a publisher. I have published ten to twelve articles in
> sixteen or seventeen years, and these are policy inter-
> pretation stuff. I've lost the cutting edge. I enjoy the
> teaching, but I don't want the rest of the full-time
> responsibility.

Another part-time faculty member also currently works as a biochemist for a major corporation. His research, while satisfying, does not fulfill his interests in teaching:

> I love teaching! I work full-time in the private sector
> for the money and because I have a chance to do re-
> search. But I wanted to grow personally and am look-
> ing to options for a postretirement career—teaching is
> high on the list. I love the challenge of dealing with
> students who aren't intrinsically interested and who
> are required to be in my class. I feel I can bring real
> world examples to help motivate and interest them in
> the study of biology.

Over and over again, we interviewed executives, health care specialists, engineers, artists, public school teachers, and others who teach in addition to their full-time careers. They teach because they love to and are rejuvenated by their students. But they often teach at considerable personal sacrifice.

> When you work full-time, it is hard to find the time
> to teach. It is hard to juggle the schedule. I teach at
> most twice a year here. Employers are supportive of
> the concept [of teaching], but the work doesn't go

away. Employers are expecting nothing in return; they are neutral. It is your choice to teach.

Part-timers in the School of Extended Education at Saint Mary's College whom we interviewed were commuting to off-campus teaching sites from homes and jobs all over the greater San Francisco Bay area, frequently at peak commuting hours.

> My personal life is very scheduled, and my children recognize this. My wife is also in health care. I schedule time with the children. I keep a calendar, and the kids know this. I am working in Pleasanton, living in Richmond, and teaching in San Francisco. But the students are also driving and preparing and they have full-time jobs.

Still, the personal price tends to be worth the costs to those with primary jobs elsewhere. As one part-timer put it:

> Teaching at _____ is the only stable part of my life. CEOs in health care have rapid turnover.

Some careerists mentioned their desire eventually to switch from full-time executive jobs to teaching positions:

> Teaching is very rewarding personally. In five or six years I would like to make a career change to full-time teaching and part-time consulting. Now I have two children.

Aspiring Academics

Aspiring academics include relatively new Ph.D.'s seeking tenure-track appointments and some Ph.D. recipients who have been teaching on a part-time basis for years in the hope of attaining a full-time, tenure-track position. Under better circumstances, they would be part of the tenured faculty. Aspiring academics also include ABD doctoral students who are simultaneously employed as part-timers.

Many of these long-term part-timers, while still retaining a wish that they could be part of the "regular" faculty, have found ways to build academic careers within their part-time status. In the most satisfactory arrangements, they have successfully put together several part-time assignments within their institutions and/or have taken leadership positions in faculty governance.

One part-timer exemplifies this group of individuals. With a Ph.D. from a leading university in 1972, he held a tenure-track position for four years before deciding to return to California. Employed in higher education for several years, he was laid off in the wake of California's Proposition 13. He then took courses in computer science at his local community college. In 1978 he returned to the university in a half-time faculty position in medieval studies and in a staff position created for him because of his knowledge of the use of computers in the humanities. Now he teaches courses in his discipline in three different departments and is also employed as a data base manager. All of his part-time assignments, when put together, are more than full-time. This ability to put together a full-time "position" out of pieces of part-time assignments is characteristic of more than a few of the part-timers we interviewed. While the pieced-together temporary assignments may constitute a full-time work load, they remain without the status, salary, benefits, and security normally associated with full-time or regular employment. At any time one of the part-time assignments can easily "disappear."

For other aspiring academics we interviewed, waiting and hoping had extended for substantial periods of time without bearing fruit. Some of these people realized that they were now falling behind the newer doctoral graduates and had become less attractive as potential full-time faculty. One assessed his situation this way:

> I am ambivalent as to whether part-time faculty should be thankful they've had an opportunity to teach or whether they should be regretful that they've pursued teaching too intensely at the expense of other things. You teach part-time here at the expense of research, and this forecloses opportunities. . . . There

are also psychological issues: part-time faculty sometimes wonder if they are living in an artificial world;
my kids think I'm a professor, but I know nothing is
guaranteed beyond the current semester. I feel I am
under scrutiny all the time. I worry about how I am
doing and am oversensitive to student reactions. Every
year, you are judged. You have to perform all the time
and can't rely on the colleagueship or goodwill of full-
time faculty. I also can't take time to do research. I
teach ten to fifteen hours each semester with hundreds
of papers, and I don't have time for research or even
to prepare properly for class. I know I've devoted too
much energy to teaching and should have done more
research. I deeply regret this choice, but [I] had no
alternative at my age and with my family commitments. I needed to provide a stable income.

This person was acutely conscious that he had essentially
foregone the opportunity for a full-time position and was now
"stuck" in a marginal role in academic life. A major reason for
being stuck is lack of geographical mobility. Another part-timer we
interviewed is teaching at a large comprehensive regional university
in an urban area. She has all her degrees, including her doctorate
from the institution where she is currently employed as a part-timer.
She started teaching part-time as a graduate student in 1978. By the
mid 1980s she had achieved a full-time teaching load while retaining part-time status.

I wanted an academic career, and this is the only way
I could do it. . . . Part-time work was the only route
to go. . . . I am not terribly satisfied. I am paying a
mortgage and am overworked to meet this obligation.
I need to work hard to survive. . . . [There is] not
enough time to do a lot of research. Also, I am committed to one institution. As a part-timer, I basically
have to take the work that is available to me. I want
to teach a philosophy course. I am teaching humanities, social sciences, English, extended education. [I

am] teaching all over the university. . . . Our experience is a mile wide but an inch deep. . . . I can use
my seniority to get part-time positions all over the
university, but I can't use it to get a tenure-stream
appointment.

These two individuals exemplify a small but important and
vocal part of our total sample: those dedicated, well-prepared individuals who still hope to move to tenure-track status but who have
pursued, for whatever reasons, the wrong strategies for achieving
that goal. They feel stuck, and their future prospects are uncertain
at best.

Other aspiring academics are more recent Ph.D.'s. Some
begin teaching part-time immediately after completing the Ph.D.
while they seek tenure-track positions. Others are teaching part-
time because of family responsibilities. While we interviewed several men who are the trailing spouses in dual-career couples (see
Chapter Two), by far the majority are women. These women are
caught in their prime childbearing years in an unresolvable conflict
between their desire to have a family and the lack of alternatives and
flexibility in an academic career. Through its rigidity, this career
system fails to use considerable available talent and also demonstrates a systemic, if not intentional, gender bias. Such bias wreaks
havoc with the lives and plans of superbly well-qualified
individuals:

I came from England where I did my B.A. I came to
_____ on a four-year fellowship to do my Ph.D. I did
not originally plan to stay here. I met someone who
became my husband, and now I'm on my second
child. The first child was born in 1987. The consequence of this decision is that my husband is in his
own business here and I am not mobile. My career
plans changed. I have been working here as a lecturer
since 1987, sometimes full-time, sometimes part-time.
I'm almost forty; my husband is fifty. We did not plan
to have children. I planned to have regional mobility
and come home weekends or whatever. I looked for a

77

tenure-track position. Then I got pregnant. Having a child changed my plans. I wasn't willing to commute long distances. Decisions have come after life changes. It has been *difficult*. I was always at the top in fellowships, scholarships. For example, I published my honors thesis as an undergraduate student. The institution loses out because I have lots more to offer than they are taking advantage of. The institution could *gain* from accommodating my needs. Until very recently I was not eligible for research grants.

In our interviews we encountered evidence of unused potential over and over again. Many women (and increasingly men, too) feel exploited by an academic career system that does not adequately address the interrelationship between the personal and professional lives of faculty and that takes advantage of their training and talent without providing rewards and incentives.

A small subset of those we interviewed were doctoral students close to completion of their Ph.D.'s and employed as part-timers. Aspiring academics who are also aspiring Ph.D. recipients can lead very hard lives. The Ph.D. candidates we interviewed had been struggling for years to earn a living by teaching part-time while finishing degrees. Said one,

> I came to the University of Minnesota to get a Ph.D. I am in my fourth year at _____ . I am also teaching at three other institutions. I am primarily here as a Ph.D. student. The relationship between jobs is rough. I don't like what I am doing. It is hard on me and has slowed down my progress on the dissertation. I have to work hard to make a minimum income to support me and my family. It would be nice to have a job in one place so I wouldn't have to run around. My wife is not allowed to work because of immigration, and we have two children. It is not easy. Our last child had major medical problems. I hope to finish the Ph.D. in a year and a half.

Another interviewee had been working on her Ph.D. for seven years. She had received her undergraduate degree in 1968, worked as a librarian, had three children, and now is divorced.

> I am going to have to skip doing academic jobs in order to get ahead in my academic career. I need the money. I am a single mother with three teenagers. ABDs teaching part-time are having a real struggle. It's a full-time job just to be employed enough to support myself in getting the Ph.D. Colleges and universities are using us as a cheap source of labor.

A final subgroup of aspiring academics are "freeway fliers," those part-timers who have teaching assignments at several institutions at the same time. They represented a small portion of our total sample of part-timers. Their "packages" of teaching assignments in multiple locations contribute to the marginal nature of their affiliation with each of their institutions and to the little that is known about them by their departments. One young man's situation illustrates the rigors of multiple teaching assignments in different locations:

> I have a lot of roots in [the area]. I don't want to relocate. I wanted to keep a foot in each door as an inroad to a full-time job. . . . I have taught part-time a lot. One year I taught at five colleges simultaneously. Thursdays I started at the university for an 8 A.M. class. Then I went [across town] for a 9:45 A.M. class, which went to 11 A.M., then to [a nearby institution] for early afternoon and to [a fourth institution] for mid afternoon. [Finally, I returned] to the university for an evening extension class. I finished teaching at 9 P.M. I think I taught well. I never sacrificed the classroom. The colleges lost the out-of-class interaction. It really compromised my personal life. But it would be too embarrassing to be unprepared for class.

Another part-timer in a large city had been teaching at three different institutions for the past eleven years, having begun her career as a part-timer more than twenty years ago. During our interview, she said,

> I used to teach seven or eight classes a semester. I'd come home and read *The Faerie Queen, Paradise Lost,* and *The Sun Also Rises* at the same time. I started retrenching. I try to coordinate. Here I have one class and work with the learning-disabled students. I also do tutoring ten hours a week. I have cut down on the work. Now I teach four courses a semester and a bit in the summer. I make $20,000. I don't think about the money. My primary job is at all three places. I am the oldest living adjunct (here). Nasty rule they have here—three-courses-a-year limit. That hurts. I used to teach two each semester and one in the summer. Doing the preparation for one class doesn't pay. But I like the variety. . . . I don't want to spend time on bureaucracy. I don't want committees. I don't like office politics. A number of things that go along with full-time work don't interest me. I would prefer the variety of three schools to the convenience of three composition courses here. I like the sense of freedom I have.

This part-timer is both a freeway flier and a freelancer. While she commented that there are aspects of the academic career she values, she also values her freedom and the variety that a series of part-time positions can offer. Thus, she provides a good introduction to our final employment group, the freelancers.

Freelancers

In our interviews, we encountered as many career profiles as we encountered freelancers. Their reasons for working part-time make sense in the context of their lives. The composite group of freelancers includes homemakers or primary care people; artists and others seeking affiliation with an institution for a variety of reasons; individuals who choose to build their careers around a series of part-time jobs that are generally interrelated but occasionally capitalize on varied skills and talents; and individuals who at the time of our interviews occupied part-time positions for reasons beyond their control. A substantial number of the part-time faculty we interviewed were freelancing to support themselves. They held a variety of "jobs," including writing, consulting, and teaching and preferred not to have ties to any particular institution or position.

One woman we interviewed exemplifies the freelancers. She had moved to a rural area as a "life-style émigré" after her husband left corporate life. She now writes education books and manuals for teachers, offers in-service teacher training as an independent contractor, holds a one-quarter-time position as director of a state energy education program, and teaches part-time at a public institution in her area. Her various jobs and roles reinforce each other; what she learns in one arena she puts to use elsewhere. Her teaching job, for example, serves as a laboratory for new ideas that she can later pass along in her writing and consulting. Although she reported being isolated from the full-time faculty and her department chair, she prefers not to have any greater involvement in the institution because she values the free time she can devote to her other roles and activities.

There are many variations on this theme. Generally speaking, freelancing part-time faculty have much to offer the colleges and universities where they teach. They have varied experiences that they put to good use in the classroom. They tend to be resourceful and are able to use their contacts and connections to benefit the college or university. All in all, they constitute a resource not easily found in other ways. The part-timers who are freelancers are also usually uninterested in tenure-track appointments. They vary in whether or not they are dependent upon their part-time positions for salary or benefits.

Some of the freelancers we interviewed were experimenting at the time. They had not yet found a career that ideally suited their needs. One of the women we interviewed has bachelor's and master's degrees and a teaching credential. She had tried full-time teaching but had not found it a viable career alternative. So she had gone to Maine to write the great American novel and run out of money!

It took me ten years to pay off the two degrees. I
worked in a press office for a U.S. senator. He lost. My
thirtieth birthday was spent in unemployment offices.
I became the communications director of a company.
Then I went to Lexington, Kentucky, as a spouse.
There I taught business writing at the university and
really liked it. But I hated Kentucky, so we moved back.
I worked for a trade association. I hate office politics,
working twelve-hour days, feeling out of control of
my life. So I went to part-time work. The head of my
department was in a class in Gaelic [with me]. She
hired me. Now I am putting together a Ph.D. program, teaching three courses, and making money as a
freelance editor. I take the summers off and work on
my fiction.

This ability and desire to handle multiple jobs and interests simultaneously was common in our interviews.

Some part-timers have already experimented and, at the time
of our interviews, were quite satisfied with their career choice to be
a freelancer. One of our interviewees had started out with a Ph.D.
in English (Shakespeare). She had gone into publishing and opened
her own consulting firm in textbook development. From there she
had moved into business communication and teaching business
writing. Recently married to a tenured faculty member, she has
continued her consulting business and teaching, in combination
with enjoying a new marriage and stepson. Experiencing a variety
of roles or jobs simultaneously meets her personal needs at this
point in her life.

At most of our site institutions we found a substantial
number of freelance studio artists. One member of the art department at a comprehensive regional university in a large city was
teaching at two other institutions and was also a professional paint-
er when we spoke with her. Because of her financial needs and the
benefits package the university offered, she commuted to the regional campus three days a week, leaving home at 5:30 A.M. and
returning at 7:30 P.M. The other two days she taught at the other
institutions. Another artist whom we interviewed talked about her

commitment to staying in a major city in order to be part of its art world, to retain her affiliations with a gallery and an art institute. She talked about how she was balancing her life between the loneliness of painting in her studio and her teaching:

> I want contact with people. I want to offer people things. It is a thrill to teach people how to draw or to help the advanced people into careers.

A music teacher at an urban community college maintained an intimidatingly energetic schedule, dividing her work among a number of activities. She told us:

> I wanted to teach at the college level and wanted time for composing, arranging, and concertizing. In addition to teaching here, I also teach at [a local] music school, serve as church choir director, give concerts around the country, and provide private music lessons. I like the flexibility part-time teaching allows me.

Conclusion

The profiles of academic and employment experience show that the bifurcated employment system that lumps all tenure-track faculty in one class and all part-time faculty in another does not nearly fit the current realities. Part-time faculty come from enormously varied backgrounds and life situations. They need a far more flexible set of options, rewards, incentives, and recognitions for their work. Some depend almost completely on their part-time teaching to survive, but others are primarily committed to other professional careers in which they are well compensated. Some part-time faculty aspire to academic careers, but others have no interest in them at all. Yet most institutions treat all part-time faculty alike. They see part-timers as marginal, temporary employees with no past and no future beyond the immediate term and give them no incentive to stay and make a commitment.

Institutions should make a greater effort to understand who

is teaching for them, what each person has to offer, and what kind of incentives and support would help part-timers make a greater contribution. For example, are aspiring academics being developed as a legitimate future pool for tenure-bearing appointments? Are career enders seeking part-time employment as an attractive transition to retirement? Are specialists, experts, and professionals recognized as an untapped resource with great potential for enriching academic programs? Could freelancers make more enduring contributions if they enjoyed a more stable employment relationship with their institutions? We found these questions rarely raised and even more rarely addressed because part-timers are treated as an invisible, indistinguishable mass and dealt with arbitrarily.

Academic Culture
and Socialization

Professorial Attitudes — An International Survey

By Philip G. Altbach and Lionel S. Lewis

The professoriate is everywhere faced with challenges. This is not the best of times in academe—many, indeed, would have us believe that it is the worst of times. The close to 20,000 professors in the 14 countries participating in the Carnegie Foundation's international survey of the academic profession—the first ever undertaken (see box)—are well aware of the problems they face in an era of worldwide fiscal constraints for higher education and increased demands for productivity.

The United States is by no means alone—the survey shows that academe worldwide faces some common problems: academics in many parts of the world are engaged in conversations about higher education reform, better articulation between the universities and the labor market, and changing patterns in research funding. Many countries also are looking for a new definition of academic work in a changing environment. Yet the survey also shows that the professoriate is remarkably sanguine about the future—even in a time of troubles. In this article, we discuss how academics in these 14 countries evaluate their lives and careers.

Context. We noted significant differences among the countries. Specific national circumstances—such as dramatic societal transformation and tension in Russia, the structural changes in higher education of the past decade in the United Kingdom, and continuing tensions between academics and the government over salary issues in Israel, to name just a few—obviously influenced the responses.

The survey was carried out at a particularly important time for the professoriate, which, for a number of years, has been

Philip G. Altbach is professor and director of the Center for International Higher Education, Boston College, Chestnut Hill, Massachusetts and is a senior associate of the Carnegie Foundation for the Advancement of Teaching. Lionel S. Lewis is professor of sociology at the State University of New York at Buffalo and author of Marginal Worth: Teaching and the Academic Labor Market, forthcoming from Transaction.

About the Survey

The survey of academics in 14 countries addressed in this article was initiated by the Carnegie Foundation for the Advancement of Teaching and carried out by research teams in each participating country in 1991 and 1992. A common methodology was used to select institutions and individuals to ensure a random sample from each country. The number of respondents per country ranged from more than 3,500 to somewhat fewer than 1,000; altogether, the total sample was close to 20,000. The 12-page questionnaire included 72 items on a variety of topics. While the questionnaire was common, questions used in some countries had variations to reflect specific national circumstances.

Academics were surveyed in order to gather information on—among other things—the demographic facts of the profession, as well as on attitudes toward teaching and learning, the governance of academic institutions, the national and international involvement of scholars and scientists, and morale. In addition, information was gathered on how academics spend their time, and about their participation in research. As a result of this survey, we now for the first time have comparable data about the attitudes and activities of the academic profession in 14 countries—and this study can provide the basis for research in other countries.

Since the Carnegie international survey includes 14 *diverse* countries, we feel that we have obtained a fairly broad understanding of the academic profession. All continents are included, and the only geographical region entirely absent is sub-Saharan Africa. The nations participating in the survey are the United States; in Latin America, Brazil, Chile, and Mexico; in Europe, England, Germany, the Netherlands, Russia, and Sweden; in Asia, Hong Kong, Japan, and South Korea; in the Middle East, Israel; and Australia. (Egypt participated in the survey but did not report data and so is not included here.)

Readers will notice that in some of the tables (1-5, 7, 10, 12, 13), one or two countries are missing. In these cases, the question specified in the table heading was not included on the questionnaire for the missing country or countries. ℘

under strain almost everywhere. Fiscal problems for higher education are evident not only in Russia, Israel, and the United Kingdom, but in all 14 of the countries we surveyed. (In the United Kingdom, respondents were limited to England and did not include faculty in Wales, Northern Ireland, or Scotland.) Evident in most of them is the somewhat unprecedented phenomenon of increasing enrollments combined with steady or even declining resources. Reassessment by policy-makers and opinion leaders of the professoriate's role in teaching and research is also widespread. At the same time, professors in a number of countries are being asked to be more entrepreneurial—for example, in bringing research grants and contracts to their institutions. The insulated world of academe is clearly undergoing significant change. There is little doubt that insights concerning how academics are coping with this strain have broad policy implications.

Fiscal Constraint. One common denominator is fiscal constraint. In only one of the countries included in our survey—Hong Kong—have economic circumstances been generally favorable during the past decade. All of the rest have seen problems ranging from modest to severe. The Asian countries included here have been least affected by economic crisis, although Japan's recession has had a modest impact on academe. Northern Europe also has been spared significant cuts, even though the economies of countries such as Germany and Sweden have experienced recession, clearly showing that there is not a necessary relationship between economic trends and higher education policy. Yet even in these countries, governmental policy has increased enrollments without adding significant new resources.

The Latin American countries in the survey have not experienced major cuts in support for public higher education. Indeed, there has been some growth—at the same time that enrollments have increased significantly. The greatest difficulties have been experienced by the English-speaking nations and Israel, where economic downturns have been accompanied by growing enrollments and fiscal difficulties for higher education. The impact in the United States has varied by state and region—with the

Northeast and California suffering most. Israel experienced cuts in higher education funding so severe that the professors engaged in a lengthy strike. Israeli academic institutions were closed at the time that the questionnaire was administered. No doubt, all of this had some effect on the nature of the responses.

To be sure, if more money and resources were available and if academic administrators did not have to say no so often, Israel's faculty morale would be higher and there would be fewer criticisms of how institutions of higher education were managed. The impact of economic crisis and political change on the Russian academics who responded to our questionnaire also must be significant, but this was impossible to gauge with any certainty. (The response rate for Russia was quite low, perhaps reflecting the unstable situation for academics.)

Australia and the United Kingdom are among the most interesting cases, since their economic downturns were accompanied by significant reforms in higher education policy. These reforms were bitterly opposed by the academic profession, and have led to dramatic changes in academe in these countries. The direction of change in both was similar: to improve productivity in postsecondary education, previously separate sectors of the system were combined, thus downgrading what had been the elite sector of higher education. The changes were especially contentious in the United Kingdom, where the conservative government dismantled the binary system—the division between the traditional universities on the one hand and the more vocationally oriented polytechnics on the other—combining all institutions into one system in which the polytechnics and other postsecondary colleges became universities. Controversial performance measures were implemented. At the same time, enrollments were increased to provide greater access, and an effort was made to rank the institutions so that research funds could be awarded to those at the top of the rankings.

Patterns of Attitudes. Few scholars and scientists are pleased with their salaries. Indeed, there is considerable dissatisfaction with earnings and quite a bit of pessimism about future prospects for improvement in this area. In only two places—Hong Kong and the Nether-

Table 1
To what extent are you satisfied with the courses you teach?

	Satisfied	Neutral	Dissatisfied
Australia	77%	16%	7%
Brazil	64	31	5
Chile	78	18	4
England	76	17	7
Germany	59	27	14
Hong Kong	72	23	5
Israel	81	17	2
Japan	54	35	11
Korea	82	15	3
Mexico	79	16	6
Russia	60	36	4
Sweden	74	21	5
United States	86	11	4

Note: The Netherlands is absent because this question did not appear on its questionnaire. Countries were omitted from tables 2-5, 7, 10, 12, and 13 for the same reason.

lands—do more than half of the faculty rate their salary as good or excellent. In six countries, fewer than 20 percent of faculty report this degree of satisfaction. (In the United States, 46 percent report this level of satisfaction, and 34 percent report it in Australia.) In some countries, a number of faculty have turned to paid consulting projects and other extramural work to make ends meet. This is especially true in Russia, where more than 80 percent of the respondents indicated that an outside income is essential to augment their salary. In Japan, too, where there is a tradition of professors in prestigious universities also teaching a course in a less renowned institution, a number of faculty hold outside academic appointments.

We noted an interesting pattern of responses to some of these questions about working conditions—academics (especially in the humanities) seem relatively satisfied with what they teach but have mixed feelings about resources given to them to carry out their work. Female and junior faculty are less likely to be satisfied with their circumstances than are male and senior professors. Clearly, the latter encounter fewer hurdles in their path and can expect fewer surprises as their careers unfold. Male and senior professors also do less teaching.

Table 2
Based on your experience at this institution, how would you assess relationships between faculty and administration?

	Excellent	Good	Fair	Poor
Australia	3%	28%	39%	30%
Brazil	6	46	35	12
Chile	3	25	48	24
Hong Kong	3	28	47	22
Israel	9	40	31	20
Japan	3	22	58	18
Korea	1	15	47	38
Mexico	6	43	37	15
The Netherlands	3	29	47	22
Russia	3	47	42	8
Sweden	4	34	41	21
United States	7	36	36	21

Table 3
If I had it to do over again, I would not become an academic.

	Agree	Neutral	Disagree
Australia	16%	18%	66%
Brazil	15	7	78
Chile	16	12	72
England	20	17	63
Germany	17	15	69
Hong Kong	17	15	69
Israel	9	6	85
Japan	16	30	54
Korea	10	14	76
The Netherlands	13	18	69
Russia	11	17	72
Sweden	8	8	84
United States	11	10	79

Specifically, faculty express general dissatisfaction with their classrooms, laboratories, research equipment, libraries, and with the technologies available for teaching, although they are more satisfied with existing computer facilities. In almost all of these areas, the faculty of five countries—Hong Kong, the Netherlands, the United States, Sweden, and Germany—are usually the most critical. Faculty more involved in research have fewer complaints about facilities than those more involved in teaching, although they report considerable pressure to be more productive as scholars and scientists. The demands for teaching are also greater than in the recent past, and a large number of respondents are perplexed that this is occurring at a time when fewer resources are available. Because of the greater workloads, many report a growing sense of unease.

In light of all of the above, it is hardly surprising that in half of the countries, two-thirds or more of the respondents report that relationships between faculty and administration are only fair or poor; in no country did even 10 percent judge these to be excellent. While being asked by academic administrators and policy-makers to do more with fewer resources, faculty are being told that they should not expect to be re-warded—financially or otherwise—for meeting ever-increasing demands. Yet, while obviously frustrated by day-to-day working conditions and by poor prospects for increased rewards, most responded that their overall morale is relatively high, saying they find intellectual pleasure in their work, and that this in large part sustains them.

It is surprising that so many academics characterize their working conditions as adequate despite both general and specific dissatisfactions with campus and societal issues. Many among the professoriate—especially female faculty—are unhappy about their lack of control over the contemporary situation and are unsure of what the future holds. Many respondents—especially Japanese, Korean, and British scholars and scientists—report their careers to be a source of considerable personal strain. In half the countries, 40 percent or more of the respondents report excessive external frustrations (though this figure is less than 20 percent in Israel). In addition, the majority of respondents in every country except the Netherlands believe that a sense of community is lacking on campus. Still, despite concern about all these aspects of their day-to-day lives, most academics indicate that they would again choose the academic profession if they were starting their careers over.

In sum, there is ample evidence that professorial working conditions are deteriorating in most of the countries included in this study. Indeed, only in East Asia and Latin America do objective circumstances seem to be fairly stable in terms of workload, salary, and the overall situation on campus. Elsewhere we find that classes are getting larger, academics are under pressure to teach more, funds available for research are declining, and salaries are not keeping abreast of inflation. In a few countries, the significant systemic reorganization has created stress for academics, while in others, including the United States, retrenchment threatens some faculty. Given these difficult conditions, we were surprised that the academic profession is as optimistic as our data indicate. The overall picture of faculty morale, however, is neither good nor bad—but often quite blurred. The professoriate around the world may express considerable discontent, but it has not lost sight of the positive aspects of academic life.

Students. In only four countries do a majority of the faculty describe their students as excellent or good. Fewer than one-third of the respondents report that their students are adequately prepared in writing and communication skills. In five countries, the figure is 20

Table 4
Please indicate the degree to which your academic discipline is important to you.

	Very important	Fairly important	Not too important	Not at all important
Australia	67	27	5	2
Brazil	95	4	1	0
Chile	87	13	0	0
England	64	29	6	1
Germany	62	29	6	3
Hong Kong	68	27	3	2
Israel	75	23	2	0
Japan	69	28	3	0
Korea	80	19	1	0
Mexico	71	26	2	0
Russia	66	30	3	1
Sweden	55	34	9	2
United States	77	21	3	0

Table 5
In my department it is difficult for a person to achieve tenure if he or she does not publish.

	Agree	Neutral	Disagree
Australia	64	15	21
Brazil	25	21	55
Chile	33	35	32
Germany	78	8	14
Hong Kong	60	16	24
Israel	81	4	15
Japan	48	23	29
Korea	38	15	48
Mexico	28	24	48
Russia	32	41	27
Sweden	58	18	24
United States	75	8	17

percent or less. In most countries, the professoriate also feels that students lack adequate training in mathematics, with U.S. faculty being the least satisfied, and those in Hong Kong being the most content with student preparation. Faculty in most countries feel that students were better prepared five years ago; only in Australia, Israel, Korea, and Sweden are they convinced that students are currently better. Female respondents have more favorable attitudes about students than do males. There is widespread agreement that too many students, except those majoring in the respondents' fields, are inadequately prepared to fully benefit from higher education.

The Importance of Academic Work. Respondents were asked to rate the importance of their academic discipline, their department, and their institution from "very important" to "not at all important." It was found that the professional loyalty of faculty is stronger than campus loyalty. In every country, the largest proportion ranked in order of importance their discipline first, their department second, and their institution third. Academics obviously value their relationships with colleagues. In only three countries, all in Latin America (where, ironically, high proportions of faculty have work

commitments off campus), are significant numbers of faculty convinced that their institution is very important. Elsewhere, the majority of respondents indicate that the institution where they hold an appointment is at least moderately important. This finding may be surprising given the modest level of mobility for faculty among institutions in most countries. Taken together, these responses make it quite apparent that the orientation of the academic profession worldwide is more cosmopolitan than local: academics indicate that they care more about their professional activities—their teaching and research—than about parochial matters. They also value contacts with colleagues on campus as well as with others in their discipline.

Faculty express some ambivalent attitudes about research. More than three-quarters in all countries—except Brazil, Russia, and Korea—note that a strong record of successful research activity is important in faculty evaluation, and a majority agree that it is difficult for someone to achieve tenure if he or she does not publish (exceptions here include Japan, Korea, Mexico, Chile, Brazil, and Russia). As a rule, the professoriate is not happy about this state of affairs. Many feel that they are under pressure to do more research than they

would like to—approximately one-third in half of the countries surveyed.

At the same time, those who write more articles and books are, sometimes by great margins and sometimes by narrow margins, more satisfied with their work life and less likely to feel vulnerable to acute and chronic pressures they encounter on campus than those who write fewer articles and books. There is a relationship between research productivity and a sense of empowerment and overall satisfaction. Many scholars feel—probably quite accurately—that research funding is more difficult to obtain in the early 1990s than in the late 1980s. This perception was most acute in England, Germany, Russia, and the United States.

Faculty worldwide do not endorse the view that teaching and research necessarily work at cross-purposes. Indeed, more faculty than not are convinced that their research has a positive influence on their teaching, and the majority of faculty in all countries, except Hong Kong, are not of the opinion that the pressure to publish reduces the quality of teaching. However, such a conflict is noted by a significant minority in Chile, England, Israel, the Netherlands, Germany, and the United States. Administrative assignments are seen as having a more negative influence on research than teaching.

Table 6
I frequently feel under pressure to do more research than I actually would like to do.

	Agree	Neutral	Disagree
Australia	31%	23%	46%
Brazil	13	17	71
Chile	38	27	36
England	34	24	42
Germany	28	17	55
Hong Kong	36	21	43
Israel	13	12	76
Japan	37	31	32
Korea	36	18	45
Mexico	20	25	55
The Netherlands	22	26	52
Russia	12	47	41
Sweden	25	21	54
United States	30	20	50

Table 7
How influential are you, personally, in helping to shape key academic policies at the institutional level?

	Very influential	Somewhat influential	A little influential	Not at all influential
Australia	2%	6%	14%	78%
Brazil	3	18	36	43
Chile	3	14	20	64
England	2	8	16	74
Germany	1	5	14	80
Hong Kong	1	6	13	81
Israel	5	7	31	57
Japan	5	24	40	31
Korea	3	8	33	57
Mexico	3	13	23	61
Russia	3	19	25	53
Sweden	5	13	18	64
United States	3	11	22	64

In common with national surveys of the academic profession, respondents report that they work hard at a variety of activities related to their academic roles. They engage in teaching, research, service, and administrative activities. There are some variations according to country, and further differences according to institutional affiliation. Most of those surveyed express a significant commitment to all of the standard faculty roles, but, as indicated, are most impatient with their administrative responsibilities. At the same time, they are also critical of administrators who have taken over these tasks.

Governance. It is well known that there are striking variations in governance arrangements from one country to another; in some countries, colleges and universities are government controlled, while in others there is a tradition of institutional independence. In most of the countries included in our survey, most academic institutions are government sponsored, although in Japan, Korea, and the three Latin American countries a majority of students study in private colleges and universities.

When we asked respondents to reflect on issues of governance, common concerns emerged. It is generally reported that there is a mixture when it comes to most of the major elements of decision-making. Since World War II, as higher education rapidly expanded, the close, more collegial and informal patterns of decision-making have to some seemed less effective, and a large proportion of our respondents are aware of and concerned about the trend toward centralized power in higher education. They are unhappy and unsure of how to cope with the more hierarchical, more rigid governance structure. As a result, faculty dissatisfaction with current administrative and governance arrangements is high—and a cause for concern. Senior faculty were more sympathetic of administrators than were junior faculty, who had more questions about the competence and goodwill of those who manage institutions of higher learning. Not surprisingly, many believe that they have the greatest influence on decision-making in their academic department or similar unit, with majorities in almost all countries feeling that they were either very influential or somewhat influential at this level. Respondents in Germany and Mexico are least likely to express this view.

At the same time, fewer than 10 percent of respondents in almost all of the countries feel that they play a key role in governance at the institutional level. Obviously, faculty around the world feel considerable alienation from the higher echelons of administration at their colleges and universities. An unusually large number express dissatisfaction with and doubts about the quality of the leadership provided by top-level administrators at their colleges and universities—Japan is the only country in which a majority of the respondents agree that top administrators are providing competent leadership. The distrust is pervasive. Fewer than half of respondents feel that they are informed about what is going on, and close to half characterize communication between the faculty and the administration as poor.

In eight countries, the majority of faculty report that academic administrators are autocratic, and in six countries, a majority agree that a lack of faculty involvement in governance is a problem. Only in the United States and Japan do more than half of the faculty feel that administrators even support academic freedom. Other questions elicit an expression of general dissatisfaction on the part of faculty. As has been suggested, the

91

Table 8
Top-level administrators are providing competent leadership.

	Agree	Neutral	Disagree
Australia	29%	26%	46%
Brazil	46	27	27
Chile	28	31	42
England	26	25	49
Germany	24	27	49
Hong Kong	23	29	48
Israel	28	31	41
Japan	60	22	18
Korea	24	31	45
Mexico	33	23	44
The Netherlands	32	42	26
Russia	30	53	17
Sweden	30	38	32
United States	39	22	38

Table 9
The administration is often autocratic.

	Agree	Neutral	Disagree
Australia	63%	23%	14%
Brazil	44	20	36
Chile	58	23	19
England	64	21	16
Germany	67	21	13
Hong Kong	64	23	13
Israel	57	24	19
Japan	40	34	26
Korea	46	30	24
Mexico	54	20	27
The Netherlands	37	38	25
Russia	43	41	16
Sweden	43	36	21
United States	58	22	20

Table 10
Is academic freedom strongly protected in this country?

	Yes	No
Australia	77%	23%
Brazil	38	62
Chile	71	29
Hong Kong	71	30
Israel	92	8
Japan	79	21
Korea	74	26
Mexico	69	31
The Netherlands	74	26
Russia	16	84
Sweden	83	17
United States	81	19

financial setbacks higher education has faced in recent years have contributed to faculty mistrust and unrest. Yet, there is clearly a need to create new mechanisms to bring faculty and administrators together to resolve problems, re-establish communications, and renew collegiality.

Academic freedom is one of the core values of higher education. Our respondents, in general, have reasonable confidence that they are protected by this principle. Large majorities in every country (except Russia) note that they are free to determine the content of the courses they teach, and similarly large numbers feel free to do research on any topic that is of interest. Academics—again, except in Russia—believe that academic freedom is fully protected in their country.

When it comes to perceptions of restrictions on what a scholar or scientist can teach or publish, some additional variations were noted. While about half of the respondents feel that there are no political or ideological restrictions on what a scholar can publish, significant numbers do feel constraints: one-third in the United States, for example, and almost 40 percent in Korea. Current debate in the United States concerning

"political correctness" might be responsible for the feeling of some in the social sciences and humanities that there are limits on expression. Although its campuses were hotbeds of activism and of repression in previous regimes, Korea is now a democracy, but it might need more time for new ideas to take hold.

Other Concerns. The issue of the evaluation of academic work is currently of considerable interest to scholars around the world. A significant proportion of faculty in all countries except Brazil, Korea, and Russia report that a strong research record is important in faculty evaluation. Understandably, those who feel the least need to publish also feel least compelled to do research. (Again, this is most true for Brazil, Mexico, and Russia.) But this is not the case at the high end of the scale. Consider, for example, Israel. Eighty-one percent of the faculty there believe that they must publish, but only 13 percent feel that they are asked to do more than they would prefer.

The responses further indicate that the academic profession supports the ideas that higher education should prepare students for work, that research and scholarship should continue to be a key part of the mission of the universi-

ty, that intellectual inquiry should be protected, and that higher education should help to resolve basic social problems so as to enable the nation to compete economically internationally.

When we asked: "Are academics among the most influential people in your country?" overall the responses did not reflect much optimism. Professors in Korea feel that they have relatively high levels of influence; those in England and Israel do not. With regard to England, one wonders what the responses would have been a decade or two ago, before the Conservative government's restructuring of the higher education system. In any case, despite the importance of colleges and universities in modern society, academics do not believe that they are among the most influential opinion leaders.

Another measure of public support for higher education is the respect academics feel in their own country. While responses vary, the general pattern again is not encouraging: about 60 percent of faculty feel that overall respect for academics is declining in their country—ranging from a high of nearly 80 percent in Brazil to a low of less than 45 percent in the Netherlands and Sweden.

Table 11
Faculty in my discipline have a professional obligation to apply their knowledge to problems in society.

	Yes	No
Australia	86%	14%
Brazil	78	22
Chile	74	26
England	79	21
Germany	93	7
Hong Kong	84	16
Israel	76	24
Japan	81	19
Korea	86	14
Mexico	86	14
The Netherlands	87	13
Russia	61	39
Sweden	68	32
United States	82	18

Table 12
Academics are among the most influential opinion leaders in my country.

	Agree	Neutral	Disagree
Australia	19%	27%	54%
Brazil	39	17	44
Chile	16	30	54
England	11	25	63
Germany	15	29	56
Hong Kong	26	36	38
Israel	12	26	62
Japan	40	46	15
Korea	63	29	8
Mexico	30	28	42
Russia	24	33	43
Sweden	30	29	41
United States	21	27	52

Table 13
In this country there is far too much governmental interference in important academic policies.

	Agree	Neutral	Disagree
Australia	57%	26%	17%
Brazil	42	23	35
Chile	17	32	51
Hong Kong	43	32	25
Israel	31	22	48
Japan	48	41	11
Korea	89	8	3
Mexico	55	22	23
The Netherlands	46	32	22
Russia	33	39	27
Sweden	25	36	39
United States	34	33	33

The professoriate in a number of countries feels that institutions of higher learning are increasingly subject to interference from special interest groups—this is particularly true for respondents from the United States, Mexico, England, Brazil, and Australia.

When asked if government interferes too much in important academic policies, positive responses varied from 89 percent in Korea to 17 percent in Chile. In Russia and the United States, about one-third of the faculty feel that there is too much government interference.

Generally, scholars and scientists are supportive of a significant societal mission for higher education and support expansion so that qualified young people can obtain access to postsecondary education. Yet, they would like to distance themselves and their institutions from government edicts and officials.

Implications. This international profile of the academic profession shows a complex web of attitudes and values. One cannot but be immediately struck by the many similarities among the faculty in these diverse countries. While there is a feeling that higher education faces many difficulties and that conditions have deteriorated in recent years, most academics are committed to the profession and to its traditional values of autonomy, academic freedom, and the importance of scholarship, both for its own sake and for societal advancement. Academics are critical of their institutions and are not especially supportive of senior administrators, yet they express remarkable loyalty to the profession and to other academics. They are clearly prepared to respond to higher education's call to contribute more tangibly to economic development and social well-being—that is, they believe they have an obligation to apply their knowledge to problems of society.

In brief, it is resiliency, determination, and a focus on the core functions of higher education that seem to characterize the academic profession. While the vicissitudes facing the profession in recent years have been considerable, the professoriate is by no means demoralized. This fact cannot be overemphasized. In all but three countries, 60 percent or more agree that this is an especially creative and productive time in their field. Professors are on the whole satisfied with the courses they teach, and—with few exceptions—are pleased with their opportunities to pursue their own ideas. The intellectual atmosphere is good; faculty do not regret their ca-reer choice and are generally pleased with their relationships with colleagues. They face the future with a concern about the direction of higher education, but they have confidence that what they do is valuable and express a continuing desire to pursue scholarship and teaching. The intrinsic pleasures of academic life obviously endure.

The Carnegie survey's portrait of the academic profession is at variance with much contemporary commentary about the professoriate. In books and articles, faculty are depicted as deeply demoralized and disaffected. In the United States and England, especially, the profession has been widely portrayed as acutely depressed. Professors are described as lacking in commitment to the academic enterprise, sullenly facing the future. While our respondents are critical of the state of the academy and are not especially sanguine about the future of the university in an era of fiscal crisis and uncertainty on many fronts, they are by no means depressed.

The considerable unanimity of views internationally is remarkable. Despite differing circumstances, the professoriate retains a considerable degree of optimism in the 14 countries included in the Carnegie survey. ▣

CHAPTER VIII

The Ties of Association

In every case, at the head of any new undertaking, where in France you would find the government or in England some territorial magnate, in the United States you are sure to find an association.

> —ALEXIS DE TOCQUEVILLE, *DEMOCRACY IN AMERICA*

For what to us is the praise of the ignorant? Let us join together in the bond of our scientific societies, and encourage each other, as we are now doing, in the pursuit of our favorite study; knowing that the world will sometime recognize our services, and knowing, also, that we constitute the most important element in human progress.

> —HENRY A. ROWLAND, ''A PLEA FOR PURE SCIENCE''(1883)

Individuals who are not bound together in associations, whether domestic, economic, religious, political, artistic, or educational are monstrosities.

> —JOHN DEWEY, *INDIVIDUALISM OLD AND NEW* (1930)

AMERICAN ACADEMIC SPECIALISTS do not long remain monstrosities—in John Dewey's vivid imagery—unbound by solid organization that promises to consolidate and further their intellectual effort. They settled a century ago upon the department as their main tool of controlled development inside universities and colleges, a unit primarily centered on individual subjects and devoted to furthering individual disciplines, while it also served as the building block of academic enterprises. But something more was needed to tighten the hold of specialization upon academic life, a device that would serve externally as a carrying mechanism for a discipline at large, a way of furthering specialties without regard to institutional boundaries. By the end of the nineteenth century, American academics en masse found that external arm in the learned so-

233

ciety or disciplinary association, a form at once specialized in scope and national in membership and orientation.

Near the end of the twentieth century, we cannot imagine academic life without this type of professional linkage. It serves many interests of academics, idealistic and practical, right down to the "flesh market" realities of job seeking. No academic specialty amounts to anything unless it has a national association, or a section of one—or, as we later see, an "invisible" substitute—to help it develop, spread its influence, and enhance its sense of solidarity. Among the associations operating in 1985, two-thirds had originated since 1940, with 150 starting up after 1960 (Table 4 and Appendix B), clear evidence of the widespread and increasing importance of this form of linkage. Disciplinary associations multiply as fast as specialties develop; they have also begun to reflect the division of academics among institutional sectors.

THE PATTERNS OF ASSOCIATION

The first distinction we need to grasp is between associations of professors and associations of administrators. The duality of disciplines and institutions in American higher education is reflected in the division of national associations into those that center on faculty interests and those that are organized around the interests of college and university administrators. Institutionally tied associations are exemplified and semiofficially capped by the American Council on Education (ACE), a "presidents' club" established in 1918 at the same time as the National Research Council (NRC) and the Social Science Research Council (SSRC). All were voluntary associations established to help link higher education and the national government.[1] While the NRC and the SSRC served as multidiscipline associations organized by and for professors, the ACE became an association of universities and colleges, hence administrator-driven, that was to serve, in part, as an association of associations. Its present locale at One Dupont Circle, an edifice in Washington, D.C., houses the headquarters of many other associations in which institutional members are represented by their top administrators, as in the powerful National Association of State Universities and Land-Grant Colleges (NASULGC) that dates itself in an earlier form as far back as 1887, or in which individuals represent a segment

234

of administration as well as their whole institutions, as in the Council of Graduate Schools (CGS), where graduate school deans, committed primarily to the welfare of graduate education, serve as members. The programs of the annual meetings of these associations do not take up academic subjects, other than, occasionally, the minor specialty known as the study of higher education. They explore not Wittgenstein and Weber, but student personnel services and strains of the college presidency. Representing the interests of administrators in the welfare of whole institutions or major parts thereof—and in personal advancement in administrative careers—an entire set of associations runs on a separate track from the discipline-by-discipline representation we find in the faculty associations.

When graduate deans, business officers, admissions officers, presidents, chancellors, and other clusters of administrators represent institutional concerns, their efforts may well serve faculty interests. They may help to increase financial resources and, generally, to enhance the good name of academia; they may specifically lobby to strengthen the humanities or the sciences. Leaders in these associations may go down two roads simultaneously, running with the faculty hare as well as with the administrator hound. But often they do not: The agendas quite naturally diverge. The administrators tune to governmental actions that would strengthen or adversely affect entire institutions. They are interested in overall institutional leadership and hence in effective administrative controls. They seek counsel on "management." Their agenda stretches from legislative actions on student aid, to relations with universities in other countries, to the never-ending battle to bring big-time collegiate sports under some semblance of control.

In contrast, faculty members operate within disciplines, either individual ones or in combinations of them—the natural sciences, the social sciences, the humanities, the arts—to influence governmental and private-sector actions that will strengthen the research and scholarly base of their own fields. The academicians are particularly strong in science councils, penetrating by means of peer review the ordinary routines of such major agencies as the National Science Foundation and the National Institutes of Health. And, most of the time, their associations turn inward upon periodic meetings in which papers are read and criticized and specialized knowledge is otherwise pursued. Hence it is not surprising that faculty

235

members and administrators from the same campus may go separate ways in representing interests in Washington, D.C., to the point where one does not know what the other is doing, and uncoordinated if not conflicting action is taken, to the surprise of all. Clark Kerr pointed out in the 1960s that the heads of campuses can readily feel things are out of control, and their own authority threatened, when professors strike their own deals in Washington.[2] One story used to illustrate the problem is about the research professor who strolled into the president's office in an Eastern private university to announce that he had just arranged, on a recent trip to Washington, for a research grant that included not only a new laboratory but an entire new building. The professor was sure the president would welcome this good news.

Natural conflict between administrator and faculty associations is exemplified in arguments over the size of "institutional overhead" in the budgeting of federal research grants. Researchers are inclined to see every dollar for overhead as one less dollar for research itself. They strongly prefer to have granting agencies limit the amount allotted to "indirect costs" that goes to the institution as a whole and hence into the hands of central administrators. On the other hand, campus administrators have constantly urged the government to raise the overhead rate. They maintain that big science has long had major hidden costs on university campuses, that "in the early days of indirect costs, everyone was under-recovering."[3] Further, science is steadily becoming more capital intensive, requiring more equipment and buildings that entail significant increased costs in depreciation, maintenance, and administration, which ought to be charged to research projects. At major private universities, the indirect cost rates had climbed by 1984 to between 65 and 70 percent, a very major addition to the allocations made directly for the research itself. Hence, income from this source becomes a major item in the overall budgets of research universities: At Stanford, "indirect cost recovery from government is characteristically the second most important income source, behind tuition but well ahead of all endowment income."[4] A million here and a million there soon add up to real money.

Sharp hostilities broke out over this issue in 1983, when the National Institutes of Health (NIH)—the principal supporter of research in the biological sciences—proposed to withhold 10 percent of indirect cost reim-

236

bursement in order to allocate more money to the research projects themselves. NIH was backed by the Federation of American Societies for Experimental Biology (FASEB), which accused university administrators, in true fighting language, of playing a "four-dimensional shell game" with indirect costs and described them as having made a "triumphant tour de force in evading the issue in the past three years." This serious conflict called out the skills of some of the best academic diplomats, who were soon at work forming another coalition, one of "university associations and scientific groups" that would help to obtain "full funding for both direct and indirect costs." FASEB reversed its position and passed a resolution calling for cooperation.[5] However, the issue is a sore point, a matter on which administrators and professors naturally divide, and on which their associational voices are prone to speak in divergent and often conflicting terms. Administrative associations and faculty associations see the world differently.

Of the disciplinary associations to which faculty members belong, some are almost completely restricted to academics, others center on the outside members, and still others blend the two. The American Historical Association and the American Sociological Association are known as academic associations: Academics heavily predominate, and the organization has a "learned-society" heritage that may have made a simple name change from "society" to "association" a wrenching decision. Such academic organizations are understood to be inside higher education, parts of the academic profession. In contrast, the American Medical Association and the American Bar Association are outside higher education, positioned in major domains of professional practice, with academics a small proportion of their members.

But the lines are rarely hard and fast, and some associations extensively mix academics and others. Academic chemists use the American Chemical Society as their primary association, but they constitute only one-third of its members; membership of the other two-thirds indicates that chemistry is a field in which the Ph.D. degree leads mainly to employment in industry. Founded in 1876, this association has evolved in a century into a complex organization that stretches quite naturally across the boundary between academia and industry. By the standards of wholly academic associations, it is huge, with a membership of 125,000, a budget of over one

237

hundred million dollars, a dozen or more journals, and a fully profession-alized administrative staff of 1,600 people (in a major building of its own in Washington, D.C.) that annually oversees 1,700 local, regional, divi-sional, and other meetings.[6] Academic and nonacademic concerns natu-rally crosshatch, for whatever the differences between the academics and the industrial chemists, they have powerful mutual interests in such spe-cialties as food chemistry, organic chemistry, and physical chemistry. This association epitomizes a longstanding and increasingly more prevalent subject-centered form of organization that bridges between higher educa-tion and other sectors of society, particularly industry. The form is now common in engineering and the sciences, including biology, as a rapidly expanding field in which Ph.D.'s increasingly spread out from the academy to posts in government and private firms.

What gradually emerged in our probing of the associational structure of the profession, particularly in the accounts that respondents provided in field interviews, is the way associations mirror the ongoing contest be-tween centrifugal and centripetal academic forces. "Splinteritis" is every-where. Each academic association finds itself subdividing into numerous major divisions along subject-matter lines, which then divide still further into subsections. As they grow substantively, incorporating more special-ties, associations sow the seed of their own fragmentation. The large as-sociations also tend to divide by institutional sector: One community col-lege president pointed out that in the Modern Language Association and in the National Council of Teachers of English, "there is usually a commu-nity college component or at least a series of workshops dealing with com-munity colleges at these annual meetings." If a major association does not strategically subdivide itself, it faces the constant threat of the loss of au-tonomy-seeking groups of specialists who move to set up their own organ-izations. In the older mainline associations that have managed to remain intact, unitary organization drifts toward a more federative form.

Interests in some fields—preeminently the biological sciences—have been so scattered and diversified from the beginning that no one organi-zation ever established hegemony. Biologists of varying specialties turned to different associations, which then became integrated confederatively from the bottom up by coming together officially in one or more mam-moth umbrella organizations. A well-informed observer of the associa-

238

tions in biology did his best to tell us how a confusing reality was composed:

> The discipline is divided in this country into perhaps a hundred subdisciplinary societies: the ecologists, the physiologists, the microbiologists, the biochemists, and so on. These societies are really independent, but there are two major groups that are umbrellas. One, [the Federation of American Societies for Experimental Biology] has seven societies, and the other group is under the American Institute of Biological Sciences. . . . There are about thirty or forty societies in that group. But, you see, there are many societies that don't belong to either one, and there are some societies that belong to both. The physiologists belong both to AIBS and to FASEB. . . . Now the American Chemical Society, although there are many subdivisions of chemistry, has stuck together as the American Chemical Society. The American Institute of Physics has all of the nine major physics societies in the country under the American Institute of Physics. The biologists are scattered.

> (*Is that because of what biology is, or is it some historical thing that happened?*) That is a very difficult question. It is historical certainly, to a degree. The chemists organized early and stuck together; and the biologists, it seems, as soon as a discipline of biology forms, there are subdisciplines which splinter off. Their jealousies and egos and territorialities become important. For one reason or another, biologists seem to have much more difficulty working together than do the physicists or the chemists or even the engineers, although the engineers are somewhat split, too. There is an American Association of Engineering Societies [total membership, one million!], which has recently been structured to pull together the electrical engineers and the chemical engineers and the mechanical engineers, and so forth, under one umbrella. The point is that in Washington . . . or [in] a national posture, you almost need a strong unified group. . . . The nation simply can't listen to hundreds of little subdisciplines, each one purporting to represent science in their field, because the fields get too small and get too specialized. It's just like medicine. Medicine is also splintered, but somehow the AMA has held together, and the American Association of Medical Colleges has held together. But the biologists probably have the worst case of splinteritis of anyone in the country. . . .

239

101

You'll find that each individual society feels that it has the key to the future. The ecologists feel that the rest of biology is really not all that important. This is the pinnacle of science. The biochemists, at the other end of the spectrum, say you get anything above the molecule [and] it just becomes hokus-pokus and phenomenological. There is, perhaps, a great deal more sheer arrogance from discipline to discipline in biology than you find anywhere else. I don't understand it completely, and I have been observing it my whole life.

In the set of disciplines known as "the biological sciences," there are numerous associational keys to the kingdom. But a good share of the groups feel they ought to associate loosely with each other in umbrella organizations, just as small individual political states often feel the need to confederate, federate, or band together as a united larger state to exert influence. In biology, however, the larger nation is inherently weak; the individual states have separate historical identities and interests. Still, superimposed upon a resource- and knowledge-rich academic base, umbrella organizations in biology offer impressive credentials. The Federation of American Societies for Experimental Biology, with a combined membership of over 20,000, can rightfully claim it is a powerful and wealthy organization. It publishes over thirty scientific journals, counts over 100 Nobel Prizes earned by its members, and is organized to do massive reports for the federal government and other authorities on food safety and food additives, toxic waste disposal, and other significant, practical issues.[7] Confederative or not, it is a major, busy corner of academia. And its identity and membership blur the lines between the pure and the applied, the private lives of academic disciplines and the public concerns of legislators and public executives.

In efforts to counter splinteritis, multidisciplinary associations interpenetrate one another. Umbrellas are raised over umbrellas. A professor of biology who had been active in the American Zoological Society pointed to the two umbrella organizations mentioned above as larger amalgams, and then noted that he belonged to and had been an officer in yet another wider umbrella organization, the American Association for the Advancement of Science (AAAS), whose interests were very diffuse and included the social sciences and beyond. He continued:

240

Then, there are global organizations. For example, there is the International Union of Immunological Societies (IUIS), which is the umbrella for all national immunological societies. For example, the American Association of Immunologists holds a seat in IUIS; so does the French Society of Immunologists; so does the British Society of Immunologists. Then there is another one . . . the International Union of Biological Societies. . . .

Umbrella is one metaphor, spider web another, and pyramid yet another that points to the many ways in which proliferating associations constitute a larger maze of linkages. Many relatively small associations do not particularly acknowledge the overtones of shelter and possible subordination inherent in the umbrella concept, yet they weave themselves around a larger national association by holding their annual meeting in the same city, presenting their own programs right before, right after, or during the meeting of the major group. In the social sciences, the Society for the Study of Social Problems (SSSP) has long attached itself in this fashion to the American Sociological Association; most of its members also hold memberships in the ASA, while backing a vehicle for more practical concerns. The Policy Studies Organization, newly sprung largely from political science and public administration, meets with the American Political Science Association, again with an extensive overlap of membership. In turn, the associational networks include pyramids within individual disciplines, as smaller regional associations feed loosely into national associations that, in turn, offer the institutional building blocks plus the members for international associations. In a confusing manner only partially caught in any one metaphor, associations structure the metainstitutional life of the academic profession.

That metastructure has begun to reflect significantly the allocation of academics to types of institutions other than research universities. In at least three major ways, the associational network is adapting to the interests of faculty located in the middle and lower rungs of the institutional hierarchy. For one, national associations themselves have been adjusting their own inner lives, since about 1970, to attract and retain faculty located in state, small private, and community colleges. More attention is paid to teaching the discipline: A teaching specialist is placed in the headquarters staff; a separate budget allocation is made for work on the problems of

241

teaching; a subdivision is organized; and space for discussion of the problems of teaching is inserted in the annual program. Second, regional disciplinary associations take on the character of a home for those who cannot get on the programs of the national associations, and especially for those unable to obtain travel funds to attend distant meetings. Regional associations are also much smaller, and their meetings in most cases seem friendlier as well as more accessible. Coast to coast, lack of travel funds is a major irritant particularly noticeable in the state-college sector. On one coast we heard: "I don't have the money to go. . . . I can't, even if I am invited to present a paper. . . . I couldn't go last year." And on the other coast: "We don't have any money within this system to send people to those things. . . . If they [the meetings] are in the neighborhood, I will go to them." The regional associations are also joined by more localized state and city counterparts, which serve as small worlds attractive to teachers and researchers of less than national renown. Those who serve as officers and as members of the many committees of these associations may receive some local and regional notice in their disciplines in lieu of national accolades.

A third, and most recent, adaptive evolution is the most telling: Disciplinary associations are now forming along sector lines. The more a sector is organizationally set off, the more do associations break off. The community college sector is, therefore, the principal center of this type of proliferation. A community college biology instructor explained how and why a sectoral association was organized in her discipline, in her part of the country, just a few years earlier:

> [We] got a notice that a group of biology professors from various two-year schools were putting together an organization. The purpose of the organization is for communication, [for] exchange of ideas between people who have the same problems, community college biologists that saw a certain type of student, a student that for one reason or another didn't go to a four-year school, either because of money or . . . often because of academic reasons. You know, what textbooks we should use at this level, and how we can use the computer in our courses, and how we can get across this idea at this level. . . . If I go to real high-powered meetings occasionally, and they speak about technologies that I

242

have no idea about anymore, being out of it, [then] I can bring back almost nothing to our students; but from these meetings I bring back a lot because they are geared for the teacher of the two-year institution.

Localization in this case took place on two dimensions simultaneously: The association is statewide instead of national, and it limits itself to the community-college part of the biology professoriate.

Such doubly local associations are both more within reach of the pocketbook, when colleges provide little or no travel funds, and more relevant to substantive interests. A social science instructor in a metropolitan community college told us he wanted to attend disciplinary meetings, but for the last four of five years he had only been able to attend one taking place in his own metropolitan area. He had gotten out of the main national association some time ago:

> I used to belong to the American Political Science Association but found in recent years there was such a disparity between what they were doing and what I was doing that I didn't find it to be terribly intellectually stimulating. . . . Given where my students are at and where they are likely to go, given their socio-economic backgrounds and their language limitations, and their heterogeneity, a lot of things that I see in the journals don't correspond very much to what I can do in class. . . . I mean, reality dictates.

Astute observers have argued cogently that community college faculty are not in a position to follow the cosmopolitan road to professionalism so heavily traveled by university professors: "The community college faculty disciplinary affiliation is too weak, the institutions' demands for scholarship are practically nonexistent, and the teaching loads are too heavy for that form of professionalism to occur." Community college faculty will either undergo more deprofessionalization, slipping further toward the weak professionalism of American schoolteaching, or they will have to bootstrap themselves into a different set of appropriate forms that "reconceptualize the academic disciplines themselves to fit the realities of the community colleges."[8] In this effort, associations and journals are crucial

243

tools. Moves in this direction have included the formation of the Community College Social Science Association and the Community College Humanities Association, together with the establishment of journals directed toward two-year college instructors in such fields as mathematics, journalism, and English.

National surveys have shown clearly that faculty members vary greatly across sectors in attendance at national meetings. In the 1984 Carnegie survey, half of the community college faculty members reported they had not made their way to a meeting during ast year, compared to about 20 percent not having done so in leading liberal arts colleges and 15 percent in leading research universities (Table 17). About one-half of leading liberal arts college faculty members and research university faculty members had attended two or more meetings, with proportions in the other sectors diminishing to one-fourth in the two-year colleges. But the other side of the coin is that, even in the community college sector, one-half of the faculty managed at least one meeting, and one out of four, by personal expense or otherwise, negotiated two or more meetings. Clearly, the urge to meet with other academics outside of one's own institution does not die even in the most adverse settings. Unfortunately, the survey data do not reveal what type of national meeting was attended or how far respondents had to travel. As national associations move their annual meetings from one city to another, a common practice, many faculty members can readily catch a meeting in their region at least every third or fourth year. And, as sector associations develop, principally in the community college area, they can find gatherings appropriate to their own cause.

In short, as the cutting edges of academic specialization become sharply honed, reality dictates that national associations centered on university professors become inappropriate for a good share of the faculty who are so involved in undergraduate teaching that they are "out of it." National meetings replete with papers reporting the latest research results are not relevant to the vast majority of community college teachers and to a large proportion of professors located in four-year institutions. We can predict further proliferation of associations localized by type of institution as well as by geographic area. Only the top third or so of the institutional hierarchy, consisting of the better colleges as well as the research universities, is thoroughly national in interest. Academics in the rest of the system find

244

TABLE 17

FACULTY ATTENDANCE AT NATIONAL MEETINGS, BY TYPE OF INSTITUTION

TYPE OF INSTITUTION	NUMBER OF MEETINGS		
	NONE	ONE	TWO OR MORE
	(PERCENT OF FACULTY)		
RESEARCH UNIVERSITIES I	15	28	57
RESEARCH UNIVERSITIES II	22	29	49
DOCTORAL-GRANTING UNIVERSITIES I	27	32	41
DOCTORAL-GRANTING UNIVERSITIES II	33	27	40
COMPREHENSIVE UNIVERSITIES AND COLLEGES I	31	32	37
COMPREHENSIVE UNIVERSITIES AND COLLEGES II	41	27	32
LIBERAL ARTS COLLEGES I	21	34	45
LIBERAL ARTS COLLEGES II	38	32	30
TWO-YEAR COLLEGES	49	26	25
ALL INSTITUTIONS	33	29	38

Total respondents, 4,863

QUESTION: "During the last year, how many national professional meetings did you attend?"

SOURCE: The Carnegie Foundation for the Advancement of Teaching, Faculty Survey 1984.

their way to types of associations their own realities dictate, including responsiveness to a local undergraduate student clientele in place of responsiveness to a national group of peers. The critical divide between students and peers as primary clientele is increasingly reflected in the associational maze of the professoriate.

245

THE ROLE OF INVISIBLE ASSOCIATIONS

A major unanticipated finding that emerged from our interviews is the extent to which university researchers themselves are sometimes finding their major national associations to be empty shells, too general in scope to be relevant to special interests, too large to facilitate interaction among like-minded peers. National associations try to cope with this problem by elaborate sectioning, creating smaller worlds of subject-centered divisions, all with formal names, their own officers and members, perhaps a small budget, and definitely their own piece of the annual programming. The internal life of one association after another in the post-World War II decades has been characterized by a tension between the centrists, who wish to maintain a unitary organization and the section leaders who are busy developing separate parts whose strength and autonomy give the whole organization a confederative cast. History rides with the separatists; there are limits to how much their interests can be appeased by well-integrated generalist organizations.

At the interdisciplinary association level, the problem has struck particularly hard at the American Association for the Advancement of Science, where attendance at annual meetings slipped over 70 percent in a decade and a half, dropping between 1969 and 1985 from 8,000 to 2,300. Association officials have reported a sense of ebbing vitality; they bemoan the lack of announced major new scientific discoveries at their meetings; that "the young scientist who is doing the exciting experiment isn't at this meeting"; that only white-haired veterans, "long past the stage of active scientific work," still come. The cause of the AAAS problem is seen to be that "the increasing specialization of science is ending the popularity of big general meetings that consider scientific and public policy issues of interest to a great range of scientists, not just those from a narrow specialty." As a result, the AAAS, looking to its own vitality and value, has been shifting its center of gravity from the annual meeting, long the flagship activity, into such activities as publishing a science magazine for laymen and programs for improving the quality of precollege science and mathematics education.[9]

At the discipline level, the American Physical Society has seen attendance at its annual meeting slip drastically, from about 7,000 in 1967 to 800

246

in 1985. The society's executive secretary has concluded that "the general meetings are just disappearing. . . . The only way to have a successful meeting is to have specialized topics," that is, meetings that are themselves limited to such specific topics as basic properties of optical materials or radio-frequency plasma heating. The society has turned to sponsoring two dozen such smaller topical conferences a year, which might be attended by 150 to 300 physicists.[10] University faculty members we interviewed concurred: I do not go "to these gigantic Physical Society meetings, but very often to smaller workshop-things"; "nobody goes to the conferences any more very much. I mean, not the standard APS meetings. I never go; very few of my colleagues go. Instead, we tend to go to special topical meetings, which are set up just for one time only."

Similarly, in biology, where the field is already radically subdivided among national associations, professors speak of seeking smaller networks, some of which can be worked up regionally:

> I tend to go to small, local meetings. There is a guild of population biologists that meets in the Rocky Mountains. There is a prairie states ecology conclave of about five local universities. I find I get to know the people better, and I actually learn more by going to these local meetings, than the big, frustrating national ones.

Another biologist at a leading university viewed meetings of the national associations as "monster meetings." He, too, sought out informal and semiformal "meetings during the year which are smaller and, therefore, more focused. Those are the preferred ones to go to." Where specialization is most advanced, academics have learned to use disposable meetings. They deformalize their networks to better adjust to the shifting contours of research interests.

In the narrowly focused world of topical meetings, we enter a vast underbrush of semiformal and informal linkages characteristic of American academia, ties that also weave, weblike, around the mainline associations. Faculty members speak of going to meet others in their "network" when they go off to attend sessions of their "division" within the national association ("the Business Policy and Planning Division of the Academy of Management is where most of the people in my network are"). Of grow-

247

ing importance also are the ties not dependent on formal associations for their footing, connections that we can view as invisible associations, in line with the fruitful concept of invisible colleges, which has been widely used in the sociology of science. The idea of an invisible college has meant a communication "network of productive scientists" that links "separate groups of collaborators within a research area."[11] We can broaden the idea so that it is not limited to "productive scientists," but instead refers more inclusively to the informal arrangements by which academics connect and communicate on campus and, especially, in the system at large.

Even at top universities, where cosmopolitan ties are strongest, informal associations, for some, may be largely local. A political scientist at a leading university reported that although he often discussed intellectual matters with one important colleague at another university 2,000 miles away, all the others with whom he sought close interaction—a goodly number— he found by roaming his own campus, branching out from his own department to a major campus institute that contained members of several departments and then on to numerous other departments:

> Right now I have just initiated some discussions with a colleague in the linguistics department, and I talked to a colleague in the anthropology department. I have been interested in the evolution of behavior, and I have gotten a lot out of a colleague in the biology department. I have occasional dealings with colleagues in the sociology department and the business school who are also interested in organization theory—and the school of public health—because we have had a group of organization theorists that has gotten together.

This professor felt that he did "a different kind of work," and therefore, did not "feel very strongly identified with any particular group." His own department was satisfactory as "a professional home," but to pursue his own research agenda he needed to fashion his own set of ties, a flexible set of local exchanges.

A major campus is a vast collection of such highly disposable individualized networks, interpersonal ties fashioned by professors with those outside as well as with those within their own departments, as they follow the thrust of their intellectual interests. The social inventions here are

248

many. "Journal clubs," one of them, was described by a professor of biology in a leading university:

> I interact with people in the medical school because there are not other immunologists in this department. . . . Right now, we're not actually connecting on a given project, though we may be starting something like that soon, but we share journal clubs. You know what journal clubs are? That is where you get together with people working in your area and review current papers from the literature that are of interest. So we share a weekly journal club with three other labs in the medical school. . . . This is fairly common in biology, at least.

Two political scientists told us about larger invisible associations of which they were a part; mentor-student ties played an important role here. One, who indicated his closest professional ties were elsewhere, not in his own department, added, "I also have Ph.D.'s all over the place. When you have been at it as long as I have, you are pretty well connected nationally." The informal can stretch to become a whole "school of people" lasting over several academic generations. The second professor spoke of having close friends elsewhere—at Cornell and Harvard and in the government—and went on to describe his main network as an informal and "highly controversial school of people . . . who are identified with a man who taught at Chicago for many years, Leo Strauss, and I am a student of students of Strauss. People who know my work think of me as Straussian."

In all the disciplines, from the humanities to the sciences, the invisible associations have a primary role in self-identity, communication, and the bonding of members of the profession. A humanist declared, "I have better relations with colleagues at other universities simply because they share my interests in Joyce, O'Casey, and Yeats, my interest in Anglo-Irish literature, and it is healthy to meet colleagues." The informal then shades into small-scale associations: "I belong to organizations within my specific field: the Committee for Irish Studies, the James Joyce Society, the O'Casey Society." At the same time, this humanities professor continued his membership in "the major organization in our field. . . . The Modern Language Association."

249

In the sciences, too, there are extended families that form around a mentor and several generations of students and research associates. In physics: "There are several groups that basically have the same parentage, which sprang from John Wheeler at Princeton University, and he had some great students who spawned some great groups. . . . That family I identify with. I wasn't a student of his, but I was a colleague and a research associate, and that's whom I identify with."

Another physics professor spoke of his professional home as being the "collection of people I sort of professionally grew up with over the last twenty years. . . . My closest collaborators tend to be people immediately around me, but all over there are people who have been close to me and have worked with me in the past." For those struggling to do research in second- and third-level universities, the dominant informal associations were all the more likely to be elsewhere, even abroad, since relevant immediate colleagues are in short supply:

> The persons that I have most contact with in terms of my research goals are not in this department. . . . [They are] people at IBM research labs, or at the Max Planck Institute in Stuttgart, and some other universities.

> [My] closest professional colleagues in the sense of people who do what I do—certainly, they are somewhere else. There is nobody here that does what I do, which is, I guess, typical, at least at a small school.

So segmented is the academic labor market that many specialists in large and small places are hired as one-of-a-kind experts. Their intellectual sustenance then depends largely on associations, informal and formal, which bridge the boundaries of their own institutions.

Weakest in associational ties, of course, are the many reluctant part-time and temporary full-time faculty, whose marginal careers leave them hanging by their fingertips to the edges of academe. They are least likely to have personal or institutional travel funds to attend meetings. They are outside or peripheral to the regular faculty circles that spawn the more informal ties. Associationally, as well as organizationally they get left out. But even here, the drive to associate does not die: Indeed, those in a common weak position have good reason to band together to support one an-

250

other, to find strength in numbers, to share tips on employment opportunities, and to have intellectual discussions. Thus, in sociology in the 1980s, "independent scholars" became a new network of the unemployed and underemployed, with officers, meetings, a newsletter, and formal affiliation with the mainline national association.

THE ASSOCIATIONAL WEBBING
OF ACADEMIC GROUPS

To solve their institutional problems, professors turn to such place-bound tools as departments and senates. To solve their disciplinary problems, they reach for subject-based associations that extend to wherever like-minded peers can be found. The larger the national system, the more academics seem to need to create such ties; they need to bring a cohort of over 500,000 "colleagues," as in the United States, down to the more manageable size of 50,000, or better 5,000 or even better 500 or 50, and sometimes 5. The more a national system is decentralized, the more academics are encouraged to turn to voluntary action, since there are no formal embracing schemes that even pretend to bring them together. Then, too, the individual and small-group autonomies of academia provide the freedom and moral authority to voluntarily associate. Even in the most managerial settings, academics do not have to ask permission from "the boss" before reaching outside their own departments, and then beyond their university or college, to fashion meaningful ties with others. There are virtually no product secrets. Academics communicate with colleagues readily and band together in formations of their own devising as soon as they face new problems or generate new bodies of knowledge. They would rather be association persons than "organization men."

Without any person or group planning it, or even setting the general direction, a division of labor has evolved in America in which postsecondary associations of institutions attend to institutional and student issues while disciplinary associations concentrate, field by field, on issues of research and scholarship. With this division, many issues affecting professors are beyond the bounds of their primary national associations: Organized institutional interests, then, readily predominate over the professional ones. When government officials and legislators, state or national, want advice

251

on "higher education," they turn to institutional heads and their associations. In turn, especially in the national capitol, the presidents' clubs develop a lobbying capacity to represent higher education. But when the state turns directly to "science"—or "the humanities" or "the arts"—do its officials turn to disciplinary groupings. And it is mainly around the needs of scholarship that professor-run associations reciprocally develop a presence as a lobby and learn to penetrate governmental agencies. The many disciplinary associations thereby fashion connections with government that bypass the institutions.

As a class of organizations, American disciplinary associations are more pervasive and powerful than their counterparts in other countries, but their power is narrowly focused. As they concentrate on the research and scholarship of direct interest to their members, they leave other aspects of higher education to administrators. The division of influence parallels the bargain struck within the authority structures of universities and colleges, but the professional base is more dampened. The associational structure reflects the simple fact that the higher the level in the American system, the more pervasive is the sway of management. Senates may be powerful locally, but there are no powerful professor-dominated senates nationally to pull academics together as a professional class.

Since specialization is what counts in the professorial network, right down to professors withdrawing from their own major associations because they view them as too general, all-inclusive associations have a difficult time. They are cast in a secondary role because they deemphasize disciplinary distinctions, swimming against the tide of the proliferating pursuit of such separations. Membership in the American Association of University Professors, for example, then seems relatively costly: One first pays membership dues to a set of regional, national, and possibly international, disciplinary associations and then squeezes the family budget still further to pay the AAUP its annual dues. For those in top places, disciplinary memberships are relatively essential; joining and serving in the AAUP is more in the nature of *noblesse oblige*, done with a sense that less fortunate colleagues in other places need a defense league to protect them against the batterings of politicians, trustees, and administrators.

When the National Education Association and the American Federation of Teachers seriously entered the picture in the late 1960s and the 1970s,

252

114

in full union dress, they not only deemphasize disciplinary distinctions but also those of status. As we have seen (Chapter VI), they run up against the stubborn fact that successful people in every discipline want the rewards of status. Thus, in a system so much given to diversity, competition, and hierarchy, there are powerful reasons why inclusive bodies in the form of unions are strongest where discipline and status matter least, and weakest where discipline and status count the most. Issues left for unions are then largely economic and managerial in a domain where leadership and stature flow to those who most effectively attend to their focused scholarship and take up the roles of salaried entrepreneurs. For their members, the disciplinary associations, able to build on a substantial consciousness of kind, are often impressive symbols of professional community. The NEA, the AFT, and sometimes the AAUP, in contrast, have only a weak base of common consciousness upon which to operate as vehicles of shared identity. Their base lies in local strains between "workers" and "management."

American higher education is simultaneously underorganized in certain respects and overorganized in others.[12] It has no national ministry and no national formal system of control. Seen in comparative perspective, it is only loosely structured by normal bureaucratic and political tools of state authority. But voluntary association then substitutes for systemwide formal organization. The substitute system is bewildering and hard to capture, quantitatively or qualitatively. It is simultaneously formal, semiformal, and informal; it is visible and invisible. Overall hierarchy is minimal: No peak association or set of ties commands all the rest. Lines of affiliation loop through and around one another, with no regard for unifying principles of order, logic, and accountability. The gaps and redundancies are too numerous to count.

American academics associate voluntarily from the bottom up. Their national network forms from the intellectual and practical interests of thousands of clusters of practicing academics scattered in the vast array of disciplines and institutions that compose the system. What the bottom does not like, the bottom disposes of. More than in other countries, the voluntary lines make for a disposable structure of coordination, thereby promoting system flexibility. Voluntary associating is a good way to have structure follow knowledge, rather than the other way around. Professionals have known for a long time that, as a general form, association is more

253

malleable than bureaucracy. It follows particularly well the many contours of academe. In the American setting, it is deeply a part of the logic of the academic profession.

Paralleling the cultural overlap identified in Chapter V, associational overlap provides some integration in an otherwise chaotic domain. Even in the most narrow specialties, professors face outward from their own campus, joining hands across organizational boundaries. They take up multiple memberships: They join specialty associations and larger disciplinary ones; they belong to a pyramid of regional, national, and international associations; they maneuver in the invisible groupings as well as the formal ones. Specialties in one discipline converge on those in another: Some molecular biologists run some of the time with physicists and chemists. As a biologist put it, "My area of research carries me into other professional societies of which I am also a member." It is hard to distinguish political sociologists from behavioral political scientists; they cross associational lines accordingly, even to occupy high office. The inclusive faculty associations, such as the American Association of University Professors, provide some additional linkage, however secondary its importance. As for liaison among the associations themselves, there are the interdisciplinary umbrella associations and the councils of the umbrella organizations.

In American academic life, where scholars are so scattered by type of institution as well as discipline, reasons for singularity and division abound. Following the division of labor, fragmentation is necessarily—as emphasized throughout this study—the dominant theme. But if there are reasons to isolate, there are reasons to associate. Academics who occupy a common corner in fields of knowledge coalesce so they will not be monstrosities of individualized isolation. As their limited associations, formal and informal, overlap one another, a larger network emerges. In a profession of professions, overlapping voluntary linkages are the nearest thing to a social structure that provides order and integration.

254

*The self is not so much a substance as a process in which
the conversation of gestures has been internalized within
an organic form. This process does not exist for itself, but
is simply a phase of the whole social organization of which
the individual is a part* (Mead 1934, p. 178).

Socialization is a concept that has concerned social scientists
throughout the 20th century. For some, socialization is a
means for achieving a sense of solidarity by the institution-
alization of shared values (Merton 1957; Parsons and Shils
1951). For others, socialization is a means for reproducing
the mores of the dominant culture (Bourdieu 1977). Some
theorists have investigated socialization as a common need
across all cultures (Levi-Strauss 1963), and others have considered the interaction between the individual psyche and
the social organization (Goffman 1959, 1967; Mead 1934).

*As a process,
socialization
is ongoing,
although it
occurs most
clearly when
new recruits
enter the
organization.*

Many anthropologists have thought of some forms of socialization as a ritualized situation (Turner 1977). Van Gennep,
for example, studied "rites of passage" that socialized individuals to the larger society (1960). These rituals were
designed to move individuals from one developmental stage
to another. The most obvious form of such rituals were those
used for adolescents who were to become adults. Educational
anthropologists (Spindler and Spindler 1989) and social
scientists (McLaren 1986; Tinto 1987) also have considered
how students become socialized to society through the educational organization.

We view socialization as a ritualized process that involves
the transmission of culture. In what follows, we elaborate on
our definition of organizational socialization and then delin-
eate the stages in which faculty become involved.

Organizational Socialization Defined
Organizational socialization is a cultural process that involves
the exchange of patterns of thought and action. As a process,
socialization is ongoing, although it occurs most clearly when
new recruits enter the organization. For new members, organizational socialization is "the process of 'learning the ropes,'
the process of being trained, the process of being taught what
is important in an organization" (Schein 1968, p. 2). And yet,
as a process, the organization's members always are involved
in socialization.

A new leader, for example, enters the institution with a significantly different vision about the organization, and those in the organization perhaps may have to reframe previously held beliefs. An individual spends a year away from the organization on a sabbatical, and upon return, has a different way of seeing the institution. And obviously, any long-term member of an organization will point out how different the organization is today than when he or she first entered. A cultural view of organizations highlights change rather than stasis. We need to consider socialization from a similar viewpoint.

Socialization's purpose is twofold. On one hand, "One of the important functions of organizational socialization is to build commitment and loyalty to the organization" (Schein 1968, p. 7). Individuals learn about the organization's culture. On the other hand, since an organization's culture is interpretive and dynamic, as new members enter the institution it is resocialized. We are suggesting that since an organization's culture exists as the product of social relations, as new members engage the organization they are able to change it (Tierney 1992b).

In this regard, our interpretation of faculty socialization differs from traditional notions that have stressed a one-directional process (Baldwin 1979; Baldwin and Blackburn 1981; Blackburn 1985). In today's diverse society an organization's participants need to re-think how faculty become enmeshed within an organizational setting. This point is crucial to bear in mind as individuals consider groups such as women or African-Americans, since they have been excluded and/or underrepresented in academe. Similarly, as young faculty enter an institution with an interdisciplinary orientation, the organization needs to respond in ways different from the past. How might the organization be transformed as significant cadres of faculty enter with different perspectives and orientations?

We have pointed out how a leader such as a college president may play a key role in reorienting the organization's culture, and hence, socialization. Long-term members also play a significant role in socializing the young. The point stressed here is that as an interpretive site of negotiation, an organization's culture has the potential to undergo change in any number of different manners due to the multiplicity of voices that exist. Socialization is a highly charged process, where different individuals and groups come together to define organizational beliefs and attitudes. Rather than simply a sense of events, it is an ongoing process which involves virtually all organizational actors.

Faculty Socialization
A new professor enters a postsecondary institution and in one way or another becomes accustomed to the organization's norms. At some institutions, faculty dress formally, while at other institutions, faculty will be found in shorts and sneakers. At one institution, faculty are expected to be in their offices a great deal of time, while at another locale, faculty offices are little more than way stations between classes. Some institutions value research and others teaching. How do individuals come to learn about these norms, and how do these norms change? Faculty socialization is one area that provides clues.

Faculty socialization is a process with two stages: the anticipatory stage and the organizational stage. Anticipatory socialization occurs largely during graduate school. The organizational stage involves initial entry and then role continuance. The organizational stage occurs when a faculty member enters the institution for the first time and comes into contact with the institutional culture. The contact between the prospective faculty member and the institutional culture occurs initially during the recruitment and selection process (Wanous 1992).

Stage One: Anticipatory Socialization
The first step in organizational socialization involves anticipatory learning on the part of the potential recruit (Van Maanen 1976, 1983). Anticipatory socialization pertains to how non-members take on the attitudes, actions, and values of the group to which they aspire.

Anticipatory socialization serves three functions: "For the individual who adopts the values of a group to which he [she] aspires but does not belong, the orientation may serve the twin functions of aiding his [her] rise into that group and of easing his [her] adjustment after he [she] has become a part of it" (Merton 1957, p. 265). At the same time, new members also begin to reframe the group to which they will belong.

During graduate training, for example, students anticipate the types of roles and behaviors they must enact to succeed as faculty members. Graduate training is where students begin to acquire the values, norms, attitudes, and beliefs associated with their discipline and with the profession at large. "As

young scholars work with professors, they observe and internalize the norms of behavior for research as well as supporting mechanisms such as peer review and academic freedom" (Anderson and Seashore-Louis 1991, p. 63).

At the same time, graduate students choose dissertation topics and areas of study that may help dramatically reorient a discipline. Native American Studies and Women's Studies are but two examples that benefited by the backgrounds of the "new recruits." These individuals interacted with the "norms" by reconfiguring them. And too, the manner in which work is done also changes as the backgrounds of these recruits change.

In examining the training of medical students, Becker et al. argued that students create their own culture which aids them in surviving medical school (1961). This culture is not necessarily geared toward adopting the future values and attitudes associated with becoming a doctor but is more short term in its orientation. They described student culture as "the working out in practice of the perspectives from which the students view their day-to-day problems in relation to their long-term goals. The perspectives, themselves collectively developed, are organizations of ideas and actions" (p. 435).

However, the development of a student culture takes place within an organizational context in which various problems, dilemmas, and situations are placed before the medical students by faculty, residents, and interns. While the short-term implications of the organizational context may be the emergence of a student culture geared toward survival, there also are significant long-term effects. The general set of perspectives that Becker and others highlight as a by-product of medical training is one facet of anticipatory socialization.

For aspiring faculty, graduate training, then, serves as a significant force in socializing students into the roles and expectations associated with faculty life. How one interacts with students and colleagues, the lifestyle one leads, and the journals, conferences, and books that one reads initially are learned from mentors and peers in graduate school.

These initial socializing experiences that new faculty bring to an institution may not necessarily match the culture of their new organization. A biologist trained at Harvard to value research may experience a mismatch of expectations if she arrives at a state college without research facilities. A United States historian who is trained to use a seminar style in teaching may be surprised if, for one reason or another, his career begins in an Islamic university that exclusively employs the lecture.

Our point is straightforward: Socialization begins prior to an individual's first day of employment. The individual learns what it means to be a member of a profession and discipline during one's training, and this learning may be at odds with what he or she ultimately finds. Since human beings constantly try to make sense of the culture, the events and messages that are provided during one's initial interaction with an institution send potent symbols. A university may not be able to alter the students' graduate school socialization, but it has vast discretion over institutional structures that frame the organizational experience.

Stage Two: Organizational Socialization

The organizational stage has two phases: initial entry and role continuance. The entry phase involves interactions that might occur during the recruitment and selection process as well as the early period of organizational learning that occurs as soon as the individual begins employment.

The role continuance phase begins after the individual is situated in the organization. The organizational stage is initially framed by activities that occurred during the anticipatory socialization of the recruit that has helped shape understandings and responses to the task demands and performance requirements (Van Maanen 1983).

When anticipatory socialization for an individual is consistent with that of the organization's culture, then the recruit will experience socialization processes which affirm the individual qualities brought to the organization. On the other hand, if the values, beliefs, and norms brought by a recruit are seen as inconsistent with the cultural ethos of the institution, then the socialization experience will be more transformative in nature: The organization will try to modify an individual's qualities.

In terms of faculty socialization, transformative processes occur when a faculty member with a research orientation enters an institutional setting where teaching takes precedence, or conversely, when a new faculty member is hired at a research university but enters with a teaching orientation. Obviously, to a certain degree, everyone goes through transformations upon entering an organization. Organizational leaders need to be conscious of what kinds of transformations are important and necessary, and what kinds are trivial.

If recruits survive the initial entry process and the experiences that go along with being a "novice," they gradually move to a role continuance phase (Corcoran and Clark 1984). Junior faculty must master the necessary academic and cultural skills to attain tenure. Tenured faculty need to become socialized to the responsibilities of academic leadership, and so on. Hence, organizational socialization is a two-phase process. Recruits first enter an organization and begin to "learn the ropes" during the initial years of their academic life and then expand their organizational role.

Most often, organizational socialization occurs informally and haphazardly. A new faculty member arrives on campus and learns from other faculty members about the in's and out's of the environment. Younger faculty learn how to act in meetings from the behavior of older colleagues. An assistant professor hears senior faculty speak constantly about the importance of publications and never mention participation in university service, so she declines to attend the faculty senate.

Although informal organizational socialization will always occur, one of the key purposes of this text is to suggest that an organization's participants need to consider more consciously how to socialize individuals to the organization's culture. When individuals do not make the organization's culture explicit to new members, they are assuming that individuals all interpret the institution's symbolic life in the same way. Our suggestion is to consider strategies that socialize the organization's participants not simply to unquestioned norms, but also to consider what those norms are and how they might need to be changed with the inclusion of new groups of faculty. Such a process means that all individuals are involved in ongoing organizational socialization and learning.

Dimensions of Organizational Socialization
Van Maanen and Schein have proposed "tactical strategies" for understanding organizational socialization (1979). By tactical, they refer to the ways that "the experiences of individuals in transition from one role to another are structured for them by others in the organization" (p. 232). The dimensions of organizational socialization are: 1) collective versus indi-

vidual; 2) formal versus informal; 3) sequential versus random; 4) fixed versus variable; 5) serial versus disjunctive; and 6) investiture versus divestiture.

Collective vs. individual

Collective socialization refers to forming a group of recruits who face a common set of experiences together. Examples of this type of socialization include soldiers during boot camp, students during graduate school, or a significant number of tenure-track faculty in a particular school or college. Distinctive colleges such as Reed College in Oregon, Deep Springs College in California, or Hampshire College in Massachusetts are examples of a unitary framework for organizational socialization, since their culture is unitary and collective as opposed, for example, to large public institutions that have a more disparate culture.

Individual socialization refers to processing new members in an isolated and singular manner. Individual socialization more aptly describes the experiences of faculty in the vast majority of colleges and universities. Faculty generally are hired on a departmental or divisional basis with little coordination across organizational boundaries. Faculty experiences throughout their tenure are generally individualized experiences. Some institutions provide campuswide orientation and/or development programs, but these are, for the most part, short-term experiences.

Formal vs. informal

A second tactical dimension of organizational socialization pertains to whether the socialization experiences are formal or informal. Formal socialization relates to those experiences where the recruit is separated from other regular members of the organization while participating in a series of specifically designed activities. Formal socialization is to what we referred previously as a rite of passage; the initiate undergoes a structured experience to pass to a new stage—complete with a new organizational status.

Informal socialization relates to more laissez-faire experiences where the norms of the organization are learned through trial and error. Faculty socialization, generally, is most typically a "sink or swim" proposition and is more informal than formal. Van Maanen and Schein elaborate on informal socialization (1979).

> *Learning through experience in the informal socialization mode . . . place recruits in the position where they must select their own socialization agents. The value of this mode to the newcomer is then determined largely by the relevant knowledge possessed by an agent and, of course, the agent's ability to transfer such knowledge* (p. 238).

If we agree that faculty socialization takes place to a significant degree through an informal process, then it logically follows that at a minimum, new faculty need experienced and caring mentors.

Random vs. sequential

Another tactical dimension relates to random versus sequential socialization. Random socialization pertains to a progression of unclear or ambiguous steps which lead to a target goal or role. While the goal may be clear, how to achieve the goal is unclear. Sequential socialization involves discrete and identifiable steps for achieving an organizational role. This type of socialization is more ordered and clear and typically falls in line with formal and collective socialization processes.

Random socialization describes processes associated with faculty evidenced by the tremendous stress, ambiguity, and confusion faculty experience in pursuit of promotion and tenure. One is never sure how much to write, how good a teacher to be, or what to do in terms of public service to attain promotion or tenure. Although the target may be clear, the process to achieve it is not. Some aspects of the promotion process in the U.S. military may be seen as examples of sequential socialization in that certain tests must be taken and passed, specific skills must be acquired, and certain educational levels must be attained before a soldier can be promoted to the next level.

Fixed vs. variable

Fixed versus variable socialization processes refer to whether the timetable related to moving through different organizational roles is fixed (precisely spelled out) or variable (vague and unclear). An example of fixed socialization is high school graduation—12 years of successful schooling typically moves someone to a new status as a high school graduate. Obtaining the Ph.D., however, might be considered a type of variable socialization, in that the process involves rites of passage that frequently are unclear and variable across individuals based on their own level of ability or accomplishment.

Usually, transitions from one role to another for faculty are a mixture of fixed and variable processes. The passage from novice through the promotion and tenure process is relatively fixed—usually six years. The role continuance that occurs when a person passes from an associate professor to a full professor is more an individualistic time frame and thus much more variable.

One is never sure how much to write, how good a teacher to be, or what to do in terms of public service to attain promotion or tenure.

Serial vs. disjunctive

Serial socialization refers to the planned training of an individual by a senior member. A disjunctive socialization process is one where no role models are available for the organizational newcomer. An untenured faculty member might be trained by a tenured professor, or a new department chair might learn from someone who has been a chair for a considerable time.

For faculty, having experienced role models seems critically important. At a minimum, individuals need peer support. This is problematic for underrepresented groups, since issues related to gender, race, and sexual orientation may make the mentoring process more difficult.

Investiture vs. divestiture

The final dimension relates to investiture versus divestiture socialization processes, which we discuss in terms of an affirming versus a transforming socialization experience. Investiture (more affirming) concerns the welcoming of the recruit's anticipatory socialization experiences and individual characteristics, whereas divestiture (more transforming) involves stripping away those personal characteristics seen as incompatible with the organizational ethos.

When newcomers take their first faculty position, two generalized institutional patterns may result. On one hand, the institution encourages and reinforces those experiences learned in graduate school (investiture). On the other hand, institutional gatekeepers might adopt a transformative stance and attempt to restructure the new member's values, norms, and beliefs (divestiture). Investiture versus divestiture processes may be enacted at the same time, but with regard to different aspects of the novice's orientation.

Subsequently, a new faculty member who did not attain tenure at a research university may be hired by a teaching-oriented institution and the faculty member's values, norms, and beliefs associated with the research function may need to be modified. The college may adopt a transformative stance toward the new faculty member's view of the importance of research. At the same time, this new member may place great value on the teaching role, and the institution likely would affirm this quality. Unfortunately, as we have noted, few real institutional mechanisms are enacted in any kind of formalized way. Instead, qualities of new faculty are affirmed or transformed through informal mechanisms that are, for the most part, imprecise and haphazard.

Another difficulty related to faculty socialization and the notions of investiture versus divestiture socialization is the fact that dominant norms, values, and beliefs tend to get reproduced. Logically, it follows that if an institution values certain characteristics, it will look for those qualities in new recruits. However, members of underrepresented groups may bring personal characteristics and anticipatory experiences that are incongruent with some of the dominant values of the organization, and the organization may enact transformative processes to modify the new recruit.

Summary

During the anticipatory stage of graduate school, the prospective faculty member's experience is shaped by four cultural influences that produce a general orientation. These cultural forces relate to disciplinary influences, professional influences, individual factors, and influences that derive from society. In the second stage of faculty socialization, the recruit begins to learn about an organization's culture, which becomes the fifth cultural force in shaping the faculty member's occupational life (see Figure 1 for a visual summary of faculty socialization).

During stage two, the newly hired faculty member arrives at an institution and must learn about the organization's culture while at the same time he or she continues to be shaped by the four other cultural influences. Organizational socialization has two phases: initial entry and role continuance. The entry phase moves the individual from the role of outsider to novice. The role continuance phase relates to the continuing relationship between the institution and the faculty member. Essential to understanding this phase in academe is the promotion and tenure process.

FIGURE 1

Faculty Socialization

STAGE ONE Anticipatory	STAGE TWO Organizational Socialization
Four Cultural Influences 1. National Culture 2. Professional Culture 3. Disciplinary Culture 4. Individual Cultural Differences	**Five Cultural Influences** 1. National Culture 2. Professional Culture 3. Disciplinary Culture 4. Individual Cultural Differences 5. Institutional Culture

	Phase One	Phase Two
	Entry	Role Continuance

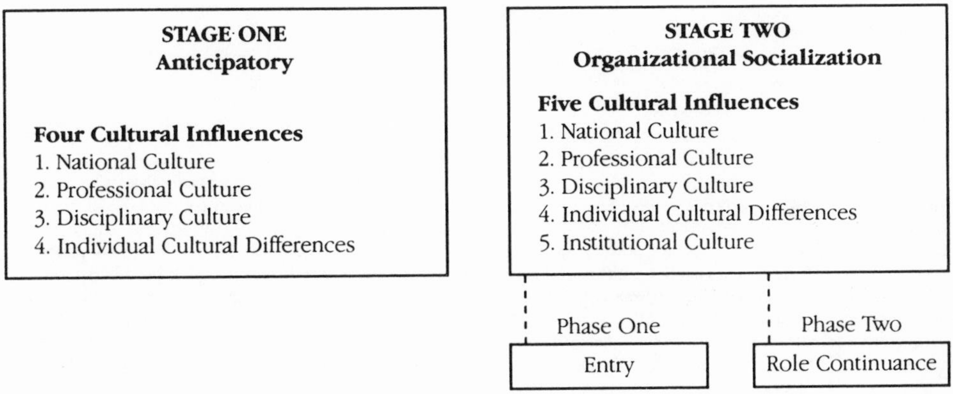

Dimensions of Faculty Socialization
1. Collective .... Individual
(group vs. singular)
2. Formal .... Informal
(isolated from organizational members or interwoven with organizational members)
3. Random .... Sequential
(unclear and ambiguous vs. ordered steps)
4. Fixed .... Variable
(specific timetable vs. no timetable)
5. Serial .... Disjunctive
(lead by role models vs. no role models)
6. Investiture .... Divestiture
(affirming of individual characteristics to transforming individual characteristics)

Tenure:
A Summary,
Explanation,
and "Defense"

William Van Alstyne

I. Introduction

In the wake of student unrest and in the presence of strong competition for the diversion of funds to other national priorities, severe demands are now being made for greater professional accountability and for greater efficiency in higher education. Unsurprisingly, tenure has been singled out as an obstacle to both of these goals and, consequently, as a blockade to educational progress. Simultaneously, the felt dissatisfaction with the general adequacy of teaching has renewed the common suspicion that tenure is a professional masquerade: that it lingers as a sophistical phrase obscuring the dark reality of uniquely selfish claims of a right to lifetime employment for the incompetent and irresponsible.

Older members of the profession may well be inclined to shrug off these critical suggestions, having heard them more than once before and remembering the careful answers that ably replied to them. (It is in fact quite true that the issue has been joined many times, *i.e.*, that the concept of tenure has never been allowed to pass unexamined, simply as part of the conventional wisdom.) Nevertheless, even if it is true that little new can possibly be said on the subject, some brief reconsideration may serve at least to rekindle a livelier understanding of a vital concept which has tended of late to suffer from a hardening of the categories.

In this small essay, I mean hardly to offer a "defense" of tenure at all. Rather, given the presuppositious character of criticism so recently heaped upon it, tenure's best defense may well inhere simply in a clear statement of what it is—and what it is not. In what follows, I believe that the statements about tenure are fully responsive to the applicable principles and standards supported by AAUP, although there is certainly nothing more authoritative about my views in this regard than those of others to whom the *Bulletin* freely extends the courtesy of its pages.

WILLIAM VAN ALSTYNE is Professor of Law at Duke University. He is the immediate past General Counsel of the AAUP and is currently Chairman of Committee A on Academic Freedom and Tenure.

II. A Summary, Explanation, and "Defense"

Tenure, accurately and unequivocally defined, lays no claim whatever to a guarantee of lifetime employment. Rather, tenure provides only that no person continuously retained as a full-time faculty member beyond a specified lengthy period of probationary service may thereafter be dismissed *without adequate cause*. Moreover, the particular standards of "adequate cause" to which the tenured faculty is accountable are themselves wholly within the prerogative of each university to determine through its own published rules, save only that those rules not be applied in a manner which violates the academic freedom or the ordinary personal civil liberties of the individual. An institution may provide for dismissal for "adequate cause" arising from failure to meet a specified norm of performance or productivity, as well as from specified acts of affirmative misconduct. In short, there is not now and never has been a claim that tenure insulates any faculty member from a fair accounting of his professional responsibilities within the institution which counts upon his service.

In a practical sense, tenure is translatable principally as a statement of formal assurance that thereafter the individual's professional security and academic freedom will not be placed in question without the observance of full academic due process. This accompanying complement of academic due process merely establishes that a fairly rigorous procedure will be observed whenever formal complaint is made that dismissal is justified on some stated ground of professional irresponsibility, to insure the fair determination of three facts:

1. that the stated cause is the authentic cause for dismissal, rather than a pretense or makeweight for considerations invading the academic freedom or ordinary personal civil liberties of the individual;

2. that the stated cause exists in fact;

3. that the degree of demonstrated professional irresponsibility warrants outright termination of the individual's appointment rather than some lesser sanction, even after taking into account the balance of his entire service and the personal consequences of dismissal.

In all of these respects, the procedural protections of tenure are analogous to fair hearing requirements even now evolving in the federal courts for the protection of various kinds of status in the public sector (including employment), to the statutory procedural protection of civil servants, and to the grievance procedures conventional in collective bargaining agreements. It has long since ceased to be true that even relatively unskilled workers in an industrial firm may be summarily fired by unilateral decision of management; statutory law limits the grounds for dismissal, recourse to the National Labor Relations Board is available for reinstatement and back pay under appropriate circumstances, and the contract itself ordinarily provides for a grievance procedure for review and arbitration of the proposed discharge. (Tenure —through its reference to more specific and rigorous forms of academic due process—usually does provide, however, a larger measure of procedural protection than is provided in the *ex post facto* review of the factory worker's grievance.)

Tenure may also be stated in the following way more clearly to indicate its basis and meaning. The conferral of tenure means that the institution, after utilizing a probationary period of as long as six years in which it has had ample opportunity to determine the professional competence and responsibility of its appointees, has rendered a favorable judgment establishing a rebuttable presumption of the individual's professional excellence. As the lengthy term of probationary service will have provided the institution with sufficient experience to determine whether the faculty member is worthy of a presumption of professional fitness, it has not seemed unreasonable to shift to the individual the benefit of doubt when the institution thereafter extends his service beyond the period of probation and, correspondingly, to shift to the institution the obligation fairly to show why, if at all, that faculty member should nonetheless be fired. The presumption of the tenured faculty member's professional excellence thus remains rebuttable, exactly to the extent that when it can be shown that the individual possessing tenure has nonetheless fallen short or has otherwise misconducted himself as determined according to full academic due process, the presumption is lost and the individual is subject to dismissal.

There are, moreover, certain circumstances in which tenure will not provide even this degree of professional security for faculty members of unquestioned excellence. Two of these circumstances may appropriately be specified to indicate further how utterly false is the claim that tenure would rather suffer hardship to an entire institution than hardship to any of its tenured staff. As many faculty members are painfully aware, declining student enrollments in certain academic departments not only have occurred with such suddenness as to raise a serious question of whether the decline is really a healthy turning away from less worthwhile subjects (rather than a simple turn of fashion), but have also precipitously reduced the demand for the services of some faculty members with particular skills in those departments. Nevertheless, assum-ing that each of the affected faculty members, even though he possesses tenure, is either unable or unwilling to retrain and equip himself to be professionally competent in some other area of the academic program with sufficient demand to sustain his employment within the institution, his services may be terminated simply by the cessation of the program itself. While the faculty appropriately must participate in any decision concerning the reduction or elimination of a given program for the same reason that it must do so when the enlargement or addition of a program may be contemplated, *viz.*, to provide some informed judgment about the educational wisdom of the proposed programmatic change, tenure provides no guarantee against becoming a casualty to institutional change.

Again, the termination of particular academic programs, not from failure of interest by students but from unavoidable conditions of financial stringency, carries with it no suggestion that the released members of the faculty have either fallen short in their duties or otherwise misconducted themselves in a manner warranting termination. Nonetheless, if there is an authentic financial emergency confronting the university, and if decisions concerning what programs must be terminated and in what order, what particular faculty members must be released and in what sequence—if these decisions are made in a nonarbitrary and reasonable way with appropriate faculty participation, then nothing at all will insulate adversely affected individuals from the hard prospect of unemployment.

Tenure, then, neither buttons up the process of institutional change nor binds the ways which each institution must consider as it copes with authentic financial distress. It is but a limited statement that each faculty member possessing it, receiving it only after a stipulated period of probationary service, is thought worthy of a rebuttable presumption of professional excellence in continuing service to the institution. Thereafter, when termination of his services is sought for any reason inconsistent with that presumption, it requires only that the burden of justification be fairly discharged under conditions of academic due process by those with whom it properly rests.

To the extent that tenure protections of full academic due process possess a marked resemblance to the procedural rights of others not involved in higher education, it is clear that tenure does contemplate an interest in professional security quite apart from its central objective to safeguard academic freedom. There is, moreover, every good reason that it should do so entirely aside from an intelligent concern to render higher education competitive with other employment opportunities by assuring that it provides at least as much job security. The more fundamental reason for the requirement of due process here as elsewhere is the desire to do justice and to avoid errors in the making of critical judgments. Even supposing that in many instances a particular charge of professional irresponsibility is neither stated in terms which anyone would claim to raise a question of academic freedom (*e.g.,* a charge that a faculty member has accepted bribes in the award of grades) nor that the charge is otherwise suspected of having been brought forward solely from an ulterior reason which itself relates to academic freedom, still the need would remain to protect the individual from unreasonable risks of error and prejudice in the resolution of that charge. The power to fire a person without a fair hearing—in this instance a hearing according to academic due process—deserves to be called "arbitrary" and to be despised, not so much on its own account as on account of its greater tendency to result in error—to yield a result utterly at odds with what we would have desired had the actual facts been known. On such a basis, we find no difficulty in understanding why an individual may not be made even to pay a fine for drunk driving in the absence of a right to fair trial which yields a civilized assurance that he did in fact violate the law. Protection of a professor from the unjust forfeiture of his position after a long period of service to the institution is surely as simple a thing to understand, and thus the appropriateness of furnishing that protection through the assurance of academic due process without regard to the nature of the charge.

Nevertheless, beyond the consideration of justice itself, it is still extremely important to understand the special relationship of tenure to academic freedom in particular. An understanding of this relationship would be worthwhile in any case, given the fact that the vast majority of contested dismissals continue to involve disputes over whether what the individual may have done is part of his academic freedom (e.g., how he discharges his duties, what he has said about the college, whether his extramural utterances are defensible within his discipline), and many others have arisen under circumstances involving the suspicion of ulterior purpose in bringing the charge—a purpose itself believed to violate academic freedom. Essentially, however, the connection of tenure with academic freedom is important to understand so as to account for the particular *form* of due process to which tenure creates an entitlement, namely, full academic due process with its emphasis upon professional peer-group participation in the first instance.

The function of tenure is not only to encourage the development of specialized learning and professional expertise by providing a reasonable assurance against the dispiriting risk of summary termination; it is to maximize the freedom of the professional scholar and teacher to benefit society through the innovation and dissemination of perspectives and discoveries aided by his investigations, without fear that he must accommodate his honest perspectives to the conventional wisdom. The point is as old as Galileo and, indeed, as new as Arthur Jensen. An individual who is subject to termination without showing of professional irresponsibility, irrespective of the long term of his service within his discipline, will to that extent hesitate publicly to expose his own perspectives and take from all of us that which we might more usefully confront and consider. Exactly as his skill and understanding advance to a point making it more likely than before that he will contribute something to the legacy of past endeavors, exactly as he will have made

an extended commitment in one given discipline diminishing his opportunities to do something else with his life or to start all over again in a wholly different kind of career, so the larger society will tend to be deprived of whatever he would have had to offer it by the very degree of chilling inhibition which it would impose through upholding institutional authority to dismiss him without full academic due process. It is the most vital function of tenure to avoid this contingency by shifting the benefit of doubt to the individual, entitling him then to full academic due process.

The shift does, indeed, do more than to provide a fair hearing in the usual sense, *i.e.*, a full hearing before disinterested parties, preceded by a statement of specific charges based upon reasonably clear standards. Rather, full academic due process locates the fulcrum of responsibility to determine in the first instance whether the tenured professor's work is professionally defensible in those with whom the risk of abuse may least dangerously be placed, namely, his professional peers.

The matter can be fairly expressed only in this way (*i.e.*, "with whom the risk of abuse may *least* dangerously be placed"), for it is true of course that there are degrees of intolerance and convention regarding the methodology and premises of "professionally responsible" utterances within academic peer groups as outside of them. Faculty committees are doubtless capable of reacting against a colleague when others would not have done so, or of favoring him when others would not have done so, and either of these may be accomplished on occasion by means against which no system can be 100 per cent foolproof. Given the necessary decision that there must be accountability somewhere, according to some standard, as initially reviewed by some group of human beings, however, the alternatives to initial peer-group hearing all seem worse where academic freedom tends so frequently to be at stake. At the same time, the entitlement of tenure to full academic due process with its emphasis upon initial peer-group hearing is not without significant checks and balances and by no means reposes final adjudicative authority within the faculty. Rather, it is characteristically hedged about by the reserved authority of the university president and trustees to reverse a judgment or to modify a sanction either favoring or disfavoring the individual, for compelling reasons and following fair review with him and with the faculty committee which initially considered the case.[1]

The sense and system of tenure, in summary, come down to this. After completing the full profile of professional preparation, an individual appointed to the faculty of an institution for the first time is neither assured of

[1] A better alternative to this system is by no means obvious. Indeed, a number of alternatives were canvassed again early this year, in a comprehensive report at the University of Utah, by a Commission including among its members students and citizens from outside the institution. Two-thirds through that Commission's Report (the text of which appears elsewhere in this issue), the first recommendation appears:

RECOMMENDATION NO. 1: The tenure system at the University of Utah should be maintained.

lifetime employment, nor is he assured of employment beyond the initial term on some general condition of good behavior, nor is he even presumed to be professionally excellent according to the institution's own standards of faculty excellence. Rather, the immediate premise of his appointment is extremely limited, *i.e.*, that he is appointed because he appears to be attractive and to meet certain needs better than others at the time, with only the assurance that he will not be fired without cause during the specified term of his initial appointment and that he will be given a fair chance to establish his excellence over a period of six years assuming, further, that the institution does not in the meantime find others whom it thinks may show greater promise or otherwise better meet its needs then he. If the institution so resolves its policy clearly, to "play the field" and to displace a nontenured appointee by appointing someone else it subsequently finds has become available and whom it regards as more attractive, it is free to do so at least if it has fairly articulated this prerogative and provides notice of and intention to exercise it, reasonably in advance of the end of a given probationary term.

Even assuming the necessity of this sort of rugged competition arrangement to assure each institution of flexibility of choice and an opportunity to resolve the excellence of its newer staff, however, it is surely clear that six years of experience with the faculty member's full-time professional service will provide the institution with ample opportunity to judge his fitness according to the standards and means of review it has established. The institution thus may not further postpone resolving whether that faculty member is now worthy of a conditional statement of continuing confidence, given the intrinsic unfairness of an ever-increasing degree of specialization and dependence on his part under circumstances where a qualified judgment respecting his fitness is clearly feasible and where a failure to resolve that judgment must continue to trammel both his personal security and his academic freedom.

Indeed, throughout his probationary terms of service the academic freedom of the appointee will necessarily have been more constrained than that of others, given the fact that he has continued to face the prospect of nonrenewal without a demonstration of adequate cause pursuant to full academic due process. The degree of dampening effect upon his academic and personal freedom has been justifiable during this time, moreover, solely on the basis that an initial appointment with "instant tenure" would have been premature and reckless, *i.e.*, it would have expressed a statement of confidence in the *demonstrated* excellence of the appointee when no such statement could intelligently be made in the absence of a reasonable opportunity to determine whether it is warranted.

Temporizing beyond six years of experience can scarcely be rationalized on such a basis, however, and thus the institution is fairly called upon carefully to decide by that time whether a conditional statement of continuing confidence is warranted—a statement of tenure. If,

upon adequate consideration, the conclusion is reached that no such statement is in fact warranted, the institution must so advise him and put an end to uncertainty by making the seventh year terminal. Otherwise, it must extend to him the benefit of the doubt for the first time, equally ending the uncertain cycle of term appointments Thereafter, while never assured that he will not fall casualty to some contingency of programmatic change in the institution or to some hard decision reflecting a financial crisis without available alternatives, he at least need not fear that he may be dispossessed of his position in the absence of demonstrated adequate cause pursuant to a hearing by his peers and the forms of fair review by the administration of his institution. So very far is this arrangement from being well calculated to establish lifetime employment, to protect the incompetent, or to conceal the irresponsible, and so mild are its features in the encouragement of professional excellence and the protection of academic freedom, I cannot think it needs defending at all. To the extent that it may, however, a defense was well and succinctly stated in the following resolution adopted by the 1971 Annual Meeting of the AAUP:

> Misconceptions of tenure are commonplace. For many groups and individuals tenure has become a conveniently simple explanation for what they perceive as a variety of educational ills. Tenure is not the cause of these ills, nor is it an incidental and self-serving privilege of the academic profession which may be casually dismissed It is the foundation of intellectual freedom in American colleges and universities and has important but frequently overlooked benefits for society at large.
> Basically tenure insures that faculty members will not be dismissed without adequate cause and without due process. From the long list of academic freedom and tenure cases with which the Association has been confronted, it is evident that many good teachers and scholars have been arbitrarily dismissed, and that many more would have been dismissed without the protection of tenure. In the absence of a manifestly more effective means for safeguarding intellectual freedom, attacks on tenure are irresponsible. Therefore, the Fifty-seventh Annual Meeting of the American Association of University Professors reaffirms the Association's commitment to tenure and insists upon its centrality as an enabling principle of American higher education.

III. A Lengthy Postscript: Academic Freedom and the Nontenured Faculty

While the need to enter a defense of tenure against the criticism that it is a shield for the incompetent and irresponsible may melt away once the actual conditions and terms of tenure have again been clarified, it may nonetheless be appropriate to add a postscript in acknowledgment of a very different kind of criticism, a criticism which finds serious fault with what is apparently the anomaly of tenure and the equal protection of academic freedom. In essence, the criticism is that insofar as the case for tenure stands or falls according to the measure of protection it yields for academic freedom, either it must be extended equally to all faculty members irrespective of their length of service, or withdrawn equally from all, (possibly then to be replaced by a uniform standard of academic due process for all, but without the invidious distinction implied by the term of "tenure" itself). If it is said that academic freedom is realistically secure for each person only to the extent that his professional status may not be placed in question without the observance of full academic due process, and if it is acknowledged that only those with tenure are entitled to full academic due process, then it necessarily follows that only those with tenure do in fact have academic freedom. On the other hand, if it is claimed that all members of a faculty are equally entitled to the free exercise of academic freedom, then it must be acknowledged either that tenure itself is not truly regarded as indispensable to the protection of that freedom or, if it is regarded as indispensable, that it must be provided for all alike. In short, the alleged equation that academic freedom = no termination without full academic due process = tenure, proves too much or too little. The anomalous combination of mutually exclusive assertions, "equal academic freedom for all, but tenure only for some," displays all the unseemliness of a motto from *Animal Farm:* all teachers are equal in their academic freedom, but some teachers are more equal than others (*viz.,* those with tenure)!

It will not do, as a response to this criticism, merely to point out that nontenured faculty members are equally entitled to full academic due process if sought to be dismissed within the specified term of their appointment. *I.e.,* it is not enough that newer appointees do in fact have "tenure" within their particular one-, two-, or three-year terms, and that any action to dismiss them within that term must be taken solely on the basis of adequate cause as demonstrated pursuant to full academic due process. The fact remains that the anxiety of prospective *nonrenewal* may be seen to chill the appointee's academic freedom in a manner unequalled for those members of the faculty with tenure.

Nor will it do quixotically to deny on second thought that tenure is really wholly unconcerned with academic freedom and that it is, rather, defended solely on the basis that it provides an appropriate degree of professional security for those of *demonstrated* excellence, *i.e.,* those who weathered an uncertain career (and kept their mouths shut) as probationary appointees for as long as six years and were found on the basis of experience to warrant a conditional expression of institutional confidence in their continuing excellence. Other kinds of incentives than tenure might satisfy the need for perquisites for the senior faculty, although possibly not so cheaply.

Rather, it may help to dissolve the dilemma first to note that while there is a difference in the *degree* of academic due process which tenure provides as compared with that to which a person lacking tenure is entitled when confronted with the prospect that his term appointment may not be renewed, the difference is not at all one of "full" academic due process vis-à-vis "no" academic due process. Indeed, recent developments in the federal courts as well as the AAUP's *Statement on Procedural Standards in the Renewal or Nonrenewal of Faculty Appointments* provide for substantial due process in cases of proposed nonrenewal. The differences of degree between the two

forms of academic due process are, in fact, essentially these:

1. Proceedings to dismiss one with tenure must be initiated by the employing institution, whereas proceedings to avoid termination of one lacking tenure who has received notice that nonrenewal is contemplated must be initiated by him;

2. The burden of proving the existence of adequate cause is upon the institution in proceedings to dismiss one with tenure, whereas the burden is upon the individual contesting notice of nonrenewal to establish at least a prima facie case either that reasons violative of academic freedom contributed to the proposed decision or that adequate consideration was not given to the merits of his reappointment;

3. The degree of formality in the total procedure is somewhat heavier in the case of one with tenure faced with dismissal than one without tenure faced with nonrenewal.

Recognizing, then, that those in probationary service are assured of *full* academic due process against the contingency of dismissal within any term of their appointment and that they are also assured of at least minimal due process against the contingency even of nonrenewal, the disparity which remains as between themselves and those with tenure is clearly not so great as first it may have appeared. To the extent that it is nonetheless an important difference, especially as it may weigh upon the exercise of academic freedom, an explanation may rest largely in the following considerations.

First, other things being even roughly equal, the degree of hardship to one threatened with dismissal after an extended commitment to a given discipline and a longer period of service in a particular institution is likely to be greater than to a younger person subject to nonrenewal after a more tentative commitment and a briefer period of service. To the extent that the degree of due process is appropriately graduated to the degree of hardship which may result from the decision in question, it is not difficult to understand on that basis alone why dismissal proceedings are accompanied by a fuller complement of academic due process than those concerning nonrenewal. Similarly, exactly to the extent that dismissal is more portentous than nonrenewal, the chilling effect on the individual's exercise of academic freedom may itself also be greater. Correspondingly, merely to insure that the same degree of academic freedom is assured equally to the individual faced with the threat of dismissal as to the one faced with the prospect of nonrenewal, a more deliberate form of academic due process may be required in the first case than in the second.

Second, there is simply no basis to hold that the fact of one's first or second short-term appointment in teaching necessarily manifests an institutional presumption of excellence which it would thereafter be the burden of the institution to overthrow when contemplating nonrenewal at the end of the term. Surely no institution ought to be held to have made a judgment about the long-term professional excellence of a first-time appointee to its faculty in view of the fact that frequently the appointment will represent the individual's first experience in teaching and there will have been no reasonable opportunity in fact so to determine his professional fitness. It is precisely the purpose of having a probationary period to enable the institution to resolve the doubt not previously resolved by actions of the individual with whom the burden necessarily rests. To extend the presumption of professional fitness back to the point of initial appointment is to be unfair toward the institution's capacity to make a judgment on the matter so early, with all the deleterious consequences of granting "instant tenure." Similarly, to extend the assurance of full academic due process back to the time of renewal of the first appointment is functionally exactly that, *i.e.*, the establishment of instant tenure.

Third, as initial appointments are usually not made with an adequate basis for assessing the individual's long-term excellence, there is correspondingly less reason to suspect that a decision not to renew such an appointment is made on grounds unrelated to a reasonable belief about that excellence. The same obviously cannot be said of those who have been found by lengthy experience to be satisfactory, however, and correspondingly their proposed termination creates a greater suspicion that ulterior reasons (*i.e.*, reasons violative of academic freedom) are more likely to be operating, thereby providing an appropriate reason for requiring fuller academic due process as a prerequisite to their termination. Stated in another way, as between the two groups a higher rate of non-renewal is less suspicious with respect to the first group

than with respect to the second and, correspondingly, incurring the higher costs of more ponderous full academic due process is less warranted by the uniform concern for academic freedom.

Fourth, as it is normally to be expected that one may become more expert in his specialty the greater amount of time and experience he will have devoted to it, the more important it becomes not to permit the public value of his academic freedom to be circumscribed precisely as he becomes more likely to make an original contribution by what he proposes to do or to say. Correspondingly, the degree of full academic due process which protects his academic freedom is more nearly likely to be worth its cost than were it uniformly available to all irrespective of their length of experience. To this extent, the earlier suggestion that tenure does reflect an attitude that greater academic freedom is warranted for those with a longer commitment within their discipline than for those with a relatively new one, is not without a basis in fact. Some may well question whether the degree of difference is really justifiable on such a basis, of course, reasonably suggesting that what is lost to the younger teacher in lack of seasoning and familiarity with his subject is more than offset by his freshness, creativity, or lack of debilitating conventionality. Perhaps the debate may rest there, at least for the moment: not on *whether* tenure, with its assurance of full academic due process should exist at all, but rather on *when* it should appropriately be conferred!

Rewards and
the Academic Marketplace

CHAPTER NINE

The Flow of Faculty to and from Academe

The American faculty is a corps of nearly 700,000 educated persons. Each year, even when higher education is depressed, thousands of people enter the academic profession, and even in prosperous years thousands leave it. The flow of these people into and out of the profession largely determines the caliber of the professoriate as defined by such qualities as intelligence, breadth and depth of learning, creativity, motivation, social responsibility, concern for students, and personal integrity. In this chapter, our purpose is to trace these flows with special attention to the sources from which academic people are drawn and to the destinations of those who leave. This subject is of great importance because, over the next twenty-five years, our colleges and universities will probably require nearly as many faculty appointments (full-time-equivalent) as there are members of the professoriate today.

The Academic Labor Market

The movement of faculty into and out of academe, both as to total number and composition, varies from year to year depending on conditions in the academic labor market. In this market, colleges and universities are the buyers, or the source of demand; educated individuals are the sellers, or the source of supply. The transactions in this market consist of appointments to faculty positions by colleges and universities and the relinquishment of these positions by faculty members. A large portion of the transactions, however, involve mere transfers from one institution to another as faculty members resign from one college or university and simultaneously accept appointments in others. From the standpoint of the present discussion, which pertains to the professoriate as a whole, such transfers are merely internal moves in a game of musical chairs. This internal mobility does not affect the number or the characteristics or the caliber of faculties in the aggregate but only the institutional location of particular individuals. The movement of faculty from one institution to another may improve efficiency by helping to place faculty members where they can be most happy and productive, but it does not change the numbers or the characteristics of the professoriate as a whole. In this and the following chapter, we shall be concerned only with the entry of individuals into academic positions *from other pursuits,* and the departure of individuals from the academic profession. We shall be looking at changes in the faculty personnel of the whole higher education system, not at the game of musical chairs within that system.

The number of faculty persons serving the nation's colleges and universities at any given time is determined primarily by the aggregate workload of the institutions, that is, by student enrollments and by research and public service responsibilities. Growth in the workload will usually lead to increases in the numbers of faculty persons; decline will usually lead to decreases. The number of faculty persons hired in any academic year will also be affected by the number of replacements for persons departing from academe through retirement, death, and resignation. The total "hires" then will equal the number of replacements plus or minus the net change in size of the faculty.

The supply of people to fill these positions depends partly on the attractiveness of the academic profession—relative to other occupations—in the matters of compensation, working conditions, and status. The supply also depends on less obvious influences such as the opportunity afforded by the profession (relative to other occupations) to serve one's fellow human beings and to engage in stimulating work.

The Supply of Faculty

The persons to fill the positions that may open up in the next twenty-five years will be drawn in part from people who will be attending graduate school with a view to entering the academic profession directly. It will be drawn also from the several million persons who will have engaged seriously in advanced study but will be currently working outside academe in a wide range of scholarly, scientific, and professional fields. Some of these people will at some time in their lives have had actual academic experience—either full time or part time. Some of them may under some conditions be receptive to offers of positions in the academic profession.

Discussions of the supply of faculty are often based on three assumptions: (1) that the inflow into the profession will consist almost entirely of young persons averaging perhaps thirty years of age who enter directly from graduate school; (2) that the outflow will consist mainly of persons retiring at a predetermined fixed age plus a few persons who become ill or die before retirement; and (3) that those persons who become academics may change institutions from time to time, but that they will remain somewhere in the higher educational system throughout their careers. It is true that many faculty members do enter the profession directly from graduate school and that many stay in the profession to retirement. Indeed, the practice of employing persons just out of graduate school is encouraged by the financial reality that in the short run such persons are less costly to the employing institutions than those who have had experience in non-academic employments. Overall, however, there are many paths from college, through graduate school, to academic appointments, and to retirement. At one extreme, a small minority of people go the whole distance without interruption. At the other extreme, a large number who attend graduate school accept positions outside academe and never become members of the professoriate. iate. Between the extremes are many whose careers are interrupted for longer or shorter periods by military service, work outside academe, family demands, travel, and other activities, but who enter the profession for a part (or several parts) of their careers.[1] Given all these possibilities it is clear that there are numerous people who hold M.A.s, Ph.D.s, and other advanced degrees and certificates who are not employed in academe, and who might under some conditions be persuaded to enter or re-enter the professoriate. These people are a latent supply which constantly hovers over the market and which may become an actual supply as conditions change. Among these people are:

1. Students of graduate and professional schools who, though planning on different careers, might be lured into academe.
2. Professional employees of government, business, and other non-academic organizations.
3. Self-employed persons who have professional training and experience.
4. Professionally trained persons not employed and not in school:
   (a) Homemakers
   (b) Persons who have dropped out of the labor force for travel, for further education, to be near a spouse, for other personal reasons, or because of discouragement.
   (c) Unemployed persons actively seeking jobs.
5. Academic administrators or other academic employees who may be qualified for faculty positions.
6. Part-time faculty who may transfer to full-time status.
7. Immigrants who are professionally trained.

---

1. Toombs (1979, p. 10) found in a survey of a sample of persons listed in *Who's Who in America* that 59 percent of academic persons had had non-academic experience during their careers and that about one-fifth of non-academic persons had had academic experience. He referred to this phenomenon as the "permeability" of the profession.

These people include practising professionals, for example, physicians, lawyers, engineers, scientists, economists, psychologists, journalists, accountants, artists, musicians, and many other persons who are learned in academic disciplines and are in other ways suitable for academic work. Indeed, there are many people in non-academic positions in government, business, and other organizations, and many self-employed persons as well, who have already had successful full-time experience as faculty members and could easily resume academic work if they so chose. And there are also thousands of persons who are serving successfully as college teachers in part-time positions and who might become full-time faculty members.

We are not suggesting that all these professional or specialized persons are, or could easily become, qualified for full-time academic appointments. Probably only a minority, but a sizable minority, might be so qualified. We certainly do not recommend that the nation rely solely or even primarily on these people for its future professoriate. But we do contend that in shaping the future of the professoriate it would be a mistake to overlook the many potential sources, to rely solely on those young men and women who are in graduate school at the time and are specifically planning academic careers.

We emphasize the diversity of potential sources for two reasons. First, during the current and possibly future depressed period in higher education, the caliber of young persons who are specifically preparing for the academic profession may not be equal to the caliber of those who joined the profession in the late 1960s and 1970s. There is considerable evidence, as we shall show in Chapter 11, that some of the best talent has been, and is being, attracted to medicine, law, business, engineering, science, and other fields and away from academic careers. The higher education community, therefore, may be well advised to extend its recruiting beyond the traditional sources. It may be able to attract people who bypassed jobs in higher education in their youth but still have a hankering to be members of the professoriate. The "lost generation" need not be lost forever. It may be able also to attract people who are seeking opportunities for career change in mid-life. Moreover, sad to say, the youthful candidates for faculty positions in the near future will include the generation that was characterized by declining test scores, inadequate high school preparation in the basic subjects, and college education with underemphasis on general education. If a wider net is cast, academic institutions will be able to overcome gaps in the age distribution of the faculty, to achieve a wider selection of women and minority groups, and to attract persons of particularly rich experience. However, we are not advocating that those young people who have chosen to prepare for the academic profession and who will be emerging from graduate school should be passed over. Rather, we are suggesting that the faculties of the future need not be drawn exclusively therefrom.

140

Because of the vast numbers of persons in the society who have had professional training and experience, there is not likely ever to be any absolute shortage of persons to fill all the academic positions. Few institutions, or even departments, are ever forced to retrench or shut down for absolute lack of staff. Temporarily, they may be compelled to fill in with part-time or superannuated people, or to employ persons less than ideally qualified. But there is seldom an absolute shortage. With suitable inducements, people can be drawn into academe on relatively short notice—as illustrated in the GI period and in the rapid buildup of the 1960s. It is also true for the long run when it is possible to add almost any number of people to the professoriate partly through the training of young people and partly through recruiting people of all ages from other pursuits. The question is not: Can all the positions be filled? Rather, it is: What *caliber* of people can be attracted to these positions?

The answer to this question depends on the prospective reward structure of the academic profession *compared with that of other occupations*. The reward structure consists primarily of compensation, working conditions, and status. It will affect young people who are deciding on which careers to prepare for and will also affect those already in the labor force who are qualified, or could become qualified, for academic appointments. In the next twenty-five years when there will be so many academic jobs to fill, it will behoove American society to provide the finances, and the higher educational community to provide the other conditions, that will make academic employment competitive with other comparable professions.

Faculty Attrition

The supply of faculty is not a one-way street. Faculty members enter academe, but they also leave, and leaving is not always via retirement (Waggaman, 1983, pp. 6–16). A full treatment of supply, in this case negative supply, requires a consideration of exit from the profession. Exit may occur in the following ways:

1. Retirement
2. Death or illness
3. Voluntary departure to accept a position in government, business, or other non-academic organizations or to become self-employed
4. Involuntary separation: non-renewal of contract, denial of tenure
5. Dropping out of the labor force
   (a) for personal reasons, for example, to care for a family or to follow a spouse who has been transferred
   (b) for travel and further education
   (c) because of boredom, discouragement, burnout

6. Transfer to administrative or other non-faculty positions in higher education

7. Transfer from full-time to part-time faculty position
8. Emigration

All of the events in the list above involve departures of faculty. Collectively they are usually referred to as *faculty attrition*. They include all departures except those involving only transfer from one academic institution to another.[2]

Annual faculty attrition measures the number of replacements that must be appointed each year to maintain the faculty at its current level. If growth of faculty is desired, the number of "hires" must exceed the amount of attrition; and if faculty retrenchment is desired, the number of "fires" may be reduced by the amount of attrition. Attrition is thus a critical factor in estimating the number of "hires" or "fires" that may be necessary or possible in any given year—even though attrition may not always conveniently involve the most dispensable people or the disciplines with redundant faculty.

Attrition varies from time to time depending upon several factors. The age composition of the faculties affects the number of retirements, departures due to illness or death, and the number dropping out from burn-out or "mid-life crisis." The ratio of women to men has, in the past at least, affected the number dropping out for personal reasons such as care of family or following spouses who are moving to jobs at new locations. Factors that influence age of retirement affect the number retiring in any given year. Institutional policies designed to push people out—policies relating to probation and tenure, dismissal for cause or financial exigency, and early retirement—will have an impact on the number of departures. Institutional practices regarding the transfer of faculty members to administrative posts will make a difference. Finally, and perhaps most important, the attractiveness of academe as a place of employment—relative to employment in business, government, and other industries—will affect the number of voluntary separations. Clearly, attrition rates are not static but vary from year to year as a resultant of all these factors. However, barring cataclysmic events such as war or deep depression in higher education, the combined attrition rate from all causes tends to be confined to fairly narrow limits and to change rather slowly. Our review of the literature on attrition as summarized in Appendix C leads us to two conclusions. First, a conservative estimate of average faculty attrition for the period 1985–2010 is about 4 percent a year. This breaks down to roughly 1.3 percent for retirement and death, and 2.7 percent for departures for all

2. See Lovett, 1984, for a fascinating account of "300 men and women who had held full-time academic positions but who had left those positions for other employment between 1976 and 1980." See also Zey-Ferrell, 1982, and Stecklein & Willie, 1982.

other reasons. Second, the future rate of attrition over the years ahead is likely to rise if the faculties grow older on the average, if the ratio of women to men increases, if institutions become more adept at forcing or enticing redundant faculty members to leave or retire, or if the gap widens between compensation and working conditions within academe and those outside. On the other hand, the rate of attrition might fall if some of these developments were reversed. Our guess is that in the years ahead—especially after 1995—the factors tending to bring about a rise in attrition will outweigh those tending to make it decline.

In the following chapter (10), we shall attempt to project the number of job openings or "hires" for faculty over the years 1985 to 2010, using varying assumptions. The future rate of faculty attrition is the dominant factor determining the likely number of job openings. In preparing these projections, we have adopted three basic assumptions regarding attrition, a low one of 3 percent per annum, a middle one of 4 percent per annum, and a moderately high assumption, which we believe to be the most plausible of the three. This high assumption includes a rising rate of attrition beginning at 4 percent in 1985, gradually increasing to 6 percent in 2000 as retirements increase substantially, and leveling off at 6 percent thereafter.

These are important figures because they dominate the estimates of the number of new faculty appointments that might be made assuming no change in the overall size of the faculty, or the number of positions that might be eliminated without involuntary separations. For example, if attrition were at the rate of 4 percent a year, the faculties could be cut by about 32 percent in ten years without any firings. The 32 percent is appreciably more than the prospective percentage decline in enrollments over the next decade. Attrition is of course not a cure-all for adjusting faculty members to declining enrollments. It does not always occur at the "right" time and in the "right" disciplines and does not always affect the highest paid members of the faculty. Yet the normal rate of departure of faculty could go a long way toward meeting the need for retrenchment.[3]

The assumed rates of 3, 4, and 4 to 6 percent refer of course to all higher education. The rates will probably differ among various types of colleges and universities, among institutions individually, and among academic disciplines. We suspect that the rates will tend to vary inversely with affluence and distinction, and be lower at major private

---

3. It should be noted that the attrition rates we are considering refer to persons leaving the profession, and do not include those moving from one institution to another. From the point of view of each institution, the game of musical chairs has a place in adjusting faculty numbers to changes in demand. For any one institution, a resignation is a resignation regardless of what happens to the individual concerned. Moreover, the game of musical chairs helps distribute the faculties among institutions where they can be most effective and opens up fresh opportunities for them, even if it does not remove individuals from the academic profession.

universities, at public flagship universities, and at well-known liberal arts colleges, and to be higher at other types of institutions. But overall, we believe that attrition rates will be higher, and the opportunities for the appointment of new faculty members greater, than is generally realized. Many of the studies of faculty attrition refer only to full-time or tenured faculty and ignore the substantial attrition among junior and part-time faculty. Indeed this attrition is under the control of the employing institutions and not wholly subject to the independent decisions of the incumbents. A vacant position created by the voluntary or enforced resignation of a full-time junior person or of two or three part-time persons creates an opening for a new full-time appointee exactly as the resignation of a tenured person creates such an opening. In such cases the ability to fill a position with a first-class, full-time appointee depends on finances, not on the availability of a position. The problem of faculty staffing is not so much an inadequate number of job openings as it is the finances and the perspicacity to fill each opening with a person of excellent capability.

The Process of Career Choice, Professional Training, and Induction

We have referred to the varied sources of supply of faculty. However, the one feature that is common to all potential faculty people is college education and advanced study. The undergraduate college, however, often plays a decisive role in students' choice of professional careers and in their decision to proceed to advanced study. Many young men and women who enter graduate (or professional) school have already acquired a taste for serious learning and have been encouraged by their undergraduate professors to "go on" to graduate school. Many colleges take pride in the percentage of their students who attend graduate school. Thus, for many, the undergraduate college is the place where at least tentative decisions about advanced study and academic careers are made. Another frequent pattern is that students on graduation from college accept jobs in business, government, the armed forces, etc., but later discover that they miss the pleasures of learning and of the campus style of life and decide to prepare for academic careers by entering graduate school. Still others enter graduate school with the intent of becoming practicing professional persons but eventually decide on academic careers. Whatever the decision-making process, the graduate and professional schools have an important role in the induction of people into the academic profession. This role is to prepare them in terms of substantive learning as evidenced by advanced degrees and to socialize them with respect to academic values, rewards, and style of life.

At the time of first entry into an academic position, the age of faculty members is seldom below twenty-five, often as high as forty or

Table 9–1. Time Required for Doctoral Studies, 1981

		Median Lapse of Time from Baccalaureate to Doctorate	
	Years formally registered for study	*Total time overall*	*Median Age at Doctorate*
Engineering, Mathematics, and Physical Science	5.7 years	7.2 years	29.6 years
Life Sciences	5.9	7.3	30.1
Social Sciences	6.5	9.0	32.0
Humanities	7.7	10.8	33.5
Professional fields offering Ph.D.	6.6	11.1	34.2
Education	7.0	13.5	37.3

SOURCE: National Research Council, *Summary Report*, 1981, pp. 32–33.

more, and probably averages around thirty-three. As shown in Table 9–1, the median length of time for which doctoral candidates are registered for graduate study ranges from six to eight years. Scientists are at the low end of the range and social scientists and humanists at the high end. Because many students do not go through graduate school without interruption, or attend part time, the total elapsed period from the baccalaureate to the doctorate ranges from seven to thirteen years. The median age of the candidates at the time the doctorate is awarded varies from thirty to thirty-seven years. These data reveal the long period of gestation involved in the education of potential members of the academy, and suggest that a lead time of roughly ten years from the baccalaureate degree on the average is needed to prepare young people for the academic profession. However, the time needed for acquiring a Ph.D. could be shortened through an acceleration scheme. For example, a financial program that would enable graduate students to attend full time (instead of part time as is now so common) would both improve graduate education and shorten the elapsed time required for the degree. Also, the recruitment of doctoral students before completion of their dissertations—as was common in the 1950s and 1960s—would reduce the time.

Generally, after recruitment by colleges or universities, doctoral recipients who enter academe face a probationary period of several years. At the end of the probationary period, they may be dropped and forced to find employment elsewhere, either within or outside academe, or they may be granted lifetime tenure as career faculty members in the employing institutions.

This process of preparation, socialization, recruitment, and probation is quite rigorous. It is not guaranteed, however, to produce a highly motivated and well-educated professoriate. This will happen only if two conditions are met: (1) that the graduate schools are able to attract people who are on the whole potentially well qualified for the profession—including an ample supply of the rare, brilliant ones who are needed to provide the intellectual leadership of the nation; and (2) that the colleges and universities are able to recruit and retain a generous share of these qualified people. If either of these two conditions cannot be met, the caliber of the academic community will sooner or later decline.

These two conditions were largely met during the Great Depression of the 1930s when opportunities in higher education were promising relative to openings in other industries and occupations. They were also met during the 1960s and early 1970s when a vast expansion of higher education occurred and much talent was attracted. In view of the long lag between choice of academic career and actual entry into the profession, the people who emerged from the graduate schools and entered academe during the 1970s and early 1980s were still of high caliber as is almost universally testified by presidents and deans throughout the nation. Indeed, a large majority continue to report that on the whole their faculties are the best ever (Minter & Bowen, 1982).

The high quality of present faculties is explained also by the ability of the employing institutions in recent years to be selective. There were relatively few academic appointments to be made and relatively large numbers of persons completing graduate programs. But as of 1985 there are early warning signs that the caliber of faculties may be beginning to deteriorate. People who would once have planned to enter academe are seeking, or have been forced to seek, other outlets for their talents and energies. Meanwhile, increasing numbers of people already in academe are beginning to think of alternative options—though as yet there is no stampede out of the profession. The faculties of 1985 may be the best prepared in our history, but after years of declining compensation and deteriorating working conditions they are not the most highly motivated in our history and do not have the highest morale. Under these conditions, the current crop of young people, as they contemplate embarking on the long journey to academic careers, may be having second thoughts. Ten years from now the caliber of persons available to the profession may have diminished. These matters will be considered in some depth in Chapter 11.

The Amazing Expansion of Advanced Study

Over the past several decades, especially since 1950, there has been a phenomenal growth in the number of persons seeking advanced degrees and in the facilities and opportunities for advanced study. Since the late 1970s, however, the growth has leveled off. For doctors' degrees, it would have declined sharply except for the entry of thousands of women into doctoral study (see Table 4–2). The growth in number of first professional degrees has continued into the 1980s. This growth has been fueled in part by the entry of thousands of women into fields such as law, medicine, dentistry, veterinary medicine, and theology. The trends in degrees awarded are shown in Table 9–2 and Figure 9–1. As a result of the growth, the population as of 1985 contains more than six million persons who have received masters' degrees, well over a million who have received first professional degrees, and 750,000 who hold earned Ph.D.s.[4] Allowing for duplication, perhaps seven to eight million persons hold one or more advanced degrees of some kind. Perhaps as many as 90 percent of these people are employed outside academe and have little interest in joining the academy. They nevertheless make up the population from which almost all academic people are drawn. It is because this population is so large that an absolute shortage of academic people is highly unlikely. Indeed, the size and diversity of this pool suggest that higher education, which requires only about 700,000 faculty members (full time and part time), could employ whatever quantity of faculty it might need—but the quality of the people it would be able to attract from the pool would depend on the compensation and working conditions it could offer and the effectiveness of its recruitment efforts.

Traditionally a majority of new faculty appointees have been younger persons who have recently completed or have been about to complete their advanced study and have chosen to seek academic employment. It is of special interest, therefore, to compare trends in the number of persons appointed to academic positions with trends in graduate enrollments and advanced degrees awarded. These comparisons are made in Table 9–2. As shown in this table, graduate enrollments, advanced degrees awarded, and faculty appointments all traced a similar pattern of growth during the period from 1950 to 1969. After 1969, graduate enrollments continued to grow, though at a diminishing rate, and so did masters and first professional degrees awarded. Ph.D.s awarded leveled off, but did not decline significantly. Meanwhile, faculty appointments took a downward trend. Clearly, academic employment became a diminishing outlet for persons with newly minted degrees. See Figure 9–1.

The comparisons may be clarified by comparing the number of Ph.D.s awarded (Table 9–2, column 5) with the number of faculty appointments (column 8). During the five years 1950–54, about 47,000 persons were recruited into the higher educational faculties. This was a relatively small number of appointments, compared with the numbers for later quinquennia, because higher education was then in the

4. These figures are estimates derived from the cumulation of historical data on the number of earned degrees awarded (with allowance for mortality). National Center for Education Statistics, *Digest of Higher Education Statistics*, 1983, p. 132; National Center for Education Statistics, *Projections of Education Statistics to 1990–91*, 1982, p. 70.

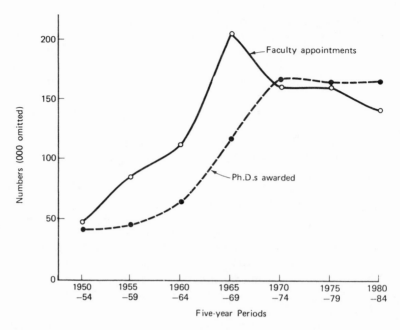

Figure 9–1. Ph.D.s Awarded and Faculty Appointments, by Five-Year Periods, 1950–84

doldrums. Yet the number of appointments exceeded the number of Ph.D.s awarded and provided a moderately brisk academic market for new Ph.D.s, especially so considering that not all of the new Ph.D.s were headed for academe. In the 1960s as the nation began to gear up for the great expansion of higher education that was triggered by Sputnik and fueled by the postwar baby boom, the number of new faculty appointments increased rapidly and steadily. During the period from 1960 to 1970, the number of new faculty appointments exceeded the number of Ph.D.s awarded by a wide margin. But in the early 1970s the tide turned. New faculty appointments declined fairly sharply while the production of new doctorates stabilized.

Non-Academic Employment of Ph.D.s

As the output of new Ph.D.s continued at around 167,000 each five-year period, or 33,000 a year (Table 9–2), exceeding slightly the number of appointments to academe, a relatively new development occurred, namely, large-scale employment of Ph.D.s outside academe. Tables 9–3 and 9–4 provide estimates of the numbers involved. The growth in

Table 9–2. Graduate Enrollment, Advanced Degrees Awarded, and Faculty Appointments, by Five-Year Periods, 1950–54 to 1980–84 (000 omitted)

1	2	3	4	5	6	7	8
					Estimated Number of Persons Appointed to Faculty Positions from Outside Academe: Over Five-Year Periods		
	Graduate Enrollment:	Number of Advanced Degrees Awarded[2]: Over Five-Year Periods					Total Appoint-ments:
Five-Year Period	Average for Period[1]	Masters	First Pro-fessional	Ph.D.s	Increase in Number of Faculty FTE[3]	Replace-ments[4]	Increase plus Replace-ments[5]
1950–54	242	298	n.a.	41	22	25	47
1955–59	336	329	n.a.	46	54	32	86
1960–64	493	488	133	65	72	41	113
1965–69	831	877	165	118	139	66	205
1970–74	1,084	1,315	241	168	77	85	162
1975–79	1,308	1,540	332	165	60	102	162
1980–84 (est.)	1,418	1,529[5]	369[5]	167[5]	32[5]	110	142

[1] National Center for Education Statistics, *Projections of Education Statistics*, 1964, p. 8; 1967, p. 19; 1976, p. 34; 1982, p. 52. American Council on Education, *Fact Book*, 1980, p. 57. Council of Graduate Schools, Jan. 1983, p. 5. Estimates of the authors by interpolation. Data do not include first professional degrees.
[2] National Center for Education Statistics, *Digest of Education Statistics*, 1982, p. 130; National Center for Education Statistics, *Projections of Education Statistics*, 1964, p. 12; 1968, p. 31; 1978, pp. 38–39; 1982, p 70.
[3] National Center for Education Statistics, *Digest of Higher Education Statistics*, 1982, pp. 105, 107; 1968, p. 56; 1964, p. 24.
[4] Computed assuming attrition at 4 percent of average number of faculty.
[5] National Center for Education Statistics, *Projections of Education Statistics*, 1982, p. 70.

employment of Ph.D.s in business, government, hospitals, private consulting, and other occupations outpaced the growth in their employment by colleges and universities. By 1985 an estimated 319,000 Ph.D.s, or 43 percent of all those holding the degree, were working outside academe.[5] This major development had the fortunate effect of preventing serious unemployment among Ph.D.s. In fact, the rates of unemployment have been surprisingly low considering that a substantial increase in the number of Ph.D.s occurred precisely when the rate of Ph.D. appointments in higher education declined sharply (as shown in Table 9–2).

5. About a half of all science Ph.D.s were employed outside academe, one-fourth of those in the social sciences, and one-sixth of those in the humanities (National Research Council, 1982, pp. 20, 50). Data are not available on the employment of Ph.D.s earned in professional fields such as education, business, engineering, computer science, clinical psychology, and communications. However, it is evident that substantial percentages of these people are employed outside academe.

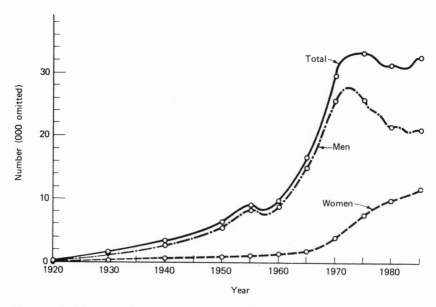

Figure 9–2. Number of Ph.D.s Awarded, U.S., by Sex, 1920–83

One may ask why doctoral production continued at a high rate after 1975 despite the worsening academic market. One reason is the long lag between entry into Ph.D. programs and receipt of the degree. Many young people undoubtedly had chosen the academic profession as undergraduates in the late 1960s or early 1970s when higher education was prosperous and then continued despite the onset of the depression in higher education. Another reason, given the long period between the baccalaureate and the doctorate, is that some candidates are entering graduate study in the 1980s planning to be ready for the academic market in the 1990s, when it is expected to pick up (Scully, 1983). Still another factor is that the women's movement encouraged and emboldened many young women to seek Ph.D.s. Figures on the number of doctorates awarded by sex tell the story (Figure 9–2). Men responded to the changing market conditions by a 18 percent reduction in number receiving the Ph.D. over the period 1975 to 1982.[6] Simultaneously, women were entering the market in unprecedented numbers. The combined effect of the declining number of men and the increasing number of women was to stabilize the total. Had women claimed only their traditional share of the Ph.D.s of 10 to 15 percent, the total would have been less by several thousand. But the most compelling reason for the continuation of doctoral production at a high rate was that opportunities outside academe did open up on a large scale. They opened up

6. See also Table 4–2.

Table 9–3. Estimated Employment Trends for Persons with Ph.D.s

	1	2	3	4	5
				Estimated	Estimated
	Number of			Number of	Number of
	Active Ph.D.s	Estimated Per-		Ph.D.s Serving	Ph.D.s
	in the U.S.	centage of	Number of	as Faculty	Employed Out-
	Population[1]	Faculty with	Faculty[3]	Members[4]	side Academe[5]
	(000 omitted)	Ph.D.s[2]	(000 omitted)	(000 omitted)	(000 omitted)
1950–51	101	37%	165	61	40
1955–56	134	39	198	77	57
1960–61	204	41	236	97	107
1965–66	273	49	340	166	107
1970–71	398	55	474	260	138
1975–76	522	58	628	364	158
1980–81	643	60	678	407	236
1984–85 (est.)	750	62	695	431	319

[1] Estimated from data covering Science, Engineering, Social Science, and Humanities in National Research Council, 1982, pp. 20, 50; and by cumulating doctorates awarded over successive 40-year periods reduced by 15 percent to allow for withdrawal from the labor force, retirement, net migration, and mortality.
[2] Estimated by the authors from many sources, especially American Council on Education, *Fact Book*, 1980, p. 118; National Education Association, 1979, p. 19.
[3] National Center for Education Statistics, *Digest of Education Statistics*, 1983, p. 103; 1964, p. 24. Includes full-time and part-time faculty.
[4] Column 2 multiplied by column 3.
[5] Column 1 minus column 4.

partly because of expansion of the market for scientists, engineers, economists, managers, and other professional persons. They also opened up simply because those with Ph.D.s are on the whole among the brightest, most energetic, and most versatile individuals in our society and tend to be attractive to employers. As Radner and Miller (1975, p. 349) commented, "The doctorate will in the future serve as a base for a widening variety of career employments."

Unemployment or Underemployment among Ph.D.s

The question of unemployment or underemployment among Ph.D.s has received a great deaal of discussion in recent years (Zumeta, 1981). Excellent data on this subject have been gathered by the National Research Council and are presented in Table 9–5. These data refer only to scientists, engineers, social scientists, and humanists and do not include persons with Ph.D.s in professional fields such as theology, business, journalism, and education. The figures are shown separately for the entire population of Ph.D.s in the included fields and for persons who have received their degrees recently. These figures leave the impression that unemployment or underemployment has decidedly not been rampant among Ph.D.s either in the scientific or humanistic fields

Table 9-4. Employment of Ph.D.s by Type of Employer and Year of Doctorate

	Year Doctorate Granted[3]				
	1960–64	*1965–68*	*1969–72*	*1973–76*	*1977–80*
Physical Sciences and Engineering[1]					
— Colleges and Universities	54.4%	47.5%	38.2%	36.1%	34.2%
— Business & Industry	34.5	38.2	46.1	50.1	52.8
— Government	7.8	10.5	10.7	9.3	7.7
— Other	3.3	3.8	4.8	4.4	5.2
Total	100.0	100.0	100.0	100.0	100.0
Life Sciences[2]					
— Colleges and Universities	67.3%	63.8%	62.6%	58.9%	62.1%
— Business & Industry	14.1	16.6	15.4	20.1	19.2
— Government	12.1	13.6	14.3	13.3	11.5
— Other	5.9	6.0	7.6	7.6	7.0
Total	100.0	100.0	100.0	100.0	100.0
Social Sciences					
— Colleges and Universities	71.2%	65.3%	62.1%	57.7%	54.0%
— Business & Industry	12.4	17.4	17.4	15.9	16.2
— Government	7.4	7.4	8.1	10.5	11.3
— Other	8.9	9.7	12.2	15.4	18.3
Total	100.0	100.0	100.0	100.0	100.0
Humanities					
— Colleges and Universities	92.9%	86.1%	85.8%	77.0%	75.0%
— Business & Industry	1.8	5.8	5.5	9.8	10.1
— Government	0.3	2.0	2.4	5.8	5.0
— Other	4.1	4.4	5.8	7.0	9.8
Total	100.0	100.0	100.0	100.0	100.0

[1] Includes mathematics, computer science, chemistry, physics, astronomy, and earth and environmental sciences.
[2] Includes agricultural, medical, and biological sciences.
[3] Because of rounding, totals do not add precisely to 100.

SOURCE: National Research Council as reported in *Chronicle of High Education*, Oct. 5, 1983.

(cf. Zumeta, 1982, pp. 335–38). The hard core of unemployment (defined as not employed and seeking work) is of the order of 1 or 2 percent,[7] an almost irreducible minimum given a less than perfect labor market. However, this is too rigid a definition of unemployment or underem-

7. A survey of Danforth scholars who had completed their work for the Ph.D. revealed unemployment rates varying by class from 0 to 3.8 percent. *Danforth News & Notes*, March 1979, p. 4.

ployment. Some of those working part time would prefer to work full time; some of those with postdoctoral appointments are in a temporary holding pattern and would prefer to have permanent jobs[8]; some of those not employed and not seeking employment would prefer to have jobs had they not been discouraged from seeking work by a slack labor market; and some of those not reporting may have been avoiding acknowledgment of their unemployment. We would guess that the true unemployment among different groups of Ph.D.s would be roughly in the range of 3 to 6 percent—still below unemployment rates for the general labor force. These figures do not spell catastrophe. They seem remarkably low when one takes into account both the tremendous outpouring of Ph.D.s in recent years and the unemployment rates in the general labor force which have varied from 7 to 11 percent in the early 1980s. These figures also convey a sense of the high ability and versatility of persons who have earned the Ph.D. They are by no means confined to academic work.

Table 9–6 presents data on rates of unemployment or underemployment as of 1981 among various academic disciplines. Though, as would be expected, the rates were higher in the humanities than in the sciences, the differences among fields were surprisingly small.

A careful study of the employment situation among humanists was conducted in 1984 by Laure Sharp under the auspices of the National Endowment for the Humanities (Sharp, 1984). Her work was based on a restudy of the excellent data collected by the National Research Council and already cited in Tables 9–5 and 9–6. Sharp summarized her results (p. vii) by saying that "This investigation leads to a more positive assessment of the overall employment picture [for Ph.D. humanists] than was suggested by press reports and anecdotal evidence about the plight of unemployed Ph.D.s . . . periodic surveys never confirmed the existence of high unemployment rates for humanists; (2.9% in 1977, 2.2% in 1979, and 1.5 percent in 1981)." More specifically, her study revealed (p. vii) that in 1981, 89 percent of the 76,000 surveyed humanists were in the labor force and that among these 2 percent were unemployed, another 2 percent were working part time and looking for full-time work, and 3 percent were working part time by choice. She noted that in no humanistic discipline were fewer than 70 percent working full time in their chosen fields; moreover, unemployment rates were not appreciably affected by the prestige of the institutions from which humanists received their degrees. Unemployment rates, she found, were not very different among different categories of Ph.D. recipients

8. Zumeta (1982a, pp. 18–19, 34–35), in a detailed study of postdoctoral research appointments, concluded that these positions, though temporary, cannot be interpreted as merely a way out for young Ph.D.s who fail to find regular employment either inside or outside academe. Rather, he suggests that for a variety of reasons, the postdoctoral appointment has become a more or less regular part of the education and training of scientists and scholars.

Table 9-5. Employment Status of Doctoral Scientists, Engineers, Social Scientists, and Humanists, 1981

	Scientists, Engineers, and Social Scientists		Humanists		Social Scientists[2]	
	All Graduates (1938–80)	Recent Graduates (1975–80)	All Graduates (1938–80)	Recent Graduates (1975–80)	All Graduates (1938–80)	Recent Graduates (1975–80)
Employed Full Time	88.5%	84.5%	83.6%	84.0%	90.0%	92.5%
Employed Part Time	—	2.7	—	8.2	—	3.1
Employed Part Time, Seeking Full Time Work	0.5	—	2.0	—	0.7	—
Employed Part Time, Not Seeking Full Time Work	2.4	—	4.0	—	2.2	—
Post Doctoral Appointment	2.9	9.7	0.7	0.9	0.7	1.2
Not Employed, Seeking Employment	0.7	1.2	1.4	2.5	0.7	1.4
Not Employed, Retired and Other	3.6	—	6.1	0.6	4.1	—
No Report	0.4	0.3	0.6	0.6	0.5	0.1
	100.0[2]	100.0[2]	100.0[2]	100.0[2]	100.0[2]	100.0[2]

SOURCE: National Research Council, *Science, Engineering, and Humanities Doctorates in the United States, 1981 Profile*, 1982, pp. 16, 30, 32, 47, 58, 61. These data include all Ph.D.s except those in Professional Fields as follows: Theology, Business Administration, Home Economics, Journalism, Speech and Hearing Science, Law and Jurisprudence, Social Work, Library and Archival Science, Education, and a few other fields.
[1] Social scientists also included in "Scientists, Engineers, and Social Scientists."
[2] Because of rounding, totals do not add to precisely 100.

Table 9–6. Employment Status of Doctoral Scientists, Engineers, Social Scientists, and Humanists Who Received Their Degrees Between 1938 and 1980, by Selected Disciplines, 1981

	Percentage Employed Part Time and Seeking Full-Time Work	Percentage Not Employed and Seeking Employment
Sciences:		
Mathematics	0.2	0.5
Computer Science	1.0	0.2
Physics/Astronomy	0.1	0.6
Chemistry	0.3	0.7
Earth & Environmental Sciences	0.8	0.8
Engineering	0.2	0.1
Agricultural Science	0.2	0.4
Medical Science	0.3	0.7
Biology	0.8	1.5
Psychology	1.1	1.1
Other Social Science	0.8	0.8
Humanities		
History	2.2	1.2
Art History	2.7	4.2
Music	3.1	2.2
Speech and Theater	1.6	0.8
Philosophy	2.6	0.6
Language and Literature		
English–American	1.5	1.2
Classical	2.6	1.9
Modern Foreign	2.8	2.1

SOURCE: National Research Council, 1982, pp. 32, 61. *Science, Engineering, & Humanities Doctorates in the United States: Profile 1981*, pp. 32, 61. These data differ from those of Table 9–5. In that table the rates are computed as percentages of the total Ph.D. population, whereas in this table the rates are computed as percentages of the relevant Ph.D. labor force, omitting retired persons, persons not seeking work, and those not reporting employment status.

though they were somewhat higher for women than for men. Sharp indicated, however, that the situation had been greatly eased by the steep decline in the number of Ph.D.s awarded in the humanistic fields—from a peak of 5,170 in 1974 to 3,560 in 1982 (p. 4).

Further enlightenment on the situation in the humanities is provided by a study conducted by May and Blaney (1981). In answering the question What happens to Ph.D.s who cannot find jobs as teachers?, their answer was (p. 83):

> They have gotten and will get other types of jobs. Most will enjoy their work as much as they would have enjoyed teaching. Very few face unemployment . . . the proportion believing themselves underemployed will be similar to that among the Ph.D.s who did find teaching jobs [p. 85]. [May and Blaney continue [p. 111] Our contention is simply that the

number of people who equip themselves to be scholars should not be a function of actual or anticipated fluctuations in the academic job market. . . . It will not be a waste if large numbers continue to earn doctorates and go on to posts in insurance companies or government agencies. In fact the cultural life of the United States will be significantly richer if the training of scholars can be divorced from the preparation of teachers and if it becomes no more extraordinary for a corporate vice-president to have a Ph.D. in philosophy than a law degree and no more remarkable for someone in business or civil service to publish a scholarly book or article than to win an amateur golf tournament or to be elected to local office. The humanities could become more integral to American life.

A revealing data set has been compiled by the National Research Council on career plans of new doctorate recipients at the time the degree is awarded. These data show the percentage of recipients having made definite career arrangements and the percentage still seeking positions. The data are especially interesting because they are stratified by field of study and are available annually over a long period, 1958 to 1982. Table 9–7 presents these data for selected years in terms of the percentage of new doctorates still seeking positions, that is, not placed, at the time the degree is awarded. As the table shows, the percentage not placed was fairly stable in 1958 and 1964, was appreciably higher in 1970, and was still higher in 1976 and 1982. Clearly, new Ph.D.s were not being snapped up instantly in the 1970s and 1980s, as they had been

Table 9–7. Percentage of New Doctorate Recipients Still Seeking Positions at the Time Degree was Conferred, by Field of Study, Selected Years, 1958–1982

	1958	1964	1970	1976	1982
Physics and Astronomy	13.3%	17.8%	22.8%	28.5%	24.3%
Chemistry	9.3	9.5	18.1	21.2	16.3
Mathematics	15.1	15.8	20.6	28.1	23.6
Engineering	15.4	16.5	24.7	27.3	25.9
Biochemistry	11.4	9.8	13.4	17.2	19.7
Other Biosciences	16.0	13.7	19.7	22.4	22.9
Medical Sciences	12.6	12.9	17.8	20.4	22.7
Psychology	18.6	14.9	20.6	28.2	28.5
Anthropology	15.1	12.0	12.4	29.4	40.5
Economics	14.8	9.1	10.9	17.7	15.7
History	15.8	9.6	13.6	34.4	34.1
English and American Literature	9.9	11.0	13.8	37.3	32.4
Foreign Language and Literature	14.8	9.3	18.8	39.1	32.5
Education	15.2	13.1	22.6	24.5	24.6
All Fields Combined	14.3	13.0	19.4	25.7	24.7

SOURCE: National Research Council, *Doctorate Recipients from United States Universities: Summary Report, 1982*, pp. 16–21.

in the 1960s. More time and effort—and presumably worry—were required in getting placed than had been common in the 1950s and 1960s. These figures also imply the necessity on the part of many aspirants of settling for second or third or tenth choices in their acceptance of job offers. Yet, as shown in Tables 9–5 and 9–6, unemployment rates have been surprisingly low. We interpret these data to mean that job-seeking among new Ph.D.s has become more difficult in recent years than it was in the halcyon 1960s, but that jobs are eventually found.

Many new doctorates have been forced to find positions outside the traditional labor markets, and more time and ingenuity have been required to seek out such positions. Thus, the change in the labor market for Ph.D.s has shown up more plainly in data on the time required for placement rather than on rates of unemployment. Table 9–7 also shows that the percentage of new doctorates still seeking positions is on the whole higher in the humanities and social studies than in the sciences, and this is no surprise.

Solmon and Zumeta (1981) in observing the increasing employment of Ph.D.s outside academe remarked (p. 22), "If Ph.D. holders have successfully demonstrated their unique productivity in nontraditional work settings during a period of their relative abundance, they may have created permanent new sources of demand for their services." This thought has an ominous ring, because it suggests that academe is likely to face increasingly intense competition with industry and other employers for the available Ph.D. talent.

Concluding Comments

This chapter has been a wide-ranging analysis of the academic labor market. It has been provocative in the sense that the conclusions reached are not wholly congruent with anecdotal accounts or journalistic reports about conditions in this market. In preparing this chapter, we have been plagued by the shortage of reliable statistics available for our purposes. We have made use of several excellent data sets of the National Center for Education Statistics and the National Research Council, but have also found it necessary to improvise by developing our own rough estimates of some of the needed information. Our main conclusions are:

First, through various forms of advanced study, the nation is creating a great and growing pool of highly educated people who engage in a multitude of professional (but non-academic) activities for which advanced study is required. We suspect that in the future there will be increasing two-way traffic between this pool and the academic community. The pool will be an increasing source of new faculty and at the same time it will confront academe with stiff competition for both new Ph.D.s and established members of the professoriate.

Second, the number of openings for new appointments to the nation's faculties is likely to be greater than is usually assumed. Our studies lead to the conclusion that attrition might average 4 percent in the years ahead to the late 1990s and might even reach 6 percent by the beginning of the 21st century. The actual attrition rate is likely, however, to be volatile because it is a function of two independent variables: conditions within academe and conditions in the economy outside academe. The worse the inside conditions, the greater the attrition; and the better the conditions outside, the greater the attrition. At the annual rate of 4 percent, over ten years about 32 percent of all faculty positions would become vacant through attrition, and over twenty-five years 70 percent would become vacant. We see the problem of faculty replacements as not so much a shortage of vacancies as a shortage of funds necessary to make solid appointments as distinguished from non-tenure-track and part-time appointments. It should be noted, however, that success in the appointment of full-time tenured faculty would ultimately result in a reduction of the attrition rate.

Third, the average lead time for preparing Ph.D.s is of the order of seven to eleven years from the date of the baccalaureate degree. Since many students make their career choices during their undergraduate years, the average elapsed time between decision to enter advanced study and completion of Ph.D. programs may easily be ten years or more. These facts suggest that the latter half of the 1980s is none too early to encourage promising young people to consider academic careers.

Fourth, the number of Ph.D.s awarded during the 1970s would probably have fallen quite sharply had the women's movement not propelled many women into Ph.D. programs. The net result of the decline in number of degrees awarded to men and the increase of number awarded to women has been a fairly stable production of Ph.D.s at just above 30,000 a year.

Fifth, despite much opinion to the contrary, unemployment rates among Ph.D.s have remained remarkably low. Though there have been differences among the various fields of study in the time and trouble involved in achieving placement, the market has not been glutted with unemployed Ph.D.s. This has been due in part to an unexpectedly resilient academic labor market and also to the increasing flow of Ph.D.s to non-academic employment. It is something of a miracle that the market has been able to absorb most of the increasing number of new Ph.D.s.

Sixth, the data suggest that people with advanced degrees have proven their versatility and employability and have successfully penetrated new markets.

One of the principal themes of this book is the need for higher education to be strongly competitive for the best talent in the labor market wherever it can be found—in the graduate schools, in the pool of professional talent, among the unemployed or underemployed. To seek the best talent is always expensive. But we would argue that in helping higher education to get through a difficult period, funding agencies should recognize the need to make faculty salaries and working conditions competitive to assure the recruitment and retention of genuine talent. In the same vein, it would be healthy for the profession and for the institutions if new job openings could be created, for example, by converting part-time positions into full-time positions, by employing more Ph.D.s on community college faculties, and through tactful forms of early retirement.

The Review of Higher Education
Spring 1988, Volume 11 No. 3
Pages 311–317

AN OVERVIEW OF THE 1987 ASHE DISTINGUISHED DISSERTATION

Change in the Academic Marketplace: Faculty Mobility in the 1980s

Dolores L. Burke

This study replicates one reported by Theodore Caplow and Reece McGee in 1958 (*The Academic Marketplace*, Basic Books). The current study uses Caplow and McGee's original research framework and materials and, like the earlier study, examines the faculty personnel system in research universities.

METHODOLOGY

First, the replication itself provides some constraints. As general guidance, I used a paper published by Professor Caplow* that classified qualitative replications in two types: (1) a challenge, to confirm or weaken results of a study, or

---

* Theodore Caplow, "La Repépétition des enquêtes: Une méthode de récherche sociologique," *L'Année Sociologique* 32 (1982): 5–22.

Dolores L. Burke is special assistant to the president at Duke University. This dissertation, done under the direction of David Dill, University of North Carolina at Chapel Hill, is soon to be published by Greenwood Press, Westport, Connecticut.

311

(2) a longitudinal study after a lapse of time to determine what changes have affected the system or subject during that period of time. These two categories are not necessarily mutually exclusive.

The research findings are based upon data obtained from 306 faculty members, primarily through personal interviews (266), but also in telephone interviews (6) and mail responses (34), with department chairs and other faculty members in the arts and sciences from December 1985 to April 1986. These individuals were at six of the universities Caplow and McGee visited in 1958; all are members of the Association of American Universities. The research used the original interview schedule, slightly modified with Professor McGee's assistance. Data analysis likewise followed the original design, with the exception that computer spreadsheets were used instead of manual coding sheets; the analysis consisted of a quantitative framework (numbers of appointments, etc.) and content analysis. (For further details, see the dissertation or forthcoming book.)

DATA COMPARISONS

The data were organized in a natural progression, starting with process (search, selection, and separation) and moving to environment in a chapter on market and policy.

The Search

Caplow and McGee noted that the most striking feature of academic hiring procedures was the time and effort that most departments devoted to appointments. They remarked that the average salary of an assistant professor was approximately that of a bakery truck driver—and his occupancy of the job likely to be less permanent—but that it took a large part of the time of several highly skilled people for a long period of time to hire him. That has not changed. The recruiting process is still an extremely time-consuming task; one chair characterized it as "gut-wrenching and tiring".**

Changes have occurred in the structure of the search; for example, the Caplow-McGee assumption that a faculty departure or retirement almost automatically triggers a faculty replacement at the same rank in the same department has given way to a pattern of considerable negotiation between chairs and deans before a position is authorized. But the *position definition* generally remains within the province of the academic department.

** This and later quotes are drawn from interview data.

Another change is that today's search is public knowledge through advertising in various forms. About half of the new assistant professors in the sample had learned about the position through an advertisement; the others had heard about the job before seeing it advertised. But the once-prevalent method of placement by a mentor in the "right place" seems to have vanished, and one chair expressed relief at no longer being "at the mercy of a senior man here who has a friend somewhere with a graduate student he wants to place".

At the senior level, advertising had little effect. The important consideration was, in the words of one respondent, "Who could we get to come?"

Throughout the search process, generally a change from the 1950s, all departmental faculty members were encouraged to read the files, express opinions to members of the search committee, and argue for the inclusion or exclusion of candidates. As one experienced chair commented: "I've been chairman here for a long time, before that chairman at another university. If there is a lesson to be learned, it is that you can never please everybody all the time, but if there is one place you have to be democratic, it's in selecting new faculty".

Selection

A major change in the selection process is the importance of the campus interview for junior candidates. Fewer than half of the assistant professors in Caplow and McGee's sample were interviewed prior to being hired. Now there is general agreement that the interview is the top rung of the recruiting ladder—the place where the candidate can perform brilliantly or self-destruct. In the current study, the routine for the campus visit was fairly standard and matched the 1950s visit in the instances where it occurred. The selection decision continues to be based primarily on the research interests and capabilities of the candidate.

As in Caplow and McGee's study, the hiring departments were quite successful in hiring the people who were their first choice. New assistant professors (a group Caplow and McGee did not interview) were satisfied as well: Only six (out of seventy-four) admitted that the job was not their first choice, and more than two-thirds of the group had rejected other offers. New assistant professors were primarily attracted to the department because their personal research interests were compatible with those of the department. They were also sensitive to treatment by the department; and astute chairs, knowing that the top layer of candidates was not deep, tried, in the words of one, "to sell the place." It was a successful technique. One assistant professor said that she was impressed by "the red carpet treatment, very fine".

For the senior candidate, there was no change from the 1950s. The campus visit might not take place at all, or it might occur in a modified form—e.g., participation in a seminar series, an invitation to consult. The department is particularly interested in a good fit, as in this case: "Ostensibly her work is good and she is younger than the other candidate and therefore thought to have more potential. But really we just liked her personally a lot better."

Separation

Termination showed a rather surprising lack of change in some respects. As would be expected, there was a larger proportion of retirements and a smaller proportion of deaths in comparison to the 1958 sample. But dismissals and resignations were proportionally about the same as in the earlier study: 25 percent dismissals for Caplow and McGee; 26 percent in the current study; 47 percent resignations in 1958, in the current study, 49 percent.

Further, my expectation that a central all-discipline promotion and tenure committee would play a greater role in tenure denials was not realized. An impressive 70 percent of the tenure denials were made at the departmental level, 67 percent for Caplow and McGee. Lower-ranked departments turned people over at a higher rate; there were only eight tenure denials in top-ten departments (about 20 percent of total denials), and none in top-five departments.

Colleagues of resigning assistant professors frequently cited intellectual isolation and intellectual incompatibility with senior colleagues as mobility motivators. A typical report would be, "They didn't offer him much more in the way of money, but he thought he would be more appreciated there." Senior people also left because of intellectual isolation or incompatibility, in their case with peers, and sometimes because of a lack of research support or a pronounced hostility in the department. Salary was rarely a motivator, consistent with the earlier study.

Important to the future of higher education in the more competitive market place of the 1990s may be the apparently increasing proportion of faculty members who leave higher education altogether—about a third of the assistant and associate professors in the current sample, as compared to a quarter of those in Caplow and McGee's sample. An example of the change in mindset that may be occurring is reflected in this quote from an assistant professor: "We undergo brainwashing in graduate school. We are attracted to academia by the lure of formulating and solving problems. But there are also problems to solve in the private sector. I may leave higher education".

Market and Policy

The market and policy category showed a great deal of change—change that is continuing. The study reflects the same market conditions noted by others recently—an opening up of the academic job market. One chair of classics said: "The market has improved and I think it will continue. I foresee days when we'll be right back where we were in the '60s and I'll be pulling people off the street." More than half the chairs in the sample across disciplines expressed similar sentiments. Effects like those of Sputnik in the 1950s were seen—one chair of physics talked about the "Toyota revolution" and several chairs of languages remarked on the positive effects of international trade. There was much mention of nonacademic competition for Ph.D.'s as in this comment from a chair of anthropology: "Ten to fifteen years ago all of our Ph.D.'s would get jobs in academia. Now only 10 to 20 percent get academic jobs. They work as research organizers, with computers in business and industry, in contract archaeology." So, a once-shrinking market has created new opportunities that will continue to compete for graduates.

Another change is more subtle—the reinforcement of the research culture in the university. Caplow and McGee recognized the increasing emphasis on research in the 1950s; this study shows that it is a shared emphasis, between employer and employee. There is no confusion about the basis for evaluation of an assistant professor nor any initial disagreement. The junior faculty member chooses a job and is chosen on the basis of research interests.

Related to the research emphasis is the tension between disciplinary and institutional attachment (or locals and cosmopolitans). This study identified a career cycle effect, with a strong discipline-oriented approach in assistant professors and with institutional and disciplinary orientation achieving more balance above that rank.

There are more participants in the current market, but the change in number does not necessarily connote a decline in quality. Of the chairs in the current sample, 35 percent said that today's candidates were better than those of some years ago, and the other 65 percent mostly said they were no worse—different, perhaps: "It's hard to put 'better' into

165

perspective," commented one, "because there are a lot more things to be trained in and as chemists they know more because there is more to be known. The science has progressed. As to whether they are better, I don't really think so."

Another difference in today's participants, though, creates the spouse employment issue, now much more pronounced than the one or two occasions noted in Caplow and McGee's interview data. "The spouse problems are terrible these days", complained one chair. "It's a factor in two-thirds of our offers." In this sample, spouse employment was a factor in almost 20 percent of the appointments and resignations. For example, in appointments, 18 percent of the women and 19 percent of the men were affected by spouse employment problems.

The new problems of the academic market place have resulted in various management strategies, apparently not present at the time of the earlier study. One manifestation is a new flexibility in the central fund used for special hires—a spouse budget line and "targets of opportunity" or "superstars." Strategic planning has produced greater control over positions, but departments, too, engage in active planning: "Every two years we go off for a weekend retreat and talk about our long-term future," reported one, "not specifically about people but about research, academics." Indeed, management—a word once anathema to academics—is an important consideration for many chairs, as in this comment: "My job as a manager is to enable people to do their work."

An outgrowth of strategic management may be the aspiration to higher rankings currently found in many departments but absent from the earlier study. Chairs were highly sensitive to rankings, and there were numerous references to "moving up," "aiming for the top ten," etc. A frequent downside to these ambitions was disgruntled senior people: "I have an iron in the fire and I hope it burns," said one. "I will leave here if I can. There is a general feeling of being unappreciated."

CONCLUSION

The findings led to identifying sources of change and nonchange in the academic marketplace. The source of change is the relationship between the organization and the social environment. Factors such as greater competition between universities and the composition of the labor market have also caused change. The source of nonchange, or inertia, is the academic department itself, where the personnel process resides, with its own extra-institutional relationship with the academic discipline. The organizational problem that emerged from the dissertation focused on the tension between department and institution, raising the question of how to integrate the departmental culture—the culture of the clan—into the broader organizational culture that seems necessary in a competitive environment.

Within the study, there was little variance on such items as type of institution (public or private) and disciplinary division (humanities, natural sciences, or social sciences). Variance occurred principally at the departmental level, indicating the control of the department over the faculty personnel process. Therefore, an important element of the departmental culture is that process. Caplow and McGee pointed out that "the process by which a department replaces its members and maintains its immortality is as nearly central to an understanding of academic institutions as anything can be." The academic organization can be strengthened through further examination, understanding, and improvement of that process.

THE VALUE OF TEACHING, RESEARCH, AND SERVICE

by James S. Fairweather

James Fairweather *is associate professor and senior research associate, Center for the Study of Higher Education, Pennsylvania State University. His interests include faculty roles and rewards, industry-university relationships, and access to postsecondary education for youth with disabilities.*

Fairweather, a Stanford Ph.D. in higher education, currently directs the evaluation of a National Science Foundation project to enhance undergraduate engineering education, and is a senior member of the National Center on Postsecondary Teaching, Learning and Assessment.

In 1984, the Study Group on the Conditions of Excellence in American Higher Education launched a national movement by calling for major enhancements in the quality of undergraduate education.[1] Ernest Boyer, president of the Carnegie Foundation for the Advancement of Teaching, later echoed the recommendations of the Study Group in his widely-discussed *College: The Undergraduate Experience in America*.[2] Positing a decline in emphasis on teaching and public service, particularly at the undergraduate level, the Study Group and Boyer urged greater attention to these "undervalued" faculty activities. Relying largely on anecdotal evidence, the reports cited instances of students who based their college choice on the opportunity to work with renowned professors only to find themselves taught by graduate students. The reports asked whether faculty members, caught up in their research, had the time to debate curricular reform, much less implement the results of the deliberations.

A decade later, the public still perceives inattention to undergraduate education at a time of increasing tuition costs. Congressional hearings on tuition costs and state legislative attempts to mandate faculty workloads reflect a perceived lack of progress.[3] Faculty members, according to the longitudinal Carnegie Foundation survey, still believe that neither administrators nor their peers value teaching.[4] Derek Bok, the former Harvard president, notes:

> Universities may be paying as much attention to the quality of education as they did 30 years ago—but the fact is that we did not pay enough attention then, and we are not paying enough attention now. Although there are smaller colleges where teaching remains the overriding priority, in the modern university the incentives are not weighted in favor of teaching and education—indeed, quite the contrary is true.[5]

The faculty reward structure expresses the relative importance that institutions accord to teaching, research, and public service. Most research on faculty rewards has focused on faculty and administrator attitudes towards the relative importance of teaching and research in promotion and tenure.[6] Department chairs, for example, universally cited teaching as a key criterion, but several studies found that faculty perceived research and publishing, not teaching, as the keys to advancement.[7]

Promotion and tenure—the usual measures of faculty rewards—occur, at most, three times during a career: promotion to associate professor, tenure (often combined with promotion to associate professor), and promotion to full professor. In contrast, salary reflects, in part, the institution's or department's *annual* evaluation of faculty work. But only a minority of studies related salaries to faculty activities. Most salary studies were descriptive. Quantitative studies asked whether faculty salaries kept pace with inflation, examined the effect of salary on potential faculty shortages, or looked at discrimination, merit pay, mobility, or institutional hiring policies.[8]

Studies of the relationships between salary and faculty activities were inconclusive. Faculty research, according to one literature review, was consistently and positively related to promotion and salary.[9] But the relationships between teaching, promotion, and salary were ambiguous, even contradictory. Different studies found teaching positively related, unrelated, or negatively related to these variables.[10]

PURPOSE

Faculty members, according to a key study, viewed teaching as an important activity, influenced by extrinsic rewards and by internal motivation.[11] The study, assuming that teaching was a positive—or at least neutral—factor in the extrinsic reward structure, recommended a focus on intrinsic rewards to enhance teaching. But was this assumption correct? To test this assumption, we examined the relationships between faculty pay and four activities: teaching and instruction, research and scholarship, administration, and public service.[12] Our research focused on three competing propositions about teaching and instruction:

- Teaching was a positive factor in compensation—the highest salaries went to faculty members who spent more time teaching and whose teaching productivity was high.

- Teaching was a neutral factor in compensation.

- Teaching was a negative factor in compensation—the lowest salaries went to faculty

members who spent more time teaching and whose teaching productivity was high.

The Study

Data from the 1987-1888 National Survey of Postsecondary Faculty (NSOPF), sponsored by the National Center for Education Statistics, permitted examination of the three competing propositions. NSOPF surveyed a nationally representative sample of 11,071 faculty members from 480 colleges and universities. The faculty sample—limited to faculty members with at least some instructional duties during the 1987-1988 academic year—was stratified by full- or part-time status and by program area. The survey obtained a 76 percent faculty response rate: 8,383 full- and part-time faculty from 424 institutions.[13] This study was confined to analysis of full-time, tenure-track faculty from *public* four-year institutions (n = 2,864), *private* four-year colleges and universities (n = 1,617), and public two-year colleges (n = 575). NSOPF examined the nature of faculty employment, job satisfaction, academic and professional background, institutional responsibilities and workload, benefits and professional development activities, compensation, academic interests and values, and sociodemographic characteristics. Our research included faculty and institutional demographics, faculty activities and workload, and compensation.

NSOPF's institutional sample was stratified by type of institution, time allocation, and salary, source of control, and size, measured by estimated number of faculty members.[14] Prior studies found type of institution to be a key determinant of workload differences, so we refined this variable to include public and private research universities that educated the majority of doctorates in the United States and that housed the majority of funded research; public and private doctoral-granting universities that also trained doctoral students and conducted research, but produced fewer doctorates and research dollars than research universities; public and private comprehensive colleges and universities that focused on undergraduate and master's-degree liberal arts and professional programs; private liberal arts colleges; other four-year institutions—predominantly private professional schools of engineering and medicine—and public two-year colleges.

Indicators

This study used basic salary paid by the institution as the principal measure of compensation. The high correlation of salary with compensation, which includes fringe benefits and other nonsalary income, and the desire to compare results with previous research, leads most researchers to use basic salary as the indicator of compensation.[15]

Prior research found that faculty workload, productivity, and compensation vary by demographic and position-related characteristics, including academic rank, discipline, gender, and ethnicity.[16] Salary and productivity, for example, were positively related to age and length of service. Variables examined in this study included age in fall 1987, gender, ethnic/racial minority status—including respondents who were Caucasian *and* of Hispanic descent, American Indian, Asian/Pacific Islander, or Black—highest degree awarded, academic rank, length of service, and program area. The study measured length of service by time in current rank—the number of years since achieving the rank held at the institution in question during fall 1987—and by the number of years at the current institution. Program area was the primary field of study in which a faculty member worked: agriculture/home economics, business, education, engineering, fine arts, health sciences, humanities, natural sciences, social sciences, and other fields. We derived an additional variable, high paying field, from ranking the average pay in each program area relative to the overall national average.[17] Some analyses controlled for the existence of collective bargaining at the respondent's institution, either public or private.

Measures of instruction-related activities and workloads included percent of time spent on teaching and instruction,[18] hours spent in the classroom per week,[19] and the type of student taught (undergraduate, graduate, or both). Time spent on teaching and instruction included teaching, advising, and supervising students; grading papers, preparing courses, and developing new curricula; and working with student organizations.

Our measure of instructional productivity was total student contact hours generated during fall 1987—estimated by summing the number of hours a class met per week times the number of students enrolled in the class across

all courses taught in fall 1987.[20]

Our indicators of research and scholarship included one measure of faculty activity and two measures of productivity. The activity—percent of time spent on research and scholarship—included research, preparing or reviewing articles or books, and attending or preparing to attend professional meetings or conferences; giving performances in the fine or applied arts; and seeking funds for research.[21] The first productivity measure—total refereed publications for the career—included articles, chapters in edited volumes, textbooks, other books, monographs, and reviews of books, articles, or creative works. Designation as a principal investigator or co-principal investigator, the other productivity measure, meant having at least one research project during fall 1987, funded by the federal government, state or local governments, foundations or other nonprofit organizations, or industry.[22]

We also estimated the percent of time spent on administrative activities and on public or community service.[23]

Scales

For faculty in four-year institutions, high positive correlations between age, time in rank, and years at current institution ($r = .65$ to $.69$), and a high negative correlation between percent of time spent on teaching and time spent on research ($r = -.62$), suggested the need to create composites prior to proceeding with multivariate analyses.[24] Two composites emerged from a principal components analysis that clustered highly correlated indicators into common groups. *Seniority* combined age, time in rank, and years at the current institution into a single scale. The second composite—*more research/less teaching*—was derived from the discovery of an "exchange relationship": the inseparability of time spent on research and on teaching—time spent on one activity came directly at the cost of time spent on the other.

We found a similar pattern for seniority among faculty members in two-year colleges. But the exchange relationship was between administration and research ($r = -.62$), not between teaching and research. This study used a composite based on this relationship—*more administration/less teaching*—for multivariate analyses of faculty in two-year colleges. Finally, the high positive correlations between hours spent in class per week and student contact hours per semester led us to join these indicators into a single composite—*classroom productivity*—for multivariate analyses.[25]

Results

Table 1 shows means and standard deviations for study variables.[26] We studied salary differences by faculty teaching, research, administrative, and service activity, after separating indicators of these variables into quartiles.[27] We also examined faculty workload

and productivity[28] by type of institution,[29] as well as correlations between measures of faculty activities and compensation. Regression models were completed by type of institution and program area.[30] Here, we first analyze how salaries varied by type of institution and program area. We then discuss our bivariate analyses, including differences between institutional type and between source of control, and examine regression models with basic salary as the criterion.

TABLE 1

MEANS AND VARIANCES FOR STUDY VARIABLES

	Public						Private		
	Four-year			Two-year			Four-year		
	Mean	SD	SE	Mean	SD	SE	Mean	SD	SE
Income									
Basic Income ($)	42,225	16,850	314	34,070	8,659	369	42,937	21,999	559
Demographic									
High Paying Field*	-.3	.8	.01	N.A.	N.A.	N.A.	-.5	.7	.02
Age (years)	48.1	9.4	.18	48.2	8.7	.37	47.4	10.0	.25
Percent minority	9.9	29.9	.56	10.8	31.1	1.31	11.3	31.6	.80
Percent male	77.9	41.5	.78	62.8	48.3	2.02	81.3	39.0	.97
Collective Bargaining	42.0	49.4	.97	79.7	40.3	1.70	15.5	36.2	.95
Job History									
Time in rank (years)	8.2	6.3	.12	8.8	6.4	.31	7.4	6.4	.16
Percent Doctorate	81.5	38.8	.73	22.3	41.6	1.74	83.2	37.3	.93
Years current job	12.9	8.7	.16	13.4	7.7	.32	11.7	8.8	.22
Teaching									
Percent time teaching	53.5	22.8	.43	74.1	19.8	.84	52.9	25.2	.63
Student contact hours									
(semester)	322.0	441.1	8.44	440.5	345.6	14.7	322.7	573.0	14.62
Hours/week in class	9.5	7.3	.14	15.7	7.2	.31	9.2	6.3	.16
Only undergraduates	9.6	29.5	.55	N.A.	N.A.	N.A.	6.5	24.7	.61
Only graduate	10.1	30.2	56	N.A.	N.A.	N.A.	14.1	34.8	.86
Research									
Percent time, research	22.2	19.3	.36	4.6	7.4	.31	21.5	20.6	.52
Publications, career	23.8	41.1	.78	4.2	18.3	.78	27.2	43.0	1.08
P.I., Fall, 1987	25.7	43.7	.82	N.A.	N.A.	N.A.	23.1	42.1	1.04
Other									
Percent time, admin.	13.9	15.4	.29	9.8	12.0	.51	14.1	14.7	.37
Percent time, service	2.1	4.2	.08	2.6	5.3	.23	1.8	3.7	.09

*-1 = below average, 0 = average, 1 = above average
N.A. = Not Applicable
SOURCE: NSOPF, 1988.

Institutional Type and Program Area

Basic compensation varied directly by type of institution in 1988 (Table 2). "Other four-year schools"—mostly engineering and medical colleges—and research universities offered the highest pay to full-time faculty members in four-year institutions, about $55,000 and $50,000, respectively. Pay descended in order from about $38,000 at doctoral-granting institutions to about $31,000 in liberal arts colleges.[31] The same relationship between faculty pay and type of institution held for private and public four-year institutions, except for an insignificant difference between pay in public doctoral-granting universities and comprehensive colleges.[32] Pay for faculty members in public two-year colleges averaged about $34,000.

Faculty members in engineering and health sciences received more than the national average basic salary (Table 3). Faculty in agriculture/home economics, business, and natural sciences were paid at the national average. Faculty in education, the fine arts, the humanities, social sciences, and other fields earned less than the national average.[33] This pattern also held true for pay in public and private institutions.

TABLE 2

BASIC SALARY (MEANS), BY SOURCE OF CONTROL AND TYPE OF INSTITUTION

	Total	SE	Public	SE	Private	SE
All four-year	$42,498	286	$42,225	314	$42,937	559
Research	49,648	533	48,292	548	52,930	1,320
Doctoral	38,478	528	37,612	587	40,405	1,152
Comprehensive	36,820	335	37,892	408	33,569	557
Liberal Arts	30,628	533	N.A.	N.A.	30,628	533
Other	55,920	2,403	N.A.	N.A.	55,920	2,403
Public two-year	34,070	369	34,070	369	N.A.	N.A.

N.A. = not applicable
SOURCE: NSOPF, 1988

TABLE 3

BASIC SALARY (MEANS), BY SOURCE OF CONTROL AND PROGRAM AREA

Program Area	Total	SE	Public	SE	Private	SE
Agri-Home Eco.	$42,680	977	$42,617	1,006	$44,500	3,678
Business	42,235	1,005	42,644	1,142	41,649	1,810
Education	36,034	576	37,234	602	30,396	1,431
Engineering	45,828	934	46,273	1,121	44,749	1,679
Fine Arts	34,452	542	35,262	668	32,657	893
Health Sciences	56,530	1,756	56,836	1,943	55,908	3,694
Humanities	36,267	372	36,951	473	35,181	598
Natural Sciences	41,825	676	42,744	809	40,141	1,198
Social Sciences	38,212	456	38,754	510	37,280	874
Other Fields	38,685	942	38,932	998	38,344	1,801

SOURCE: NSOPF, 1988

Faculty Activities and Pay

Are faculty activities rewarded differentially? Previous research suggests that research and scholarship are valued more highly than teaching in promotion and tenure, but the relationship between teaching and faculty pay is less clear.[34] This section examines the bivariate relationships between basic salary and indicators of teaching, research, administration, and public service, by type of institution and source of control.

1. Teaching/Instruction

Teaching-related activities included percent of time spent on teaching and instruction, hours in class per week, student contact hours per semester, and type of student taught.

Pay and percent of time spent on teaching and instruction were inversely related in all types of public four-year colleges and universities (Table 4). Faculty members who taught for less than 35 percent of their time in 1988 received an average of about $54,000; colleagues who taught for three-quarters or more of their time received about $35,000.[35]

Private institutions overall displayed the same inverse relationship, but offered a somewhat broader pay range—from about $59,000

for faculty members in the 35 percent or below category to about $33,000 for colleagues in the 72 percent or more group.[36] By type of institution, this pattern held true in private research universities, doctoral-granting universities—save for the two middle quartiles—comprehensive universities—save for one category—and "other four-year" schools.[37] Time spent on teaching and instruction was not related to pay at liberal arts colleges. Pay was not related to time spent on teaching at public two-year colleges.[38]

Overall, pay decreased with hours spent in class for faculty members in public[39] and private four-year institutions.[40] Faculty members in public and private doctoral-granting institutions who taught for less than six hours and eight hours per week, respectively, received more pay than their colleagues. Faculty members in public[41] and private comprehensives followed the pattern for the entire sample.[42] In liberal arts colleges and other four-year schools, pay decreased when hours spent per week in class rose above eight and six hours per week, respectively. Pay was unrelated to time spent in class in public two-year colleges.

Public research universities displayed a U-shaped pattern: faculty members who taught the fewest hours in class per week

TABLE 4

BASIC SALARY (MEANS), BY SOURCE OF CONTROL, TYPE OF INSTITUTION, AND TEACHING-RELATED VARIABLES: PUBLIC AND PRIVATE FOUR-YEAR INSTITUTIONS

| | Percent of Time Spent on Teaching and Instruction | | | | | | |
	<35%	SE	35-52%	SE	53-71%	SE	>71%	SE
Public								
All four-year	$54,091	979	$42,753	481	$37,826	442	$35,429	408
Research	55,850	1,222	46,290	700	43,223	879	38,880	1,348
Doctoral	46,475	2.031	38,898	972	33,957	761	33,193	964
Comprehensive	53,054	2,376	39,053	776	35,459	536	35,041	444
Private								
All four-year	$58,916	1,809	$43,318	1,048	$36,239	603	$32,725	505
Research	61,838	2,409	50,636	1,923	42,892	2,078	36,229	2,183
Doctoral	46,087	4,067	39,914	1,941	39,904	1,513	36,407	2,184
Comprehensive	42,048	3,877	33,779	1,172	32,008	627	32,228	717
Liberal Arts	*	*	30,908	1,283	30,672	976	30,023	708
Other Four-Year	67,202	4,639	54,345	4,833	40,876	2,184	38,869	2,254

TABLE 4 (continued)

	Number of Hours Per Week Teaching Class							
	<6	SE	6-8	SE	9-11	SE	>11	SE
Public								
All four-year	$50,167	830	$42,349	486	$37,776	433	$37,574	512
Research	51,916	1,019	46,296	676	40,253	943	47,880	1,794
Doctoral	45,130	1,757	36,381	898	36,148	782	34,204	1,142
Comprehensive	47,465	2,112	38,657	819	37,263	603	35,341	473
Private								
All four-year	$52,101	1,417	$44,602	1,063	$38,521	1,117	$35,536	766
Research	56,028	2,040	52,374	2,220	42,992	2,676	46,430	3,682
Doctoral	40,474	2,952	43,120	1,635	38,131	2,084	38,103	2,704
Comprehensive	36,142	2,471	39,222	2,032	33,188	748	30,758	590
Liberal Arts	33,897	2,176	33,142	1,295	29,708	1,023	29,139	679
Other Four-Year	60,928	3,924	46,531	3,232	*	*	49,180	4,121

	Number of Student Contact Hours per Semester							
	<110	SE	110-217	SE	218-359	SE	359>	SE
Public								
All four-year	$48,648	817	$40,213	466	$37,890	449	$41,279	604
Research	51,669	1,024	43,706	789	43,660	1,031	50,247	1,250
Doctoral	40,323	1,475	38,365	1,069	34,587	902	36,836	1,153
Comprehensive	45,921	2,021	37,452	596	36,057	520	36,304	589
Private								
All four-year	$50,124	1,312	$35,711	617	$37,200	915	$46,840	1,351
Research	55,623	2,083	44,489	1,785	50,909	3,471	54,580	3,109
Doctoral	39,386	2,884	37,964	1,491	41,673	2,266	43,384	2,512
Comprehensive	31,908	1,888	33,505	938	32,502	656	36,972	1,763
Liberal Arts	30,742	1,472	30,649	852	29,524	775	32,945	1,663
Other Four-Year	61,512	3,628	*	*	*	*	54,649	3,833

	Type of Students Taught					
	Undergraduate	SE	Both	SE	Graduate	SE
Public						
All four-year	$44,753	967	$40,219	296	$55,680	1,819
Research	47,390	1,449	46,370	564	54,487	1,951
Doctoral	41,644	1,836	36,025	574	55,491	3,990
Comprehensive	41,517	1,500	36,785	351	63,738	7,637
Private						
All four-year	$42,742	1,961	$40,262	579	$57,770	2,092
Research	51,532	4,145	49,899	1,432	62,305	3,500
Doctoral	*	*	39,132	1,224	*	*
Comprehensive	*	*	32,030	483	*	*
Liberal Arts	31,296	2,793	30,565	533	N.A.	N.A.
Other Four-Year	*	*	57,598	3,351	54,457	2,495

* Too few cases for reliable estimate
N.A.: Not applicable
SOURCE: NSOPF, 1988

received the highest salaries, followed by faculty members who spent the most time in class, and then by colleagues who spent intermediate numbers of hours in class. Pay in private research universities decreased as instructional time increased—eight hours per week was the breakpoint. This discrepancy between public and private research universities may reflect differing policies on instructional workloads.

The relationship between pay and student contact hours per semester was U-shaped in public[43] and private four-year institutions.[44] Faculty members who generated the fewest contact hours received the highest salaries. Salaries decreased for faculty members with intermediate numbers of contact hours, but then increased for colleagues with the most contact hours. This pattern may reflect higher pay for faculty members who taught the least and for colleagues whose teaching responsibilities consisted of a small number of large lecture classes, a typical practice in higher paying fields, including engineering.

Faculty members in public research universities followed the overall pattern.[45] But pay decreased as student contact hours increased in public doctoral-granting universities, public comprehensives, and private research universities—key breakpoints were 217, 110, and 110 contact hours, respectively.[46] Pay was unrelated to student contact hours in private doctoral-granting and comprehensive universities, liberal arts colleges, and other four-year schools. But public two-year colleges showed a positive relationship between pay and student contact hours.[47]

Faculty members in public[48] and private four-year institutions[49] who taught only graduate students in 1988 received more pay than colleagues who taught undergraduates or both graduate and undergraduate students. This pattern held true in each type of public institution,[50] and in private research universities.[51]

2. Research/Scholarship

Measures of research and scholarship included percent of time spent on these activities, refereed publications for a career, and being a principal investigator on an externally funded research project.

The more time spent on research and scholarship, the higher the pay for faculty in public[52] and private colleges and universities over-

all (Table 5).[53] But this relationship did not hold for faculty at public[54] or private research universities,[55] liberal arts colleges, private comprehensives, and community and junior colleges.[56]

For full-time faculty members in public[57] and private institutions,[58] the more publications, the higher the compensation. This pattern held true in every type of public[59] and private college or university,[60] including comprehensives, liberal arts colleges, and even community colleges.[61]

Being a principal investigator on an externally funded research project meant earning a substantially higher basic salary in 1988 for faculty in public and private four-year institutions.[62] This pattern held true for faculty at all types of public institutions,[63] private research universities, and other four-year institutions.[64]

3. Administration and Service

Faculty members who spent the most time on administration[65] earned the highest basic salaries at public[66] and private four-year institutions[67] (Table 6). This pattern held true in all types of public four-year institutions,[68] varied substantially in private schools, and did not hold at community and junior colleges.[70] Time spent on service was not related to pay for faculty at public two- and four-year institutions. At private four-year schools, the most active faculty members received the least pay,[71] but this pattern did not hold by type of institution.

4. Correlational Analysis

Table 7 shows the intercorrelations between salary and teaching, research, administration, and service by type of institution. Pay and time spent on teaching and instruction were negatively related in all types of four-year institutions, except private liberal arts colleges. Hours spent in class per week was negatively, though weakly, related to pay for private institutions and for most publics [72] Student contact hours generated per semester was positively, though weakly, related to pay in each type of private institution except research universities, which showed a negligible correlation. Student contact hours were positively, though modestly, related to pay for faculty in public research universities and two-year colleges, but were unrelated to pay in other publics. Teaching only undergraduate students

TABLE 5

BASIC SALARY (MEANS), BY SOURCE OF CONTROL, TYPE OF INSTITUTION, AND RESEARCH-RELATED VARIABLES: PUBLIC AND PRIVATE FOUR-YEAR INSTITUTIONS

	Percent of Time Spent on Research and Scholarship							
	<5.0%	SE	5.0-15.9%	SE	16.0-33.9%	SE	>33.9%	SE
Public								
All four-year	$37,704	572	$40,267	543	$43,239	647	$46,806	656
Research	46,017	1,998	46,732	1,148	48,861	1,061	49,044	821
Doctoral	34,555	1,200	36,714	840	36,190	1,126	42,328	1,429
Comprehensive	36,414	574	38,042	722	38,512	807	40,657	1,395
Private								
All four-year	$35,984	1,022	$38,579	886	$45,486	1,177	$51,841	1,293
Research	44,839	5,160	52,969	3,642	56,559	2,698	52,405	1,556
Doctoral	34,113	2,356	38,746	1,554	40,696	1,609	43,733	2,887
Comprehensive	34,052	1,087	33,757	838	31,458	1,074	37,360	2,519
Liberal Arts	30,389	943	30,281	789	29,615	1,191	*	*
Other Four-Year	46,424	4,946	52,394	5,356	58,935	4,089	60,713	4,480

	Number of Refereed Publications (Career)							
	<2	SE	2-10	SE	11-29	SE	>29	SE
Public								
All four-year	$35,328	709	$37,741	442	$42,909	484	$52,807	704
Research	43,021	2,346	42,172	1,041	45,242	800	54,672	889
Doctoral	30,625	1,145	33,086	864	38,654	772	48,953	1,461
Comprehensive	34,419	823	36,515	497	41,920	751	47,940	1,605
Private								
All four-year	$30,282	571	$36,842	593	$42,791	889	$61,258	1,608
Research	38,944	3,268	40,693	1,949	46,204	1,755	66,018	2,185
Doctoral	30,372	1,237	38,568	1,359	41,590	2,198	47,623	2,833
Comprehensive	30,233	730	32,989	602	35,805	1,563	44,460	2,744
Liberal Arts	26,242	732	31,625	815	36,922	1,199	*	*
Other Four-Year	34,544	2,005	48,678	2,819	50,683	3,338	67,574	4,672

	Status as Principal Investigator (PI) on Research Project			
	Not PI	SE	PI	SE
Public				
All four-year	$39,686	314	$49,608	801
Research	45,217	591	52,947	1,079
Doctoral	35,470	535	44,193	1,704
Comprehensive	37,283	427	42,525	1,277
Private				
All four-year	$39,384	544	$54,966	1,655
Research	50,574	1,715	56,469	2,008
Doctoral	38,871	993	47,320	4,933
Comprehensive	33,331	580	36,288	1,931
Liberal Arts	30,536	566	31,572	1,494
Other Four-Year	49,456	2,448	68,240	5,240

Too few cases for reliable estimate
SOURCE: NSOPF, 1988

TABLE 6

BASIC SALARY (MEANS), BY SOURCE OF CONTROL, TYPE OF INSTITUTION, AND ADMINISTRATIVE AND SERVICE-RELATED VARIABLES: PUBLIC AND PRIVATE FOUR-YEAR INSTITUTIONS

	Percent of Time Spent on Administration							
	<5.0%	SE	5.0-9.9%	SE	10.0-19.9%	SE	>19.9%	SE
Public								
All four-year	$38,700	533	$40,459	630	$40,989	502	$48,349	768
Research	44,336	1,066	47,177	1,076	45,465	859	55,256	1,221
Doctoral	35,934	1,064	37,886	1,499	36,653	845	40,211	1,291
Comprehensive	35,985	663	34,788	645	37,210	651	43,558	1,142
Private								
All four-year	$38,109	989	40,331	1,182	42,825	898	48,855	1,325
Research	46,973	2,723	54,700	3,317	48,482	1,834	60,016	2,579
Doctoral	34,824	2,477	39,160	2,477	42,852	1,816	43,051	2,490
Comprehensive	31,964	932	32,127	1,017	30,954	880	38,956	1,395
Liberal Arts	32,517	1,291	27,012	906	30,782	797	32,430	1,288
Other Four-Year	*	*	*	*	58,716	3,516	62,272	5,733

	Percent of Time Committed to Public Service			
	<5.0	SE	≥5.0	SE
Public				
All four-year	$42,291	335	$41,636	885
Research	48,294	576	48,272	1,781
Doctoral	37,497	627	38,406	1,657
Comprehensive	37,932	441	37,548	985
Private				
All four-year	$43,444	600	$37,319	1,257
Research	52,673	1,374	*	*
Doctoral	40,325	1,213	*	*
Comprehensive	33,872	609	31,634	1,244
Liberal Arts	30,655	569	30,388	1,536
Other Four-Year	57,019	2,552	*	*

* Too few cases for reliable estimate
SOURCE: NSOPF, 1988

was positively, though modestly, related to pay in public and private comprehensives, and in public doctoral-granting universities, and negatively related to pay in other four-year schools. Teaching graduate students was much more positively related to pay at each type of institution.

Time spent on research and scholarship was positively related to pay in public and private doctoral-granting universities, liberal arts colleges, and "other four-year" schools. Publishing was strongly, positively related to

pay at each type of institution except community colleges. So was being a principal investigator on an externally funded grant, except in private comprehensives and liberal arts colleges.

Spending time on administration was positively related to pay at all types of schools except liberal arts colleges. Time spent on public service was unrelated to pay, except at "other four-year" schools where the relationship was negative.

Indicators of teaching activity and productivity were thus either negatively related, or unrelated, to pay, save for the small, positive correlation between hours spent in class and pay for faculty in public research universities. Conversely, time spent on research and scholarly productivity were positive indicators of pay. These results were remarkably stable across source of control—public and private— and type of institution.

Combined Relationships

Bivariate relationships, though suggestive, can mislead. Seniority may influence the positive correlation between career publications and compensation, for example. We therefore employed multiple regression models with basic salary as the criterion to examine the combined relationships between faculty and institutional demographics, length of service, faculty activity and workload, and faculty productivity with pay. The regression models accounted for between .30 and .60 of the variance in basic salary across the analyses, which focus separately on type of institution,

source of control, and program area.

1. Type of Institution

Publishing, next to working in a high-paying field, was the strongest predictor of pay for faculty members in public research universities. Next came time spent on administration, followed by seniority, and gender. Teaching only graduate students, being a principal investigator, and spending more time on research, less on teaching were also positively related to pay. Student contact hours was the only measure of teaching with even modest predictive value.

Private research universities showed a remarkably similar pattern. Publishing record and time spent on administration were the strongest positive predictors, followed this time by high paying field. Seniority, gender, and teaching only graduate students were positively related to pay. So was spending more time on public service, unlike the results for public institutions. Student contact hours was unrelated to pay.

TABLE 7

CORRELATIONS BETWEEN FACULTY WORKLOAD AND PRODUCTIVITY WITH BASIC SALARY, BY TYPE OF INSTITUTION

	1	2	3	4	5	6	7	8	9	10
Public										
All four-year	-.40	-.02	.07	.05	.27	.19	.38	.26	.23	-.04
Research	-.32	.11	.14	-.02	.17	.05	.34	.21	.17	-.04
Doctoral	-.32	-.10	-.04	09	.30	.17	.43	.26	.11	.04
Comprehensive	-.36	-.06	.01	.07	.33	.07	.23	.12	.34	-.01
Public two-year	-.06	-.04	.12	N.A.	N.A.	.07	.06	N.A.	.10	.00
Private										
All four-year	-.46	-.15	.06	.00	.28	.25	.46	.30	.21	-.11
Research	-.36	-.04	-.04	-.02	.22	.01	.44	.12	.25	.04
Doctoral	-.18	-.13	.09	.05	.20	.13	.19	.21	.09	-.03
Comprehensive	-.25	-.13	.12	.19	..38	-.01	.21	.06	.36	-.05
Liberal Arts	-.07	-.14	.04	.02	N.A.	.13	.32	.03	.05	-.08
Other four-year	-.41	-.04	.02	-.10	-.04	.10	.35	.32	.28	-.19

1 = Percent of time on teaching/instruction
2 = Number of hours teaching in class per week
3 = Student contact hours per semester
4 = Taught only undergraduate students
5 = Taught only graduate students
6 = Percent of time on research/scholarship
7 = Number of refereed publications, career

8 = Principal investigator on research project, Fall, 1987
9 = Percent of time on administration
10 = Percent of time on service

N.A. = Not Applicable

SOURCE: NSOPF, 1988.

Length of service was the strongest positive predictor of faculty pay in public doctoral-granting universities. Two research variables—teaching only graduate students and publishing—followed; spending more time on research and less on teaching also showed modest predictive power. Holding the doctorate, working in a high paying discipline, and gender were other strong positive predictors. Weaker positive predictors included teaching only undergraduates, spending more hours in class per week, and spending more time on administration. Only seniority and publishing significantly predicted pay in private doctoral-granting universities.

Seniority, followed by teaching only graduate students and spending more time on administration, dominated the list of positive pay predictors in public comprehensive colleges and universities. Demographic characteristics—holding the doctorate, working in a high paying field, gender, being a member of a racial or ethnic minority group, and working in a school that bargained collectively—showed substantial predictive ability. So did publishing, spending more time on research and less on teaching, and spending time in class.

Private comprehensives showed a similar profile. The only differences were the stronger relationship between pay and publishing, the positive relationship between student contact hours and pay, and the negative relationships between hours in class with pay, and between time spent on service and pay.

Important positive indicators of pay in liberal arts colleges included seniority, holding the Ph.D., and gender. Also helping: spending more time on research and less on teaching, publishing, spending less time in class while generating more student contact hours, and spending more time on administration.

Faculty in "other four-year" schools, principally medical and engineering schools, were rewarded for publishing, bringing in grant money, and spending time on administration. Being in an institution with collective bargaining also predicted higher pay. Seniority, holding the Ph.D., gender, and collective bargaining were positively related to pay in community and junior colleges. The only behavioral indicator of pay was spending more time on administration.

Table 8 summarizes the regression results by type of institution and source of control.

Seniority (all publics, four out of five privates) and demographic characteristics, including gender (all publics, three out of five privates) and high paying field (all publics, two out of five privates) were important pay predictors. Publishing (all publics, four out of five privates), spending more time on research and less on teaching (all publics, two out of five privates), teaching only graduate students (all publics, two out of five privates), and spending more time on administration (all publics, four out of five privates), were the most consistent positive behavioral predictors of pay. Hours spent in class was positively related to pay in public doctoral and comprehensive institutions, and negatively related to pay in two out of five types of private schools.

The research and scholarship-oriented model, these results suggest, dominated the reward structure at each type of four-year institution regardless of mission, including comprehensive and liberal arts colleges that historically emphasized undergraduate education. Teaching activity and productivity was largely a neutral or negative factor in pay, except for the modest positive relationship between pay and time spent in class or student contact hours generated at public institutions.

2. Program Area

To examine faculty rewards across discipline, regression analyses were carried out by type of academic program. Dummy variables indicating type of institution and source of control were added to the analyses. The results are discussed in descending order by average salary of the program area. (Table 9)

Publishing and teaching only graduate students were positive predictors of basic salary for faculty members in the health sciences. So were time spent on administration and gender. Engineering faculty were rewarded for doing more research and less teaching, publishing, and being a principal investigator on an externally funded grant. Senior faculty members received more pay than junior counterparts. Highly paid faculty members in agriculture and home economics had seniority, and were likely to be male and to hold the doctorate, to spend more time on administration, and to obtain external research funding. For business faculty members, publishing and holding the doctorate were positively related to pay.

Faculty members in the natural sciences

TABLE 8

SIGNIFICANT PREDICTORS OF BASIC SALARY—FOUR-YEAR AND TWO-YEAR INSTITUTIONS

	1	2	3	4	5	6	7	8	9	10	11	12	13	14	15
Public															
Research	R square = .38 N (unweighted) = 883														
Beta	3081	2679		6474			1453			1469	1359	3376	1115	3929	
Beta-Std.	.17	14		.29			.09			.10	.07	.24	.07	.22	
P level	.0001	.0001		.0001			.02			.002	.03	.0001	.02	.0001	
Doctoral	R square = .51 N (unweighted) = 499														
Beta	5181	1680		2130	2532		1547		1197	5056	2035	4111		989	
Beta-Std.	.37	.13		.16	.13		.09		.10	.27	.13	.21		.07	
P level	.0001	.0002		.0001	.0001		.03		.01	.0001	.001	.0001		.04	
Comprehensive	R square = .50 N (unweighted) = 960														
Beta	4759	1889	750	2309	3528	3959	1445			7603	1395	2493		2742	
Beta-Std.	.34	.15	.06	.21	.19	.15	.10			.30	.08	.12		.22	
P level	.0001	.0001	.01	.0001	.0001	.0001	.0003			.0001	.004	.0001		.0001	
Two-year	R square = .35 N (unweighted) = 371														
Beta	4885	868		1320		2712								1727	
Beta-Std.	.53	.09		.15		.12								.17	
P level	.0001	.03		.02		.008								.0004	
Private															
Research	R square = .52 N (unweighted) = 236														
Beta	4013	2954		7044						3583		5398		8561	3429
Beta-Std.	.19	.11		.25						.22		.33		.33	.12
P level	.001	.02		.0001						.0002		.0001		.0001	.02
Doctoral	R square = .36 N (unweighted) = 145														
Beta	3476											2540			
Beta-Std.	.27											.15			
P level	.001											.01			
Comprehensive	R square = .58 N (unweighted) = 438														
Beta	4156	1515		4502	2715	-3285	4757	1804	4454	2810	2040			981	-866
Beta-Std.	.35	.13		.26	.07	-.17	.15	.10	.19	.14	.08			.08	-.07
P level	.0001	.0002		.0001	.03	.0001	.0002	.007	.0001	.0001	.02			.05	.04
Liberal Arts	R square = .46 N (unweighted) = 341														
Beta	4847	2124	-1002	1331			-2185	3828			3357	5144		1695	
Beta-Std.	.45	.20	-.09	.15			-.15	.12			.20	.18		.15	
P level	.0001	.0001	.04	.001			.006	.03			.0001	.0001		.006	
Other Four-year	R square = .51 N (unweighted) = 103														
Beta							17308			-6436		7733	7373	11923	
Beta-Std.							.26			-.32		.37	.27	.31	
P level							.005			.003		.002	.005	.0003	

1 = Seniority
2 = Male
3 = Minority
4 = Highest degree—doctorate
5 = High paying field
6 = Union
7 = Number of hours teaching in class per week
8 = Student contact hours per semester
9 = Taught only undergraduate students
10 = Taught only graduate students
11 = More research/less teaching
12 = Number of refereed publications, career
13 = Principal investigator on research project, Fall, 1987
14 = Percent of time on administration
15 = Percent of time on service

N.A. = Not Applicable

SOURCE: NSOPF, 1988.

TABLE 9

SIGNIFICANT PREDICTORS OF BASIC SALARY, BY PROGRAM AREA—FOUR-YEAR INSTITUTIONS

	1	2	3	4	5	6	7	8	9	10	11	12	13	14	15
Agr./Home Eco. R square = .58 N (unweighted) = 157															
Beta	4495	3167		3636									3368	3476	
Beta-Std.	.33	.27		.22									.28	.26	
P level	.0001	.0001		.001									.0001	.0002	
Business R square = .45 N (unweighted) = 154															
Beta				2304							15964				
Beta-Std.				.16							.38				
P level				.04							.0001				
Education R square = .52 N (unweighted) = 341															
Beta	5107	1403	877	1053		2611	-2255		-1191		4961		1251		
Beta-Std.	.45	.15	.08	.10		.12	-.16		-.09		.28		.12		
P level	.0001	.0004	.04	.02		.005	.001		.03		.0001		.008		
Engineering R square = .46 N (unweighted) = 134															
Beta	3152		-1664							3061	4009	2417			
Beta-Std.	.29		-.17							.21	.26	.22			
P level	.001		.03							.03	.002	.01			
Fine Arts R square = .45 N (unweighted) = 232															
Beta	4253			1340		5530				4075		2952		1464	
Beta-Std.	.42			.18		.27				.21		.14		.15	
P level	.0001			.002		.0001				.001		.01		.02	
Health Sciences R square = .63 N (unweighted) = 185															
Beta		8533								5060		14084		5641	
Beta-Std.		.36								.27		.38		.23	
P level		.0001								.0001		.0001		0001	
Humanities R square = .48 N (unweighted) = 939															
Beta	5295	1013		1386		1731	-3792	4088				1900		1851	-1473
Beta-Std.	.45	.09		.11		.07	-.19	.12				.15		.16	-.10
P level	.0001	.0002		.0001		.009	.0001	.0001				.0001		.0001	.0004
Natural Sciences R square = .49 N (unweighted) = 441															
Beta	4502					4208				1612	1618	3326	2029	4472	
Beta-Std.	.30					.13				.12	.12	.31	.15	.25	
P level	.0001					.001				.007	.03	.0001	.0005	.0001	
Social Sciences R square = .50 N (unweighted) = 648															
Beta	5267	1015	1158	1665	980	3731	1042	1944							
Beta-Std.	.41	.08	.07	.07	.08	.26	.08	.17							
P level	.0001	.006		.02	.05					.006	.0001		.01	.0001	
Other Fields R square = .52 N (unweighted) = 271															
Beta	5246			1782	8438		-4177	6305				3662	2288		
Beta-Std.	.32			.12	.24		-.14	.16				.24	.10		
P level	.0001			.02	.0001		.02	.001				.0001	.03		

1 = Seniority
2 = Male
3 = Minority
4 = Highest degree—doctorate
5 = Doctoral-granting institution
6 = Union
7 = Number of hours eaching in class per week
8 = Student contact hours per semester
9 = Taught only undergraduate students

10 = Taught only graduate students
11 = More research/less teaching
12 = Number of refereed publications, career
13 = Principal investigator on research project, Fall, 1987
14 = Percent of time on administration
15 = Percent of time on service

N.A. = Not Applicable

SOURCE: NSOPF, 1988.

were rewarded for following a graduate-oriented research behavioral model—publishing, bringing in funded research projects, spending more time on research and less on teaching, and focusing on graduate instruction. Spending more time on administration, seniority, and working under a collective bargaining agreement were also positively related to pay.

Spending fewer hours in class while teaching more students was positively related to pay for faculty in "other fields." Publishing, obtaining research funding, seniority, holding the doctorate and working in a doctoral-granting institution were also positively related to salary.[73]

Faculty members in the social sciences who received the highest pay, like their colleagues in the natural sciences, emphasized publications, more research and less teaching, administration, and attaining funded research dollars. Seniority, gender, holding the doctorate, and working in a doctoral-granting institution were also positively related to salary. Positive demographic correlates with pay for faculty members in the humanities included seniority, gender, and holding the doctorate. Having more publications, spending more time on research and less on teaching, and spending fewer hours in class per week while generating more student contact hours were also positively related to basic salary. Working in an institution under collective bargaining and spending time on administration were positively related to pay. But pay and spending time on public service were negatively related.

Senior male faculty members in education who worked in institutions with collective bargaining agreements received the most pay; membership in an ethnic or racial minority and holding the doctorate were also positively related to salary. So were publishing, spending fewer hours in class per week, and devoting more time to administration. But teaching only undergraduates was negatively related to pay. Seniority, holding the doctorate, and working under a collective bargaining agreement were positively related to basic salary for faculty members in the fine arts. Spending more time on administration, teaching only graduate students, and publishing also translated into higher pay.

The predictors of pay for different program areas thus did not vary by source of control—public or private—or, for the most part, by type of institution. Publishing was the most frequent predictor of pay—nine out of ten program areas. Other recurring measures of research activity positively related to pay included obtaining funded research projects—five out of ten program areas—and spending more time on research, less on teaching—four out of ten program areas.

Indicators of teaching productivity and workload were usually unrelated or negatively related to pay. Hours spent in class per week was related to pay in only three program areas; the relationship was negative. The positive correlation between pay and student contact hours generated in two of three program areas suggests the wisdom of teaching larger classes. Teaching only graduate students was positively related to pay in three program areas. Spending time on administration, on the other hand, was a positive indicator of pay in seven out of ten program areas.

Working in an institution under collective bargaining was positively related to pay in education, fine arts, the humanities, and the natural sciences. Collective bargaining may therefore be a particularly important resource for faculty members in lower paying fields. Seniority and holding the doctorate predicted income in eight and seven out of ten program areas, respectively. Being a male had the same effect in five out of ten.

CONCLUSIONS

Research and scholarship—as well as seniority and gender—were key determinants of faculty pay, regardless of institutional type or mission, source of control, or program area. Except for community colleges, where experience and length of service predicted higher pay, faculty members who spent more time on research and who published the most were paid more than their teaching-oriented colleagues. Norms developed during graduate training, usually in doctoral-granting, research institutions, resist the different norms applied during employment. Also, apparent differences in mission between, for example, comprehensives and research institutions, may not be real: research productivity was an equally important pay determinant at nondoctoral institutions and at elite research universities. Our findings mainly supported proposition two—teaching was a neutral factor in pay—and proposition three—teaching was negatively related to pay. The only support for proposition one was the modest positive relationship between classroom productivity and pay in public four-year institutions.[74]

Making teaching the primary function of faculty life requires a radical shift in faculty reward structures, even at institutions that profess the centrality of undergraduate teaching. Even modest efforts to revitalize undergraduate education or to restore a balance to teaching in the faculty reward structure, directly confront the prevalent view—that faculty members should be judged principally by their research and publishing activity.[75]

AUTHOR'S NOTES

Data were collected under a contract supported by the National Center for Education Statistics. Grants from TIAA-CREF and from OERI, U.S. Department of Education (as part of the National Center on Postsecondary Teaching, Learning and Assessment) supported the analyses. The views expressed in this paper are solely those of the author.

NOTES

[1] Study Group on the Conditions of Excellence in American Higher Education, 1984.

[2] Boyer, 1987.

[3] Jacobsen, 1992; Huber, 1992, for example.

[4] Carnegie, 1989.

[5] Bok, 1992, 16.

[6] See, for example, Carnegie, 1989.

[7] Russell, Cox, and Boismier, 1990, 12-13, on department chairs. Bowen and Schuster, 1986, Cook, Kinnetz, and Owens-Misner, 1990, and Peters and Mayfield, 1982 on faculty perceptions.

[8] Inflation: American Association of University Professors, 1989; Armey, 1983; California State Postsecondary Education Commission, 1989; College and University Personnel Association (CUPA), 1986a, 1986b; Dillon and Marsh, 1981; Hansen, 1985; Keister and Keister, 1989. Shortages: Bowen and Sosa 1990; Fairweather, 1989; Lozier and Dooris, 1988. Discrimination: Daymont and Andrisani, 1984; Elmore and Blackburn, 1983; Gordon and Morton, 1974; White, 1990. Merit pay: Koehler, 1986. Mobility: Breneman and Youn, 1988; Burke, 1988; Ehrenberg, Kasper, and Rees, 1991; Matier, 1990; Solomon, 1978. Hiring policies: Wyer and Conrad, 1984.

[9] Kasten's 1984 review included Fulton and Trow, 1974; Katz, 1973; Rossman, 1976; Siegfried and White, 1973; Tuckman, Gapinski, and Hagemann, 1977; Tuckman and Hagemann, 1976; Tuckman and Leahy, 1975.

[10] Positive: Hoyt, 1974; Kasten, 1984;Katz, 1973; Koch and Chizmar, 1973; Rossman, 1976; Salthouse, McKeachie, and Yin, 1978; Siegfried and White, 1973. Unrelated: Tuckman, Gapinski, and Hagemann, 1977; Tuckman and Hagemann, 1976. Negative: Marsh and Dillon, 1980.

[11] Berman and Skeff, 1988; see also O'Connell, 1983.

[12] Bowen and Schuster, 1986, suggest this categorization.

[13] Russell, Fairweather, Cox, Williamson, Boismier, and Javitz, 1990, 97-98.

[14] Type of Institutions: Carnegie, 1987. Confirmation as Key variable: Fulton and Trow, 1984.

[15] NSOPF asked, "For the calendar year 1987, what were your gross earnings before taxes for your basic salary at this institution?" Studies that used basic salaries as a compensation indicator: CUPA, 1986a, 1986b; Dillon and Marsh, 1981; Gordon and Morton, 1974; Hansen, 1985; Katz, 1973; Keister and Keister, 1989; Siegfried and White, 1973.

[16] Rank: Fulton and Trow, 1974; discipline: Fulton and Trow, 1974, Gordon and Morton, 1974; Hansen 1985; gender: Daymont and Andrisani, 1984; Gordon and mortorn, 1974; ethnicity: Gordon and Morton, 1974.

[17] High paying field was scored as follows: 1 = program areas with average salaries above the overall mean (engineering and health sciences), 0 = program areas with average salaries at the overall mean (agriculture/home economics, business, natural sciences), -1 = program areas with average salaries below the overall mean (education, fine arts, humanities, social sciences, other fields).

[18] See Baldridge, Curtis, Ecker, and Riley, 1978; Fulton and Trow, 1974.

[19] See Bayer, 1973; Fulton and Trow, 1974.

[20] See Bayer, 1973.

[21] See Baldridge et al., 1978; Ladd and Lipset, 1975.

[22] See Ladd, 1979.

[23] See Baldridge et al., 1978; Bayer, 1973.

[24] Correlations greater than ±.30. Basic salary: percent time, teaching (-.43); publications, career (.42). Age: time in rank (.67); years at institution (.69). Time in rank: years at institution (.65). Percent time, teaching: taught only graduate students (-.34); percent time, research (-.62); publications, career (-.31); principal investigator (-.36); percent time, administration (-.42). Hours in class: student contact hours

(-.45). Percent time, research: publications, career (.33); principal investigator (.41).

25 Composite variables: rotated weights for principal components, four- and two-year institutions (only weights >.10 and <.97 reported, starred weights = meaningful contributor to component, source: NSOPE, 1988): Four-year institutions: percent time, teaching: more research/less teaching (-.83*); percent time, administration (-.41); percent time service (-.11). Percent time, research: more research/less teaching (.95*); percent time, administration (-.30). Time in rank: seniority (.88*). Age: publications (.85*). Two-year institutions: Age: male (-.10); classroom productivity (.12); minority faculty member (-.14); publications (-.12); seniority (.77*). Time in rank: minority faculty member (.11); seniority (.84*). Years in current job: seniority (.89*). Percent time, teaching: percent time, research (-.38); highest degree—doctorate (-.32); more administration/less teaching (-.63*). Hours in class per week: male (.13); highest degree—doctorate (-.23); more administration/less teaching (-.13); classroom productivity (.76*); seniority (-.12). Student contact hours: highest degree—doctorate (.17); classroom productivity (.90*). Percent time, administration: percent time, research (-.15); percent time, service (-.14); more administration/less teaching (1.00*).

26 The criterion for minimally acceptable level of significance for statistical tests was p < .05. When multiple pairs were compared simultaneously, such as in the comparison of each program area mean with the overall average, the acceptable significance level was increased by the Bonferroni adjustment (i.e., dividing the level of significance by the number of multiple comparisons). The presentation of t-test results for mean differences or for differences between proportions is as follows: t(comparison reference) = t-value, p-value (level of significance), where, for example, the comparison might be research universities versus comprehensive colleges and universities [referred to as t(res/comp)]. The relevant symbols are: res = research universities, doc = doctoral-granting universities, comp = comprehensive colleges and universities, lib = liberal arts colleges, other = other four-year institutions, cc = two-year or community colleges. The footnotes only show statistically significant differences.

27 The distributions of some variables did not permit use of quartiles for analyses. Few faculty members in four-year institutions spent much time on service, so the variable was split into two parts: respondents who spent more than five percent of their time on service, and respondents who spent less than five percent. For faculty members in two-year colleges, percent of time spent on research, percent of time spent on service, and total publica-

tions (career) were split into three groups: one-half of two-year college faculty in the first group and the remainder into the top two quartiles. This procedure was required because almost one-half of all two-year college faculty neither spent any time on research or service, nor published.

28 Population estimates from survey data were based on weights derived from the inverse of the probability of a faculty member in a particular type of institution being selected. The probability of selecting a faculty member for the sample was a function of the odds of an institution being selected from the universe of accredited postsecondary institutions, the probability of a faculty member being selected from the population of faculty within his or her institution, and the sampling rate for employment status (full- or part-time) and program area (Russell, Fairweather, Cox et al., 1990, 99).

29 Previous research demonstrated the importance of controlling for type of institution in analyses of faculty behavior (Baldridge et al., 1978; Bayer, 1973; Fulton and Trow, 1974; Ladd, 1979).

30 Estimates of regression coefficients were unbiased. A study of residuals showed no evidence of heterosedasticity or for the need to transform variables. The analysis of residuals showed no evidence of interaction effects or for the need to explore quadratic or other polynomial equations.

31 $t(other/res) = 2.55$, $p < .05$; $t(res/doc) = 14.89$, $p < .001$; $t(doc/comp) = 2.65$, $p < .01$, $t(comp/lib) = 9.84$, $p < .001$.

32 Private: $t(res/doc) = 7.15$, $p < .001$; $t(doc/comp) = 5.34$ $p < .0001$, $t(comp/lib) = 3.81$, $p < .001$. Public: $t(res/doc) = 13.30$, $p < .001$.

33 $t(education) = -10.05$, $p < .001$; $t(engineering) = 3.41$, $p < .001$; $t(fine arts) = 13.13$, $p < .001$; $t(health sciences) = 7.89$, $p < .001$; $t(humanities) = 13.28$, $p < .001$; $t(social sciences) = 7.96$, $p < .001$; $t(other) = 3.87$, $p < .001$.

34 Promotion: Bowen and Shuster, 1986; Boyer, 1987; Carnegie, 1989. Pay: Kasten, 1984.

35 All types of publics: $t(35/35-52) = -10.39$, $p < .001$; $t(35-52/53-71) = -7.55$, $p < .001$; $t(53-71/72) = < 3.99$, $p < .001$. By type of institution: Research: $t(35/35-52) = <6.34$, $p < .001$; $t(35-52/53-71) = -2.73$, $p < .01$; $t(53-71/72) = -2.70$, $p < .01$; Doctoral: $t(35/35-52) = -3.36$, $p < .001$; $t (35-52/53-71) = -4.00$, $p < .001$; Comprehensive: $t(35/35-52) = -5.60$, $p < .001$; $t(35-52/53-71) = -3.81$, $p < .001$.

36 $t(35/35-52) = -7.46$, $p < .001$; $t(35-52/53-71) = -5.86$, $p < .001$; $t(53-71/72) = -4.47$, $p < ,001$.

37 Research: $t(35/35-52) = -3.63$, $p < .001$; $t(35-52/53-71) = 5.13$, $p < .001$; $t(35-52/53-71) = 2.54$, $p < .05$.

[38] Basic salary (means), by teaching-related variables at public two-year colleges (Source: NSOPF, 1988): Percent time, teaching: < 65% = $34,585 (SE=706); 65-75% = $34,519 (SE=670); 76-89% = $31,984 (SE=874); > 89% = $36,107 (SE=688). Hours per week teaching in class: <12 = $34,124 (SE=790); 12-14 = $35,150 (SE=881); 15-18 = $34,017 (SE=623); > 18 = $33,450 (SE=702). Number of student contact hours per week: < 262 = $32,872 (SE=717); 262-376 = $32,543 (SE=731); 377-504 = $34,287 (SE=806); > 504 = $36,804 (SE=628).

[39] t(6/6-8) = -8.13, p < .001; t(6-8/9-11) = -7.02, p < .001.

[40] t(6/6-8) = <4.23, p < .001; t(6-8/9-11) = -3.94, p < .001; t(9-11/12) = -2.20, p < .05.

[41] Research: t(6/6-8) = -4.60, p < .001; t(6-8/9-11) = -5.21, p < .0 -4.91, p < .001; t(218-359/360) = 4.50, p < .001.

[44] t(110/110-217 = -9.94, p < .001; t(218-359/360) = 5.91, p < .001.

[45] Research: t(110/111-2170 = -6.16, p < .001; t(218-359/360) = 10.62, p < .001; Doctoral: t(110-217/218-359) = -2.70, p < .01; Comprehensive: t(110/110-217) = -4.02, p < .001.

[46] Research: t(110/110-217) = -4.06, p < .001.

[47] t(262/505) = 4.13, p < .001.

[48] t(grad/undergrad) = 5.30, p < .001; t(grad/both) = 8.39, p < .001.

[49] t(grad/undergrad) = 5.24, p < .001; t(grad/both) = 8.06, p < .001.

[50] Research: t(grad/undergrad) = 2.92, p < .01; t(grad/both) = 3 82, p < .001; Doctoral: t(grad/undergrad) = 3.15, p < .01; t(grad/both) = 4.83, p < p < .001. Comprehensive: t(grad/undergrad) = 2.86, p < .01; t(grad/both) = 3.53, p < .001.

[51] Research: t(grad/undergrad) = 1.99, p < .05; t(grad/both) = 3.28, p < .01.

[52] t(5/5-15) = 3.25, p < .01; t(5-15/16-33) = 3.52, p < .001; t(16-33/34) = 3.87, p. < .001.

[53] t(5-15/16-3×3) = 4.69, p < .001; t(16-33/34) = 3.63, p < .001.

[54] Doctoral: t(16-33/34) = 3.37, p < .001; comprehensive: t(5/34) = 2.81, p < .01.

[55] Doctoral: t(5/16-33) = 2.31, p < .05; t(5/34) = 2.58, p < .01; Other: t(5/34) = 2.14, p < .05.

[56] Basic salary (means), by research-related variables at public two-year colleges (Source: NSOPF, 1988): Percent time, research/scholarship: < 1%= $34,155 (SE=521); 1-4%= $32,857 (SE=724); > 5%= $34,491 (SE=744). Number of refereed publications (career): 0=$32,749 (SE=515); 1-2=$35,319 (SE=890); > 2= $36,266 (SE=765).

[57] t(2/2-10) = -2.97, p < .001; t(2-10/11-29) = -7.88, p < .001; t(11-29/30) = -13.75, p < .001.

[58] t(2/2-10) = -7.97, p < .001; t(2-10/11-29) = -5.57, p < .001; t(11-29/30) = -10.05, p < .001.

[59] Research: t(2-10/11-29) = -2.34, p < .05; t(11-29/30)= -7.88, p < .001; Doctoral· t(2-10/11-29) = -4.80, p < .001; t(11-29/30) = -6.23, p < .001; Comprehensive: t(2/2-10) = -2.18, p < .05; t(2-10/11-29) = -6.00, p < .001; t(11-29/30) = -3.71, p < .001.

[60] Research: t(2-10/11-29) = -2.10, p < .05; t(11-29/30) = -7.07, p I < .001; Doctoral: t(2-10/11-29) = -4.46, p < .001; t(2/30) = -5.58, p < .001; t(2-10/30) = -2.88, p < .01; Comprehensive: t(2/2-10) = -2.91, p < .01; t(11-29/30) = -2.74, p < .01; Liberal Arts: t(2/2-10) = -4.75, p < .001; t(2-10/11-29) = -3.65, p < .001; Other: t(2/11-29) = -2.12, p < .05; t(11-29/30) = -2.26, p < .05.

[61] t(0/1-2) = -2.50, p < .05.

[62] All publics: t(PI) = 11.54, p < .001; All privates: t(PI) = 8.94, p < .001.

[63] Research: t(PI) = 6.28, p < .001; Doctoral: t(PI) = 4.88, p < .001; Comprehensive: t(PI) = 3.89, p < .001.

[64] Research: t(PI) = 2.23, p < .05; Other: t(PI) = 3.25, p < .01.

[65] Department chairs without instructional duties were excluded from these analyses.

[66] t(5/5-9) = -2.13, p < .05; t(10-19/20) = -8.02, p < .001.

[67] t(10-19/20) = -3.77, p < .001.

[68] Research: t(10-19/20) = -6.56, p < .001; Doctoral: t(10-19/20) = -2.31, p < .2.31, p < .05; Comprehensive: t(5-9/10-19) = -2.64, p < .01; t(10-19/20) = -4.83, p < .001.

[69] Doctoral: t(5/20) = -3.15, p < .01; Comprehensive: t(10-19/20) = -4.85, p < .001.

[70] Basic salary (means), by administration and service-related variables at public two-year colleges (Source: NSOPF, 1988): Percent time, administration: < 2%= $33,729 (SE=751); 2.0-5.1%= $33,829 (SE=797); 5.2-100.0%= $34,320 (SE=749); ≥ 11.%= $34,615 (SE=725). Percent time, public service: 0= $34,563 (SE=471); 1.0-3.5%= $33,214 (SE=989); ≥ 3.6%= $33,934 (SE=747).

[71] t = 4.40, p < .001.

[72] The exception: public research universities where time spent in class per week showed a positive, though weak, relationship to pay.

[73] Doctoral-granting institution: Beta = 8438; standardized Beta = .24; P level = .0001.

[74] These results are consistent with prior research that showed teaching as a negative or a neutral factor in pay. Marsh and Dillon, 1980; Tuckman,

Gapinski, and Hagemann, 1977; Tuckman and Hagemann, 1976.

[75] Boyer, 1987, and Bowen and Schuster, 1986, respectively.

REFERENCES

American Association of University Professors, "The Annual Report on the Economic Status of the Profession, 1988-89," *Academe*, 75 (2) (1989)

Armey, R.K., "Comparing Real Income: The Faculty and the Administration, *Change*, 15 (1983), 36-40.

Baldridge, J.V., Curtis, D., Ecker, G, and Riley, G., *Policy Making and Effective Leadership* (San Francisco, Calif.: Jossey-Bass, 1978).

Bayer, A.E., *Teaching Faculty in Academe: 1972-1973*. *ACE Research Reports*, 8 (1973), 1-68.

Berman, J., and Skeff, K.M., "Developing the Motivation for Improving University Teaching," *Innovative Higher Education*, 12 (2) (1988), 114-125.

Bok, D., "Reclaiming the Public Trust," *Change*, 24 (2) (1992), 12-19.

Bowen, H.R., and Schuster, J.H., *American Professors: A National Resource Imperiled* (New York, N.Y.: Oxford University Press, 1986).

Bowen, W. G., and Sosa, J.A., *Prospects for Faculty in Arts and Sciences* (Princeton, N.J.: Princeton University Press, 1989).

Boyer, E.L., *College: The Undergraduate Experience in America* (New York, N.Y.: Harper and Row, 1987).

Breneman, D.W., and Youn, Ted I.K., *Academic Labor Markets and Careers* (New York, N.Y.: Palmer Press, 1988).

Burke, D.L., *A New Academic Marketplace* (Westport, Conn: Greenwood Press, 1988).

California State Postsecondary Education Commission, *Faculty Salaries in California's Public Universities, 1988-89* (Sacramento, Calif.: California State Postsecondary Education Commission, 1989).

Carnegie Foundation for the Advancement of Teaching, *A Classification of Institutions of Higher Education* (Princeton, N.J.: Carnegie Foundation for the Advancement of Teaching, 1987).

___ , *The Condition of the Professoriate: Attitudes and Trends, 1989* (Princeton, N.J.: Carnegie Foundation for the Advancement of Teaching, 1989).

College and University Personnel Association, *National Faculty Salary Survey by Discipline and Rank in State Colleges and Universities, 1985-86* (Washington, DC: College and University Personnel Association, 1986a).

___ , *National Faculty Salary Survey by Discipline and Rank in Private Colleges and Universities, 1985-86* (Washington, D.C.: College and University Personnel Association, 1986b).

Cook, E.P., Kinnetz, P., and Owens-Misner, N., "Faculty Perceptions on Job Rewards and Instructional Development Activities," *Innovative Higher Education*, 14 (2) (1990), 123-130.

Daymont, T., and Andrisani, P., "Job Preferences, College Major and the Gender Gap in Earnings," *Journal of Human Resources*, 19 (1984), 408-428.

Dillon, K.E., and Marsh, H.W., "Faculty Earnings Compared with Those of Nonacademic Professionals," *Journal of Higher Education*, 52 (1981), 615-623.

Ehrenberg, R., Kasper, H., and Rees, D., "Faculty Turnover at American Colleges and Universities: Analyses of AAUP Data," *Economics of Education Review*, 10 (2) (1991), 99-110.

Elmore, C.J., and Blackburn, R.T., "Black and White Faculty in White Research Universities," *Journal of Higher Education*, 54 (1983), 1-15.

Fairweather, J.S., "Academic Research and Instruction: The Industrial Connection," *Journal of Higher Education*, 60 (1989), 388-407.

Fulton, O., and Trow, M., "Research Activity in Higher Education," *Sociology of Education*, 47 (1974), 29-73.

Gordon, N., and Morton, T., "Faculty Salaries: Is There Discrimination by Sex, Race and Discipline?" *American Economic Review*, 64 (1974), 419-427.

Hansen, W.L., "Salary Differences Across Disciplines," *Academe*, 71 (4) (1985), 6-7.

Hoyt, D.P., "Interrelationships Among Instructional Effectiveness, Publication Record, and Monetary Reward," *Research in Higher Education*, 2 (1) (1974), 81-89.

Huber, R.H., *How Professors Play the Cat Guarding the Cream*, (Fairfax, Va: George Mason University Press, 1992).

Jacobsen, R.L., "Colleges Face New Pressure to Increase Faculty Productivity," *Chronicle of Higher Education*, 38 (April 15, 1992), 1.

Kasten, K.L., "Tenure and Merit Pay as Rewards for Research, Teaching, and Service at a Research University," *Journal of Higher Education*, 55 (1984), 500-514.

Katz, D.A., "Faculty Salaries, Promotion, and Productivity at a Large University," *American Economic Review*, 63 (1973), 469-477.

Keister, S.D., and Keister, L.G., "Faculty Compensation and the Cost of Living in American Higher Education," *Journal of Higher Education*, 60 (1989), 458-474.

Koch, J.V., and Chizmar, J.F., "The Influence of Teaching and Other Factors Upon Absolute Salaries and Salary Increments at Illinois State University," *Journal of Economic Education*, 5 (1) (1973), 27-34.

Koehler, W.F., "From Evaluations to an Equitable Selection of Merit-Pay Recipients and Increments," *Research in Higher Education*, 25 (1986), 253-263.

Ladd, E.C., Jr., "The Work Experience of American College Professors: Some Data and an Argument," *Current Issues in Higher Education* (Washington, D.C.: American Association of Higher Education, 1979).

Ladd, E.C., Jr., and Lipset, S M., *The Divided Academy* (New York, N.Y.: McGraw-Hill, 1975).

Lozier, G.G., and Dooris, M.J., *Is Higher Education Confronting Faculty Shortages?* (Houston, Tex.: Institute for Higher Education Law and Governance, 1988).

Marsh, H.W., and Dillon, K.E., "Academic Productivity and Faculty Supplemental Income," *Journal of Higher Education*, 51 (1980), 546-555.

Matier, M.W., "Retaining Faculty: A Tale of Two Campuses," *Research in Higher Education*, 30 (1990), 39-60.

O'Connell, C., "College Policies Off-Target in Fostering Faculty Development," *Journal of Higher Education*, 54 (1983), 662-675.

Peters, D.S., and Mayfield, J.R., "Are There Any Rewards for Teaching?" *Improving College and University Teaching*, 30 (3) (1982), 105-110.

Rossman, J.E., "Teaching, Publication, and Rewards at a Liberal Arts College," *Improving College and University Teaching*, 24 (4) (1976), 238-240.

Russell, S.H., Cox, R.C., and Boismier, J.M., *A Descriptive Report of Academic Departments in Higher Education Institutions* (Washington, D.C.: U.S. Department of Education, 1990).

Russell, S.H., Fairweather, J.S., Cox, R.S., Williamson, C., Boismier, J., and Javitz, H., *Faculty in Higher Education Institutions* (Washington, D.C.: U.S. Department of Education, 1990).

Salthouse, T.A., McKeachie, W.J., and Lin, Y., "An Experimental Investigation of Factors Affecting University Promotion Decisions," *Journal of Higher Education*, 49, (1978), 177-183.

Siegfried, J.J., and White, K.J., "Teaching and Publishing as Determinants of Academic Salaries," *Journal of Economic Education*, 4 (2) (1973), 90-98.

Solomon, L.C., "Turnover of Senior Faculty in Departments of Social and Physical Science and Engineering," *Research in Higher Education*, 8 (1978), 343-355.

Study Group of the Conditions of Excellence in American Higher Education, *Involvement in Learning: Realizing the Potential of American Higher Education* (Washington, D.C.: U.S. Department of Education, 1984).

Tuckman, H.P., Gapinski, J.H., and Hagemann, R.P., "Faculty Skills and the Salary Structure in Academe: A Market Perspective," *American Economic Review*, 67 (1977), 692-702.

Tuckman, H.P., and Hagemann, R.P., "An Analysis of the Reward Structure in Two Disciplines," *Journal of Higher Education*, 47 (1976), 447-464.

Tuckman, H.P., and Leahy, J., "What is an Article Worth?" *Journal of Political Economy*, 83 (1975), 951-967.

White, C.S. "Salary and Gender Discrimination in a Public Institution," *CUPA Journal* 41, (1990), 17-25.

Wyer, J.C., and Conrad, C.F., "Institutional Inbreeding Reexamined," *American Education Research Journal*, 21 (1984), 213-225.

Yuker, H.E., *Faculty Workload: Research, Theory, and Interpretation*, ASHE-ERIC Higher Education Research Report No. 10 (Washington, D.C.: Association for the Study of Higher Education, 1984).

Faculty at Work: Teaching, Research, and Service

JE   Robert Boice

New Faculty as Teachers

In the midst of growing concerns for college teaching [1] we produce more and more useful advice about ways to improve instruction [8]. Yet, we know almost nothing about how (and how quickly) professors establish their teaching styles. And, it follows, we too rarely consider strategies for dealing with their teaching in its formative stages.

This article depicts the experience of new faculty as teachers over periods of one and two years and across two large campuses. It shows a surprisingly slow pattern of establishing comfort and student approval, of moving beyond defensive strategies including overpreparation of lecture content, and of looking for supports in improving teaching. The few prior efforts at observing new faculty have been enlightening but limited to smaller groups, to fewer observations, or to nonteaching activities [3, 5, 6].

The aim of this study, though, is not simply to document the teaching experiences of new faculty but to answer four related questions. First, do initial teaching patterns, adaptive and maladaptive, tend to persist? Second, what can we learn from the experiences of new faculty who master teaching quickly and enjoyably? Third, how does success in teaching correspond to prowess in areas including the establishment of collegial supports and of outputs in scholarly writing? And, fourth, how do initial teaching experiences compare at a "teaching" (comprehensive) and at a "research" (doctoral) campus?

Robert Boice is director of the Faculty Instructional Support Office and professor of psychology at the State University of New York, Stony Brook.

Journal of Higher Education, Vol. 62, No. 2 (March/April 1991)

Methods

The four cohorts of new faculty described here came from two campuses, (1) a comprehensive university with some thirty-five thousand students and about one thousand faculty and (2) a doctoral campus with some fifteen thousand students and some one thousand faculty. Both campuses hired similar numbers of new tenure-track faculty during the study years of 1985 to 1990, from fifty to seventy per year.

Cohorts

Table 1 shows the composition of the four cohorts, two of them from the former campus and two of them from the latter campus. Cohorts 2 and 3 overlapped as the author transferred his faculty development programs from the first campus to the second during 1988–89.

At Campus 1, all but one to three new faculty per cohort volunteered for interviews conducted in their offices over successive semesters. The few individuals who did not participate were inaccessible because of their commitments off campus. At Campus 2, all but twelve to fifteen new faculty per cohort volunteered to participate in the same format of interviews. Campus 2, much less publicly committed to teaching than Campus 1, differed most obviously in the influence of department chairpeople; at Campus 2 (but never at Campus 1), five of some forty chairs advised their new faculty not to participate in a program that might interfere with research productivity.

In most other ways the two groups of new faculty were alike. They came to campus with similar levels of scholarly productivity, of teaching experience, and of doctoral credentials from prestigious universities. New faculty at both campuses also declared an interest in teaching well and in establishing themselves as visible members of their disci-

TABLE 1

Distribution of Background Types of Interviewees across Cohorts for Both Campuses (number of participants during second years are shown parenthetically)

	Background Category		
Year cohort began, Campus 1	Inexperienced	Returning	Experienced
1987	14 (10)	5 (3)	29 (28)
1988	19 (14)	2 (2)	47 (46)
Year cohort began, Campus 2			
1988	19 (17)	6 (5)	16 (15)
1989	25	4	11

plines. However, newcomers at Campus 1 differed in that they expressed an interest in avoiding the pressures for publication existing at research universities such as Campus 2.

At both study campuses, a critical distinction emerged between types of new faculty. They differentiated themselves as (a) inexperienced (with less than two years beyond the doctorate, (b) returning (from careers outside academe and/or teaching), and (c) experienced (including full-time teaching at another campus).

The most obvious difference between the two campuses was teaching load. Campus 1 had an official load of twelve classroom hours a week (that is, four separate courses per semester). Most of its new hires received three hours of release time in year 1 on campus; thereafter, only a minority of successful applicants who demonstrated productive beginnings continued to receive reduced teaching loads. Campus 2 had a two-course (or six hours a week) load except for some humanities faculty who carried three courses. The majority of new faculty at Campus 2 in the science areas had teaching loads of one course or less for their first year or two on campus.

The key faculty under study here are the inexperienced newcomers and returning newcomers; experienced new faculty serve as comparisons. Most inexperienced and returning new faculty in this sample had minimal experience as classroom teachers during graduate school ($N=$ 17 at Campus 1 and $N=12$ at Campus 2 taught their own classes as graduate students). Fewer still reported any systematic training including teaching practica ($N=8$ at Campus 1; $N=5$ at Campus 2).

Interview Formats

The interview format resembles that used in prior research with new faculty by a variety of researchers [7]; copies can be obtained from the author. Each participant in this study was interviewed during successive semesters. Essentially, I asked new faculty about their experiences and plans as teachers, colleagues, and scholarly writers. These visits to new faculty, however, consisted of much more than preplanned interviewing. Interactions usually lasted one hour, often longer, always in informal fashion with prods for open-ended answers beyond responses to structured questions. Thus, except for replies to set questions, individuals chose what to emphasize and develop.

Participants were recruited by means of phone calls in which they were asked to give an hour of their time for a confidential interview about their experience as a new faculty member on campus. Where new faculty expressed ambivalence about participating, the author visited them during their posted office hours to repeat the request. This modicum of social pressure was sufficient to enlist almost all faculty who would otherwise not have participated; the result was a representative sample of individuals who volunteered and who, invariably, indicated satisfaction in having done so. As indicated above, this strategy worked except in some cases at Campus 2 where chairs (distributed across campus) had cautioned their new faculty not to participate.

A critical condition for all new faculty was the assurance that I would not relate information about the participation or answers of individuals to anyone. Administrators, who routinely asked about the involvement or responses of individual faculty, were given the kinds of generalized and/or anonymous results reported here.

My own role in this study was multifaceted and reflects my training, first as an ethologist and then as a psychotherapist; that is, I interacted with new faculty as an observer, researcher, helper, and colleague. I began initial interviews by explaining this complexity of interactive stances as part of explaining the project's purpose. No one expressed discomfort with my multifaceted role or with the prospect of waiting to learn the results of repeated interviews in manuscripts like this one.

Results

Interview formats produced both qualitative and quantitative results. Interviewees responded to requests to rate experiences on 10-point Likert scales (for example, rate your recent comfort in the classroom), to specify experiences including teaching practices (for example, number of colleagues with whom they discussed teaching), and to elaborate on quantitative answers (for example, "how do you suppose students would describe you as a teacher?").

Analysis of these interviews is presented in terms of successive semesters on campus. Within each semester (for example, the first semester on campus), data are presented as a conglomerate of all cohorts studied; then, contrasts are drawn between backgrounds (as inexperienced, returning, and experienced), and between campuses. Where appropriate, individualistic patterns of new faculty are described to give a sense of how new faculty (1) experienced problems and supports as teachers, (2) showed ready promise as successes or as failures at teaching, and (3) responded to opportunities for help as teachers.

First Semester

Initial contacts with new faculty at orientation workshops (before the onset of formal interviews) revealed various common concerns. Because both campuses required publication for tenure, newcomers supposed that they would feel more pressured to write than to do anything else during coming semesters; they worried that teaching would suffer in the process. No one at orientation expressed concerns about social supports; in the exuberance of meeting other new faculty, campuses seemed easy places to make friends. Moreover, new faculty just arriving on campus often reaffirmed their attraction to academe as a place where autonomy is highly valued (as in this typical comment during orientation by an inexperienced new faculty member at Campus 1):

> I'm not sure that I need this sort of thing [that is the orientation day]. I have people I can rely on back at —— if I need them, but I think I know what I need to do. [In response to my question about whether she would be interested in having a mentor on campus?] No, I think I am too busy for that . . . and I'm not sure what such a person could tell me. That's why I decided to become a professor; I like to have good people around me but I prefer to manage on my own.

By the midpoint of the first semester, when interviews were well underway, two surprising realities had set in. First, a lack of collegial support and of intellectual stimulation dominated complaints. Second, investments in lecture preparation dominated workweeks. Writing and other things that "could wait" were put aside until new faculty had time and energy left over from teaching.

Collegial support. One specification of new faculty's experience can be seen in analyses of reported collegial help in terms of advice about teaching (see table 2). Three results stand out. First, general levels of

TABLE 2

Percentage of New Faculty Reporting High Overall Levels and Specific Kinds of Collegial Support in Terms of Advice Offered by Senior Colleagues

Category		Campus 1	Campus 2
High overall support:	1987	48% (N = 23)	
	1988	48% (N = 33)	42% (N = 17)
	1989		40% (N = 16)
Type of advice:			
None:	1987	10% (N = 5)	
	1988	19% (N = 13)	18% (N = 7)
	1989		20% (N = 8)
Gossip and politics:	1987	54% (N = 26)	
	1988	50% (N = 34)	59% (N = 24)
	1989		47% (N = 16)
Teaching-related:	1987	4% (N = 2)	
	1988	3% (N = 2)	4% (N = 2)
	1989		6% (N = 3)

collegial support evidenced as advice were anything but universal; senior faculty were unlikely to say much beyond initial small talk. Second, most of what they did say that could have been credited as informative and supportive tended to be far more gossipy than new faculty would have preferred. And third, of all the kinds of advice and support, counsel about teaching was least often reported (table 2). This comment from an inexperienced newcomer at Campus 1 was normative:

> No, no one has said much about teaching. Mostly, I've been warned about colleagues to avoid. A lot of it is gossip and complaining. I can only think of two specific things that have been said about teaching here. One is how bad the students are . . . about how unprepared and unmotivated they are. The other one, that maybe two people mentioned, was a warning about the need to set clear rules and punishments on the first day of class. All in all, I'm pretty disappointed with the help I've gotten.

This inattention to teaching surprised new faculty at both campuses. Inexperienced and returning faculty were not confident that they knew how to teach (although their senior colleagues seemed to assume that they did). Almost all new faculty felt that they should have gotten more concrete help such as syllabi from courses that preceded theirs. And, the majority of new faculty at both campuses reported that they had not been given appropriate strategies for coping with difficult students, especially those who disrupted classes or who might complain to departmental chairs. (At each campus, rumors spread quickly about new faculty who suffered embarrassment and other punishments as a result of such complaints).

Another way of documenting inattention to teaching can be seen in a single datum: Less than 5 percent of new faculty in their first semesters at either campus could identify any sort of social network for discussing teaching. Moreover, no new faculty were in departments where colleagues met occasionally to discuss teaching (in ways akin to departmental discussions about, say, the scholarly literature).

These questions about support produced another surprise. At both campuses, nurturance was no greater for inexperienced and returning faculty than for experienced newcomers, despite the seemingly greater need of the former. At Campus 2, curiously, experienced new faculty reported receiving by far the most useful advice and encouragement; this was part of a general pattern where already accomplished professors were welcomed by their new colleagues.

When I asked new faculty about what sort of help they needed most as teachers, the answer was nearly universal: they imagined that the hardest tasks would be learning the appropriate level of lecture difficulty for students. The follow-up question, about how senior faculty could provide such help, produced a hint about why new faculty were passive in soliciting assistance. That is, new faculty could not imagine how anything short of direct classroom experience could provide the answer they needed.

Another question asked for specific plans to coteach. New faculty's plans (12 percent and 20 percent intentions to coteach for the two cohorts at Campus 1; 8 percent and 4 percent at Campus 2) and the results of those plans (less than 3 percent at both campuses for new faculty who were actually in class simultaneously with another instructor) evidenced little use of this collegial device for helping new faculty acculturate to teaching a new population of students.

Finally, new faculty in inexperienced and returning categories commonly reported some distress over their senior colleagues' attitudes about teaching. At Campus 1, interviews with new faculty produced this rank-ordered list of what they disliked about their seniors: (1) burnout, (2) overconcern with campus politics, (3) complaints about campus resources, and (4) negativism toward students. Campus 2 produced the same list except for the omission of the first complaint.

Taken together, senior faculty at both campuses seemed unable, unasked, or unwilling to provide the kinds of modeling as teachers that new faculty found themselves wanting as semester 1 progressed. At Campus 1, only five new faculty specified senior colleagues who acted as models of a sort (three instances were department chairs). At Campus 2, only 6 such specifications were made (three of them for chairs). Casual comments from chairs suggested a reason why they were more likely than other senior colleagues to offer help; they felt obligated to give advice where other faculty might have felt they were overstepping their bounds. The majority of chairs, however, expressed the same Social Darwinistic logic that I heard from their senior colleagues; that is, the best faculty seem to figure these things out on their own.

Work and plans. Close behind concerns for a lack of collegial supports came distress over workloads. Table 3 shows that new faculty, in their predictions of typical workweeks during semester 2 anticipated a balance of time spent on lecture preparation and on scholarly writing. A curious quality of these estimates was that they only remotely reflected ongoing patterns at the midpoint of semester 1. New faculty including the two experienced associate professors quoted here, the first at Campus 1 and the second at Campus 2, invariably described their beginning patterns as temporary aberrations:

TABLE 3

New Faculty's Median Estimates of Typical Workweeks, in Hours per Week, during the Coming Semester (Semester 1, Year 1)

Academic Activity	Year Cohort Began			
	1987 (Campus 1)	1988 (Campus 1)	1988 (Campus 2)	1989 (Campus 2)
Teaching	9.0	8.0	4.5	5.0
Lecture Prep	13.0	13.0	8.0	7.5
Scholarly Writing	13.3	14.0	7.0	9.0

As soon as I have my classes under control, I'm going to spend a lot more time on my writing. I need to get at least two papers finished (actually one just needs revision) this semester. [In response to my question about how ready he was to teach his classes?] I have taught these courses before. And, I spent some time this summer going over my notes. I thought that I would be spending very little time preparing for classes. But now I find that I'm doing a lot of modification. I'm trying to simplify some things. And, much as I always have done . . . now that I think about it . . . I find myself always trying to improve the content of my notes. I want to be sure that I'm up-to-date.

I'm not settled down yet. I'm still trying to figure out what will work with students here. So, my typical workweeks, as you call them, are not typical yet. I find myself spending much more time than I planned on my classes. I want to find a way to make the students a little less obviously bored and disinterested. Once I do that I will get back to writing and the other things I have to do.

Self-descriptions as teachers. Here again, the result was remarkably uniform across groupings when new faculty were asked to list their strengths as teachers. My rank-orderings of the most common answers sorted themselves into categories of kindred responses:

1. I am well-prepared and knowledgeable (Campuses 1 and 2)
2. I am interested in students (Campus 1)
   I am good at explaining/conceptualizing (Campus 2)
3. I am good at explaining/conceptualizing (Campus 1)
   I am a motivator (Campus 2)

In this context, new faculty implied what they considered the basis for good teaching in terms of this uniform estimate: good teaching equals clear, knowledgeable, and, possibly, inspiring lectures.

Self-generated lists of weaknesses as teachers produced this rank-ordering:

1. I ask too much of students (Campus 1)
   None (Campus 2)
2. None (Campus 1)
   I ask too much of students (Campus 2)
3. I am disorganized (Campuses 1 and 2)

Fewer than four new faculty in any of the four cohorts studied here indicated an awareness that their teaching prowess could depend on more than issues of content and of clear, enthusiastic presentation. Given that the majority of new faculty already saw themselves as doing adequately or better in these regards, three other outcomes may have been foregone.

For one thing, a near majority of new faculty had no plans for improving their teaching (and all but a few who did specified improvements to content, organization, and motivation). For another thing, fewer than four faculty per cohort described their classroom styles as anything more than what Fink [5] and others have labeled "facts-and-principles lecturing." And, finally, only two newcomers at each campus had firm plans to visit the classrooms of colleagues for tips on teaching. When asked to explain this disinterest, the remaining respondents answered much like this inexperienced new hire at Campus 2:

> Frankly, I never thought of it. I'm not sure what I would learn. I really think it's a matter of simply learning what the students here can handle and of lowering my standards in general. Besides, I'm not sure I would be welcome in my colleagues' classes.

Second Semester

In general, second semesters proved disappointing for new faculty. They felt no more settled-in, successful at teaching, or productive at writing than they had in semester 1. For most of these new faculty, semester 2 was the nadir of reported experience at their new campuses and in their recall of overall careers.

Collegial support. Estimates of collegial support declined for all groupings in semester 2. Table 4 shows this result in terms of new faculty who rated collegial contacts as generally poor. Ratings in this category during semester 1 had been at least 10 percent higher for all groups except the inexperienced members of cohort 2.

The drop in perceived collegiality by semester 2 seemed to have a reliable concomitant. New faculty talked openly about a growing sense of disillusionment — usually as in this excerpt from the comments of an inexperienced new hire at Campus 1 (cohort 1):

TABLE 4
Semester 2 Ratings of Collegiality as Poor

Year Cohort Began	Background of New Faculty		
	Inexperienced	Returning	Experienced
1987 (Campus 1)	30% (N = 3)	50% (N = 1)	64% (N = 18)
1988 (Campus 1)	15% (N = 2)	50% (N = 1)	57% (N = 27)
1988 (Campus 2)	33% (N = 6)	83% (N = 5)	25% (N = 4)
1989 (Campus 2)	40% (N = 10)	50% (N = 2)	27% (N = 3)

I'm beginning to see how hopeless things really are here. I don't think I was told how bad things are here and I hold the older people — the same people who painted such a rosy picture during my interview — responsible. It makes me feel all the more alienated here . . . all the more determined to just do my work quietly and to leave as soon as I can.

Table 4 mirrors another related dimension of disappointment for new faculty; feelings of intellectual understimulation continued into semester 2, more so for new faculty at Campus 1. Consistent with that difference, newcomers to Campus 1 held generally lower estimates of the professional competence of their senior colleagues. As before, one grouping contradicted the experience of loneliness and understimulation — the experienced faculty hired at Campus 2.

Reports of understimulation went beyond collegial prods to reflect and write; by semester 2 it grew to strong salience as a factor that might undermine newcomers' commitment to teaching. This concern was equally prominent at both campuses and it often took the form of these comments from returning faculty at Campuses 1 and 2:

One thing I worried about in returning to a campus job was whether I could handle the teaching. I guess I didn't presuppose that I would get lots of help but I certainly didn't expect to be surrounded by colleagues who don't seem to care about teaching. When I talk about it in the department I feel like I am violating a rule of silence.

One big reason why I left my job at ——— was because I thought I would enjoy teaching. Now I wonder how I can avoid becoming just as negative about teaching as this campus is. It isn't just that people don't care; teaching is seen as a negative and as something that we rarely discuss except to complain about.

Self-descriptions as teachers. Changes in self-descriptions were almost nonexistent, except in the few new faculty who had become participants in the author's faculty development programs by semester 2 (N

= 14, 18, 8, and 17 over the four cohorts who participated in programs that coached them through changes in teaching assumptions and practices). Whereas participants persisted in the short run as facts-and-principles lecturers, during semester 2 they began to list plans for changes in teaching, such as setting learning goals and effecting critical thinking. Even so, the transition to trying new tactics came slowly; most new faculty who planned to improve their teaching wanted to wait until year 2, when they would presumably be less busy and more confident.

Work patterns. In semester 1, new faculty of all groupings predicted changed work patterns that would allot equal time to teaching and to scholarly writing (table 3). Table 5 shows that the reality of demands for time had changed little since the initial interviews. By semester 2, averages for lecture preparation remained far higher than deemed desirable by new faculty; Campuses 1 and 2 reported a mean exceeding twenty-one hours and sixteen hours, respectively, across all experience types. Even the small subgroup of newcomers to science departments at Campus 2 (with teaching loads of one course or less) routinely expressed surprise that they had spent three to four hours a week preparing for each hour of classroom presentation. Another surprise for new faculty who paused to calculate their work loads was the realization that core workweeks were only about thirty hours long.

Thus, anticipations of spending far more time at writing by semester 2 went unfulfilled. Original estimates of workweeks with a balance of hours per week spent on teaching and writing persisted at a ratio of at least 15:1. Most surprising, these imbalances were as characteristic of experienced faculty as of other new hires at both campuses.

New faculty's immediate concern with this pattern related to a near absence of scholarly and grant writing. The result was an increasing frustration with teaching as a task whose demands overshadowed its rewards. But, with prods during these interviews to reflect about the

TABLE 5

Actual Core Work Weeks during Semester 2 (cf. table 3) in Mean Hours

Academic Activity	Year Cohort Began			
	1987 (Campus 1)	1988 (Campus 1)	1988 (Campus 2)	1989 (Campus 2)
Teaching	8.5	8.2	4.0	4.1
Lecture Prep	23.7	21.0	17.2	16.1
Scholarly Writing	0.8	0.6	1.1	1.3
Committees	3.3	2.8	4.0	3.8

reasons for spending so much time preparing lectures, new faculty realized their own contributions to the problem. That is, the majority of them spontaneously admitted to overpreparing in the sense of having too much material to present without hurrying their lectures and in terms of trying to be too perfectionistic beyond the level that could be rewarded in most classes.

A final pattern characterized new faculty in regard to habits. Despite having no immediate plans to effectively change their workweeks, new hires invariably predicted more productive and effective schedules in the near future. Moreover, nearly all new faculty saw upcoming summers as times when they would, at last, catch up on writing.

Teaching evaluations. During semester 1, all but a few new faculty (eleven at Campus 1 and eight at Campus 2) declined offers made during the first interview to help them conduct early, informal student evaluations of their teaching. The stated reasons at both campuses are typified in this comment noted from an inexperienced new hire at Campus 2:

> I already do that in my own way. I ask students to tell me how I am doing
> . . . and if they have any questions. I think I'm doing fine in that regard. So
> I don't really see the need to go through this.

By semester 2, at both campuses and across all groupings, poor teaching ratings became a reality for the majority of new faculty. Table 6 shows that most new faculty were rated as mediocre according to campus-generated, compulsory teaching evaluations administered at the end of semester 1. In terms of this measure, new faculty reported that they generally fared far worse as teachers than they had anticipated.

Although this result held across campuses, two limitations merit mention. First, faculty at Campus 2 were less surprised at their generally poor ratings; their students, especially undergraduates, were seemingly more open in expressing their dissatisfaction during classes in

TABLE 6

New Faculty Who Received Student Evaluation Scores (Global) below Departmental Means (Semester 1)

	Background of New Faculty		
Year Cohort Began	Inexperienced	Returning	Experienced
1987 (Campus 1)	57% ($N = 8$)	75% ($N = 4$)	57% ($N = 16$)
1988 (Campus 1)	57% ($N = 8$)	50% ($N = 1$)	43% ($N = 20$)
1988 (Campus 2)	67% ($N = 12$)	83% ($N = 5$)	56% ($N = 9$)
1989 (Campus 2)	68% ($N = 17$)	67% ($N = 2$)	64% ($N = 7$)

terms of bored expressions, audible conversations among themselves, and exiting classes early. In retrospect, new faculty at Campus 2 reported realizing that they should have paid more attention to obvious signs that students would rate them unfavorably. Second, nearly half of new faculty at Campus 2 did not receive the printouts of the analyses of their student evaluations during semester 2. Even though this campus had made special efforts to devise and institutionalize a student evaluation device in the few years prior, it had not followed up to see that faculty were getting the results.

Although Campus 1, which prided itself for caring about teaching, did a far better job of getting feedback from its teaching evaluations to faculty, it did little better in supplementing printouts with consultation from chairs or colleagues. That is, only a handful of new faculty at either campus ($N = 5$ and 4, respectively) were counseled by departmental colleagues about what their numerical ratings meant or how they translated into alternative ways of teaching.

Third Semester

New faculty in semester 2 expected that their return to campus after summer vacation would mark the end of campus experience as one of busily catching up. They hoped to be rested and ready to assume a less harried schedule. Once again, realities differed from plans.

Even before contacts were reestablished in the third interview, casual meetings left the impression of disappointing progress during first summers. As a rule, new faculty did not settle down to productive writing as planned; instead, they spent most of the summer resting up from what they generally described as the busiest, most stressful year of their lives. Then, when and if they felt compelled to do something productive with the last parts of their first summers, they most often spent them in preparing and revising course plans and lectures. The stated reason (typified in this note from an inexperienced newcomer at Campus 1) was this:

> What I realized when I finally felt like getting back to work was that I needed to be better prepared for my classes than I was last year. I realize that as long as I'm struggling to have good enough notes and problems, I will never get around to writing.

Almost without exception, newcomers reported feeling another disillusionment upon returning for year 2: They still did not feel that they were a real part of campus.

Collegiality. By around the midpoint of semester 3, reports of collegial support had reached new (albeit still modest) heights. New faculty during my visits usually offered an explanation like this one made by an experienced newcomer to Campus 2:

> You have to realize that I don't always do this. When I have a better class, one that is better prepared and better prepared to participate, then I can focus around break-out groups and that sort of thing. Besides, to be honest with you, I don't feel all that confident here yet. These students are not shy about letting professors know when they don't like something.

In fact, by semester 3 little had changed for most new faculty as teachers. When asked, as in semester 1, what plans they had for improving as teachers, the answers at both campuses reflected the rank-ordering listed earlier in this article: (1) none, (2) teaching at lower levels of difficulty, and (3) preparing lectures with better and more organized content).

Student evaluations. Given the formalized student rating systems for teaching used at both campuses, new faculty got no printouts about semester 2 until semester 3. Two things stood out in my discussions of these ratings with new faculty: first, student ratings (except for some of the teachers with student-oriented styles mentioned earlier and for a near majority of experienced new faculty) had not improved. Second, new hires reported feeling ambivalent about these generally discouraging results. On one hand, the ratings seemed so remote in time that they could be dismissed as irrelevant to teaching in what had since become more comfortable surrounds. On the other hand, the ratings seemed finally to force many new faculty to admit that this was an unanticipated, unhappy state of affairs that had to be addressed. Resulting plans, seen just above, suggested little immediate promise for improved teaching.

Work patterns. Disappointments about teaching were matched, for most new faculty, by frustrations with continuing imbalances in work-weeks. The result of assessing the self-reported workweeks of new faculty in semester 3 produced a result closely similar to that already seen for semester 2 (table 5). Despite firm expectations to the contrary, new faculty generally persisted in patterns where teaching preparation dominated other activities.

Plans. By the third semester, new faculty uniformly set more modest goals for productivity and for balance of teaching preparation with other activities. Still, they continued to hope that the time would come soon when they could put the priority of teaching behind them (as in this comment from an inexperienced new hire at Campus 1):

> I just need to get to the point where I feel that I am in control of my classes. I mean that my notes and overheads have to be better organized. I mean that the materials have to be at a level appropriate for students. [In response to

203

continued to complain about loneliness and understimulation, but they were often better able to identify colleagues with whom they had regular and substantial interactions. Nonetheless, this phenomenon was not universal. Two groups evidenced no gains in collegial support for activities including teaching: returning faculty at both campuses, and experienced faculty at Campus 1. Their comments about this continuing predicament are echoed in this remark by a returning full professor at Campus 2:

> No point kidding myself; I'm a bit hurt by it all. I thought that by now I would have some friends . . . or at least some colleagues who feigned an interest in what I'm doing. But evidently, this is how things are going to be. I'm just going to have to make the best of a bad situation. It's hard to want to spend time at things like teaching when no one here seems to care.

And where collegiality had improved, changes came from sources other than those expected by new faculty (beyond the senior faculty who invited a minority of new hires for one-time, welcoming dinners in their homes). As a rule, inexperienced newcomers found the collegiality they valued most from other new faculty. An oft-heard comment in this context: "Its like the blind leading the blind."

Self-descriptions as teachers. In the main, self-descriptions continued unchanged. The great majority of new faculty in their second year on campus still saw good teaching (including their own aspirations for excellence) in terms of little more than content and enthusiasm. The hoped-for trend toward more involvement in faculty development programs (and in goals for more active student learning) had grown only slightly (to nineteen and eleven in cohorts 1 and 3, the two groups studied into year 2). By semester 3, six more individuals identified themselves as having brought more enlightened concepts of teaching to campus than they had displayed or even discussed during year 1. This was usually evidenced as an inclination to have parts of classes devoted to student participation. The single reason stated for this delay was waiting to feel settled as teachers before taking risks.

The great majority of new faculty in year 2 persisted in describing their classroom styles as strict facts-and-principles lecturing. My visits (with prior permission of new faculty and with my appearances at unpredictable times) to the classrooms of samples of ten of these faculty at each campus confirmed these self-descriptions. A similar sampling of new faculty who claimed to be using student-oriented approaches (see Weimer [8] for a definition of this concept), in contrast, confirmed self-descriptions in only slightly more than half my visits. These self-described innovators who were lecturing in "content only" fashion

my question about when he would know that his notes were well-enough prepared?] Good question. Maybe never; I might always be repreparing my notes. [In response to my question about when he would feel comfortable about balancing teaching preparation with other activities such as social life and writing?] I think, really, that will come when students seem to like what I'm doing . . . and when I like what I'm doing.

Again, new faculty were asked to specify their plans for improving their teaching. Rank-orderings of their most common responses produced responses nearly identical to those listed for prior semesters. In brief, beliefs about the best ways of finding improved teaching, classroom comfort, and student acceptance revolved around notions of better lecture preparation and lowered standards. Increasingly, though, new faculty in their third semester were attributing their negativism about improving teaching to students, specifically to their lack of preparation and motivation.

Fourth Semester

Although new faculty continued to predict that each new semester would bring the sense of feeling accepted and "on track" for career goals, semester 4 rarely brought those desired results. Instead, semester 4 brought another self-rated low for new faculty. Exceptions to this rule were inexperienced new faculty who found strong bonds with other junior faculty that promised scholarly productivity, inexperienced new faculty at Campus 1 who participated in campus faculty development programs, and experienced newcomers at Campus 2 who had reestablished research productivity. In contrast, the new faculty who showed the most obvious signs of maladjustment were returning new faculty. As a rule, then, the socialization periods at these two campuses lasted well beyond the fourth semester.

Collegiality. Overall, new faculty at both campuses rated collegial support as lowest in semester 4. Returning new faculty, as just indicated, were most vocal in making this complaint. As indicated in the following comment from Campus 1, they had usually come from settings where they experienced more friendly and appreciative colleagues:

> Sometimes I feel like a failure here. No one cares what I'm doing . . . except in the critical comments I got in my annual review. They make a big deal of my one poor teaching rating but not one of them has offered to help. This system would be considered madness in industry. They wouldn't go to the trouble to recruit a doctoral-level specialist and then watch him or her fail.

In a preliminary sense, semester 4 may have been a critical period of sorting out people who would establish happy bonds with their campus and those who would remain estranged. Overall, about half the new faculty studied into semester 4 showed signs of establishing social networks and of finding comfort with job demands such as teaching. While they as a rule, had not yet found the kind of balance mentioned several times in this manuscript, they were anticipating it in seemingly more realistic ways.

Student ratings. Semester 4 brought feedback on student ratings of new faculty's teaching in semester 3, the juncture at which some new faculty reported expecting a turnaround in student appreciation. But this did not happen on the average; increases over semesters 1 and 2 were slight except for participants in faculty development programs, for a group of self-starters to be described later, and for most experienced new faculty.

Three things about new faculty's reactions to these ratings stood out in interviews in semester 4. First, new faculty now tended to attribute disappointing ratings to their students' inabilities to handle challenging material. Second, new faculty almost never (except for the minority who participated in faculty development programs) sought out advice for ways of translating ratings into alternative styles of teaching. Third, even in the face of two disillusioning ratings, new faculty generally supposed that their usual plans for improvement (that is, better organization, lowered standards) offered the best likelihood for improved ratings.

Self-descriptions as teachers. Consistent with what we have just seen, new faculty showed few changes from earlier answers about their self-images as teachers. One slight change at both campuses was the valence associated with teaching: increasingly, teaching was depicted as even less fun than it had been in semester 1. A related change: some interviewees, especially returning new faculty, volunteered the possibility that they would never be considered good teachers. These preliminary admissions were not, however, accompanied by a sense of relief; these were people who apparently wanted to teach well and who did not find comfort in the prospect of chronically mediocre ratings.

Work patterns. By this fourth interview, new faculty generally expressed dismay with how they were allotting their time. With the exceptions of small groups who were making regular time for scholarly productivity, new faculty showed work weeks similar to those seen earlier (table 5). On the average, new faculty at both campuses were producing manuscripts at rates well below the mean of one-plus per year necessary to meet usual expectations for tenure decisions. For the first time, new faculty in this unbalanced pattern openly expressed resentment toward the demands of teaching as they saw them. That is, teaching, despite its signal lack of rewards, seemed to demand preparation to the exclusion of other important things.

Plans. At the end of their second year on campus, new faculty placed heavy expectations on the coming summer session. Here again they hoped to catch up on neglected activities, especially regarding social life and writing. But this time new elements crept into interview comments. New faculty no longer reported being as busy and stressed as they had been in semesters 1–3; they supposed that they would not have to spend the coming summer resting. Moreover, plans for writing seemed more realistic; suddenly, plans were accompanied by realizations that, for most interviewees, *any* writing of substance would be progress. Thus, plans now specified, say, mornings at writing and afternoons at family outings (and not the entire days imagined in plans made a year earlier). This excerpt from my notes on an inexperienced newcomer to Campus 2 reflects the tone of trying to be realistic amidst a disillusioning semester:

> Things are overdue, that's for sure. Maybe this summer will be the turning point. I have to make something work; I have to take better care of myself and of my career. Students may have to accept me for what I am. . . . I am not perfect, but I try hard to bring good material to class. And, when I think of it, I may have to accept myself for what I am. I certainly have to accept the fact that I'm not producing great scholarship at a great rate. But I think that I will produce some good stuff, slowly but surely. [In response to my question about what, assuming that progress, would remain as important goals for year three on campus ?] That's easy. I need to work harder to find friends, maybe even collaborators. I need to feel like I belong here.

Comparisons of Novice and Veteran Teachers

As I analyzed the results of interviews over semesters, I integrated them with other observations. For example, my repeated sampling of the classroom performances of inexperienced new faculty ($N = 8$), of returning new faculty ($N = 3$), and experienced new faculty ($N = 6$) suggested surprisingly few differences in superficial teaching styles during semesters 1 and 2. That is, most faculty new to campus, regardless of level of experience as teachers, were lecturing in facts-and-principles style. All but a few newcomers obviously focused on presenting lots of content organized in terms of concepts and lists. All but a few lectured in rapid-fire fashion. The obvious difference between veteran and novice teachers emerged in other dimensions including more classroom comfort and confidence for the former.

By semesters 3 and 4 nearly half of the teachers veteran to teaching had further relaxed their styles to include somewhat more student participation. During comments to me after class, these experienced professors described the change as feeling settled and comfortable with the students. Curiously, experienced new faculty who evidenced no apparent changes in classrooms from year 1 reported having experienced similar improvements in comfort, not necessarily in regard to students but in terms of worrying about their teaching. For them, the transition evidenced itself as a reduction in feeling pressured about lecture preparation.

Inexperienced and returning new faculty generally reported no such transitions in comfort or in time saved during years 1 and 2 at either campus. They were, according to my observations and their interview comments, still teaching in facts-and-principles style during semester 4. And by their own admissions, they were still primarily concerned about avoiding punishment (for example, widely known complaints made by students to campus administrators). They were continuing, in their own description, to teach defensively.

How persistent is this general pattern? In a pilot study with two cohorts at Campus 1 immediately preceding the cohorts studied here, I found that inexperienced ($N = 18$ and 13) and returning ($N = 3$ and 6) new faculty persisted in this same pattern during their first three and four years on campus. Even where they had, on occasion, ceased overpreparing lectures (usually by semesters 5 or 6), they stuck to the same facts-and-principles style that had characterized their performances in semester 1.

Another bit of evidence already mentioned corroborates the notion that faculty tend to stick to initial styles: the majority of experienced new faculty sampled here were lecturing, by their own reckoning, in the same facts-and-principles manner they had used as novices. Curiously, only a few of them were able to specify any significant changes as teachers beyond (a) increases in the confidence that results from experience and (b) decreases in the demands that they made on students in terms of assignments and tests.

These data stimulated two related inquiries: what characterizes novice professors who seem to start as excellent teachers and what causes other colleagues to move in similar directions by their second year on campus?

Inexperienced Newcomers Who Found Quick Comfort

I selected three inexperienced new faculty in each cohort who began as exemplary teachers. Criteria for inclusion were: clearly superior students ratings as teachers; my own classroom ratings (of comfort, enthusiasm, organization, student rapport and involvement, clarity of presentation, and active student learning); and new faculty's own self-descriptions as comfortable, as innovative, and as interested in active student learning.

Analysis of my notes about these twelve individuals produced the following list of characteristics that, in combination, distinguished them from their peers:

1. Positive attitudes about students at these state universities
2. Lectures paced in relaxed style so as to provide opportunities for student comprehension and involvement
3. Low levels of complaining about their campuses including collegial supports
4. Evidence of actively seeking advice about teaching (especially the mechanics of specific courses), often from a colleague in the role of a guide or mentor
5. A quicker transition to moderate levels of lecture preparation (that is, less than 1.5 hours per classroom hour), usually by semester 3
6. A generally ($N = 4$ at Campus 1; $N = 3$ at Campus 2) superior investment in time spent on scholarly and grant writing (mean = 3.3 hours per workweek)
7. A greater readiness to become involved in campus faculty development programs ($N = 2$, 3, 2, and 3, respectively, over the four cohorts).

Ten other new faculty who were not fast starters made transitions that brought them to obvious comfort and well above average student ratings during year 2. All but four of the individuals who met this description were experienced new faculty. The four inexperienced newcomers in this category evidenced gradual movement toward items 1–3 of the list above; by semester 3 and 4, for example, they were complaining less about colleagues and students. These new hires, however, did not seem to seek out the collegial support characteristic of the sample just described. Instead they showed a determination to adjust on their own.

New Faculty Active in Campus Faculty Development Programs

Although new faculty were routinely contacted in the repeated interviews that formed the basis of this manuscript, only a minority of them followed up on admonitions to participate in campus faculty development programs. As a rule, new hires told me that they felt too busy to participate; most said that they would participate once they felt settled in, particularly after acquiring a sense of control over their teaching. Indeed, junior faculty at both campuses who counted as regular participants in campus faculty development programs most often came from cohorts in their fourth through sixth years on campus. The reason for this general delay in participation seemed clear: junior faculty admitted waiting until the pressures of meeting standards for tenure were near.

Nonetheless, the apparent benefits for new faculty who participated in faculty development programs (for example, workshops on teaching and writing, feedback on classroom performance and student evaluations including early and informal ratings, and prearranged interactions with exemplary senior faculty for advice on activities including teaching) were substantial. Earlier we saw that participants were highly represented in the group that found immediate comfort and success at teaching. Although these new faculty were vocal in attributing their successes and comfort to participation in development programs, they might well have achieved similar progress by virtue of their seemingly more optimistic styles.

Participation in campus faculty development programs did not obviously affect tendencies to lecture in facts and principles style, at least during the first two years on campus. Only two of the new faculty picked as exemplary made significant inroads into involving students in class discussion that exceeded 15 percent of class time or in teaching higher-order skills in ways that included writing-intensive courses.

What short-term participation in faculty development did seem to affect was classroom comfort and time management. That is, these participants evidenced less overpreparation for lectures, more relaxed pacing during lectures, more comfort with lecturing and with students, fewer complaints about busyness, and more time on scholarly writing. Consistent with these differences, participants displayed more confidence about their careers, more satisfaction with teaching, and quicker assimilation to their new campuses.

Discussion

The main premise of this article, namely, that we need to know more about how new faculty establish teaching styles, was generally confirmed. The study of new faculty from two large campuses suggested the following generalities about how new faculty begin as teachers:

1. They teach cautiously, equating good teaching with good content [8]. Thus, most faculty observed here stuck to what Axelrod [2] designated a facts-and principles style of lecturing.
2. They teach defensively, so as to avoid public failures at teaching [4]. New faculty routinely worried aloud about criticisms of their

teaching, especially the sort that would earn repeated listings in reports of tenure committees. This meant that new faculty tried to get their facts straight; whatever else, they did not want to be accused of not knowing their material. Other factors, such as students who seemed to complain capriciously and maliciously, seemed beyond the control of new faculty.

3. They often blame external factors for teaching failures as indicated in student ratings. Three of the most common of these attributions were to poor students, heavy teaching loads, and invalid rating systems.

4. They are passive about change and improvement [5]. They assume that casual comments from students (and perhaps from colleagues) are sufficient to gauge prowess at teaching. They reluctantly seek outside help from resources including faculty development programs. And when asked to specify plans for improvement, even in the wake of poor ratings and admitted dissatisfaction, they are unable to specify alternatives beyond improving lecture content and making assignments and tests easier.

5. New faculty's primary goals as teachers revolve around time management and punishment; they do not expect to enjoy teaching until they no longer have to spend large amounts of time preparing for it and until it no longer offers prospects of public criticism. Only then, they suppose, can they attend to subtle aspects of teaching, such as moving beyond a facts-and-principles format (perhaps by teaching critical thinking).

6. Experienced new faculty claim that their defensive and factual styles of teaching are regressions from how they had taught recently at other campuses. They too complained of worrying about public complaints and about heavy investments in new lecture notes.

7. New faculty establish comfort, efficiency, and student acceptance only slowly if at all. In preliminary studies at Campus 1, large groups of new faculty were systematically interviewed and observed for periods as long as four years. Only a minority made verifiable progress in any of these areas except for lessened preparation time. Broader progress in the samples studied here were limited to the handfuls of new faculty who persisted as participants in campus faculty development programs.

Although this evidence for the effectiveness of faculty development programs must be considered preliminary, it offers bright promise in an otherwise dreary picture of how new faculty develop as teachers. It suggests, as we just saw, that new faculty can be aided in finding balance; the study samples did less overpreparing, they got students more involved in classes, and managed more productivity on scholarly projects. Moreover, participating new faculty received significantly higher student ratings, the measure used for administrative assessments of teaching at both campuses.

A related conclusion of this article concerns the generality of the findings just reviewed across two campuses with different priorities for teaching. That is, new faculty at the campus with little public emphasis on teaching showed the same tendencies as their counterparts at the "teaching campus." Specifically, the two groups were closely similar in terms of:

1. An initial concern for teaching well and for earning the respect and gratitude of students.
2. Worries about eliciting public complaints about their teaching and strategies of teaching more for correctness than for innovation and student learning.
3. A tendency to prepare more lecture material than could be presented and assimilated in comfortable fashion, usually in a facts-and-principles format.
4. A tendency to plan few changes in teaching beyond easing standards for students who were seen as the main problem in teaching well.
5. Putting off scholarly writing until feeling settled as teachers.

Curiously, the two campuses had similar demands for publication rates (that is, about 1.0 to 1.5 manuscripts accepted in refereed outlets per year, depending on department).

Another point expands this preliminary picture. There was no observable difference in teaching performance between new faculty at the two campuses. This observation extended beyond classroom performance and students ratings in approximately similar rating forms; it included stated interests in teaching, time spent with students outside class, and attempts to seek help in improving teaching. No doubt, this finding would surprise faculty at the teaching campus who commonly asserted the teaching superiority of their campus in comparison with research campuses.

What this kind of direct and sustained examination of new faculty as teachers can tell us, then, is that professors often begin in styles that persist in disappointingly narrow fashion. One suggestion in this study is that we might do better to safeguard new faculty from all but private and formative evaluations of their classroom performance for a year or two. Such precautions might reduce the reliance of new faculty on facts-and-principles formats of lecturing as defenses against possible criticisms.

A second suggestion concerns faculty development. Involving new faculty in programs that helped them refrain from overpreparing facts and that assisted them in finding comfort with increased student participation produced two measurable improvements here. One was improved comfort and ratings as teachers; the other was improved comfort and productivity as productive scholars.

The final suggestion is that we can learn something of value about how new faculty could develop as teachers from observing individuals who excel quickly. These colleagues assumed unusually positive and proactive stances, especially in terms of seeking help.

What remains to be seen is if university campuses will provide the kinds of safety, supports, and formative feedback that appear essential to early comfort and success at teaching. In my experience as a faculty developer and consultant at a variety of campuses, management favors conditions that produce poor morale and tolerates the resulting low productivity. Why? Part of the reason, I suspect, owes to the autonomy so highly valued in academe; we tend to let new faculty "sink or swim" on their own, perhaps so that they can take full credit for their work. But the rest of this neglect has roots in our externalized world view. We have yet to learn much about ways of making our own work more effective and satisfying.

References

1. Association of American Colleges. *Integrity in the College Curriculum: A Report to the Academic Community.* Washington, D.C.: Association of American Colleges, 1985.
2. Axelrod, J. *The University Teacher as Artist: Toward an Aesthetics of Teaching with Emphasis on the Humanities.* San Francisco: Jossey-Bass, 1973.
3. Boice, R. "New Faculty as Colleagues." *International Journal of Qualitative Studies in Education*, in press.
4. Eble, K. E. "Preparing College Teachers of English." *College English*, 33 (Winter 1972), 385–406.
5. Fink, L. D. *The First Year of College Teaching.* San Francisco: Jossey-Bass, 1984.
6. Sorcinelli, M. D. "Faculty Careers: Satisfactions and Discontents." *To Improve the Academy*, 4 (1985), 44–62.
7. Turner, J. L. and R. Boice. "Starting at the Beginning: Concerns and Needs of New Faculty." *To Improve the Academy*, 6 (1987), 41–55.
8. Weimer, M. *Improving College Teaching.* Jossey-Bass, 1990.

FACULTY RESEARCH

Publish or perish" became a hackneyed phrase many years ago. Faculty spoke it more in jest than in seriousness, for they knew that most of their colleagues wrote little or nothing and still survived to live out their academic career. Today, however, publishing has replaced teaching as the principal faculty role in universities and has become an increasingly important criterion for promotion, tenure, and career success in four-year colleges. More faculty are publishing more articles and books in a mushrooming mass of journals and presses.

Several now attack this flood of literature, claiming that most of it is trivia. The critics allege that most of what appears in print never should have been written or published, that faculty simply grind out verbiage to fatten their vitae so as to qualify for the next step up the academic ladder. Faculty carve a single piece of research into bits so that one possibly decent publication instead becomes three or four fragmented articles. High-quality work has all but disappeared. So the critics say.

On the other side, even those who complain the loudest acknowledge the importance of research and our need for new knowledge. They know we have health and social problems needing solutions. They recognize the technological competition this country faces from other nations of the world. They grant the fact that our universities generate more research than all other agencies combined. They see too that this research is not designed to destroy nature or life, although other very different groups of concerned individuals believe that this is precisely what faculty research does to animals in the name of health and the weapons of war, in the name of biology, physics, and engineering.

Today's more competitive academic environment endangers a faculty member's chances for success. A career depends upon becoming known for one's work. Teaching, as important as it is, remains a local phenomenon. One can earn a reputation at home as a distinguished pedagogue. Very rarely, however, does that reputation extend beyond the immediate campus. Moreover, teaching excellence seldom brings national recognition to the institution, a goal high on the administration's list.

Besides wanting to pass their knowledge on to the next generation and to get young people excited about ideas and learning, those who choose the professorial career do so because research attracts them. Research is solving puzzles, doing it all day, every day. It's fun. If successful, one derives a modest income from it, enough to buy books and to pay for the children's music lessons.

Successful research differs from excellence in teaching. Research affects one's career. Recognized scholars, individuals whose reputations transcend the local college or university, judge a researcher's creations. Disciplinary leaders around the world award the prizes, confer on a faculty member a reputation that cannot be gained from colleagues at home. Published research leads to promotions and tenure. Higher salaries come with publications. Administrators like you. Neighbors see your picture in the local paper. Seeing your name in print supplies a momentary high. Many good things happen to those who publish.

In order to appreciate the magnitude of the academic publishing business, we briefly step back to sketch a partial picture of what has happened in the world of scholarship since World War II—a true watershed period— before looking at the evidence and passing judgment on the critics' claims. As noted above, teaching, not research, used to be the central faculty role. When Jencks and Riesman (1968) wrote *Academic Revolution,* university faculty were shifting their priorities. Jencks and Riesman called this change the "professionalization of faculty." Commitment to their professional associations and to their colleagues around the world challenged faculty members' institutional allegiance.[1] They found excitement both in new discoveries and in the dissemination of what they had learned. Nisbet (1992) has written of his graduate school days at Berkeley, describing how he joined the faculty upon completion of his Ph.D. during the Great Depression and how life changed at his university after World War II. There was no doubt in his and his most distinguished peers' minds in the 1930s that they would do research as one of their duties. However, being an excellent teacher, preparing outstanding lectures—these came first for even the most famous of the faculty at Berkeley. War research fell heavily on the universities, from covert operations such as radar to the atomic bomb. Washington money continued after 1945 to win the technological races with friendly as well as hostile nations. The pendulum has not swung back. As administrators and faculty acknowledge, research is the name of the game.

A few figures illustrate the magnitude of the knowledge production industry and the role universities have played in it, how it has changed, and to what degree.[2] To begin, the number of university presses doubled between 1948 and 1958. The 727 titles these presses published in 1948 increased to about 2,300 in 1966 (Douglas, 1992, p. 97). Between 1978 and 1988 more than 29,000 new scientific journals were launched (*Chronicle of Higher Education*, March 28, 1990, p. A13). Mooney (1991, p. A17) reports that during 1989–1990 there were a million refereed articles and 300,000 books, chapters, and monographs published.[3] A faculty member, on average, contributed one article and the equivalent of half a book (chapter or monograph) each year. (Research university professors averaged twice that output.) At the same time, the amount of available space for faculty publications has not been uniform across the disciplines. Between 1972 and 1988, journal pages for psychologists grew at a half-again faster rate than the number of psychology faculty. That is, there was about 50 percent more journal space in which psychology faculty could publish in 1988 than there was in 1972 (Bieber & Blackburn, 1993). Over this same period, publication space for English faculty decreased and competition for it increased. For example, *Publications of the Modern Language Association* (*PMLA*) now prints only half as many articles per issue as it did 20 years ago.

Besides publication differences among the disciplines, two fascinating studies show that the places where knowledge is produced are anything but randomly distributed around the world, including within the United States. When Deutsch, Platt, and Senghaas (1971) were examining the conditions that led to the 62 most significant scholarly contributions in the social sciences around the world between 1900 and 1965, they noted that the majority came from very few locations. Of the 101 different scholars involved in these 62 landmark contributions, the majority were Europeans until 1929; after 1930 the majority were Americans. For the entire 65 years the total number of scholars included 53 Americans, 44 Europeans, and 4 from other locations. Three centers—Chicago, Cambridge (Mass.), and New York—were the residences of more than half of the American professoriate contributors. Washington (D.C.), Ann Arbor, and New Haven provided another quarter (p. 458). That is, three-fourths of these landmark discoveries took place in but a handful of universities.

As we saw in chapter 2, place of work strongly predicts scholarly output. More recently, *Science Watch* counted all scientific papers indexed by the Institute for Scientific Information's *Science Citation Index* during 1991, about 600,000 of them. Approximately 25 percent came from people in but 25 cities, 14 of them in the United States. The *Scientist* (1993, p. 15) reproduced that article. Table 4.1 from it provides the details.

Between 1981 and 1991 the average growth in the number of scientific

Table 4.1   The World's Research-Rich Cities

Rank	City	1991 Papers	Rank	City	1991 Papers
1	Moscow	14,541	14	Houston	4,911
2	London	14,051	15	San Diego–La Jolla, CA	4,740
3	Boston-Cambridge, MA	12,480	16	Stanford–Palo Alto, CA	4,201
4	Tokyo	11,582	17	Seattle	4,055
5	New York	8,551	18	Berlin	4,040
6	Paris	7,964	19	Ann Arbor, MI	3,907
7	Los Angeles	6,601	20	Montreal	3,895
8	Bethesda	6,233	21	Toronto	3,887
9	Philadelphia	6,183	22	Cambridge, England	3,850
10	Osaka, Japan	5,408	23	San Francisco	3,773
11	Washington, DC	5,388	24	Kyoto, Japan	3,679
12	Chicago	5,174	25	Oxford, England	3,597
13	Baltimore	4,933			

Source: Scientist (1993), p. 15, reproducing data from *Science Watch*/ISI's *Science Citation Index* (1991).

papers produced at these locations was about 25 percent. One might expect research activity to be high in cities such as Boston-Cambridge (with Harvard, the Massachusetts Institute of Technology, Boston College, Boston University, and the University of Massachusetts–Boston, as well as 50 other higher-education institutions), New York (with Columbia, New York University, Cornell Medical Center, and several other universities), and Chicago (with the University of Chicago, Northwestern, the University of Illinois–Chicago, Loyola, DePaul, and Roosevelt). But Baltimore is essentially Johns Hopkins (although the University of Maryland–Baltimore is also there); Stanford–Palo Alto *is* Stanford; and Ann Arbor *is* the University of Michigan. Single institutions can be highly productive organizations when staffed with talented faculty, when resources are adequate, and when colleague interaction is valued.

What has created this worldwide explosion of knowledge? Most likely a number of factors—societal needs and requests; competition among universities to be recognized as the best (with faculty publication rates determining the standings); attempts to satisfy faculty members' intrinsic desires while incidentally providing extrinsic rewards. The multiplication of journals is the most understandable phenomenon. As knowledge grows and more people participate in its production, interesting subbranches of inquiry emerge. They grow, and mitosis sets in. Journals spring up to handle the new specialties that arise. The newly founded fields grow. Then they split, an inevitable process. New questions spawn other journals for communicating with colleagues on the current state of the enterprise.

Do faculty play the game the critics accuse them of? Sure, some do. Others try to solve what they and others believe are the important problems. We see the vast majority of faculty in the latter category.

What about the quality of this tremendous outpouring of new knowledge? Here the answer is not easy. From Deutsch, Platt, and Senghaas (1971) and the data from the *Scientist* (1993) we see that quality and quantity go together, a fact researchers have established by correlating numbers of articles with citations received. (See chapter 2.) Bieber, Blackburn, and De Vries's (1991) effort to establish the criteria for high-quality publications basically failed, especially in English literature (one of the three disciplines studied). Faculty agreed that rhetorical style is an essential criterion for an English essay, but they did not agree on what constitutes good style. Quality is a social construct and no doubt will always have a debatable element. One knows it when one sees it, even if its criteria cannot be specified. (See Pirsig, 1974, p. 179.)[4]

On the other hand, one need only scan the leading social science journals of the past 15 years and contrast them with today's to see a significant upgrade in quality.[5] Faculty today would not submit most of the articles published then, or even write them in the first place. Theory has become richer; databases are larger and more reliable; new methodologies have become available; computing power and techniques have advanced; and faculty training is more sophisticated. Everything supports higher-quality output.

The consequences are many. The knowledge explosion has affected the entire higher-education enterprise on nearly every front: expenses (the costs for library subscriptions to the old standard journals have risen, and there is pressure to subscribe to the new ones as well); the length of faculty education and training; the need for continuing education to keep abreast; the machinery the university now must have and regularly repair and update. Most important of all, publishing has affected faculty lives and careers. We designed our theoretical framework to increase the understanding of faculty in the research role. The studies we now report are ones that test and use our framework with research behavior and, most frequently, with products as the outcomes.

Here we present the results of five studies in which faculty research is the outcome. Each is taken directly from research papers we presented at national conferences (Lawrence, Frank, Bieber, Bentley, Blackburn, & Trautvetter, 1989; Lawrence, Blackburn, & Trautvetter, 1989; Blackburn, Bieber, Lawrence, & Trautvetter, 1991;[6] Trautvetter & Blackburn, 1990; Lawrence, Bieber, Blackburn, Saulsberry, Trautvetter, Hart, & Frank, 1989). The first details an analysis of faculty in eight Res-I universities, our first and most exhaustive test of the theoretical framework. The second extends the test of the theoretical framework to two additional institutional types. The third includes all institutional types and adds two more kinds of research output. The fourth uses the framework to explore sex differences in research output in the sciences. Before presenting the fifth study, which introduces a longitudinal component to the research, we briefly report the outcomes of three other studies using the framework with other databases. We close the chapter with a summary of the personal and contextual variables that correlate with faculty research output and present strategies institutions might adapt should they wish to increase individual and unit research accomplishments.

Faculty in Research I Universities

As noted in chapter 2, the existing research on scholarly productivity has focused primarily on the direct effects of sociodemographic, career, and sometimes organizational factors. A handful of scholars have investigated the relationships between productivity and selected faculty perceptions of their employing institutions or of higher education in general—that is, their social knowledge. Even fewer have explored the relationships between productivity and a faculty member's personal educational values and beliefs. Although useful in a predictive sense, these studies do not adequately explain the process by which a faculty member's sociodemographic characteristics, career (educational background, status), perceptions (self-knowledge and social knowledge), and behaviors affect publication rates. Our explanatory causal framework identifies both direct and indirect effects of the variables that best portray such a process and provide key insights into the motivation of productive researchers. (See chapter 1.)

Current research also lacks longitudinal data on faculty perceptions, behavior, and productivity. Although a few researchers have described productivity changes through time-ordered analyses using citation indexes and vitae (Allison & Stewart, 1974; Long, 1978; Reskin, 1985), these studies fall short of explaining how individuals relate to their environments and how these interactions may change and influence scholarly output over time. For example, Allison and Stewart's notion that some professors achieve early recognition for their work, and that this reputation gives them an edge over their peers in competition for funds and publication (the accumulative advantage process), was based on cross-sequential analysis of citation indexes and not longitudinal data.

The data assess the influence of key environmental and individual variables on the rate of publication (last two years). We trace the effect of each variable within the constructs of our framework. We now describe our database.

Data and Sample

The data for the first study described here come from "Faculty at Work," a national survey of faculty conducted by the National Center for Research to Improve Postsecondary Teaching and Learning (NCRIPTAL) from November 1987 through January 1988.[7] (See appendix H.) We drew the faculty sample (N = 4,240) from the nine Carnegie classification categories (Carnegie, 1976) and across eight disciplines selected to represent a cross-section of the liberal arts (English and history for the humanities; biology, chemistry, and mathematics for the natural sciences; and psychology, political science, and sociology for the social sciences). We carried out our survey sample selection in two stages. First, we stratified institutions by Carnegie category. Then we estimated both the number of faculty members in each category and the percentage of all faculty in the United States who fell into each category. Second, we selected institutions at random until the final sample corresponded to the national distribution of faculty across Carnegie classification categories.[8]

We used only respondents from Res-I institutions in this test of the theoretical framework, because the major portion of publications are from these faculty. The resulting sample is of sufficient size (N = 637) to examine many of the individual/environment relationships specified in the framework. The faculty distribution across the disciplines is biology, 13.5 percent; chemistry, 12.1 percent; mathematics/statistics, 10.1 percent; English, 13.8 percent; history, 12.1 percent; political science, 10.7 percent; psychology, 13.2 percent; and sociology, 9.6 percent. The sample is predominantly male (78.5 percent), white (90 percent), and tenured (71.6 percent). The majority earned their highest degree in a Res-I institution (73.8 percent) and achieved the highest degree offered in their fields, namely, Ph.D., J.D., or M.D. (95.5 percent).

Individuals vary in both chronological age (mean = 47.2, standard deviation = 9.6) and career age (defined as the number of years elapsed since earning the highest degree: M = 18.5, SD = 9.6). Their ranks are assistant professor (19.5 percent), associate professor (24.8 percent), and professor (55.7 percent). Further, sufficient numbers of respondents had been reviewed for tenure or had been promoted between 1985 and 1987 (N = 85) to permit meaningful analysis of the effect this environmental response had on social knowledge, behavior, and productivity.

221

In addition to standard sociodemographic and career indices, the survey instrument contains measures of faculty perceptions of their universities and of their own efficacy (sense of organizational influence/personal control, competence), values and beliefs, and psychological dispositions. The instrument includes a variety of items that assess current distribution of effort, current rate of publication, and prior rate of publication (up to 1985). These publication output measures allowed us to distinguish between the individual's past publication performance (a career variable in the framework) and current rate of publication (an outcome variable), and therefore to test the effect of prior accomplishments on current performance. Unlike most previous surveys, our rate of publication is a continuous variable. It provides a refined discrimination among respondents.[9]

Variables

The theoretical framework evaluated in this study includes six of the nine theoretical constructs specified in figure 4.1: sociodemographic characteristics, career, self-knowledge, social knowledge, environmental response, and productivity.

We used discrete measures (e.g., sex, race, age, discipline, university where employed) and factors to test the framework. We derived the factors by submitting all survey items that assessed each of the six constructs to varimax factor rotation analyses. The factor analyses isolated the following measures and factors:

Three measures of career: (1) status, (2) past productivity record, and (3) graduate education background

Twelve factors defining four theoretically distinct types of self-knowledge: (1) self-competence, (2) self-efficacy, (3) values and beliefs, and (4) dispositions

Thirteen social knowledge factors that fell into three categories: (1) inferences about the organization as a whole (e.g., what the university values), (2) perceptions of administrators, and (3) perceptions of faculty

Under environmental responses, four factors defining both local and off-campus feedback the last two years: (1) awarded promotion/tenure, (2) hours of clerical assistance, (3) hours of graduate student assistance, and (4) requests to review manuscripts for publication

Nine behavior factors: (1) service on dissertation committees, (2) attendance at local research lectures/seminars, (3) involvement in off-campus activities, (4) publication/proposal effort (number submitted during the last two years), (5) time given to research in the current term, (6) work effort, (7) collaboration with colleagues, and (8 and 9) two factors representing different configurations of classroom teaching activities

Figure 4.1   Variables Used in Testing the Theoretical Framework

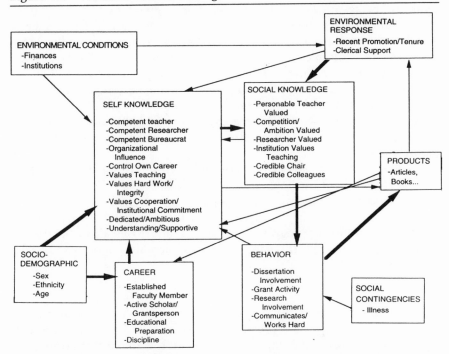

Note: See note to figure 1.1 for interpreting thicker and thinner arrows.

We used all 41 factors and the discrete measures of sociodemographic characteristics in the testing of the framework. Appendix B describes the measures from each of the six variable sets that entered the regression analyses. (The teaching variables are the focus of chapter 5.)

Data Analysis

The causal theoretical framework posits that each set of variables will directly affect the one it precedes. For example, sociodemographic characteristics will influence career, career will influence self-knowledge, and so on. It also assumes that the influence of career, self-knowledge, and social knowledge variables on current publication rate will be indirect. These variables are being mediated by the variables that follow them in the causal sequence. For example, the effect of social knowledge on publication would be mediated by behavior.

We estimated the direct and indirect effects of each construct in the framework by means of a stepwise multiple regression analysis. To estimate the direct effects, we regressed publication rate for the past two years—total number of professional writings published or accepted for publication during this time period—against all causally antecedent variables in the theoretical framework. In this analysis we entered each set of endogenous variables—for example, sociodemographic, career, self-knowledge, social knowledge, environmental response, and behavior—one at a time.[10]

We employed standard path analysis to estimate indirect effects. Each of the endogenous variables was regressed against the causally antecedent variables in the framework. This regression analysis was repeated for each of the variables subsumed under career, self-knowledge, social knowledge, and behavior.

The theoretical framework is longitudinal. However, the data set represents only one point in time, with some retrospective information. As a result, only certain temporal relationships can be tested. These are indicated by the thicker arrows in figure 4.1. In addition, two of the exogenous variables, determined primarily from forces that are outside of the framework, are not included in this analysis: environmental conditions and social contingencies.[11]

Results

Table 4.2 summarizes the results of the stepwise multiple regressions. The beta weights can be interpreted as direct effects.[12] The relative size and sign of the standardized beta weights indicate the amount of positive or negative change in publication output—the dependent measure—that is attributable to each predictor variable with the influence of every other variable in the equation held constant.

Direct Effects

The data in table 4.2 show the amount of variance in each of the variables that is predicted by all of its antecedents as well as the betas for each of the predictors. By way of illustration, column 6 indicates how much variation in the measure "established faculty member" is attributable to the sociodemographic variables by displaying the betas for each of the sociodemographic variables that entered the equation. Following standard practice, we discuss only those betas with a magnitude of .05 or greater that are statistically significant at $p \leq .05$.

The theoretical framework assumes that sociodemographic characteristics may directly affect career and self-knowledge, or that the effects on self-knowledge may be mediated by career. (The indirect effects are discussed in the next section.) The findings suggest that being female may have directly influenced discipline affiliation (columns 9–15). Women are in English (column 11) and psychology (14), but not in chemistry (9). Being a woman also had a strong negative effect on being an established faculty member (beta = $-.904$, $p \leq .001$), a factor including career age, rank, tenure status, and administrative experience.

The data also show that chronological age had significant direct effects on three self-knowledge variables: self-competence, values/beliefs, and disposition. Older faculty members rated themselves lower on research competence and ambition (columns 17 and 24) and reported strong teaching values (21). Race had a direct positive effect on research competence (17). Asian Americans expressed high research competence. Disposition measures (24, 25) had a negative effect on sense of control over one's career (20).

The percentage of explained variance for the career variables predicting self-knowledge ranged from 25.6 percent for research competence (column 17) to 3.7 percent for teaching competence (16). The established faculty member (6) and active scholar/grantsperson (7) variables were the strongest publication predictors. Both had positive direct effects on professors' self-ascribed research ability (research competence, 17) and tendency to be ambitious, competitive, perseverant, and dedicated (dedicated/ambitious, 24). Standing within the university (established faculty member) also led professors to believe they exerted organizational influence (19). In contrast with earlier studies, which conclude that such power is awarded primarily on the basis of scholarly reputation (Fulton & Trow, 1974), professors' cumulative research record (active scholar/grantsperson, 7) did not affect their perceptions of organizational influence (19). However, in keeping with extant research (Lawrence & Blackburn, 1985), the active scholars/grantspersons appear to have less regard for teaching (21).

Among the self-knowledge variables, the self-efficacy, value, and personal disposition variables had the strongest influence on social knowledge. In particular, the impression is that competitiveness and ambition are valued traits (explained variance is 26.2 percent). Professors' sense of control over their careers predicted their perceptions of the credibility of university administrators and faculty colleagues (columns 32 and 33). The faculty members' own valuation of teaching (21) influenced these perceptions of department/unit chairs and colleagues.[13] The largest direct effect on social knowledge was exerted by a disposition variable. Faculty who described themselves as ambitious, competitive, dedicated, and perseverant thought their universities valued these characteristics (29).

The environmental response variables did not have strong direct effects on social knowledge.

The social knowledge variables were not strong predictors of behavior. However, the data indicate that career and self-knowledge variables have

Table 4.2 Path Analysis Data

	6	7	8	9	10	11	12	13	14	15	16	17	18	19	20	21
1 Female	-.904c	-.047	-.046	-.105a	-.056	.160c	-.017	-.061	.092a	.041	.034	-.081a	.021	-.109a	-.001	.025
2 DAsian	.015	.017	.031	-.015	.022	.004	.014	.020	-.044	-.034	.035	.125b	-.016	-.005	-.087a	-.044
3 DOther	.007	-.048	.014	.067	.120b	-.016	.015	-.048	-.059	.019	.033	.071	.011	-.041	-.139b	.000
4 DBlack	-.017	-.086a	-.005	-.023	.012	.043	.042	.030	.068	.033	.056	.021	.032	-.003	-.078	-.002
5 Age	.767c	-.021	.075	-.007	.001	.042	.056	.055	.007	-.024	-.077	-.184b	-.013	-.172a	-.134a	.252c
6 Estab. faculty											.133	.167b	.018	.284c	.016	.006
7 Active scholar/ grantsperson											.000	.401c	-.127b	.044	.179c	-.306c
8 Edu. background											-.002	-.036	-.126b	.056	.037	-.061
9 DChemistry											-.009	-.030	-.076	.031	.080	-.053
10 DMath											.002	-.212c	.158b	-.151b	-.044	.023
11 DEnglish											.116	-.034	-.035	-.009	-.130a	.141a
12 DHistory											.124a	.055	-.057	.017	-.044	.081
13 DPolitical science											.090	.050	-.007	.025	.018	-.012
14 DPsychology											.068	-.045	-.048	-.066	.110a	-.041
15 DSociology											-.004	.021	-.038	-.042	-.017	.008
16 Competent teacher																
17 Comp. researcher																
18 Comp. bureaucrat																
19 Org. influence																
20 Control over career																
21 Values teaching																
22 Values hard work/ integrity																

		R2
23	Values cooperation/inst. commitment	.626
24	Dedic./ambitious	.012
25	Understanding/supportive	.010
26	Recent promotion/tenure	.017
27	Clerical support	.019
28	Personable teacher valued	.028
29	Competition/ambition valued	.005
30	Researcher valued	.012
31	Inst. values teaching	.018
32	Credible chair	.005
33	Credible colleagues	.037
34	Diss. involvement	.256
35	Grant involvement	.049
36	Research involve.	.089
37	Communicates/works hard	.146
38	Two-year pub. rate	.226

Continued next page

Table 4.2—*Continued*

	22	23	24	25	26	27	28	29	30	31	32	33	34	35	36	37	38
1 Female	.039	-.118a	.069	.014	.076	-.021	.003	.001	-.031	.073	.090	.064	-.039	-.230	-.076	.010	-.008
2 DAsian	.013	.067	.075	.025	.016	.042	.002	-.043	.046	-.019	.036	.057	.034	-.064	-.011	-.041	.013
3 DOther	-.048	.077	.045	.025	.003	.005	.004	-.046	.015	.006	.032	.089	.073	-.103	-.022	.047	.022
4 DBlack	.058	.086	.133b	.136b	.006	-.009	.076	-.018	.033	-.040	.032	.029	-.024	-.007	-.076	-.040	.032
5 Age	-.046	-.022	-.335c	-.062	-.089	-.228b	.079	-.072	.095	-.087	.041	.110	.176	-.315a	.001	-.109	.100
6 Estab. faculty	-.011	.153a	.261c	.082	-.337c	.380c	.075	.047	-.115	.113	.071	-.141	-.071	.106	.042	-.006	-.049
7 Active scholar/ grantsperson	.058	.043	.218c	-.128b	-.011	.083	-.084	-.074	-.086	.046	-.059	-.084	.180b	.243c	.010	.138	.172a
8 Edu. background	.067	-.010	.068	-.024	.062	.008	-.067	.026	-.009	-.047	-.055	.048	.015	.038	-.098	-.039	-.112
9 DChemistry	.057	.121a	.078	.070	.031	.084	-.144	-.006	-.065	-.031	-.011	-.106	.222b	.016	.045	.035	.029
10 DMath	-.100	-.135a	-.150b	-.084	-.013	-.143a	-.139	-.165a	-.104	.077	.010	-.123	-.081	-.182	-.068	.191a	.094
11 DEnglish	.091	-.020	-.022	.092	-.008	-.028	-.032	-.103	-.166a	.056	.065	-.090	.004	-.161a	-.111	.117	.174a
12 DHistory	.077	.025	-.039	.014	.036	-.043	-.089	-.159a	-.163a	-.015	-.039	-.084	.020	-.204a	-.114	.284b	.032
13 DPolitical science	.152a	.019	.104	.010	-.103	-.091	-.087	-.160a	-.245b	.009	-.034	-.163a	.129	-.235b	.000	.214a	.036
14 DPsychology	.057	.061	-.076	.101	-.014	-.029	-.105	-.044	-.063	-.055	.018	-.099	.151	-.243b	.000	.102	.027
15 DSociology	.061	.067	-.055	.039	-.070	-.128a	-.153a	-.099	-.115	.060	.096	-.038	.113	-.163a	-.020	.139	-.005
16 Competent teacher							.024	-.033	.161a	-.027	.068	-.027	.030	.084	.004	-.067	-.038
17 Comp. researcher							.103	-.131	-.017	.077	.034	.054	-.050	.186b	.099	.091	.047
18 Comp. bureaucrat							.026	-.157a	.028	-.043	.027	-.003	-.045	-.046	.031	.000	-.062
19 Org. influence							.046	.002	.150a	-.082	.209c	.181b	.042	.075	.051	.036	-.014
20 Control over career							.000	.073	.093	-.103	.100	.011	.139	.034	.014	-.031	.044
21 Values teaching							-.127	.017	-.014	.003	.085	.027	-.009	-.090	-.451c	-.019	.134
22 Values hard work/ integrity							.058	-.094	.095	.044	-.044	.640	-.098	.052	.072	.000	-.073

228

23 Values cooperation/inst. commitment							.111	.032	.117	.009	.149b	.150b	.036	.004	-.031	.041	-.123
24 Dedic./ambitious							.033	.419c	-.062	.071	.035	.066	-.066	-.041	-.117	.235b	.016
25 Understanding/supportive							.079	.140a	.047	.020	.074	.033	.187a	-.014	.011	-.012	.020
26 Recent promotion/tenure							.143a	.070	-.001	.011	.035	.017					
27 Clerical support							.011	-.113	.040	.095	.123a	.127a					
28 Personable teacher valued													-.130a	.039	.025	-.002	.054
29 Competition/ambition valued													-.039	.057	.141a	-.045	-.046
30 Researcher valued													.092	-.113	.047	-.004	-.032
31 Inst. values teaching													-.041	.050	-.127a	.005	.050
32 Credible chair													.134	-.087	.106	.042	-.086
33 Credible colleagues													-.146	.018	-.088	.022	.083
34 Diss. involvement																	.315c
35 Grant involvement																	.328c
36 Research involve.																	.382c
37 Communicates/works hard																	.283c
38 Two-year pub. rate																	
R2	.062	.103	.177	.064	.222	.103	.130	.262	.237	.159	.217	.185	.298	.377	.453	.247	.502

Note: The letter D before a variable's name (e.g., DAsian, DChemistry) indicates that it was a dummy variable in the data analysis.
a: $p \leq .05$.   b: $p \leq .01$.   c: $p \leq .001$.

significant betas for one or more of the behaviors that do directly affect productivity (columns 34–37).

As predicted, professors' current research behavior had the strongest direct effects on their publication rates during this time period. The betas for the behavior variables ranged from .283 for communicates/works hard (37) to .382 for research involvement (36). All betas were significant at $p \leq .001$.

Indirect Effects

The causal theoretical framework postulates that the effects of socio-demographic, career, self-knowledge, and social knowledge variables on publication rate would be mediated by behavior. In other words, these variables would have direct effects on behavior variables that in turn enhance publication rate. The framework assumes that faculty members will develop strategies to increase their publication rates based on their understanding of themselves and their environment. The strategies manifest themselves as different behaviors, all of which lead directly to publication. Therefore, to understand the motivation process, one must trace the antecedents of the different behaviors.

The data presented in table 4.2 support the general proposition that behavior mediates the influence of the antecedent variables on current publication rate. All predictor variables (column 38) account for 50.2 percent of the explained variance in publication rate.[14]

The data displayed in table 4.3 show that in the initial stages of the hierarchical regression, the increase in percentage of the explained variance was significant as we added each successive set of variables. (See the bottom row of the table.) When behavior variables were added, the effect of cumulative research record (active scholar/grantsperson) diminished substantially, from a beta of .338 to .172. However, the increase in percentage of explained variance remained significant. Constructs placed earlier in the framework have little predictive value once we take into account constructs that are temporally closer to the outcome. This finding supports the ordering of the theoretical framework.

Table 4.4 shows which of the predictors exert their influence through the four different behaviors, namely, dissertation involvement, grant involvement, research involvement, and communicates/works hard. We report the data in this manner to show both changes in the amount of predicted variance in each behavior and changes in the direct effects of variables as they enter into the regression in the causal sequence.

Beginning with dissertation involvement, the findings indicate that three career variables and one self-knowledge variable have stable effects on this behavior. Active scholars/grantspersons, faculty members with appoint-

Table 4.3   Variations in Publication Rate Predicted by Variable Sets

	1	2	3	4	5
Sociodemographic					
Female	−.073	−.050	−.034	−.040	−.008
Asian	−.005	−.011	−.024	−.022	.013
Other	−.002	.004	.012	−.012	.022
Black	−.052	−.010	−.008	−.015	.032
Age	−.062	−.078	.009	.017	.100
Career					
Established faculty member		.047	−.014	−.024	−.049
Active scholar/grantsperson		*.452*	*.333*	*.338*	*.172*
Educational preparation		*−.136*	*−.143*	*−.151*	−.112
Chemistry		.094	.083	.101	.029
Mathematics		−.066	−.032	−.014	.094
English		.031	.049	.062	*.174*
History		−.039	−.048	−.024	.032
Political science		.000	−.009	.005	.036
Psychology		−.019	−.026	−.012	.027
Sociology		−.053	−.041	−.026	−.005
Self-knowledge					
Competent teacher			−.002	.005	−.038
Competent researcher			*.149*	.129	.047
Competent bureaucrat			−.078	−.071	−.062
Organizational influence			.061	.073	−.014
Control over career			.097	.094	.044
Values teaching			−.066	.079	.134
Values hard work/integrity			−.061	−.061	−.073
Values cooperation/commit.			−.080	−.090	−.123
Dedicated/ambitious			.048	.039	.016
Understanding/supportive			.079	.084	.020
Social knowledge					
Personable teacher valued				.053	.054
Competition/ambition valued				.026	−.046
Researcher valued				−.053	−.032
Institution values teaching				.037	.050
Credible chair				−.005	−.086
Credible colleagues				.017	.083
Behavior					
Dissertation involvement					*.315*
Grant involvement					*.328*
Research involvement					*.382*
Communicates/works hard					*.283*
Percentage of explained variance	1.0	28.7	*34.7*	35.6	50.2

Source: NCRIPTAL survey.

Notes: Numbers are standardized betas. Bold, italicized entries are at $p \le .05$.

231

Table 4.4 Variations in Behavior Predicted by Antecedent Variables

	Dissertation Involvement				Grant Involvement				Research Involvement				Communicates/Works Hard			
	1	2	3	4	1	2	3	4	1	2	3	4	1	2	3	4
Sociodemographic																
Female	-.075	-.062	-.050	-.039	-.079	-.024	-.030	-.230	-.123	-.091	-.069	-.076	-.021	-.003	.011	.010
Asian	.009	.013	.034	.034	-.038	-.051	-.076	-.064	.017	.022	.006	-.011	.002	-.008	-.040	-.041
Other	.024	.034	.055	.073	-.089	-.074	-.086	-.103	-.086	-.059	-.043	-.022	.064	.070	.054	.047
Black	-.051	-.027	-.027	-.024	-.011	.028	.012	-.007	-.105	-.066	-.054	-.076	.001	-.001	-.027	-.040
Age	.115	.145	.161	.176	-.289	-.363	-.309	-.315	-.104	-.105	.018	.001	-.111	-.226	-.130	-.109
Career																
Estab. faculty member		-.046	-.083	-.071		.129	.117	.106		.037	.016	.042		.117	.011	-.006
Active scholar/ grantsperson		.187	.201	.180		.293	.246	.243		.169	-.019	.010		.283	.155	.138
Educational prep.		.035	.039	.015		.034	.009	.038		-.069	-.078	-.098		-.052	-.047	-.039
Chemistry		.272	.247	.222		.048	.041	.016		.039	.025	.045		.041	.027	.035
Mathematics		-.037	-.035	-.081		-.204	-.193	-.182		-.160	-.133	-.068		.134	.198	.191
English		.023	.023	.004		-.132	-.134	-.161		-.214	-.165	-.111		.145	.147	.117
History		.056	.054	.020		-.155	-.166	-.204		-.179	-.172	-.114		.322	.314	.284
Political science		.142	.152	.129		-.178	-.203	-.235		-.017	-.030	.000		.257	.233	.214
Psychology		.210	.171	.151		-.224	-.232	-.243		.039	.005	.000		.075	.095	.102
Sociology		.154	.152	.133		-.156	-.154	-.163		-.048	-.046	-.020		.151	.160	.139
Self-knowledge																
Competent teacher			.057	.030			.158	.084			.021	.004			-.071	-.067
Competent researcher			-.065	-.050			.089	.186			.085	.009			.108	.091
Comp. bureaucrat			-.040	-.045			-.065	-.046			.012	.031			.004	.000
Org. influence			.063	.042			.007	.075			.015	.051			.015	.036

232

	1	2	3	4	5	6	7	8	9	10	11	12	13	14	15	16
Control over career			*.174*	.139			-.006	.034			.047	.014			-.047	-.031
Values teaching			.018	-.009			-.096	-.090			*-.428*	*-.451*			-.004	-.019
Values hard work/ integrity			-.125	-.098			.058	.052			.033	.072			-.010	.000
Values coop./commit.			.023	.036			-.015	.004			-.070	-.031			.027	.041
Dedicated/ambitious			.021	-.006			-.002	-.041			-.059	-.117			*.222*	*.235*
Understanding/ supportive			*.162*	*.187*			.011	-.014			.028	.011			-.013	-.012
Social knowledge																
Personable teacher valued				-.130				.039				.025				-.002
Competition/ ambition valued				-.039				.057				*.141*				-.045
Researcher valued				.092				-.113				.047				-.004
Inst. values teaching				-.041				.050				-.127				.055
Credible chair				.134				-.087				.106				.042
Credible colleagues				-.146				.018				-.088				.022
Percentage of explained variance	2.6	17.8	23.9	29.8	7.9	29.1	33.1	33.7	3.6	18.0	36.8	45.3	8.1	14.1	22.4	24.7

Source: NCRIPTAL survey.

Notes: Numbers are standardized betas. Bold, italicized numbers are at *p* ≤ .05 for betas and change in variance explained.

233

ments in the sciences, and individuals who describe themselves as understanding and supportive were more likely to supervise dissertation research. The combination of variables fits with the process of accumulative advantage described by Allison and Stewart (1974). The findings from the present study show that professors with strong cumulative records as researchers (active scholars/grantspersons) were more likely to be supervising dissertations. Chairing dissertations can be a strategy used by these faculty to increase their publication rates. Dissertation activity frequently leads to articles co-authored with students whose dissertations are part of faculty members' ongoing research programs. It can also be the case that students seek faculty with strong records to chair their dissertations.

The findings vis-à-vis grant involvement underscore this interpretation. The data show that active scholars/grantspersons are more likely to spend time on the preparation of proposals than on other research activities. However, the findings also suggest that people engage in activities they believe they do well in. In the final regression of the path analysis, faculty members who thought they were competent researchers were more involved with grants than were those who rated their research competency low. Furthermore, the betas for the sciences were positive, and the betas for the humanities were negative.[15] One could infer from these discipline findings that people engage in grant activities when they think the probabilities for success are greater—for example, more funding is available for the sciences—or when the funds are needed for support people and equipment to conduct research.

Although chronological age exerted a substantial negative impact on current grant involvement, its direct effect was reduced as the self-knowledge and social knowledge variables entered the regression. Perhaps older professors in research universities who are not engaged with grant proposals do not feel as competent as researchers when compared with younger professors.

Research involvement, the amount of time given to research in the present term, exerted the strongest direct effect on current publication rate (beta = .382, $p \leq .001$; column 36 in table 4.2). It appears that those who allocate time to research use it in ways that result in publication. It is, however, such a general measure that few antecedents predict it. The variable with the most significant direct effect, "values teaching" (column 21 in table 4.2), had a negative influence (beta = $-.451, p \leq .001$). This instance may be the clearest example of personal values resulting in a decision to devote effort to activities other than research (probably teaching, but perhaps committee and service work). Apparently faculty make this decision irrespective of their inferences about the organizational climate, because the respondents' personal values did not directly affect their perceptions of their institution's emphasis on teaching. (See column 31 in table 4.2.)

Last, the behavior "communicates/works hard" (working long hours, talking about research at conferences and over the phone) has a link to a personality trait. Although writers have speculated about how a professor's personality might influence productivity, there has been little direct empirical research on the question (Baldwin & Blackburn, 1981; Chambers, 1964; Knapp, 1963; Roe, 1964; Zacharias & Mathis, 1982). Our data indicate that the self-ascribed tendencies to be dedicated, perseverant, ambitious, and competitive (dedicated/ambitious) had a significant direct effect on time spent communicating with colleagues about research and pursuing professional activities (communicates/works hard). Communication may involve collaboration on research that leads directly to publications—or arguably, those who are ambitious may also be inclined to communicate with persons who might provide funding or technical assistance that would enable them to carry out their research.

Discussion

The causal theoretical framework evaluated explained 50 percent of the variance in publication rate during a two-year time period. By far the strongest predictors of publication rate were the actual activities (behaviors) professors engaged in during this time. The data suggest, however, that individual differences in career patterns as well as competence, values and beliefs, disposition, and perceptions of the organization lead professors to distribute their effort in different ways. The data also show that self-knowledge exerts an indirect effect on productivity as mediated by behavior.

Because our framework is temporal, the retrospective data did allow us to assess the impact of an individual's previous research accomplishments on current rate of publication. The findings corroborated earlier studies, concluding that professors with strong cumulative research records tend to be more prolific publishers. The data also fit with other research on expectancy theory and work motivation in that the self-knowledge and social knowledge variables together accounted for as little as 4.6 percent and as much as 27.3 percent of the explained variance in grant involvement and research involvement, respectively (Wahba & House, 1981). Even though the overall impact was not great, the type of influence exerted by these two sets of variables is important in understanding why certain individuals engage in different behaviors.

One provocative inference follows from an examination of the impact of self-knowledge and social knowledge on current publication rate. Self-knowledge variables (primarily research competence) explained 6 percent of the variance in rate, whereas social knowledge accounted for less than 1 percent of the predicted variance and actually suppressed the direct effect of respondents' sense of research competence. Staw (1983) argues that an organization's reward system can become detrimental when an activity is overemphasized. The incentive that is inherent in the activity itself may be diminished and be replaced by the extrinsic reward that is given for performance. In brief, professors may begin to engage in research not because they enjoy the process itself but because it is the basis for merit salary increases and promotion.

With over 50 percent of the variance accounted for—an appreciable increase from the typical 15 percent reported in earlier studies—we claim an initial success. Our theoretical framework has incorporated a number of important variables.

Research in Three Institutional Types

In this second study we determine if our theoretical framework of publication productivity applies to professors in two additional institutional types—doctoral and comprehensive colleges and universities. The analyses enable us to address several important questions about the extent to which organizational factors, individual differences in preparation, prior activities, and perceptions influence faculty publication, and to take preliminary steps toward developing generalizations about what motivates professors to publish.

Several factors have hampered attempts to develop a theoretical framework of faculty motivation that is relevant to different types of institutions. Key limitations include the lack of identical measures from individuals in the same disciplines but different postsecondary institutions, and the scarcity of longitudinal data. Although a few researchers have described productivity changes through time-ordered analyses using citation indexes or curriculum vitae (Allison & Stewart, 1974; Hammel, 1980; Long, 1978; Reskin, 1985), these studies fall short of explaining how individuals relate to their environments and how these interactions may change and influence scholarly output over time. For example, the notion that some professors achieve early recognition for their work, and that this reputation gives them an edge over their peers in competition for funds and publication—the accumulative advantage process—was, as we noted above, based on cross-sequential analysis of citation indexes and little additional longitudinal data (Allison & Stewart, 1974).

The faculty in our NCRIPTAL sample from research universities (N = 601), doctoral universities (N = 366), and comprehensive colleges and universities (N = 1,004) were similar in terms of sociodemographic characteristics and disciplinary affiliations. (See table 4.5.) However, the average two-year publication rates varied across settings. The research university faculty had the highest rate (M = 6.1, SD = 6.6), followed by doctoral faculty (M = 4.0, SD = 5.3) and comprehensive faculty (M = 2.1, SD = 3.7).[16]

Each factor analysis resulted in a different number of factors as well as different factor structures for each institutional type. However, the intercorrelations among factors were small for all institutions (coefficients ranged

Table 4.5   Distribution of Institutional Samples across Sociodemographic Variables

	Res-I	Doc-I	Comp-I
Number of institutions	7	6	26
Number of faculty respondents	601	366	1,004
Percent female	17.9	19.4	19.2
Percent Ph.D.	97.7	93.7	86.7
Discipline (%)			
Biology	14.2	10.5	13.9
Chemistry	12.2	10.5	10.8
Math/statistics	10.7	11.9	14.6
English	14.9	20.2	20.4
History	12.9	13.9	10.8
Political science	10.8	10.0	8.4
Psychology	13.6	15.0	13.4
Sociology	10.7	8.0	7.7
Rank (%)			
Assistant professor	15.4	15.7	18.6
Associate professor	24.8	31.4	31.2
Full professor	58.5	52.9	49.9
Other	1.4	0.0	0.3
Appointment (%)			
Regular appt. w/ tenure	82.7	81.6	82.3
Regular appt. w/o tenure	14.6	15.9	15.4
Other	2.7	2.5	2.3
Race (%)			
Caucasian/white	94.8	95.8	93.5
Black, Asian, and other	5.2	4.2	6.5
Number of pubs. in last two years			
Mean	6.1	4.0	2.1
SD	6.6	5.3	3.7

Source: NCRIPTAL survey.

from $r = -.20$ to $r = .20$). Consequently, it seems reasonable to assume that the factors were measuring different aspects of each of the framework's constructs; that is, they were not related. We entered a total of 61, 67, and 68 variables into the regressions for Res-I, Doc-I, and Comp-I institutions, respectively. In all instances social knowledge subsumed the largest number of variables (24 for Res-I's, 22 for Doc-I's, and 21 for Comp-I's). The fewest variables were under career (3). We define each in appendix B.[17]

We accounted for environmental conditions by running separate regressions for each of the Carnegie institutional types. Our procedure assumes that the colleges and universities within each category are sufficiently similar in terms of mission, the quality of students and faculty, and institutional resources for research. While variations within a group undoubtedly exist, they are likely to be less than the differences between institutional types. The publication output (table 4.5) demonstrates appreciable differences on the key outcome variable. (See the next to last row for the average number of publications in the last two years per faculty member.)

Effects of Theoretical Constructs on Productivity

Res-I Institutions

The results of the regression analysis with publication rate (total publications in the last two years) as the outcome variable are shown in table 4.6.[18] The variables entered into the regression accounted for 58.5 percent of the explained variance in publication rate at Res-I universities.

Table 4.6 and other similarly structured tables in this chapter are to be read as follows. There are two numerical entries for each institutional type. The one in the first column shows the percentage of the variance in the outcome variable (percent effort given to research) that is attributable to the other (predicting) variables as each is entered into the regression analysis. The second column shows the significance level for each variable that was found to be significant at $p \leq .05$ after all of the variables had been entered into the regression analysis. A value of $p \leq .05$ means that a value of the magnitude shown would occur by chance less often than 5 times out of 100.

The variables were entered in the order of the framework, that is, as they are displayed in the tables when read from top to bottom. Sometimes we entered the entire set of our construct measures as a single step. (That is the case for table 4.6.) Other times we entered the variables one at a time. (That is the case for table 4.8.) The tables show the total explained variance at each successive step. Once the percentage of explained variance is above 2 percent, it is significant at $p \leq .05$, the exact value depending upon the size of the sample for that institutional type: the larger the number of faculty, the smaller the percentage can be and still be significant. When the entry of a

Table 4.6 Predicting Percent Effort Given to Research

	Res-I		Doc-I		Comp-I	
	% Var.	p	% Var.	p	% Var.	p
Sociodemographic	0		1		1	
Female						
Race				-.05		
Age				.001		
Career	**29**		**41**		**13**	
Academic discipline		.01		.05		
Active scholar/grantsperson				.001		
Educational preparation						
Established faculty member				-.01		
Self-knowledge	**36**		**51**		**28**	
Committed to teaching		.01		-.01		
Values cooperation/ inst. commitment		-.01				
Values disciplined-focused teaching		-0.5				
Values scholarship		-.01				
Competent researcher				.01		
Responsible faculty member						
Environmental response	**36**		53		**30**	
Journal editorial work						.05
Social knowledge	38		62		31	
Credible colleagues		.05	47			
Faculty committed to teaching			47	.001		
Students are motivated			**50**	-.01		
Teacher control needed			50	.05		
Course relevance important			51	.05		
Credibility of alumni				-.05		
Students are competitive				.05		
Well-rounded teacher valued				-.01		
Ambition/dedication valued				.001		
Salary equity				-.01		
Institution values scholarship				.001		
Behavior	**58**		**78**		**39**	
Grant preparation		.001				.001
High research effort		.001		.001		.001
Communicates/works hard		.001				
Applying for fellowship		.001		.01		
Attends local res. seminars		.001				
Dissertation work				.001		
Org. decision making				-0.5		

Source: Lawrence, Blackburn, Trautvetter (1989).

Note: Bold, italicized entries are at $p \leq .05$.

variable into the regression produces a significant increase in the percentage of variance accounted for, the value appears in bold italics.

By way of illustration, note the first entry for Res-I institutions in table 4.6. When all three sociodemographic variables—sex, race, and age—were entered, the percentage of variance accounted for was less than 1 percent, and hence zero is entered. That is, these variables had no effect on the outcome variable. In addition, none proved to be a significant predictor after all of the variables had been entered, so no entry is recorded in the p (probability) column for female, race, or age.

The second entry was the set of career variables—academic discipline, active scholar/grantsperson, educational preparation, and established faculty member. They significantly increased the percentage of variance accounted for to 29 percent. After all of the variables had been entered into the analysis, discipline was statistically significant at $p \leq .01$. When a minus sign precedes a p value (as it does, e.g., on three of the self-knowledge variables), it means the opposite (here, e.g., that more prolific publishers do *not* highly value cooperation and institutional commitment). The entry of the self-knowledge variables increased the percentage of the variance accounted for to 36 percent, but this was not a statistically significant increase. (The number therefore appears in the table in regular type.) At the end one sees that 58 percent of the variance in the publication rate of research universities was attributed to the entire set of variables.

Behavior variables most strongly predicted publication rate. All of the behavior variables were strong predictors ($p \leq .001$). Specifically, faculty members who published more during the two years prior to the survey had been actively involved in the preparation of grant proposals and had given more time to research and less to teaching. The prolific publishers had also spent more time working and communicating with colleagues about scholarly and research issues or had been actively engaged in applying for fellowships. Faculty members who attended seminars or made presentations about their research on their own campuses also published at a higher rate.

The results further suggest that the behavior variables mediated the direct effects of the career, self-knowledge, and social knowledge variables. The direct effects of faculty members' educational preparation and cumulative publication or grant record—all publications and proposals submitted before 1985—weakened and dropped out completely when behaviors were entered. On the other hand, the effects of selected measures of self-knowledge and social knowledge became significant only after the behaviors were entered. A personal commitment to teaching had a positive effect on publication, suggesting that productive publishers may also have a concern about their teaching. The negative sign for "values scholarship" indicates, however, that persons who prefer to spend time on activities that enhance their teaching knowledge or skills are not necessarily publishing. The emergence of the social knowledge factor "credible colleagues"—a perception that one's colleagues give valuable feedback on both one's teaching and one's scholarship—suggests that the behavior "communicates/works hard" enhances its effect. Professors who find their colleagues' critiques useful apparently communicate with them more often about research activities.

Doc-I Institutions

The variables entered into the regressions appear to be particularly potent within the doctoral universities, accounting for 77.5 percent of the explained variation in current publication rate. The results indicate that at least one measure of each of the theoretical framework's constructs influenced publication. The strongest predictor was a behavior variable, high research involvement. This factor means that a professor was giving more time to research and less to teaching in the current term, and had been actively submitting grant proposals and articles for publication over the last two years. Next came a second behavior, dissertation work, a factor that shows a faculty member's high level of involvement in students' doctoral research and comprehensive examinations. Self-knowledge in the form of greater commitment to research than teaching, signified by the negative sign for "committed to teaching," continued to influence publication rate from initial entry through the final step in the regression. Likewise, a career factor, active scholar/grantsperson, representing one's cumulative research record as of 1985, exerted a continuous influence on publication rate, although its effect diminished. On the other hand, chronological age (a sociodemographic variable) became an important predictor only when behavior entered the framework and indicated that older professors were publishing at a higher rate. Last, "institution values scholarship," the perception that one's university encourages scholarship (social knowledge), also had a positive impact on publication rate.

Generally speaking, the systematic controls on behavior enhanced the impact of the other variables in the framework. The only variable that entered the regression and did not remain through the last step was journal editorial work, a factor indicating involvement in reviews and editing submitted articles. The fact that seven of the social knowledge variables came to exert significant effects on publication rate after we controlled for behavior indicates, however, that these important views of students and organizational climate are not transmitted through the behavior variables specified in this regression.

Comp-I Institutions

The framework's theoretical constructs account for 39 percent of the variance for Comp-I institutions, a highly significant amount even though less than for the other two types. Two behavior variables—grant preparation, signifying active involvement in grant preparation, and high research effort, signifying high involvement in research over the past two years—provide the strongest publication predictors. While their strengths were not especially large, both were significant at $p \leq .001$. The only other variable that remained in the final regression was an environmental response factor, journal editorial work. It identifies faculty members actively involved in reviewing articles for journals and serving on the editorial board of a journal. This factor was significant at $p \leq .05$ but is not a strong predictor.

As for the other components of the framework, only one socio-demographic variable, age, appeared in step one but did not account for a significant amount of the explained variance. (The negative value indicates that younger faculty in Comp-I's published more.) No sociodemographic variable remained after all variables had been entered into the regression.

Active scholar/grantsperson, a career variable representing people who were actively publishing books and articles and submitting grant proposals, was initially statistically significant, but its direct effects were mediated when the behavior variables were entered. Further, the strength of the career measures diminished at each succeeding step. Their strength weakens with the addition of the variables in the subsequent theoretical categories.

Three self-knowledge variables—values discipline-focused teaching, competent researcher, and committed to teaching—initially entered the regression. The two teaching factors have negative signs. To the extent that teaching and research are in competition with one another—that is, are opposite ends of a continuum—one interprets the negative teaching signs as positive research ones. No variables subsumed under the social knowledge construct were significant. The direct effects of social knowledge also disappear when behavior variables are entered at the end. The increase in explained variance at each successive step was significant at $p \leq .01$, except for when social knowledge was introduced. This finding further suggests that faculty perceptions of their environment relate to their personal values, competence, and psychological dispositions.

Discussion

The results of this study support the proposed theoretical framework for understanding faculty publication differences. The variables taken into account predicted 77.5 percent, 58.5 percent, and 39.0 percent of the variance

242

in two-year publication rates in the doctoral, research, and comprehensive institutions, respectively. As each group of variables entered into the regression, the amount of explained variance increased in a linear fashion. However, except for the career and behavior variables, which always produced significant changes in the explained variance, the size of the increase was not always significant.

In Res-I's the self-knowledge, environmental response, and social knowledge variables together accounted for very little variance in publication rate. None of these variable groups produced a significant change in the productivity measure. In the Doc-I's the self-knowledge measures produced a significant change in the amount of predicted variance, but environmental response and social knowledge measures did not. Both the self-knowledge and environmental response variables increased the explained variance in publication rate within the Comp-I's.

Although the items in this factor are not identical for all three institutional types, the career variable active scholar/grantsperson stays as an important predictor. This finding suggests that past role performance does indeed influence current productivity. A self-knowledge variable, commitment to teaching, is the same factor for all institutions, but among research university faculty it has positive direct effects on publication, and among the doctoral faculty it has a negative effect. One behavior, the high research involvement factor, was important in the comprehensive and doctoral institutions. However, only three of the behavior items in this factor were the same. These items indicate that faculty who devoted more time to research than to other activities, and who conversed with others about research, also submitted larger numbers of manuscripts for publication. Overall, the theoretical framework taps important constructs for different institutional settings and shows that one needs to take into account where faculty members work when making inferences regarding their motivations toward research and publishing.

We defer further generalizations and implications for practice until the conclusion of the next study. It extends the framework to all institutional types.

All Institutional Types and Other Indicators of Research

We now turn to expanding the framework's applicability to include all institutional types and to two additional indicators of research. We retain typical scholarly publications—articles, book chapters, research proposals and reports, submitted and accepted professional writings—as the product indicator. We add one other behavior as a dependent variable: making conference presentations. A conference presentation may or may not have a formal paper. Even if it does, it may not result in a published article or monograph. In our theoretical framework, then, conference presentations are behaviors, not products. Conversations with colleagues about research processes and progress are important behaviors. A research product can result.

The productions of scholarly publications were once the almost exclusive domain of research and doctoral universities. Today, however, faculty nearly everywhere perceive pressure to obtain external funding, conduct research, and publish their findings. Liberal arts college faculty with their strong teaching mission also find that good teaching evaluations may not suffice to obtain tenure.

The increasing emphasis on the faculty research role may be the result of administrators' desires for enhanced institutional reputation and economic stability. It could also be the outgrowth of an increased interest on the part of faculty in conducting research as a consequence of their graduate school training. Regardless of the reason, more faculty at all institutional types indicate that they would prefer to give more of their work effort to research than they currently give. The needed extra time, they say, would take away from the effort they now give to service. They would prefer the effort they give to teaching to stay about as it is (Carnegie Foundation for the Advancement of Teaching, 1989a).

Consequently, empirical studies that have the research role as their focus are important. We need to know the relative effect of different kinds of motivators on faculty behavior, specifically on their propensity to engage in research.[19]

We used responses from faculty in our same nine Carnegie institutional types. Our institutions span the spectrum of faculty role expectations, from very little research and medium-sized classes with no graduate student assistance in community colleges to a significant research effort and graduate seminars mixed with large classes and supervising teaching assistants in research universities. Before analyzing three specific outcome components of the study, we first used the percentage of effort the faculty member gave to the role as the dependent variable. This procedure allowed us to ascertain the degree to which the sociodemographic, career, self-knowledge, and social knowledge variables explained the faculty behavior of conducting research. We then employed this behavior variable as a predictor for the product (scholarly publications) and the two role-specific behaviors (conference presentations and conversations regarding research).

We begin by giving a broad picture of what the faculty in this study are like. Table 4.7 displays selected sociodemographic, career, self-knowledge, and social knowledge variables by institutional type.

Table 4.7 Selected Demographic, Career, Self-Knowledge, and Social Knowledge Variables (Percent)

	Res-I	Res-II	Doc-I	Doc-II	Comp-I	Comp-II	LAC-I	LAC-II	CC
Number	597	244	360	251	996	135	194	263	845
Female	18	23	19	19	19	23	30	35	30
Graduate school	78	60	59	56	51	38	52	32	33
Lecturer	1	0	0	0	0	0	0	1	1
Instructor	0	0	0	0	0	1	0	3	18
Assistant prof.	15	30	16	26	18	26	29	24	10
Associate prof.	25	35	31	32	31	26	29	31	26
Professor	58	35	52	42	50	47	42	41	43
Career age (actual)	19	17	18	17	18	19	17	16	18
Interest in research	79	68	51	49	25	13	26	14	7
Personal pref. for research	42	36	34	31	19	8	14	9	4
Institutional pref. for research	39	36	32	31	20	15	20	15	10

Source: NCRIPTAL survey.

The sociodemographic and career variables reveal what other studies have demonstrated: that women are underrepresented, more so in universities than in liberal arts and community colleges (see chapter 2); and that Ph.D.-producing universities, especially Res-I's, have more faculty who graduated from Res-I universities (Breneman & Youn, 1988). The top select their faculty from the top. Most who earn their Ph.D.'s from Res-I's want to be on the faculty in a Res-I. The combined factors lead to a highly inbred faculty in Res-I's.

Career age is similar across institutional types. Since the average age of earning the highest degree is about 29 years, the average actual age of these faculty is approximately 47 years. Res-I's and -II's have a markedly higher percentage of full professors, an indication that research matters most in these universities. Rapid promotion and a competitive environment favor those who are successful in this role.

"Interest in research" means that these faculty have said they have a higher interest in research than in teaching, but not that they have no interest in teaching, and vice versa. By way of illustration, 75 percent of Comp-I faculty (100 percent minus 25 percent) have a higher interest in teaching than in research. Most, however, still have some interest in doing research, just as the 25 percent whose greater interest is research maintain an interest in teaching. The very high percentages for interest in research in research universities and the low percentages in Comp-II's, LAC-II's, and CCs conform to expectations.

Personal preferences for time given to research follow the same pattern. University faculty agree on perceived institutional preference for research effort and personal preference for research effort. However, in the two- and four-year colleges, personal preference for research effort is less than what faculty believe the administration wants. The discrepancies can be a source of stress.

In summary, colleges and universities differ appreciably on the variables the framework uses to predict research behavior and output. (Appreciable variation also exists among institutions within a Carnegie category.) The study, then, tests the framework's ability to enlighten us about faculty with differing characteristics in a variety of work environments.

Table 4.8   Predicting Percent Effort Given to Research

	Res-I		Res-II		Doc-I		Doc-II	
	% Var.	p	% Var.	p	% Var.	p	% Var.	p
Sociodemographic								
Female	1		1		1		1	
Career								
Grad. inst. rating	1	-.02	1		1		3	
Career age	5		8		6		4	.04
Assistant professor	5		9		6		5	.00
Associate professor	6		12		9		10	
(Male full prof.)								.00
Self-knowledge								
Self-competence	16	.02	15		26	.02	40	.00
Self-efficacy (infl.)	17		16		26		41	
Ambit./compet./commit.	17		16		26		44	
Research interest	20		23		28		46	
Preference for research (% effort)	35	.00	48	.00	47	.00	62	.00
Social knowledge								
Inst. pref. for research (% effort)	37	.00	52	.01	47		67	.00
Support services and colleagues	38		52		47		68	.01
Support, grant ($s)	38		53		50	.01	69	
Credence to chair/dean	38		53		50		69	-.03
Colleague commitment to research	39		53		51		69	

Source: Blackburn, Bieber, Lawrence, and Trautvetter (1991).

Regression Results

Table 4.8 shows the results of the regression analysis with the outcome variable being percentage of effort given to research. First we see that the theoretical framework strongly predicts percentage of faculty effort given to research across all institutional types. The percentage of the explained variance in effort given to research ranges from 23 percent in LAC-II's—institutions that neither emphasize nor reward research—to 80 percent in Comp-II's, with an overall average above 50 percent.

However, not all variables turn out to be significant predictors. For example, the sociodemographic and career variables, the ones almost exclusively used in prior research on faculty productivity, rarely account for the effort given to research. Gender never does. The self-knowledge and social knowledge variables, however, do predict well. People who want to give

Table 4.8—*Continued*

Comp-I		Comp-II		LAC-I		LAC-II		CC	
% Var.	p	% Var.	p	% Var.	p	% Var.	p	% Var.	p
0		4		0		2		1	
1		7		1		2		1	
1		*13*		3		4		1	
2		13		4		5		2	
3		13		4		5		2	
	.00								
23	.00	*21*		*18*		*19*	.01	*22*	.01
24		25		18		20		23	
25		*30*	.05	21		20		24	
31	.00	*40*		24		20		*32*	
41	.00	*74*	.00	*35*	.01	20		*53*	.01
42	.02	*80*	.00	*41*		23		*54*	
42		80		42		23		*54*	
43	.00	80		42		23		*54*	
43		80		42		23		*54*	
44	.01	80		44		23		*54*	

time to research, feel that they are able researchers, and believe that research is a high institutional priority are the ones who allocate the most time to their research, a finding that is true across most college and university types (8 of 9, 6 of 9, and 5 of 9, respectively).

For example, we can see that the very high 80 percent explained variance in Comp-II's results principally from the faculty members' personal preference concerning how much time they wish to give to that role. The explained variance increased from 40 percent to 74 percent when that single variable entered the regression. Yet there are publication differences across institutional types, with faculty at Res-I's far outpublishing their counterparts along the Carnegie classes of institutions. Comp-II faculty's preferred effort, then, is not resulting in a proportionate number of publications. They must suffer frustrations.

These findings indicate that it is important for an institution to establish a climate conducive to what it values if it wishes to achieve its goals. If the organization wants increased faculty research output, there must be a clear message from above that such is the case. In addition, the institution must make it obvious that faculty research is being rewarded. Those who successfully serve this goal will receive visible honors, titles, raises. The scholarly record of new hires will be made public.

Turning to table 4.9, where the outcome variable is publications, the behavior variable effort given to research—now a predictor variable—significantly increases the amount of publication output accounted for in three institutional types (Res-I's, LAC-I's, and LAC-II's) but lowers it for two others (Doc-II's and Comp-II's). Self-competence and financial support through obtaining grants are the strong predictors of publishing. The former is significant in all institutional types and the latter in all but LAC-II's and Comp-II's. The entry of self-competence into the equation produces a significant percentage predictive increase for faculty in every college and university type. When grant support entered the regression, it produced a significant increase in the variance accounted for in six of the nine institutional types.

Of the sociodemographic and career variables, only two appear as significant predictors: career age (in three cases) and rating of institution granting the highest degree (two times). What is new here is that it is the younger faculty who are publishing more—the negative coefficient for significant career age means the opposite of older—an outcome different from all prior national surveys of faculty. At the same time, being a male full professor is a significant predictor of publication in five institutional types. It is also of interest that being a graduate of a non-Res-I predicts higher publications. What this discovery suggests is that if you have not graduated from a Res-I but you are a prominent publisher, research institutions will hire you. The finding also demonstrates that Res-I's are not necessarily the exclusive, snobbish clubs many accuse them of being. Faculty in Res-I's have not been growing appreciably for two decades now. These institutions are not hiring anywhere near the number of Ph.D.'s they graduate. Res-I's have been, and still are, the leading Ph.D. producers. They graduate many more than they can add to their staff. It would be a simple matter to have a faculty of 100 percent Res-I graduates, *if* that status was their goal. Here we see that Res-I's value performance over graduate school pedigree when it comes to whom they have on their staff.

We note that gender again fails to predict (except negatively in Comp-I's, meaning that males, coded the opposite of females, produce more there). Most earlier studies found that men published more than women. Also contrary to earlier expectations, interest in research did not predict actual output. We used this self-knowledge variable in a study on teaching (see chapter 5) and found it to be a strong predictor of effort given to teaching (Blackburn, Bieber, Lawrence, & Trautvetter, 1991). Self-efficacy, the ability to influence having one's work published, predicts only for faculty in Res-I institutions. Apparently faculty at the top believe that their status gives them the power to have a piece accepted for publication, a hegemony their colleagues in other institutions do not claim. As generally acknowledged researchers, their peers call on them to write chapters for books they are editing. They can influence the publication of their products. However, what proportion of their work effort they believe the institution wants them to give to research has no impact.

The strong role that having grants has in predicting faculty publication rate suggests that those institutions that want to increase this kind of output need to consider ways they can assist faculty members prepare acceptable proposals. Proposal writing requires skills and support for doing it. The task is about as difficult and complex as is writing up the research that flows from the grant support. Experts can teach others the fine points of grant writing, but they cannot do the writing for the faculty. The author has to know the subject and the state of the art, what research is needed, and how it can be creatively undertaken. Those outside the specialized field cannot design the research.

In addition to learning how to prepare grant proposals, the faculty member needs time and assistance. Relief from an assignment, help from advanced students who can locate key sources, and some seed money to gather critical pilot data and equipment are some of the things the institution can supply at a relatively low cost. If successful grant-getting senior faculty will pair themselves with upcoming researchers and show them the way, this is

Table 4.9 Predicting Publications

	Res-I		Res-II		Doc-I		Doc-II	
	% Var.	p	% Var.	p	% Var.	p	% Var.	p
Sociodemographic								
Female	1		1		1		1	
Career								
Grad. inst. rating	5	-.01	1	-.02	1		3	
Career age	7	-.01	10	-.01	5		4	
Assistant professor	10	-.01	19	-.01	6		5	
Associate professor	17	-.04	27		13		16	
(Male full prof.)				.01				
Self-knowledge								
Self-competence	41	.00	37	.05	34	.01	47	.00
Self-efficacy (infl.)	44	.01	37		34		47	
Ambit./compet./commit.	44		38		36	.04	49	
Research interest	44		39		36		50	
Preference for research (% effort)	45	.00	40		38		51	
Social knowledge								
Inst. pref. for research (% effort)	45		41		39		51	
Support services and colleagues	46	.01	41		39		51	
Support, grant ($s)	55	.00	44	.04	47	.00	57	.00
Credence to chair/dean	55		45	.05	47		57	
Colleague commitment to research	55		45		47		57	
Behavior								
Effort given to research (% time)	55		48	.02	48		57	

Source: Blackburn, Bieber, Lawrence, and Trautvetter (1991).

an effective tactic to increase the number of faculty securing grants and subsequently publishing. Evidence shows that the size of the grant is not the critical condition. Even small amounts of money can induce faculty to pay back with a publication or two. Receiving support challenges them to deliver.

At the same time, the institution that chooses to have faculty increase their research output needs to be patient. Even after grant-writing skills have been mastered, it is several years from an idea, a submitted proposal, and funding to research carried out, written up, accepted for publication, and printed. Five years would be the typical minimum time lapse.

As for the outcome variable, namely, making presentations on campus and at conferences—activities that require preparation of research, but not

Table 4.9—*Continued*

Comp-I		Comp-II		LAC-I		LAC-II		CC	
% Var.	p	% Var.	p	% Var.	p	% Var.	p	% Var.	p
1	-.02	5		1		1		1	
1		9		3		1		1	
3		18		4		3	-.02	1	
5		19		4		10		1	
7		19		4		10		1	
	.01						.01		.01
44	.00	49	.00	54	.00	55	.00	51	.00
44		49		55		56		52	
44		51		55		56		52	
45		52		56		57		53	
46		53		56	.01	57		54	.01
46		53		56		58		54	
46		53		57		59	-.05	55	
51	.00	55		59	.03	59		58	
51		55		59		59		58	
51		55		59		59		58	
51		59	.02	59		59		59	.05

necessarily publications—the amounts of explained variance are still appreciable, much higher than they are in the typical faculty study, which most often used only sociodemographic and career variables. (See table 4.10.) The amounts are not, however, as high as they were for published articles, books, and the like. (Average is 32 percent vs. 55 percent.) The predictors are much the same. Self-competence is significant in six college and university types, and financial support (having grants) in four.

A new finding for this outcome measure is that in five institutional types, male full professors are the conference presenters, on campus and away. Conferences often include symposia and special presentations. These events favor the senior faculty who have earned a sound reputation for their research. They will also be on the program with their research papers, because

251

Table 4.10 Predicting Conference Presentations

	Res-I		Res-II		Doc-I		Doc-II	
	% Var.	p	% Var.	p	% Var.	p	% Var.	p
Sociodemographic								
Female	1		1		1		1	
Career								
Grad. inst. rating	1		1		1		1	
Career age	6	-.01	7		3		2	
Assistant professor	7		7		3		2	
Associate professor	12	-.04	10		4		11	
(Male full prof.)		.00		.03		.02		
Self-knowledge								
Self-competence	23	.01	16		14	.04	25	
Self-efficacy (infl.)	25		16		14		25	
Ambit./compet./commit.	25		17		14		27	
Research interest	25		17		14		27	
Preference for research (% effort)	25		17		15	.04	28	
Social knowledge								
Inst. pref. for research (% effort)	25		17		15		29	
Support services and colleagues	25		17		15		29	
Support, grant ($s)	29	.00	18		20	.01	32	.03
Credence to chair/dean	30		19		23	.01	33	
Colleague commitment to research	30		19		23		36	.01
Behavior								
Effort given to research (% time)	30		20	.02	24		36	

Source: Blackburn, Bieber, Lawrence, and Trautvetter (1991).

most remain active throughout their career. Being a full professor predicts this activity.

Conference activity most often lies outside the institution. Regional and national meetings are beyond administrators' ability to influence, even if they wanted to. These are the professional disciplines at work—national, not in-house, operations. Administrators are welcome to participate in them and can be on the program, if they are active scholars. The organization can encourage faculty members' participation in disciplinary associations and can reward them by providing dollars for attendance, even sweetening the stimulus with additional amounts to those having their research papers accepted in a peer-review process.

Professional conferences are also the source of new ideas for faculty—

Table 4.10—*Continued*

Comp-I		Comp-II		LAC-I		LAC-II		CC	
% Var.	p	% Var.	p	% Var.	p	% Var.	p	% Var.	p
1		3		1		2	0.04	1	
1		3		3		2		1	
3		5		1		2		1	
5		9		1		4		2	
6		9		1		4		5	-.04
	.00						.02		.05
18	.00	15		18		32	.00	23	.00
18		16		20		32		25	.05
18		16		20		33		26	
18		21		21		34		26	
18		21		21		34		27	.01
19		22		23		35		27	
19		22		23		35		28	
21		25		23		36		31	.00
21		30		25		37		32	
21		30		25		37		32	
22		30		28		37		32	

from the paper-presentation sessions and, even more important in the view of many, from the conversations faculty have with peers elsewhere who are doing related work, the talks that take place in the halls, bars, and restaurants. While making research presentations adds to the status of the individual faculty member, it also enhances the reputation of her or his department and college or university, goals the individual and the institution share.

The third outcome measure of research activity—collegial conversations and frequency of talking about your research with colleagues at professional conferences or by phone—produced unanticipated results. Besides providing a high percentage of the explained variance accounted for—38 percent, on the average, larger than for professional presentations—a broader assortment of predictor variables emerged. (See table 4.11.)

Table 4.11 Predicting Conversations Regarding Research

	Res-I		Res-II		Doc-I		Doc-II	
	% Var.	p	% Var.	p	% Var.	p	% Var.	p
Sociodemographic								
Female	1		1		1		1	
Career								
Grad. inst. rating	3		1		1		1	
Career age	7	-.01	6		7	-.02	3	
Assistant professor	8		8		9		3	
Associate professor	13		15		11		8	
(Male full prof.)		.03				.00		
Self-knowledge								
Self-competence	33	.00	25		27	.01	24	
Self efficacy (infl.)	36	.01	25		27		25	
Ambit./compet./commit.	38	.00	27		27		31	.02
Research interest	38		27		28	.03	32	
Preference for research (% effort)	38		27		28		32	
Social knowledge								
Inst. pref. for research (% effort)	38		28		29		32	
Support services and colleagues	39		30		29		34	
Support, grant ($s)	40	.01	30		32	.01	39	.01
Credence to chair/dean	41		35	.01	32		39	
Colleague commitment to research	41		35		33		40	
Behavior								
Effort given to research (% time)	41		37		33		40	

Source: Blackburn, Bieber, Lawrence, and Trautvetter (1991).

Self-competence and financial support (grants) still dominated the explanations (in six and four of the institutional types, respectively). For the first time gender and ambition/competitiveness became significant predictors (in two and three institutional types, respectively). It may be that some people who are not part of the "old boy" network and are striving to improve their lot in the academic pecking order of institutions are using communication links to increase their publication output. For instance, a woman may have few female colleagues on her campus and so calls them elsewhere for a host of reasons. However, note that male full professors also engage in this activity, for they know how valuable colleague critiques and ideas are.

As private an enterprise as research is, in the end it is a social event. One shares what one has learned and benefits from the reviews one receives. As

Table 4.11—*Continued*

Comp-I		Comp-II		LAC-I		LAC-II		CC	
% Var.	p	% Var.	p	% Var.	p	% Var.	p	% Var.	p
1		1		1		6	.01	1	.01
1		2		1		7		1	
4		19	-.01	5		8		1	
4		22		5		8		2	
4		22		6		8		2	
	.00		.05						
19	.00	34		31	.01	24		19	.01
20	.02	35		32		25		22	.05
20		37		32		25		26	.00
20		37		36		26		26	
20		42		36		29	.01	31	
20		43		37		29		31	
20		43		37		29		31	
24		45		37		30		32	.04
24		47		38		32		33	
24		47		38		32		34	
25	.00	47		40		34		34	

Storer (1966) argues, until expert peers judge a creation, nothing meaningful has been brought into the world. That ambitious, competitive, perseverant people are ones who talk with other experts is therefore not surprising. That women use phones to test ideas and obtain information also makes sense, in that sometimes it is easier to talk with people at a distance than at home if the environment is the chilly one many women say characterizes their department. Lincoln (1992) learned that a computer network may be especially advantageous for women. On line, neither their self nor their voice registers. As far as the correspondent on the Bitnet message system knows, they might even be male. Men's negative stereotypes of women as researchers do not have the same chance to emerge. Male faculty have found the computer network "efficient" (their words), whereas women praise its ability to link them with people they could not otherwise communicate and share research ideas and information with. Women want to succeed in this career, but they have not been doing so as well as men. Communicating with others pays dividends.

Administrative actions here are clear, simple, and inexpensive. The computer and modem have replaced the typewriter as standard equipment, in offices both on campus and at home. Some faculty still need to learn how to use them, or be converted. Today's typical university provides many ways for faculty to learn these skills. The cost-conscious and perceptive administrator will not try to save small amounts of money by restricting long-distance phone calls or cutting back on computing allocations. Rather, he or she will be looking for ways to motivate faculty who are not conversing with faculty elsewhere to do so.

Discussion

In summary, then, the widespread strength of the explained variance argues powerfully for the usefulness of the theoretical framework. On several occasions self-knowledge and social knowledge variables significantly predicted behaviors and products, much more frequently than did socio-demographic or career variables.

We have also learned about how faculty behave and what they value. We see that they act quite autonomously. As far as their research effort and products are concerned, what they believe the institution wants them to do in this role, and particularly how much effort they should give to research, does not affect how much effort they give or how much they produce. Nor does their interest in research matter, at least in the way we measured it. It may be that the personal and professional satisfaction faculty receive from successful research effort would better explain what they produce other than books, chapters, and the like, constructs our data do not have. Percentage of effort preferred was a strong predictor and can be considered an indicator of personal valuation of the activity.

Still, research continues to be a lonely business on these campuses. Faculty do not believe they can influence the acceptance of their work to the degree they believe they can affect student learning. (See chapter 5.) Their lack of credence in their chairs' and deans' comments on their research suggests that administrators have little influence on their research success.[20] They do not even believe that having colleagues committed to research has anything to do with their own research accomplishments.

Finally, for the most part, research rewards lie outside the home institution. The organization can facilitate the faculty member's efforts but cannot guarantee them. Wise administrators will continue to support faculty research in the ways we have suggested, even if the faculty members do not recognize their important contributions.

Sex Differences in the Sciences

Our analyses so far that involved regressions have treated sex as a dummy variable.[21] This is how studies of this kind typically proceed. However, treating the sex variable in this way limits the information acquired, because one cannot compare the relative strength of the constructs for the two sexes. The following study separates men from women and examines and contrasts the relative strengths of the predicting variables for each sex. We selected faculty in the sciences—biology, chemistry, and mathematics in our database—because of the current concerns regarding the need for more women in these disciplines. (See the discussion in chapter 2.)

Our data allow us to address selected gaps in this research. The specific question being addressed here is this: What are the relationships and differences for female and male full-time faculty in the natural sciences with regard to the predictive power of our framework's career, self-knowledge, social knowledge, and behavior variables regarding scholarly publication rate?[22]

Because of the small sample sizes for female scientists, we used a variation of the Carnegie system. We established the following three categories so as to obtain a larger sample size distribution: category 1, research universities I and II; category 2, doctoral universities I and liberal arts colleges I; and category 3, doctoral universities II and comprehensive universities and colleges I and II.[23] This procedure places together those institutions that are most alike in faculty research output and support for research. The three categories run from high to low and allow us to control for work environment and to test if place of work in part explains female and male productivity. The categories also tend to equalize the number of women in each collection. The subsamples of women in biology, chemistry, and mathematics and institutional categories are of sufficient size for the analyses being performed.

We used factor analyses and scaling when appropriate to increase the strength and reliability of some of the variables. The dependent variable was the number of articles published over the last two years. Appendix C lists the factor items.[24]

The data analyses proceeded through two stages. First, we ran descriptive and simple statistical tests to discern gender discrepancies within and among the three institutional categories and disciplines. Next, we employed separate stepwise multiple regressions by gender to observe the sex differences and the relationships among the constructs used for predicting publication rate. Since there were two independent samples, we can determine the significance of the differences in the variables' strengths. Furthermore, the regressions provide information about how much variance in publication rate the constructs explain for each sex.

Table 4.12 shows the similarities and differences in terms of some of the construct variables. The samples from each category are composed as follows: category 1, accounting for 28.9 percent of the study sample, is 88 percent male; category 2, 18.7 percent of the sample, is 81 percent male; and category 3, 52.4 percent of the sample, is 86 percent male.

Three general observations: (1) women are the minority in all three disciplines across the institutional categories, (2) more female faculty are found in biology than in the other two natural science disciplines, and (3) a higher percentage of assistant professors are women in all institutional categories.

A few sex differences exist in the three institutional categories. Career age in categories 1 and 2 is consistently lower for women. In Doc-I and LAC-I institutions (category 2), women in biology and math have a lower career age than men; however, women in chemistry have more faculty experience. In general, the men are more likely to be full professors.

In addition, male faculty members in the natural sciences are generally more likely to be graduates of Res-I institutions, to have the Ph.D. degree, and to produce more publications. The average two-year publication rates varied across institutional settings as well as disciplines. Res-I and -II (category 1) faculty have the highest rates, followed by Doc-I and LAC-I (category 2) faculty.

No sex differences exist in personal preference for effort allocated to research or actual effort allocated to research. Sex differences occur in perceived institutional preference for time allocated to research, but no pattern appears.

Table 4.13 shows the results for the separate regressions run against publication rate for each sex. The table contains a middle column of t-statistics. These are positive (female greater) or negative (male greater) numbers that test for the comparative strength of the predicting variables. When it is greater than 1.95 (either positive or negative), the difference is significant at $\leq .05$.

The explained variances in publication rate (last two years) for women and men in the two regressions were 71 percent and 62 percent, respectively. In addition, the constructs that predict these variances frequently differ for the two sexes.

Overall, professorial rank (assistant professors publish less), past publication experience (high past publishers publish more), and research self-competency account for female publication performance. The latter two produced the highest increase in explained variance for the women. Perceived research self-competence stands out as the major difference for female faculty members. The more competent female faculty believe themselves to be, the more they publish; if they do not have this valuation of themselves, they publish less.[25] Rank (assistant professors publish less), career age (less experienced faculty publish more), past publication experience (high past publishers publish more), and actual allocation to research effort (a behavior) account for the variance predicting male publication performance.[26] Career and self-knowledge variables produced the highest explained variance change for publication rate by the women.

We also calculated the differences between the variable strengths of the two independent samples. A positive t-statistic for a particular variable means that the variables had a stronger effect on women. There were only three significant variables that both regressions have in common. The effect that was stronger for women was research self-competency. However, being an assistant professor and past publication experience showed stronger effects for the men.

These strong findings require further elaboration. First, it is important to note that neither discipline nor place of work was a significant predictor. No matter which institutional category, and hence no matter which institutional type, the predictors were the same. Said another way, in the case of a woman's research efficacy, it matters not at all if she is in a rich, moderate, or weak research environment; those who believe they are competent researchers will be the higher publishers, and vice versa.

Furthermore, research self-competency remains significant even when we controlled for past publication rate. Prior publication rate, therefore, is not contributing to the impact of self-competence on current publications.[27] It is the current self-valuation, not earlier success, that matters. Like the successful composer with a blank score on the desk or the mathematician with a clean chalkboard on the wall, the researcher knows that the forthcoming creation may fall short. The symphony may receive negative reviews; the mathematician may flounder in the attempt to prove the theorem; nothing comes forth. Certainly earlier successes provide clues on how to proceed. However, the confidence to try something new depends upon current valuations of the self, on how the individual assesses her or his competence. With prior failures as well as successes, the past is not as strong an indicator as is the valuation of the moment.

The strength of the research-efficacy variable can also be seen by noting the variables that did not predict when all were in the regression. Highest

Table 4.12 Gender Characteristics by Institutional Category and Discipline, 1988

	Category 1						Category 2						Category 3					
	Biology		Chemistry		Math		Biology		Chemistry		Math		Biology		Chemistry		Math	
	F	M	F	M	F	M	F	M	F	M	F	M	F	M	F	M	F	M
Number	19	98	6	96	10	67	19	49	9	51	8	55	30	156	18	131	28	173
Percent	16	84	6	94	13	87	28	72	15	85	13	87	16	84	12	88	14	86
Career age																		
Mean	11	18	12	20	19	20	15	20	24	18	15	20	13	20	16	20	12	19
SD	9	10	11	12	15	10	9	11	9	9	20	9	8	10	8	9	9	9
Rank																		
Instructor	—	—	—	—	10	—	—	—	—	2	—	—	—	—	—	—	4	—
Assistant professor	44	14	33	21	30	17	63	8	44	20	50	20	23	14	29	15	50	19
Associate professor	39	32	—	17	20	19	11	22	44	22	13	33	43	27	29	20	36	38
Full professor	11	53	67	63	40	65	26	69	11	57	38	47	33	59	41	65	11	43
Lecturer	6	1	—	—	—	—	—	—	—	—	—	—	—	—	—	1	—	—
Highest degree																		
Bachelor's	—	—	—	—	10	—	—	—	—	—	—	—	—	—	—	—	—	—
Master's	5	1	—	—	20	—	11	—	11	—	25	6	7	6	11	4	39	15
Ed.D.	—	—	—	—	10	—	—	2	—	—	13	6	3	1	—	3	11	11
J.D. or M.D.	—	—	—	—	10	—	—	2	—	—	—	2	—	1	—	—	—	1
Ph.D.	95	99	100	100	50	100	90	96	89	100	63	87	90	92	89	93	50	74
Graduated from Res-1 inst. (%)	74	75	50	71	56	72	63	47	50	62	38	47	27	44	39	55	44	47

Preference for research (% effort)																		
Mean	46	44	43	44	36	39	30	31	28	31	22	23	25	23	22	22	17	16
SD	16	16	7	14	9	19	16	15	16	20	11	16	14	16	17	15	13	13
Inst. pref. for research (% effort)																		
Mean	39	41	40	38	42	42	20	24	22	29	17	23	24	20	15	21	17	20
SD	17	17	15	16	13	17	13	15	13	24	18	17	22	15	14	14	11	14
Research effort allocation (%)																		
Mean	31	34	37	35	28	25	18	16	18	22	14	14	14	14	11	13	8	10
SD	19	20	10	16	21	16	24	12	7	19	11	14	15	13	14	14	8	12
Number of prof. writings accepted in last two years (1985–87)																		
Mean	4	7	8	9	3	4	2	3	2	6	2	2	2	3	1	2	1	2
SD	4	6	5	7	3	3	4	4	3	11	2	3	2	6	1	4	1	3

Source: NCRIPTAL survey.

Note: Category 1 = Res-I and -II; category 2 = Doc-I and LAC-I; category 3 = Doc-II and Comp-I and -II.

261

Table 4.13 Regression Results for Female and Male Faculty Predicting Two-Year Publication Rate

	Female				Male		
	R2	p	Beta	t-stat.	R2	p	Beta
1. Career							
x Career age	.58*		-0.05	0.25	.56*	.009	-0.06
x Assistant professor		.005	-2.13	-0.71		.031	-1.43
x Associate professor		.034	-1.45	-0.85			-0.76
x Inst. where one graduated		.040	0.99	0.58			0.64
x Past publication experience		.000	2.19	-2.15		.000	2.83
2. Self-knowledge							
Assistant professor	.69*	.024	-1.57	-0.03	.59*	.019	-1.54
Past publication experience		.000	1.48	-2.53		.000	2.34
x Research self-competency		.001	1.30	1.02		.002	0.84
3. Social knowledge							
Assistant professor	.71		-1.61	-0.07	.59	.021	-1.54
Past publication experience		.000	1.58	-1.66		.000	2.27
Research self-competency		.002	1.46	1.28		.007	0.79
Personal disposition			-0.06	-1.40		.043	0.41
x Perceived inst. pref. for res.			0.00	-1.73		.008	0.04
4. Behavior							
Assistant professor	.71	.045	-1.68	-0.02	.62*	.012	-1.66
Career age			-0.03	0.45		.047	-0.05
Past publication experience		.000	1.60	-1.48		.000	2.22
Research self-competency		.001	1.50	1.68		.035	0.61
x Effort allocated to research			-0.01	-2.89		.000	0.07

Source: Trautvetter and Blackburn (1990).

Notes: An asterisk indicates significant R2 change. x indicates the variables entered at each step. *p* is the significance level (*p* values ≤ .05 were recorded). Betas are unstandardized coefficients.

degree and rating of graduate school institution, along with discipline and institutional type (career variables); morale, disposition to conduct research, perceived career success, personal preference for research effort (self-knowledge); colleague support, having grants, perceived institutional preference for research effort (social knowledge)—while some of these variables were significant when first entered, none remained significant when all were present. Actual percentage of time given to research (behavior) had a small but significant strength. However, when comparing men with women, it produced the largest difference between the sexes (t = −.289, *p* ≤ .01). For men, effort was much stronger. Past publication experience (career) had the next largest t-value in the differences. Male scientists with stronger past

262

publication records published more. Other current publication performance predictors that were stronger for men than for women before the behavior variable was added were perceived institutional preference for research and personal disposition (ambitious, competitive, perseverant)—attributes often associated with masculinity. These results tend to corroborate beliefs that men are more driven and competitive than women (Hamovitch & Morgenstern, 1977) and enjoy the research image more than their female colleagues do (Fulton & Trow, 1974).

These findings are also consistent with Bandura's (1982) explanations for why individuals may stop trying to achieve a given goal (in this case, publishing): (1) they lack a sense of personal control, (2) they expect their behavior to have no effect on an environment perceived to be unresponsive, and (3) they expect not to be rewarded for their efforts. Women may publish less because they feel a loss of personal control (efficacy) and receive less recognition and fewer rewards than men do.

Some previous studies that include natural scientists also show that female scientists do not think they are taken seriously and believe they are less competent than their male colleagues (Etaugh & Kasley, 1981; Frieze & Hanusa, 1984; Ramaley, 1978; Widom & Burke, 1978; Zuckerman & Cole, 1975). Linn and Hyde (1989) believe that sex differences in confidence may contribute to differential career access. Women interested in science and mathematics display lower confidence than men at early stages of the educational pipeline, generally during the high school years, even though their grades are high (Dossey, Mulles, Lindquist, & Chambers, 1988; Eccles, 1984). This lower perceived competence can easily continue through the years, even in the face of a strong academic record.

Many implications follow. What this study implies is that if one wants to understand better what explains the productivity of female academics, one must investigate female academics as female academics, not in comparison with men. It is time to set aside the notion that the existing, essentially male, model is the standard to measure women by. We urge a fresh line of inquiry. We have learned about what affects men. We have also learned that many male attributes do not predict for women.

We need to develop instruments grounded on the growing literature on what is distinctive about women. For example, we need to test variables such as support (e.g., a significant other, financial security, a mentor, a professional partner), networks (e.g., occupation of gatekeeper positions, off-campus professional activities, access to the power elite), available work time (e.g., good health, reduced family obligations), and career goals (e.g., success without vicious competitiveness, freedom from the constraints of traditional research).

So far we have said nothing about discrimination and harassment in the workplace. We trust that administrators are already increasing the likelihood of female success by eliminating the more blatant violations. The chilly climate for female academic scientists can be made warmer. Doing so may channel more women into science and into academe. (At the conclusion of this chapter we discuss in more detail management strategies for accomplishing individual and collective success in research.)

Other Studies

Here we synoptically present findings from three other studies that used our framework but different databases. Two use data from the NSOPF88 national faculty survey conducted by the National Center for Educational Statistics, and one uses the 1989 national survey data collected by the Carnegie Foundation for the Advancement of Teaching. These are the two most recent available data banks.

Using the NCES database, Wenzel and Blackburn (1993) obtained percentage of explained variance in publication rate ranging from 15 percent for medical school faculty to 85 percent for nursing faculty (with 30 percent for engineering, 31 percent for natural sciences, and 35 percent for health sciences). In the main the strongest predictors were the same as those found above for arts and science faculty. For the most part these are lower values. Moreover, the variables often differ from those used in this chapter. The differences may result from the peculiar nature of these professional fields, and from the fact that the NCES database has very few of the theoretical framework's key variables in its questionnaire.

Wenzel, Crawley, and Blackburn (1993) used the 1989 Carnegie database. They accounted for 51 percent of the explained variance for business school faculty and 37 percent for engineering school faculty when publication in the last two years was the outcome variable.[28]

Crawley, Wenzel, and Blackburn (1993) used the NCES database to predict grant procuring as the output variable, a different dependent outcome. Twenty-four percent of the explained variance was accounted for. In the same way that prior publication rate was a strong predictor for current publications (number of scholarly articles in the last two years), so was prior proposal writing a strong predictor for grant getting. The lower value most likely resulted from the same limiting factors Wenzel and Blackburn found with this database.

Because they sampled faculty our NCRIPTAL survey did not, these databases were appreciably deficient in items that get at self-knowledge and social knowledge variables, yet they still obtained higher percentages than

264

the earlier research on faculty did. Hence, the studies give indirect support to the basic structure of our framework. As Long (1987) pointed out so well, while researchers relish the large Ns needed for more sophisticated statistical analyses, if one has not tapped the critical variables, the sheer number of cases does not advance the ultimate research goal.

An Institutional Case: Some Longitudinal Data

This longitudinal study employs interviews that allow the theoretical framework to account for what faculty tell us about their careers and how the university "works." While the number of respondents is small, the reported experiences supply new insights into why faculty behave as they do.

A research university's institutional prestige inextricably depends on faculty research accomplishments. Universities design their faculty selection and promotion processes to recruit and retain productive scholars. The reward systems provide ongoing incentives for faculty members to conduct research (Blau, 1973; Long & McGinnis, 1981). Yet despite these efforts, individual grant activity and publication output sometimes drop off or never quite attain institutionally desired levels (Fox, 1985b).

Here we focus on institutional incentives and on select career variables in order to examine their effects on faculty publication rates. We use longitudinal data to explore several questions. When an individual achieves the goal of becoming a full professor and academic promotion incentives no longer exist, do behavior and productivity change? Do faculty members from the humanities, social sciences, and natural sciences differ in their respective perceptions of the organization, their distribution of effort to research and administrative activities, and their rate of publication? Are there differences between career cohorts that may be the consequences of variations in their socialization by the university?

This analysis focuses on the productivity-feedback loop of the framework and on select career and self-knowledge variables that may influence its components (social knowledge, behavior, productivity, and environmental response). The higher-education literature suggests that (1) promotion and merit salary are highly correlated with publication in research universities, and (2) faculty from different disciplines and career cohorts may have different socialization experiences that lead to variations in behavior and productivity (Pfeffer, Leong, & Strehl, 1977; Tuckman & Leahey, 1975).

We collected data at two points in time, 1976 and 1986, from a panel of male faculty members in a Res-I university's liberal arts college.[29] Of the 75 individuals originally interviewed in 1976, 49 were reinterviewed in 1986.

265

Of these 49, 33 provided productivity data. These 33 comprise the panel set used in the longitudinal analysis. The subjects—16 humanists (from the disciplines of English, philosophy, classical studies, history, and romance languages and literature), 10 social scientists (economics, psychology, political science, anthropology, sociology, and speech), and 7 natural and physical scientists (biological sciences, computer science, and mathematics)— were appointed as assistant professors at the institution in one of three years: 1960, 1965, or 1970. There were both tenured and untenured respondents at the first time of data collection. By 1986 all 33 had been tenured, but not all had achieved the rank of full professor (full professor N = 27, associate N = 5, and assistant N = 1).

At both points in time, data were collected through in-depth interviews lasting approximately two hours and covering a range of issues. The interview questions elicited the respondents' perceptions of their department and college or university, including their explanations for key events that had occurred during the decade between interviews. They also talked about themselves (e.g., their values, interests, and competencies as researchers, teachers, and members of the "community"). They openly discussed their experiences with, and responses to, the merit and promotion systems of the institution.

Although the interview protocols used at the two points of data collection were not completely identical, they did include repeat measures on several variables, including those addressing the respondents' self-knowledge, social knowledge, and behavior. Responses to these repeat items and data from curriculum vitae constitute our data set.

We used the information collected in 1976 and 1986 to assess differences between faculty with dissimilar career experiences as well as individual change over time. We compared faculty from the three fields and from the three career cohorts at the two times with respect to their social knowledge, behavior, and productivity. In addition, we compared the publication rates of faculty members who were full professors in 1976 with that of assistant and associate professors in 1986. We also assessed individual changes in publication rate for two time periods: 1960–1976 and 1977–1986.

The repeat measures that are available permit assessments of faculty members' understanding of role expectations for the different ranks, criteria applied in tenure and promotion decisions, and degree of organizational consensus about these criteria (social knowledge). These measures are all scaled variables in which the respondent indicated the fraction of 100 percent allocated to each criterion or activity and the degree of consensus on a scale of 1 (low) to 6 (high). The distribution-of-effort indicator (behavior) is also a scaled variable. Individuals indicated how much of their full-time appointment they gave to teaching, research, and service. We used curriculum vitae to assess level of administrative responsibilities and publication output (productivity). We counted only those administrative responsibilities that involved assigned or reimbursed time (e.g., department chair, program director, dean, vice president). Publication output includes articles published in refereed journals, books authored and edited, chapters in books, and reviews. We used the rate of promotion—number of years in each rank—and number of promotions attained between 1960 and 1986 to define environmental response. We used other data available at the times of data gathering qualitatively to describe other framework constructs, primarily self-knowledge, that may contribute to variations in research effort and publication output.

To answer the questions posed, we divided respondents into several subgroups based on professorial rank, field, and year of initial appointment at the university. We calculated individual and collective publication rates in the first case by dividing a faculty member's total publications while in a given rank by the number of years the individual was in that rank. We defined the field and cohort publication rates, respectively, as the average for all respondents in the humanities, social sciences, or natural or physical sciences, and for all individuals appointed in 1960, 1965, or 1970. We calculated individual administrative responsibilities, like publication rates, as the number of assignments carried out by an individual during the time period of a particular rank; similarly, administrative responsibilities are also calculated for fields and career cohorts. We used frequency distributions and means to describe differences within and among faculty subgroups. In addition, t-tests evaluate the significance of differences between groups and the change in individual publication rate between 1976 and 1986.[30]

Analysis by Point of Promotion

The first analysis sought to identify differences in productivity between faculty members who had achieved the rank of full professor and those who had yet to achieve this rank. By 1976, 20 assistant professors had been promoted to full professor. By 1986 seven more individuals had attained that rank. In 1976 full professors produced twice as many publications as the non–full professors. In 1986 full professors produced over three times as many publications as their non-full-professor counterparts.

Since the 1986 full-professor group includes both respondents that held this rank in 1976 and those who became full professors sometime between 1976 and 1986, we made additional comparisons. We compared the productivity rates, as measured in both 1976 and 1986, for individuals who were full professors at both times of data collection with those of individuals who became full professors after 1976. The productivity rate of the two groups was not significantly different. Furthermore, individuals who were full professors in 1976 did not decrease in productivity after the incentive of promotion was removed. There was no significant decrease in productivity among the seven faculty who achieved full-professor rank between 1976 and 1986. Last, at both times of data collection there was a significant difference in the productivity rate between the respondents who were full professors in 1976 and the group that had never been promoted to full professor.

Analysis by Field

In 1976 and 1986 faculty in all fields—humanities, social sciences, and natural and physical sciences—generally agreed on the percentage of time they thought should be spent on research, teaching, and service for the tenure decision. For promotion to full professor, the natural and physical scientists preferred less emphasis on research and more on teaching and service than did the social scientists and humanists. However, these differences were not significant. With one exception there were no statistically significant differences among the fields in the percentage of time these faculty actually gave to research, teaching, and service in either 1976 or 1986. Also in 1976, for all three fields the percentage of time given to research and teaching decreased (not significantly), and the amount of time given to service increased, with the promotion from assistant to associate professor. With the move to full professor the percentage of time spent on research by the humanists and natural scientists also decreased, while the social scientists' time on research increased slightly. Similarly, time spent on teaching decreased for the humanists and social scientists and remained constant for the natural scientists.

The 1986 reports of behavior, however, do not replicate the 1976 reports. As faculty moved from the rank of associate to full professor, the time spent on research remained constant in the humanities and social sciences; it increased in the natural sciences. In all three fields faculty spent more time on research in 1986 than in 1976. In 1986 the humanists and social scientists also spent more time on service and less on teaching, while the natural scientists spent more on teaching and less on service.

Faculty reports of their perceptions of university expectations for distribution of effort (social knowledge) in 1976 and 1986 did not differ significantly among fields, with the exception of time given to teaching as an assistant professor. However, perceptions of expected effort did differ from reported behavior. Overall, faculty believed that the university expected them to spend a greater percentage of their time on research and a smaller percentage on service than they actually spent.

Analysis by Cohort

1960

Nine individuals comprised the 1960 cohort—three natural and physical scientists, two social scientists, and four humanists. Their average number of publications per year decreased with each successive change in rank. Similarly, the range in publication rate decreased as rank changed. This indicates that over time these individuals' annual output became more homogeneous.

With respect to administrative involvement, the research productivity of those involved varied. Some increased; more decreased.

1965

The 1965 appointment cohort was the largest, with 20 faculty members: 4 natural and physical scientists, 7 social scientists, and 9 humanists. Productivity rates as assistant and associate professors were, on the average, not much greater for this group than for the 1960 cohort. However, the average time in rank was longer than the average for the 1960 cohort at both the assistant and associate levels.

Of the 16 full professors in the 1965 cohort who achieved that rank prior to 1986, 14 had some type of administrative responsibility during their time with the university. Of these 14, 11 held administrative responsibilities as associate professors. Comparatively, only one person in the 1960 cohort had any administrative responsibility as an associate professor. For the most part, those individuals who had played administrative roles as associate professors continued in those roles after being promoted.

Members of this cohort had been highly active administrators. Only 6 of the 20 individuals had had no administrative responsibilities. Of these six, three never achieved full professor. The three individuals who were non-administrator full professors (one from each field) were clearly "producers," averaging just short of 4.5 publications per year since their final promotion. Conversely, the 3 least productive (averaging only one publication every three years) of the 14 full-professor administrators all had administrative responsibilities at least three years prior to being promoted. This suggests that administrative contributions may have played a role in their final promotion.

1970

Of the four individuals who constituted the 1970 cohort, one was a social scientist and three were humanists. Three were full professors, while one of the humanists remained an associate professor. These four individuals spent

269

more time in the rank of assistant professor than did the members of the other cohorts.

Among the three who were full professors in 1986, their average publication rate as associate professors was the highest of the three cohorts, while their time in rank as associate professors was the shortest. As full professors these three produced, on the average, 2.6 publications per year (again the highest).

The one associate professor never produced a scholarly publication and still achieved the rank of associate professor. The fact is an exception but lends credence to the faculty perception that the tenure decision is based on scholarly potential while the final promotion decision is based on actual productivity.[31]

Discussion

The comparison of faculty from different fields showed little variation in their personal values, perceptions of the institution's role expectations, and priorities in personnel decisions. It may well be, as Blau (1973) suggests, that the recruitment, retention, and reward processes have resulted in a faculty that, by and large, share a common set of values and beliefs emphasizing the importance of scholarship. The cohort analysis suggests, further, that the normative expectations with respect to publication rate may be escalating as each successive appointment cohort moves through the promotion process. The most recent cohort—individuals appointed in 1970—spent more time in rank as assistant professors when compared with the 1960 and 1965 cohorts. On the other hand, the publication rates of the 1970 cohort were higher for each of these time-in-rank periods. The question remains whether this heightened output is a result of social knowledge (the inferences about what was expected), or self-knowledge (the personal attraction to the research process among those hired and promoted), or environmental conditions (a conscious administrative decision to keep people in rank longer).

The evaluation of differences between faculty who are professors and those who are not suggests that the motivation to publish derives more from intrinsic factors than from the extrinsically mediated promotions and rewards. Some individuals exhibit definite spurts of productivity around the time of promotion. However, the statistical comparisons of groups indicate that the incentive value of further promotion may not be a factor in determining publication rate. The assessments of individual change in publication rate between 1976 and 1986 corroborate this interpretation, as output at the two times was similar.

The theoretical framework that frames this investigation provides possible explanations for the findings vis-à-vis promotion and publication output. Some of the respondents who had only recently been promoted to full professor in 1986 explained that when they became associate professors, they inferred from observing their predecessors that administrative performance would be taken into account in the promotion decision. However, when they were reviewed, they were told that their scholarly records were weak. Consequently, they reduced their administrative loads, increased their publications, and were promoted. In brief, their social knowledge was modified on the basis of an environmental response. Achieving the rank of full professor was important to them, and they changed their behavior so as to achieve it. Their publication rate increased, and they were promoted.

On the other hand, there were some individuals who were, in their own words, "unpromotable associate professors." The feedback on behavior and productivity they received led them to believe that the institution did not value their substantive areas of interest or the scholarly activities they preferred (social knowledge). Their affect and comments during the interviews suggested that the importance of becoming a full professor had diminished. They seemed to have decided to do things that were personally meaningful (self-knowledge) even though such activities did not fit with organizational priorities and often led to a negative environmental response (e.g., having no doctoral students as assistants or graduate courses to teach).

We quote from Bieber, Lawrence, and Blackburn (1992):

> In their interviews with University of Minnesota faculty, Clark, Corcoran, and Lewis (1986) coined the phrase "promotion-delayed" for a group of associate professors who had held this rank several years beyond their peers who had already been promoted to full professor. Our associate professors are also never likely to be promoted, as they attest, and primarily due to deficient research output. Declining productivity, coupled with the university's heightened emphasis on research, has exacerbated an increasingly "awkward" situation. By 1987–88, few faculty and administrators believed resuscitation possible and anxiety relievable.
>
> In 1976 and earlier, the associate professor whose rate of publication and grant acquisition declined, but did not stop altogether, would eventually be promoted, assuming a record of good teaching, active work with doctoral students, contribution to the department in curricular decisions, and/or overall service for the university. It might take 12 years (instead of five or six) but one would retire as a full professor. If the associate professor went into administration and continued to teach, but did not continue his program of scholarship, he would retire without the final promotion.
>
> By 1987–88, however, a department knew it could not send a candidate to the college's executive committee for promotion to full professor whose vita would not have qualified the same individual for promotion to associ-

ate professor (and tenure). Being turned down for promotion at the college level is more than losing face and reputation. A common understanding among faculty is that it endangers the department's ability to acquire future hiring funds. These delayed-promotion faculty receive below average raises each year. While their scholarly production is not likely to change, they continue to teach key courses, and students rate them and their courses highly. Discomfort with the situation, however, increases with each passing term.

Some full professors who jumped all the hurdles and are still on track question the wisdom of a single standard for the final promotion. Departments do not always have consensus on the issue even though they do agree on the criteria for tenure and promotion to associate professor. (Either an influential article in a top journal or a well-received book from an established press is the sine qua non and minimum requirement.) What is to be lost, some professors ask, from granting the promotion? Dollars do not have to accompany the new rank. Maintain the merit system, they urge, but remove the stigma of being "frozen in rank." This is not "softness" or an absence of standards; it simply would produce a better climate for everyone. After all, not promoting them does not change their behavior, and having them around as friends and peers who have "failed" is painful for all parties.

For the most part, the acerbity expressed in our conversations by these promotion-delayed individuals focused on the unidimensional character of the promotion process—significant publications in both quality and quantity. They acknowledge following the teaching and service route and knowing their preferences and decisions carried consequences—fewer chances for teaching advanced seminars, fewer strong doctoral students selecting them for dissertation chair, no promotion. Yet, despite some bitterness, these faculty were generally pleased they had the options they did—doing what they wanted with the security tenure provides. In addition, their departmental colleagues appreciate that their friends, many of whom joined the ranks at the same time with them and have close bonds from those initial experiences, carry the introductory courses and genuinely and conspicuously care about students.

Nonetheless, second-class citizenship status must carry some unpleasant consequences when one looks in the mirror every morning and anticipates the day's upcoming realities: knowing that the secretary will be too busy typing grant proposals for the coterie of research faculty to prepare your examination (so you will have to do by yourself that for which you used to have assistance); that you will not be dining at the faculty club with the prospective new faculty candidate now on campus; that you will still be teaching the introductory course even if the new candidate is hired so as to allow her or him time to develop a research program; and that there is a forthcoming announcement by the chair that extra dollars (still not enough) will be available for those presenting research papers at the national conference—but you will pay to attend out of your own pocket. They are like Professor Victor Jakob, who, while teaching Newtonian physics in the German university early in this century as quantum mechanics was winning the day (in Russell McCormmach's novel, *Night Thoughts of a Classical Physicist,* 1982), realizes his status when the custodian stops cleaning his chalkboard.

Longitudinal data allowed us to explore an important component of our theoretical framework that survey, cross-sectional data cannot—namely, the effects of environmental response. We see here that the changing—or perhaps more accurately, intensifying—university emphasis on research and making career success dependent upon it clearly became a part of the faculty's social knowledge. For most, their productivity went up, irrespective of the fact that no promotion reward was available. Some chose not to alter their research behavior and productivity, or they decided they could not. They remained associate professors.

We also witness the framework functioning well in the interview process and in the examination of the qualitative data this methodology produces. Career, self-knowledge, social knowledge, behavior, and productivity as constructs guided the interview protocol and interpretation of the responses. We now collect what has been learned in this chapter and interpret what it means for faculty and their colleges and universities.

Fostering Success

As we have seen, faculty career success depends more and more on conducting and publishing research. As we noted earlier, the shift in emphasis has spread to faculty in all institutional types, including those primarily dedicated to instruction. More faculty have a higher interest in research than in teaching compared with 25 years ago. Interest and desire, however, do not by themselves lead to publishable products. Nor does effort expended. They may be necessary conditions, but they are not sufficient ones. Know-how and skills—expertise in the discipline and with methodologies—must also be in hand. These need to be learned and mastered. Not everyone can do it. In addition, there is the creative act, seeing something in a new and/or different way, a talent no one can be taught, nor can anyone predict who will have it.

How can would-be researchers and those responsible for providing the most supportive environment for successful research be helped? We return to the studies cited in chapters 2 and 3 that report correlates of faculty research and add them to what we have learned in this chapter. The corre-

273

lates suggest some measures individuals and institutions can undertake to increase the likelihood of success.

Of course, some correlates are with unchangeable characteristics and past experiences. They are valueless when it comes to changing one's success. One's race or sex is a given, and so is where one went to graduate school, all of which correlate with publishing. Some contextual correlates also lie outside the individual's or administrator's ability to alter but still need to be recognized. For example, we have seen more than once the need to control for academic discipline. Academic specialties generally differ as to what they produce and how. Department demography also affects faculty standards and expectations (Pfeffer, 1981).[32] One can alter atypical age distributions only by hiring and firing or retiring staff. Larger departments are more productive than smaller ones (Gallant & Prothero, 1972; Wispe, 1969), but obviously one does not simply increase the number of faculty in a unit in order to make it more productive.

So we turn to factors that are changeable—faculty attributes and administrative strategies. One thing faculty can do is to fashion their research agenda to their advanced-course teaching, or vice versa, so that what their students deal with in class directly connects with what they themselves are researching and writing about. Students' questions and comments can trigger ideas, and the resulting new insights can enrich the course and the instruction.

Having gone to a less rigorous university, or to one where techniques or library resources were inadequate for doctoral work, does not mean one cannot update oneself. A sabbatical, leave, or postdoc year at a leading university can produce marked changes. Being in an environment where scholarly activity abounds not only sharpens research skills but also motivates one to engage in creative work. So can joining with a colleague; it leads to co-authorship. Simply making a contract with another faculty member to complete a piece of work by an established time sets right habits in motion and leads to finished products. In this vein, and contrary to advice from parents, it is more productive to be doing many things at once than to concentrate on a single one. Highly productive faculty have many irons in the fire, if for no other reason than that when you get stuck on one project— and paralysis always sets in somewhere along the way—you can turn to another and move it along until a good solution flashes across the brow.

Write every day, even if only a few sentences find their way to the page and even if you later alter or delete them. Make writing the highest priority, the activity that comes before all others, the first thing you do in the day, not something you save for the late evening hours. A blank sheet of paper can freeze the productive juices. Stop in the middle of a paragraph you know how to finish so that when you return tomorrow, the pen or the keyboard need not struggle to make its first marks. Like more mundane activities, creative work becomes more successful when it becomes habitual. A little success breeds satisfaction that in turn leads to more success. Wildavsky's (1989) *Craftways: On the Organization of Scholarly Work* opens many windows for the individual wanting to bring ideas to fruition.[33]

One also needs to have faith in the peer-review process. The top journals and presses, the ones everyone wants to have publish her or his work, have the leading scholars as their reviewers. They find the flaws you did not know were there. Develop a tough skin, for rejection occurs more often than acceptance. Improve what you have done. However, do not go to a vanity press. It is better not to publish anything at all than to have a review of your work that begins, "This is a bad book. It never should have been written," and then goes on for two pages to demonstrate why. Your work will probably be misjudged more than once in this business, but for the most part, the system sorts out for us what deserves reading and what does not. Keep faith in the system.

Turning from what individuals can do to how administrators can increase the publication output of their unit and assist individual faculty to do more and better work, the matter of course depends upon the current situation. The current faculty will normally search for and recommend candidates for hiring when the unit is in a position to add a new member either to fill a vacancy or because of planned expansion. However, the dean still has final control over the selection. The faculty choice may be an exciting young person full of ideas and well on the way to completing the dissertation—in short, one with strong potential. However, the evidence shows that past performance is the best predictor of future output. The already published individual with the Ph.D. is by far the better bet. The dean should act accordingly, especially today, with so many already productive individuals in the market.

The right start matters immensely for new faculty. Having the new assistant professor teach a seminar in her or his specialty rather than being assigned the large introductory course can make a tremendous difference. Add to that student assistance, critical equipment, and psychological support, and one can get the individual off on the right foot. Being sensitive to the differences between the underrepresented is also important. The minority or female faculty member is more likely to be the isolated one, not in on the important conversations, not learning how one does things in this place. Getting that person teamed with a senior colleague who is also sensitive to the special needs of women and minorities requires administrative know-how, but that is not so very difficult to acquire.

Pelz and Andrews (1976) learned in their studies of scientists in organizations that units can become more productive when work groups compete with one another in healthy ways. They also learned that group membership needs to be changed from time to time if the good-spirited competition is to continue. If one group always wins, the others will stop playing the game, and total productivity goes down. (See also Andrews's [1979] edited book on work groups in European research centers.) Deans and chairs can facilitate work arrangements of these kinds. They can also support research output by felicitous scheduling. Creative work most often requires large blocks of time. Scheduling that results in no classes on some days and more on other days, rather than some every day, supports the research effort. While chancellor at the University of Wisconsin–Oshkosh, Birnbaum (1975) introduced a year-round academic calendar of optional short semesters and credits for preparing self-taught instructional packages that allowed entrepreneurial faculty to create blocks of time for themselves. The faculty members' efficacy, their ability to control their time—that most important element faculty continually fight for—clearly enhanced their output even more. They could determine their schedule and maximize it for their own ends.

Rewards also pay dividends. While intrinsic motivation must be high, faculty do respond to what they see and believe the organization honors. Tien and Blackburn (1993) learned that faculty publication rates rise as promotion time approaches. A higher status is a reward faculty work for. At the same time, the correlation between administrative leadership and faculty publications is zero, even negative (Hill & French, 1967). Faculty do not see the chair as having anything to do with their research success. So be it. Wise chairs will not attempt to dispel the untruth or try to take credit for what they nourished. Perhaps their dean will take note of what has been accomplished. Heydinger and Simsek's (1992) monograph contains many worthwhile suggestions for increasing faculty productivity.

Last, the wise dean will also evaluate chairs on the basis of their success in raising the unit's output and input (in the form of grants, awards, and the like). That dean, or higher-level administrator, will also pass judgment on those below on the basis of how many minority and female faculty succeed, and how well. For all faculty, but especially for the underrepresented people who are often isolated and alienated, the day of simply adding individuals to the unit and expecting them to survive alone—tossing them into the department and seeing if they sink or swim—is over. Research output is a collective enterprise. It needs not only to be seeded and cultivated; it needs nurturing.

Our theoretical framework continues to illuminate faculty productivity through a variety of inquiries—qualitative as well as quantitative. We turn next to research on the teaching role.

Chapter 4. Faculty Research

1. This is not the first time the discovery of scholarship has affected faculty and the country's higher-education institutions. In the last half of the 19th century, some Americans traveled to Germany for advanced study and a Ph.D. They came home infected with scholarship. Some became the prime movers who produced the American university (Veysey, 1965). While they created a new type of institution, research did not become central until the period on which we concentrate.

2. To tell the complete story would require another book, not our aim.

3. These are mind-boggling numbers. How is one to keep abreast of current scholarship even in one's own specialty? In a neighbor's? In the larger context? The Renaissance scholar, the person who knows everything about everything, is not a foregone dream. It is a biological impossibility.

4. Bieber, Blackburn, and De Vries (1991) had somewhat better success for physical chemists, but the data were too sparse to allow definitive conclusions. The differences are understandable. In Kuhn's (1970) terminology, chemists enjoy comparatively high paradigm agreement and a high consensus on experimental procedures. Literary criticism continues to foment a state of turmoil in the humanities.

5. That these journals reject about 85 percent of the manuscripts they receive,

most of which are from leading scholars in the field, provides another indicator of raised standards and hence higher quality. Many rejects find their way into print in the next tier of periodicals and possibly raise the quality level of those less respected journals.

6. A revision of this paper has been published in *Research in Higher Education*. See Blackburn, Bieber, Lawrence, and Trautvetter, 1991.

7. This same source serves for most subsequent inquiries reported in this and the following chapters.

8. A full technical report (Blackburn & Lawrence, 1989) is available from the Inter-University Consortium for Political and Social Science Research (ICPSR), University of Michigan.

9. A plateau effect creates problems with categorical publication data because many faculty in research universities are in the top category, one that is typically stated sometimes as "11 publications or more" and sometimes as "20 or more." The variable loses its power to discriminate because the actual number remains unknown. For example, a woman publishing 25 times in two years receives no higher a score than a colleague publishing 11 times.

10. The theoretical framework assumes that environmental responses are the result of behavior and productivity at one time (T_1) and influence subsequent behavior and productivity at a later time (T_2) to the extent that organizational feedback modifies social knowledge and self-knowledge. Therefore, we only use environmental responses to predict social knowledge.

11. The data set permits approximation of one aspect of environmental conditions, namely, shared beliefs about the institution. However, we decided that the views of faculty in eight disciplines were inadequate to operationalize this construct. Furthermore, we lacked factual data on the institution. However, each institution is a separate variable. Since there were no survey items about family or involvement in non-work-related activities, we could not estimate the effects of social contingencies.

12. After this critical demonstration of our theoretical framework, we will present the statistical testing data in a much simplified form. We will also lead the reader through the first of these forthcoming regression analyses. In this note we will deal with betas and what their magnitudes and plus or minus signs mean.

When a regression analysis is run, one set of numbers that comes out are called betas. There is a beta for each variable, a number ranging from -1.0 to $+1.0$. The number is an indicator of the strength of that variable in predicting the outcome variable when all of the other variables are held constant. That is, the beta tells the direct effect of the predicting variable on the dependent variable— most often, in this chapter, publications. The program also gives the significance level for the beta, and we can see if it is, say, less that .05, the level we have been using. The limitation of this "pure" beta is that its magnitude depends upon the scale used to measure the variable. When these are not the same for all variables, you cannot compare the beta for one variable with that for another and know if the larger beta really is a stronger predictor. For example, a score of 4 on a seven-point scale is not relatively as high as is a 3 on a four-point scale, yet the beta for the former will be larger. What programs do, then, is convert the scores for every variable to the same scale. The order of the scores stays exactly the same during the conversion so that the highest is still the highest, the next remains next highest, and so on. The converted scores are called standardized betas; that is, they are all on the same yardstick. Standardized betas are what we have in the table. Now the betas can be compared with one another regardless of the differences in variable scales. Larger numbers are stronger predictors.

SATs are an example of standardized scores. No matter how many items are on the test, the scores are converted to a scale from 200 to 800, math and verbal. A 685 on the math is higher than a 550 on the verbal quite irrespective of the actual number of questions answered correctly on either examination. GREs, IQs, and other human measures are put into standardized form so that effects can be estimated.

No plus or minus sign before a beta means that the beta is greater than zero. It also means that that variable is a contributor to the explained variance. For example, we coded female = 1 and male = 0. When the beta alongside sex is positive (no plus or minus sign), it means that being female predicts the outcome. If the beta has a minus sign in front of it, then being male is the predictor.

13. This finding may be due in part to the fact that the items with the strongest loading on the administrator and faculty factors had to do with teaching evaluation.

14. As already noted, the behavior variables had the largest betas.

15. We expected a positive beta for psychology, for there has been grant money in that discipline. However, the Reagan years were hard on the social sciences, and that is when the survey was conducted.

16. Note that the standard deviations are larger than the means in all three cases. This indicates that the distributions are skewed, and in this case that there are more faculty producing no or few publications that are counterbalanced by a small number of faculty producing a large number. The distortion from a normal curve is greatest for the Comp-I faculty.

17. There are enough new variables not used in the first test paper (described in the previous section of this chapter) that the reader should consult this appendix.

18. This analysis closely parallels the preceding one. However, (1) environmental responses are different, and (2) we report only the variables that entered the regression analysis. Consequently, the findings differ slightly (e.g., percentage of explained variance here is 58 percent vs. 50 percent in the test of the theoretical framework). We include the Res-I institutions again in this form so that comparisons can be made with other institutional types.

19. We make distinctions between the concepts of research and scholarship. On our survey instrument that yielded the data analyzed here, we defined *research* as an activity that results in a product—an article, for example. We defined *scholarship*, on the other hand, as professional growth, time spent enhancing knowledge or skill in ways that may not necessarily result in a concrete product—

activities such as library work, reading, exploratory inquiries, or computer use. We explore this behavior in detail in chapter 6.

20. Faculty may credit their administrators with securing the resources needed for success, but we do not have that information.

21. *Dummy* is the technical statistical term for dealing with categorical variables, ones that do not have a scale (like, say, interest in research, where one can score the degree of interest over varying degrees, say from 5 being very high to 1 being very low). One is either female or male, and any number assigned to the sex variable has no meaning of higher or lower. Yet the statistical technique requires numbers, not words. We arbitrarily, but consistently, have coded female as 1 and male as 0. This makes sex a dummy variable, and the numbers produced by the program come out either positive (i.e., with no sign) for female or negative for male.

22. This investigation uses the term *natural sciences* for the three disciplines unless a difference occurs among the disciplines that needs to be noted. Furthermore, since part-time faculty and those at two-year institutions differ substantially as a group from their full-time four-year-institution counterparts in background, training, and work activities (Finkelstein, 1984a), this inquiry limits itself to full-time academics at four-year colleges and universities.

23. Since over 80 percent of faculty in two-year institutions and liberal arts colleges II do not publish at all (Ladd, 1979), we excluded the faculty in these institutions.

24. When appropriate, Cronbach reliability tests were run on the variables and are reported.

25. We cannot conclude causality. Women who publish may in turn increase their research self-competence and publish even more.

26. It at first seems contradictory that more experienced and lower-ranked male professors publish more. However, the lower-ranked professors can also be the more experienced female faculty members who have been trapped in lower ranks but are high publishers.

27. For example, some past publications may be invited chapters in books, writing that most often does not involve new research.

28. These are the first studies using faculty in professional schools.

29. The fact that the individuals selected in this study are all male was not controlled for by the researchers; it is an artifact of the original sample frame. The sample was chosen exclusively on the basis of year of appointment as assistant professor.

30. See the original paper (Lawrence, Bieber, Blackburn, Saulsberry, Trautvetter, Hart, & Frank, 1989) for the tables and statistical data. With such small numbers, traditional data analyses are weak. Our aim here is to witness the theoretical framework's power in dealing with primarily qualitative data. (When we do report differences, they are statistically significant unless we note otherwise.)

31. The perception of today's faculty differs significantly. Now faculty believe that promotion to associate and to full professor are equally rigorous and depend upon scholarly publications being both plentiful and of high quality.

32. Julius and Krauss's (1993) collection of papers on an aging workforce will be helpful to administrators dealing with an older faculty constituency.

33. If an institution has an Andrew J. Wiles on its faculty, then there is no problem. His devotion of seven years to one mathematical proof (Fermat's last theorem) bespeaks personal traits beyond genius. See McDonald (1993).

JE Shirley M. Clark
Mary Corcoran

Perspectives on the Professional Socialization of Women Faculty

A Case of Accumulative Disadvantage?

Disproportionately fewer faculty women than men achieve high levels of success in academe. Although falling well short of parity, women have made small gains in hiring in the past several years, but securing an entry-level position and sustaining a successful academic career are two quite different things [11, 12, 24]. According to Cole [7], women who have persevered are survivors who have gone against the grain of occupational stereotyping to enter a primarily male profession. For those who have defied the tough odds of the gatekeeping processes, their occupation has always had a position of primary importance relative to marriage, family, and other pursuits. In spite of the salience of the career to faculty women and the lengths to which they go to sustain it, there is the well-documented issue of differential progress [1, 7, 11, 12, 24, 33, 36]. The problem is especially acute in elite, research-oriented institutions and in the ranks of tenured faculty [2, 32]. Possible explanations include overt and subtle sex discrimination, differential interests and preferences for teaching rather than research, lack of sponsorship and collegial networks, and others suggesting accumulative disadvantage in the structure of the occupational career.

Studies of social stratification in academe have paid most attention

This research was supported by funds from the University of Minnesota Graduate School Grant-in-Aid of Research Program and the College of Education.

Shirley M. Clark is professor of education and sociology and Mary Corcoran is professor of higher education and educational psychology at the University of Minnesota.

Journal of Higher Education, Vol. 57, No. 1 (January/February 1986)

to men. Occasionally, quantitative data were gathered on the status of women as well. However, as Cole has noted in discussing limitations of his own substantial work, "there is a conspicuous absence of qualitative interviews with female scientists" [7, p. 15]. He further argues that it is time to describe in detail and to analyze the informal structure of activities and experiences of young scientists (academics) "that set in motion and sustain an accumulation of advantages and disadvantages" [7, p. 130].

Our objectives are both theoretical and policy-oriented. From study of faculty career vitality at a large, research-oriented public multiversity, illustrations will be drawn to demonstrate the applicability of a literature-based model of professional socialization to the career experiences of academic women. Selected hypothetical "explanations" for the different progress of women will be explored within the context of the connected, three-stage model, using content from focused, open-ended interviews with women respondents. Guiding our inquiry into academe's social stratification are the following questions: What experiences have women had in the anticipatory socialization and the entry stages of a career that have gender salience? Specifically, how were sponsorship processes (advising, mentoring, collegial) experienced by these women? What processes of accumulating advantages or disadvantages affected career progress and satisfaction for these women? Did these women perceive sex-based discrimination relative to educational preparation and employment processes, review procedures, assignments, rewards and recognition?

We then seek to illuminate processes of differential socialization that result in an accumulation of advantages and disadvantages affecting academic careers. Subjective perceptions of women respondents who were part of sample groups in the institutional study will be presented as illustrative excerpts shedding light on the forms of particularistic treatment and experience that are not easily quantified. The socialization framework will be extended by considering the "Matthew" and "Salieri" effects and the sponsorship process. Finally, we present concluding statements about the value of this approach for understanding the status problems of women and suggest some policy implications arising from the case data.

Professional Socialization

Socialization models have been postulated as being particularly useful for understanding sex differences in academic careers [7]. Conceptualizations of work socialization are variously termed organizational, occupational, or professional, but all direct attention to the setting in which the socialization of adults to work occurs. It is important to note that "at any age, socialization is a two-fold process; from the perspective of the group, socialization is a mechanism through which new members learn the values, norms, knowledge, beliefs, and the interpersonal and other skills that facilitate role performance and further group goals. From the perspective of the individual, socialization is a process of learning to participate in social life" [29, p. 422].

Although extensive research and theoretical work dealing with socialization in professional schools (especially health sciences fields) has accumulated, few studies of faculty role socialization have been done. One relevant comparative occupational study is Lortie's *Schoolteacher* [23], an ethnography of a feminized occupation that probes how career decisions are made, what the strengths and weaknesses of the preparation programs are for long-term role performance, how shared relations with peers relate to professional success, how expectations of performance affect its quality, how reward and opportunity systems are structured, and more. Sociologists have identified several dimensions or strategies of organizational socialization and their consequences for the individual and the organization [40, 41]. A framework (see Figure 1) derived from the professional literature that envi-

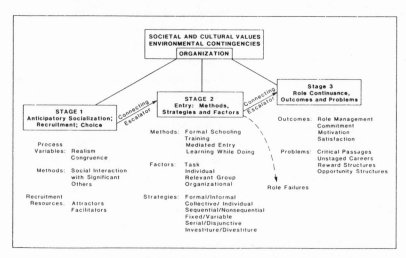

FIG. 1. Stages of Professional Socialization. SOURCE: Partially based on a scheme in Feldman [10] and a revised version of Figure 1 from Mary Corcoran and Shirley M. Clark's "Professional Socialization and Contemporary Career Attitudes of Three Faculty Generations," *Research in Higher Education,* 20 (No. 2, 1984), p. 134; used by permission from Agathon Press, Inc.

sions the individual as moving through three stages of experience is central to this study [6, 9]. Becker and Strauss [3] have used the metaphors "flow," "stream," and "escalators" to convey the relatedness of the stages.

Anticipatory socialization, recruitment, and choice is the first of the three stages. It includes the process by which persons choose occupations and are recruited to them, gradually assuming the values of the group to which they aspire and measuring the ideal for congruence with reality [10, 23, 26, and 43]. The second stage is occupational entry and induction; it includes or is preceded by formal schooling, preparation, or training for the occupation, and/or mediated entry, and/or learning while doing. For faculty members, the focus is on extensive formal training in graduate school, which also provides anticipatory socialization and a site for recruitment as well as facilitation of professional role commitment [42]. During this process, which includes passage into the status of neophyte faculty member, a variety of socialization strategies come into play [40, 41]. Particular emphasis is given here to the so-called "Matthew" effect and the sponsorship process.

The early stages of professional socialization are especially important, according to a social–psychological theory that attitudes, values, and beliefs tend to stabilize in young adulthood and to become less likely to change as persons grow older [15]. The aging-stability thesis emphasizes the importance of the early period of the career for developing commitment to work, for stimulating motivation, and for internalizing occupationally relevant attitudes and behaviors that sustain productivity and continued achievement throughout the career.

If all proceeds well, the third stage of role continuance is achieved. The new member has a set of internalized role specifications, a sense of satisfaction with work, and a high degree of job involvement and commitment. She or he is carried along within the structure of the career to later stages, which may involve the maturing, more independent professional in sponsoring, socialization, or other organizational leadership roles and generative activities.

The "escalator" metaphor is useful because it suggests that the career route may not be safe, smooth, or clear, particularly when careers are unstaged beyond an early point; when reward and opportunity structures seem to offer less than was expected; when problematic elements of the organization's environment and broader social context intrude; or when "functionally irrelevant statuses" (gender or race, for example) are believed to affect evaluation [28].

The "Matthew" Effect: Accumulated Advantage or Disadvantage

The brunt of the sociological literature on scientific elites holds that scientists who are placed in structurally advantageous positions as a result of outstanding role performance accrue certain advantages due to attaining these positions. For example, there are accumulating advantages and visibility for being in an outstanding academic department as a graduate student. Merton [27] and Zuckerman [44] have described this process with Nobel laureates; in these cases, honored standing was converted into other occupational assets. The term "Matthew" effect is an allusion to Christ's description of accumulating faith: "For whosoever hath, to him shall be given, and he shall have more abundance; but whosoever hath not, from him shall be taken away even that he hath" (King James Version, Matt. 25:29). Merton, Zuckerman, Cole [7], Lorber [22], and others who have used the quotation are referring to social status advantages: a case of the rich getting richer and the poor getting poorer as time (or the career in this case) goes on.

The "Matthew" effect tends to be considered fair. The "advantaged" scientist, after all, faces a series of challenges along the way. Success seems to be the result of a funneling process: many begin the race, some drop out along the way, some finish in record time, others finish very slowly. Cole and Cole [8] explain that, because they apprentice in top departments and interact with productive, influential scientists, and because they have superior resources to carry out research, some male scientists have social advantages and rewards attributable to a strategic location and to interactions with high-status people. These advantages affect their achievement in positive ways.

The other side of this process that potentially influences the careers of women academics may be termed accumulative disadvantage. If women do not enroll in the best graduate programs, do not receive parity in financial aids, do not become protégés of productive, established academicians, do not have resources to carry out their research and scholarly work, do not penetrate the collegial networks where useful advice, advocacy, and patronage are dispensed, and so forth, they may begin with initial disadvantage and find that it grows with time. When they are reviewed for tenure and promotion, their publication records may be inferior to those of men; in turn, if they have not accomplished much research, the funding gatekeepers may decide that there is little justification for granting financial support since the record of accomplishments is marginal. However plausible this reason-

286

ing may be, we do not have a full picture from the literature of the hypothesis of accumulative disadvantage as it applies to the career histories of women faculty. Cole suggests that "the processes of accumulative disadvantage may well begin at a far earlier age for women, and there may be processes that impede the progress of women which are not easily quantifiable" [7, p. 81].

An interesting modification of the "Matthew" effect is the "Salieri" phenomenon. In a recent paper, Lorber [22] discusses the interactive processes that keep women in academic medicine from positions of power and describes the "Salieri" phenomenon. She alludes to Peter Shaffer's play, *Amadeus* [35], in which Mozart's lack of social graces gives Salieri, the court composer and gatekeeper of musical patronage for the Emperor Joseph, the occasion to prevent Mozart's extraordinary accomplishments from receiving recognition. Salieri does recommend Mozart to the Emperor for a post, but he makes sure that the salary is set quite low. In the process, Salieri makes a pretense of being a benefactor to Mozart. Mozart, unhappy with the poor salary, is unaware that his career is actually blocked rather than advanced. Instead, he is grateful for the efforts which Salieri has made on his behalf. Not until after his death could Mozart's works be judged on their own merit, apart from the "functionally irrelevant" characteristic — lack of social graces — which so disturbed the prominent Salieri. Applying the "Salieri" phenomenon to the performance and behavior of academic women, we might consider that they are judged by a dominant, inner circle of men and may not measure up because of their social status. Women may not be blocked out entirely, but their progress is limited to a relatively low level of advancement in male-dominated occupations and societies.

Sponsorship

In *Fair Science,* Cole [7] calls for a detailed examination of the process of sponsorship in science to uncover significant differences in the training of women that are not easily captured in quantitative analysis. He doubts that the search for gross patterns of bias is likely to produce fruitful results. Rather, what is proposed is an analysis that would examine the nature of the relationship between women and their faculty advisors, the extent to which opportunities to learn to do scientific work are made available to women, the degree to which opportunities to participate in conferences, to enter the professional network, to collaborate on scholarly work, are offered to them. To be considered are both the claim that "intergenerational ties maintain a discipline's universe of discourse" [31, p. 143], thereby contributing to the development of scientific knowledge, and the practical career matters of obtaining good jobs, promotions, and salaries.

"Sponsorship," "role modeling," and "mentorship" are concepts whose time has come, as demonstrated by the attention devoted to them in the popular literature and the many recommendations devised to intervene in career development. "Professionals must have had one, been one, or be seeking one if they are to advance their careers" [37, p. 692]. The attention to mentoring, particularly, has reached (in one writer's term) "mania" proportions [4] in that readers are told that success depends "not only on what you know but whom you know" [21, p. 23]. This faith in the mentoring relationship, as a specific, two-person, mentor-protégé relationship, is not entirely supported by available research, according to Merriam's [25] critical review of the subject. Likewise, in an earlier, more encompassing review, Speizer [37] concluded that "role models," "mentors," and "sponsors" are concepts that still need to be defined and studied; until more methodologically sound studies are done, the concepts are suggestive rather than proven.

Although "sponsorship," "mentorship," and "role modeling" have not been defined with precision, for our purposes, sponsorship will include advancement of a favored protégé, mentoring and/or coaching a novice through the informal norms of the workplace and/or discipline. This process is thought to be important for upward mobility and career success in adult development generally, in business, in the professions, and specifically, in academic settings. Kanter [18] and others have recognized its importance even in "rationalistic" bureaucratic structures. Lorber argues that medicine, dependent as it is upon peer regulation, provides a good example of the processes of sponsorship and boycott—the "heart of the sorting process which results in colleague networks homogeneous in competence and ethicality" [22, p. 6]. As a further consequence, this profession becomes homogeneous in social characteristics such as race (white) and religion (Protestant). Oswald Hall's classic study of physicians in a Canadian community [16] established that novice physicians (these included the few women in his sample) who were not sponsored by influentials had "friendly careers," but they never achieved the higher status, income, or leadership of the protégé group.

As we relate ideas of sponsorship to academic women, definitional problems notwithstanding, a series of questions come to mind: Are women less likely to pursue their graduate programs in the top departments in their fields? Are women's efforts to do scholarly work discouraged? Are women channeled into teaching-oriented institutions as they move into entry-level positions? Do they receive less post-degree help from advisors? Data collected from women in an exploratory study of faculty career vitality may sharpen images in an unclear picture of how sponsorship affects the sexes in academe.

An Exploratory Institutional Case Study

As part of an institutional case study of faculty career vitality at the University of Minnesota, Twin Cities campus, lengthy interviews with 147 faculty members were conducted during 1980–81 and 1981–82. Faculty respondents were drawn from four fields: the College of Biological Sciences, the physical sciences and mathematics departments of the Institute of Technology, and the social sciences and humanities departments of the College of Liberal Arts. Both reputational and stratified random sampling procedures were used to assure representation of the full range of faculty productivity in teaching, research, and service. All of the faculty respondents were tenured associate or full professors whose median age was in the forties. Eleven percent, or twelve respondents, were women. Although this number is quite small, it is representative of the actual proportions of tenured women in the sample fields on the Minneapolis campus.[1]

The interview guide consisted of more than fifty, mostly open-ended, questions on subjects such as (1) the decision to pursue an academic career; (2) graduate school dimensions of career socialization; (3) career stages and socialization as a faculty member; (4) work interests and preference orientations; (5) dimensions of productivity and success; (6) morale, satisfaction, and perceptions of change; and (7) appraisals and future considerations.

The applicability of the study is limited because of its attention to one case of a specific institutional type (research-oriented multiversity) and to only four fields, biological sciences, physical sciences and mathematics, social sciences, and humanities. It is arguable that there are different patterns of treatment for women in fields where they are token representatives of their sex and in fields where they are better represented, but there is little actual data regarding these differences and conflicting hypotheses abound. For example, Cole [7] asserts that

---

[1] Percentages of tenured women (of total tenured faculty cohort) in each field group at Minnesota according to the February 1984 personnel listings are: 5.06 percent in biological sciences; 4.38 percent in the Institute of Technology; 11.46 percent in the social sciences, and 22.56 percent in the humanities in the College of Liberal Arts.

one could argue that few women in a field do not represent a threat to the men in power, and so women are treated equitably. Conversely, one could argue that, in fields with few women, levels of sex discrimination are significant, for discrimination is not as visible or as frequently punished and men may be more apt to define women as incapable of doing the requisite work.

We turn now to the subjective perceptions of women respondents about their experiences in the anticipatory and entry stages of their careers.

Anticipatory Socialization: Women and the Career Choice

Among the significant others who influenced the career decision of respondents were parents, high-school teachers, and faculty members. We draw from the interviews three disparate selections to illustrate, first, the self-imposed limitations in choosing a graduate school, and second and third, the impact of parental support or lack thereof for career planning. In Berg and Ferber's [4] review of studies of men and women graduate students, it is alleged that women are less confident than men, are more conservative in choosing a graduate school, complain of lack of ability as a barrier to success, often lack maternal support for their choices, set lower goals for themselves, and receive less encouragement from male faculty. A woman scientist explains how she made her decision about which graduate school to attend:

> There were at that time maybe twenty good graduate departments in the country in my field. I probably applied to about half a dozen, and I got accepted at all of them. I didn't apply to what I called the top echelon because I was good academically, but I was a woman and I had some reservations. And I didn't want to go to Harvard or Princeton; I was from the Midwest, and socially I did not think I would be happy in those places. I received financial aid, I think, at all but one. And one of those places was _____. Actually, it turned out they made the best offer; that's why I went there.

Her mother's example and advice and a particular undergraduate teacher provided support for another faculty woman's decision to move ahead:

> She had married while she was in graduate school and dropped out to have three children. She felt that it probably would have been better if she had finished and had a career, but then she went back to having a career after I went to college. So she always told me that I should go right through! And that if I wanted a family, that I should combine it somehow, and I shouldn't give up my career for a family. So I think that she was a very big influence. I also had a teacher at my undergraduate school

who was a woman—I was very impressed with her, and I think I identified with her, too.

Another distinguished woman talks of the mixed messages she received about graduate study and an academic career, even though she came from an academic family, and how this confusion kept her in graduate school but prevented her from clearly deciding to pursue an academic career:

> I wanted to be a scientist, but I didn't decide that I wanted to be a faculty member because I thought that would be impossible because I was female. I went to college at _____ and to graduate school at _____, where there were no women faculty members. I come from an academic family and the way in which I was brought up was with the belief that this was not a career open to women. Period.
>
> In fact, my father felt very strongly that women should not go to graduate school because they were taking up a place that a man should occupy and he had potential and used his education—whereas women did not, so they should not go. So I'd say I made the decision to be a faculty member when I was thirty-five and was actually offered a job as a faculty member.

In response to further probes, she explained:

> My father was a professor and a scientist, so there was a lot of talk about science and a lot of approval for people who were academics and who were intelligent and well educated. So I was getting a lot of positive reinforcement for the idea that it would be desirable to be an academic, or to be a scholar, while at the same time getting the negative message that I shouldn't do this. It was rather confusing.

Later on, some little encouragement was forthcoming:

> I would say in college, I remember talking to one of the deans, and she quite surprised me by saying that she thought that women who had combined marriage and a career were probably the happiest. That was the first positive statement I'd heard from anyone that this was an option. At this time, I was trying to make up my mind to go to graduate school, but you see I wasn't really making up my mind to have a career. I would say outside my family I didn't get much positive reinforcement about this, either. I think I met a few people later on, after I had my Ph.D., who gave me positive reinforcement. Needless to say I'm very angry about this, thinking back on it.

These selections suggest, on the one hand, the early disadvantages that spring from negative or conflicting messages from significant others about career choice and planning, as well as the potential disadvantage of a conservative choice of a graduate department. On the other hand, strong support for combining career and family aspirations was perceived as important, positive reinforcement from persons who mattered. In each of these excerpts and, indeed, throughout the interviews with women, the consciousness of gender and career is explicit, contrasting to the lack of expressed concerns about "being a man" or "combining marriage and career" among the men faculty respondents.

We turn now to dimensions of graduate school preparation: the role relationship of the advisor and the advisee, its impact, the departmental environment, and the role of peers during formal training, induction, and after.

Work Entry: The Sponsorship of Women

Formal preparation of the faculty member takes place through graduate education in the departments of research-oriented universities. The department inducts students into the discipline, transmitting skills, knowledge, and a structure of values, attitudes, and ways of thinking and feeling. Trow asserts that the effects of this socialization "are often very strong, providing an individual with the perspectives and orientations that guide a lifetime of academic teaching and research" [39, p. 15].

The basic forms and functions of graduate education are similar across disciplines, but the actual processes vary among disciplines and departments, and even within departments among pairs of students and advisors. This situation is certainly true for men as well as for women, as our interview data attest. The result is that different environments and contexts for learning are experienced and that little is known of this variety even by academics themselves. Field differences in student environment (e.g., in history as compared to psychology), as well as sex differences in student experiences, have been reported by Hartnett [17]. The disadvantages faced by women students in finding sponsors and mentors, given the ratios of female faculty to female students in most graduate programs and fields, have been examined recently by Berg and Ferber's institutional case study of the University of Illinois at Urbana–Champaign [4]. They suggest that this disadvantage is an inevitable result of rising proportions of women students without related change in the sex composition of faculties. Particularly in male-dominated fields, women graduate students at Illinois reported knowing far fewer men faculty members well and experiencing junior collegial relations with men faculty far less often than did their male peers. It seemed clear to the researchers that "students and faculty of the same sex interact most comfortably" [4, p. 639]. In an earlier study by Katz and Hartnett [20], graduate students regarded their relations with faculty members as the single most important aspect of the quality of their graduate experience; sad to say, many also reported it as the single most disappointing aspect of their graduate experience.

One talented woman reflects on the absence of women role models in her environment, a typical experience of many of the respondents:

> I had a man advisor. Something that was very significant to me during this time was that there was only one woman who taught in the graduate school there, and she offered courses that were outside the field that I was working in. So the whole time I never did work with any women professors. And this did have a clear impact on me, and I began to think, "Where do I fit in the system if there are no women in it, or very few?" And at that time, there were no women full professors in my department. So that was a very negative kind of message that I was getting. The subject was never talked about, the fact that some of us were women and some of us were men. We were treated as though we had no gender whatsoever. And yet I could see that there was a big difference in the institution in terms of what happened to women and what happened to men. My advisor was and is a very kind man, and someone I respect a great deal. His expectations, as far as I could determine, were that I do well, that I work hard and write well and be conscientious, and that's about it. And he pretty much left me on my own to do that.

When this respondent was asked whether her advisor or other faculty members provided any specific encouragement to her to pursue an academic career, she expressed the bind she felt between marriage and career success:

> I think when I look back on it that I got a set of double messages about my career. In fact, some people said very explicitly to me that I should not get married. Or that, if I did get married, I would ruin my career, or that I would not have a career. I found this sort of painful at the time, and I did get married in the course of graduate school. But three different professors suggested to me more or less openly that I would lose it all if I got married. On the other hand, the other side of that message was, "You're so good that you deserve to go on and do well." I couldn't see how I was supposed to live the life that they imagined me leading, or at least it was not the life I planned to live. But I didn't know how to reconcile my notion of what a career for me might be and their notion of what a career for me should be.

Not being taken seriously is a problem some women encountered:

> I think the expectation was that the women, since no woman had ever

graduated from there, were just kind of taking some courses because our husbands were doing something else. Well I did a couple of things that made an impression on them, and they began to treat me more seriously. One is that I was the only one that finished the first semester without incompletes. And at the end of the first year, they gave me a summer fellowship which I didn't apply for and I had never heard of; they just decided that I had done the best job and so they gave me a scholarship. The other thing I did toward the end of my first year was that I had done an honors thesis in my undergraduate school which used some very elementary statistics, and in my statistics class we were talking about something and I raised my hand, and said "Well is that why I got such and such kind of results when I did this paper before?", and so the class started talking about it and my professor encouraged me to recalculate these things. And then he sort of said after that, "Oh you're serious about this, I thought you were just kind of hanging around here." And this professor was on my dissertation committee and became sort of my major mentor figure. So I worked on this article and submitted it; since it was in history, submitted it to a history journal and revised it, and it was accepted. Then people really started to notice me. What I'm trying to say is that they didn't have particularly high expectations at first, but they began to raise them very rapidly, especially this one person. And then they started to make comments about how, "Boy, they've sure taken a sow's ear and made a silk purse." They had a lot of fun telling the history department that I'd published an article in their leading journal, and they hadn't taken me as a graduate student, and so then it was this mutual patting themselves on the back and patting me on the back, that kind of thing.

Another woman, who admitted to being very ambivalent in the past about her own, now very successful career, began her relationship with her advisor in the following way:

When I came up here, it was not to be a graduate student. He was looking for a research assistant. I always loved research. And I applied for that job. And we had quite a go-around when we first met. It was a very hostile kind of interview between us. He wanted to know if I had any authoritative medical evidence that I couldn't have children. And I said I certainly didn't. Then he said, well what would you do if you got pregnant? I said, I'd quit you. In a shot. And I was very offended. And he, of course, did not like my attitude either. And so it ended on this rather sorry note, and I thought I would never hear from him again. Well, a month later I got this letter from him and he said I have examined the qualifications of all the people who have applied for this job, and you are the most qualified and if you want it, it is yours. Which was pretty white of him considering in those days they thought women would never finish graduate school, and men were stable and sturdy.

Doubting that she would be committed to her field because women's lives were likely to include marriage, the advisor of this woman provided help begrudgingly:

I was in graduate school between '65 and '69, and I was one of one or two other women in the graduate department at the time I was there. I definitely felt that my advisor's attitude towards me, his expectations of me, were highly dependent on my sex. He was never mean to me in any way, but I always felt that he had one or two other students, men, and it wasn't until they were out of the way (I was third in line) that he would spend some time with me. It was very near the end of my thesis, and I think he really wasn't expecting much to come out; he was very surprised at the end.

When she was attempting to obtain a postdoctoral position, she solicited his help:

When I was looking for a job, I actually asked my thesis advisor, "Won't you do anything for me? Aren't you going to help me get a job?" And he said, "Well now you do the work, you go out and you write the letters and write to all the places you're interested in and if any of them respond, then tell me and I'll follow it up." But this was quite different from what he did for the two men. He said to me in effect, "Okay, so I go out and I do this for you. And I get you a good job. And after a year or so you run off and go get married, and never do any work again. How am I to feel? I have stuck my neck out for you." And I said, "I personally didn't think that was any more reason against me than it should be against someone else. What guarantee did he have that two years from now those guys were going to be great guns?" My thesis had been probably better than theirs in some ways. But he was afraid that basically he was sticking his neck out because I was a woman. He made that very specific.

As her reputation in her field grew, however, her advisor changed his mind about her:

My advisor and I are on excellent terms now. It might have sounded like I'm bitter at him. At that time, I was very bitter. But since then, he's just been absolutely gushing. He's very proud of me, and he's very quick to tell me that and to tell all the people that I was his student.

Not all of the women reported discriminatory treatment from their men advisors, although several did. For a more positive experience, this woman describes her advisor as a "real dynamo" who held "very high expectations and standards for the students":

Of course, in fact, I was a little intimidated by him because he was just so outstanding in every way. He knew so much, and he was so productive, and it was hard to think of being like him, or even working with him, but by the time I came to have to make the decision about who would be my advisor, he seemed the logical person, because he was interested in what I was interested in. We had a very formal relationship, I think. I never worked with him on his project, though he invited me to, because I felt very strongly that I should do my own thing. But it was a very good choice, I think, and he was excellent in helping me through, and reading everything very quickly, and getting me lots of good advice, and then he helped me get a job when I got out by writing recommendations. Then when it came time to make the transition here, he wrote letters and called people and so that was very helpful. But in terms of my career development, I've moved away from some of my original interests, and he's moved further in another direction.

Generally, the women respondents reported receiving some assistance, at least at a minimal level, from their advisors in obtaining positions after the doctorate was achieved. Frequently, however, this involved channeling or tracking women into certain positions and men into others, as perceived by these two respondents:

This process was basically what is known as the Old Boy system. And I think what happened is that the director of placement would recommend to various people at other institutions which candidates they might seriously consider. So I had no insight into where they thought I should go, except that I figured out, I think pretty accurately after the fact, that they thought I should go to a small liberal arts college. They tended to channel most of the men into the larger and sometimes more prestigious research-oriented institutions, and the women tended to be placed in small liberal arts colleges. Often these were colleges with wonderful reputations but known as teaching colleges rather than research colleges.

The chairman of the department at that time pretty much told people where they would go to teach and that is one of the things that I resent now, that I was discriminated against as a woman. The plum jobs went to two men, and my advisor told me that there was a job at St. Cloud State, and I said I would never go there. Then he said, "Well there's a job at Iowa State," and that did seem like a reasonable place for me to go. There was also one in Utah. Now my colleagues, my peers, were going to Princeton, and I'm sure that it was because I was a woman, because I certainly had done as well in the program as my male peers. So there wasn't much encouragement and in fact, looking back, there was a sense of my being pushed into second-rate jobs. I was lucky that my husband was given incredible direction by his advisors, and he went to _____, and then I was able to get a job on my own, without any help from my department.

The channeling of women academics into colleges emphasizing teaching rather than research puts women at a disadvantage in beginning their research and scholarly work, in building their reputations as scientists and scholars. As Zuckerman [44] and Cole [7] put it, this is the "triple penalty" principle in operation, which states that certain groups (here, women) "suffer not only from direct discrimination and cultural definitions that define certain careers as inappropriate, but also from being placed initially into second-rate structural positions, which makes it difficult or impossible for them to produce the outstanding work that is necessary for moving out of such positions" [7, p. 79].

Peer relationships are an important part of socialization, for it is with peers that informal discussions, exchanges of aid and support, and friendships facilitate the learning that, in the present, tempers the "ordeal" aspects of professional preparation and, in the future, prepares the student for collegial structures. Women faculty have peers who, for the most part, are men. Their consciousness of that fact stands out in the following comments:

> The first year, one of those ways in which I was pretty miserable was that I didn't have any friends among those students. It seemed that there were mostly single males, and I was a married woman, and you know that they didn't quite know how to relate to me, and so they just didn't. And then, over the first summer, these men all got girlfriends, or they got married; they became more able to interact as couples. And so then I started to see a lot of them socially, and their main way of relating to me was kind of like my brother used to relate to me. So they were important after the first year . . . that was really a way to get socialized.

> Well, when I was a student, we had a study group for the prelim, and I worked with two other men. There were hardly any women at all in the program, and so if you wanted to have relationships like that, they had to be cross-sex, because there was no one else by the time you reached the Master's. Beyond the Master's program, most of the women wound up dropping out. And that prelim study group kind of stands out in my mind, because it went on for a whole year; the prelim was the big milestone at _____. The third year would just be studying for this prelim, and we used to meet every week, and go through all these reading lists, and talk about the ideas, and that was very good. Both of them wound up being good friends of mine, and that's continued even now.

Working in relative isolation characterized some graduate study environments:

> Graduate students as I remember them in my department, worked very hard, and they tended to work in isolation. They didn't do what I have heard has happened at other institutions, try to undermine each other's work. There wasn't that kind of nasty competition. On the other hand, they didn't share their work very much with their friends. We really didn't talk much about the papers we were writing or the subjects we were interested in, and there was a kind of reticence in that area. I'm now making contact again with some of the people I was with in graduate school, a lot of them women, and discovering that we have similar interests and

297

sometimes it's very specific, in this field for instance. Those friendships are sort of latent and are now blossoming. We're also now able to share our work.

Many of the situations in which gender was conspicuous for women as graduate students (primarily male peers, primarily male faculty advisors, a predominantly male departmental milieu, problems of allocating time to both family and work, and so forth) continued to be experienced by many as they moved from the graduate school into postdoctoral or entry-level academic positions. There were certain pitfalls, for example, with colleagues and sponsors. One of the women who moved into a postdoctoral position found she needed to manage problems of dependency with a sponsor-colleague. As she explained it:

> A faculty member at another university provided me with encouragement and positive career advice. And he also gave me some financial support. Finally, I ended up being a postdoctoral fellow in his lab. Only I wasn't resident, I was living in another city where my husband was, and he was quite tolerant of that situation. So that was positive support from that one person who was more of a colleague than a mentor. I was very suspicious of accepting too much of this kind of help because, although I was very naive, I'd somehow caught on very early to the dangers of attaching myself to any such sugar-daddy type person who might absorb me into his research reputation. And with this man that did happen with some of the work that I did with him as a postdoc. There were certain hostilities between us for a while because I knew he was giving seminars and talking about the work I'd done, and so I extricated myself from that situation. I was very careful about not putting myself in a position of dependency. How I knew this I haven't quite figured out because I didn't see any role models for the situation, but I somehow knew that it was a danger for a young woman scientist.

Another woman, when asked about her perceptions of colleagues' expectations of her when she moved into her first faculty position, described her role as an outsider to a male culture.

> It wasn't clear to me what was expected of me, particularly at the small college where I held my first position. My experience there was not good. In part, because I was one of the very few full-time faculty members, the first full-time woman faculty member in my department. There really was difficulty among my male colleagues in associating with a woman as a colleague. I think they literally did not know how to talk to me, and as a consequence often just did not talk to me. They would ignore me. They would not invite me to have lunch with them, which was a very ordinary experience there. They all go up to the campus cafeteria and eat together. And it took me a long time to realize that they would walk past my office and ask the next person and never ask me. Late in my years there, when

this finally dawned on me that I was being treated differently, I asked one of my colleagues why this was so. And he said, "You know what would happen if I asked you to lunch." I said, "No," and he said, "People would talk." And it wasn't until then that I began to understand how deeply conventional that society was and how much I was a strange element in it. That many people saw me as a subject of gossip if they associated with me. So that made me very uncomfortable. Also I had a baby my first year there. So then I was not only one of the very few full-time women on the faculty, I was the only full-time woman faculty with a young child, in a society where all mothers of young children stayed at home. I also felt a kind of disapproval of my working and taking my daughter to a baby sitter for six hours a day. They never did articulate what they expected of me.

Societal expectations of wives and mothers bore heavily upon a woman who began her career thirty years ago. She commented:

I did feel a very important role, like I was a pioneer when I started thirty years ago. And that was to show women that you could work and have successful kids, and it was this whole syndrome which is not much about being a woman and stuff. This whole thing of the working woman was neglecting her kids was looked down on. And I had to prove, I thought, that I could have good kids and work. And I worked very much; I mean I did all the outside things too. Scout leading, which I really enjoyed, it's one of the things that makes me a good teacher, I think. But I did all of those and I had the orange juice unfrozen every morning; that's a joke in our family!

Even, however, for the more recent women doctorates, the early stages of career often combined with childbearing, childcare, and required coordination with the husband's similarly emerging career, as demonstrated in the following response:

You know, it was the dual-career, family business again, coordinating moves, and it just happened that my husband finished his degree one year before I did, and he wanted to take a post-doc position, so we planned to move to the area where his institution was located, and at that point, I had finished all of my dissertation research, but I hadn't written it yet. I had written parts of it, and I was also pregnant. So it seemed a reasonable idea at that time, and jobs were plentiful in those days, and there were a number of schools in the area, so I didn't consider it a very great risk to just move there, and then see what happened, and my plan was that I wouldn't be employed for a while, and I would finish my dissertation, I would have my baby, and then at some time maybe during the next year, I would try to get some employment. . . . I had the baby in February, and at that time I was working very hard at trying to do the writing, and that was going well. But I was feeling very distressed at being alone in this unfamiliar place without friends or relatives, and having this new baby, and being cut off from professional colleagues. I was feeling very isolated, so I decided that I really had to get a job, even though I had thought I might not work so soon. So I applied around the area, and very soon I got a job on a part-time basis. I finished my dissertation during that first year, and then I was on a tenure track. It was rather strenuous, because I had this new baby, and I was trying to finish my dissertation and also preparing new classes that I hadn't taught before. I remember feeling like I was exhausted a lot of the time, getting low-grade colds and sore throats, and infections and things, and not being able to shake them. My husband was very helpful, and that wasn't the problem, but it was just too much for both of us.

She goes on to indicate that early crises brought on by "role overload" abated:

After that first year, things really settled down, and then by the second year, I was feeling like I was able to handle it, and things weren't so stressful. I started sending things off to be published, got a grant proposal in, and then the people in my department were very supportive and really accommodating to my needs for special hours, arrangements, and things like that. I thought that was very nice to help. With women, these family concerns always enter in.

Being husbands and fathers rarely affects men's occupational involvement and commitment to the extent that women's marital and family roles affect their professional work engagement. Wifehood and maternity compete for resources that must be allocated among occupational and domestic spheres [30]. This allocation may create career discontinuity if it results in withdrawal from the workplace for child-bearing and child care. Withdrawal may result in obsolescence of skills, loss of competitive position, attenuation of professional networks, and social isolation [13]. As if this were not problematic enough, the evidence suggests that women, regardless of marital and family status, tend to be marginals or outsiders to the male world of academe (in most field areas) to some greater or lesser extent. Outsiders are excluded from, or have limited access to, informal networks of communication that carry significant professional information. They, in turn, may feel awkward and self-conscious in the male milieu and further remove themselves from informal interactions. In devising strategies for change, it is important to consider the structure and processes within academe that are male-biased and to propose changes that will do more than simply increase the ratios of women on college and university faculties.

300

Conclusions

In many respects, American women faculty have succeeded in improving their status in this century. The earlier hostile climate of opinion about women's place, about married women working, about women's intellectual and creative capacities to become scholars and scientists has been neutralized. Women have many opportunities to pursue careers. It is also true that at least some types of institutions, including research universities, have hired more women as regular faculty than in the pre-World War II era. And these structural changes in academe seem to have been accompanied by social changes that have helped reduce sex discrimination — at least in its most blatant forms. A decade of concerted activity by women's interest groups, with the help of the federal government and the courts, has strongly influenced practices if not attitudes at many institutions. If one takes a long-term perspective, that is good news indeed.

The bad news seems to be that women have not completely overcome the effects of the "triple penalty." Among women like those we studied, who are in their thirties, forties, and fifties, there are reports of difficulties in first overcoming cultural barriers to entering academic careers. Second, during the training for and entry phase of their careers, there were particularistic experiences with advisors and others who doubted the women students' potential for, or likelihood of, having an academic career that would include research productivity. Third, structural impediments to success (in the form of opportunities for "best" positions and full participation in the collegial culture and networks) were easily recalled and described by many of the women respondents in the faculty career vitality study.

Qualitative data richly illustrate the utility of theoretical conceptualizations of professional socialization for understanding the quantitatively based sex differences in academic careers that have been established in numerous empirical studies. The idea of accumulated advantage or disadvantage, as suggested by the "Matthew" effect or the "Salieri" phenomenon, seems useful for understanding processes in academe that lead similarly talented graduate students into highly productive careers or less productive ones. Models of causal chains might be drawn up and tested once we better establish the nature of the relationships, choices, and interactive processes of advantage or disadvantage. We tend to think that the "Salieri" phenomenon (when gatekeepers to career advancement permit access but control achievement) is an interesting extension of sponsorship conceptualizations warranting further study. The diminished status of women's "triple penalty" and women's opportunity for so-called "friendly careers" in academe today suggests that, although women are no longer excluded, their place may be limited to some middle-range of career success.

Sponsorship—which is so important to vital faculty careers, as we learned from the larger study from which data about the women respondents are drawn [6]—needs a great deal of research and policy attention in the case of women. Descriptions of advisor behavior ranged from the very instrumentally helpful to the relatively unhelpful and even sex-biased. The cross-sex nature of most of the advisor, peer, and eventually, collegial relationships problematically affects the quality of the relationships in many instances.

As Finkelstein [11, 12] has noted, institutions of higher education are not, in and of themselves, able to attack sex-linked differential patterns of childhood socialization and family expectations directly. However, they are in a position to address practices and processes within academe that result in inequities and marginality in women's careers as graduate students, as neophyte scholars, and as full-fledged faculty members. We believe that sponsorship should be a more deliberate process, in which advisors and colleagues would relate to women and men according to universalistic principles appropriate to a meritocratic community—but this is more easily said than done while women represent a proportional minority of the professoriate.

Finally, at the outset we accepted Cole's [7] descriptions of faculty women as "survivors" of a series of tests, challenges, and obstacles leading to and through their occupational lives. This assertion is in no way an exaggeration when applied to the women respondents in the faculty career vitality study. They have had to be successful academics, or they would not have persisted to tenured status and senior rank at the University of Minnesota, where several enjoy distinguished reputations in their fields. Yet in their descriptions of earlier experiences with advisors and colleagues, there was evidence of early preparation or career disadvantage. By their middle- and late-middle age, they overcame those early disadvantages of lack of sponsorship or little sponsorship, exclusion from the collegial culture, and significant "role-overloading" with marital and child-care demands. Many questions then arise as to how initial disadvantages were overcome, what kinds of careers these women might have had under more favorable circumstances, and what impact such earlier experiences have had on the mature, role-maintenance stage of their careers, relative to morale, commitment, work engagement, and satisfaction. We hope these questions will stimulate further inquiry into women's careers in the social system of academe.

References

1. Astin, H. S., and A. E. Bayer. "Sex Discrimination in Academe." In *Academic Women on the Move,* edited by A. Rossi and A. Calderwood, pp. 139–79. New York: Russell Sage, 1973.

2. Baldridge, J. V., D. V. Curtis, G. Ecker, and G. L. Riley. *Policy Making and Effective Leadership.* San Francisco: Jossey-Bass, 1978.

3. Becker, H. S., and A. L. Strauss. "Careers, Personality and Adult Socialization." *American Journal of Sociology,* 62 (November 1956), 253–63.

4. Berg, H. M., and M. A. Ferber. "Men and Women Graduate Students: Who Succeeds and Why?" *Journal of Higher Education,* 54 (November/December 1983), 629–48.

5. Bernard, J. "Women's Educational Needs." In *The Modern American College,* edited by A. W. Chickering and Associates, pp. 256–78. San Francisco: Jossey-Bass, 1981.

6. Clark, S. M., and M. Corcoran. "Professional Socialization and Faculty Career Vitality." Paper read at the American Educational Research Association, Montreal, Canada, April 1983.

7. Cole, J. R. *Fair Science: Women in the Scientific Community.* New York: The Free Press, 1979.

8. Cole, J. R., and S. Cole. *Social Stratification in Science.* Chicago: University of Chicago Press, 1973.

9. Corcoran, M., and S. M. Clark. "Professional Socialization and Contemporary Career Attitudes of Three Faculty Generations." *Research in Higher Education,* 20 (1984), 131–53.

10. Feldman, D. "A Contingency Theory of Socialization." *Administrative Science Quarterly,* 21 (September 1976), 433–52.

11. Finkelstein, M. "The Status of Academic Women: An Assessment of Five Competing Explanations." *The Review of Higher Education,* 7 (Spring 1984), 223–46.

12. ———. *The American Academic Profession: A Synthesis of Social Scientific Inquiry Since World War II.* Columbus: Ohio State University Press, 1984.

13. Fox, M. F., and S. Hesse-Biber. *Women at Work.* Palo Alto: Mayfield Publishing, 1984.

14. Fury, K. "Mentor Mania." *Savvy* (December 1979), 42–47.

15. Glenn, N. D. "Values, Attitudes, and Beliefs." In *Constancy and Chance in Human Development,* edited by O. G. Brim, Jr. and J. Kagan, pp. 596–640. Cambridge: Harvard University Press, 1980.

16. Hall, O. "Types of Medical Careers." *American Journal of Sociology,* 55 (1949), 243–53.

17. Hartnett, R. T. "Sex Differences in the Environments of Graduate Students and Faculty." *Research in Higher Education,* 14 (1981), 211–27.

18. Kanter, R. M. *Men and Women of the Corporation.* New York: Basic Books, 1977.
19. ———. "Changing the Shape of Work: Reform in Academe." In *Current Issues in Higher Education: (1) Perspectives on Leadership,* pp. 25–27. Washington, D.C.: American Association for Higher Education, 1979.
20. Katz, J., and R. T. Hartnett. "Recommendations for Training Better Scholars." In *Scholars in the Making,* edited by J. Katz and R. T. Hartnett, pp. 261–80. Cambridge: Ballinger, 1976.
21. Kraft, B. S. "Substantial Need for Professional 'Mentoring' Seen by Project on Women." *Chronicle of Higher Education,* 11 January 1984, p. 23.
22. Lorber, J. "Women as Colleagues: The Matthew Effect and the Salieri Phenomenon." Paper presented at American Sociological Association Meetings, Detroit, 1983.
23. Lortie, D. C. *Schoolteacher: A Sociological Study.* Chicago: University of Chicago Press, 1975.
24. Menges, R. J., and W. H. Exum. "Barriers to the Progress of Women and Minority Faculty." *Journal of Higher Education,* 54 (March/April 1983), 123–44.
25. Merriam, S. "Mentors and Proteges: A Critical Review of the Literature." *Adult Education Quarterly,* 33 (Spring 1983), 161–73.
26. Merton, R. K. *Social Theory and Social Structure.* Revised ed. Glencoe: The Free Press, 1957.
27. ———. "The Matthew Effect in Science." *Science,* 199 (January 5, 1968), 55–63.
28. ———. In conversation with Jonathan Cole, as reported in pp. 81–83, Cole, J., *Fair Science: Women in the Scientific Community.* New York: The Free Press, 1979.
29. Mortimer, J. T., and R. Simmons. "Adult Socialization." *Annual Review of Sociology,* 4 (1978), 421–54.
30. Mortimer, J. T., and G. Sorensen. "Men, Women, Work and Family." In *Women in the Workplace: Effects on Families,* edited by D. Quarm, K. Borman, and S. Gideonse. Norwood, N.J.: Ablex Publishers, forthcoming.
31. Reskin, B. F. "Academic Scholarship and Scientists' Careers." *Sociology of Education,* 52 (July 1979), 129–46.
32. Rossi, A. "Status of Women in Graduate Departments of Sociology." *The American Sociologist,* 5 (1970), 1–12.
33. Sandler, B. R. "You've Come a Long Way, Maybe—Or Why It Still Hurts to Be a Woman in Labor." *Current Issues in Higher Education,* 11–14, Washington, D.C.: American Association for Higher Education, 1979.
34. Sarason, S. B. *Work, Aging and Social Change: Professionals and the One Life-One Career Imperative.* New York: The Free Press, 1977.
35. Shaffer, P. *Amadeus.* New York: Harper and Row, 1980.
36. Simon, R. J., S. M. Clark, and K. Galway. "The Woman Ph.D.: A Recent Profile." *Social Problems,* 15 (Fall 1967), 221–36.
37. Speizer, J. J. "Role Models, Mentors and Sponsors: The Elusive Concepts." *Signs,* 6 (Summer 1981), 692–712.
38. Trow, M. (ed.). *Teachers and Students: Aspects of American Higher Education.*

A volume of essays sponsored by the Carnegie Commission on Higher Education. New York: McGraw-Hill, 1975.

39. ———. "Departments as Contexts for Teaching and Learning." In *Academic Departments,* edited by D. E. McHenry and Associates, pp. 12–33. San Francisco: Jossey-Bass, 1977.

40. Van Maanen, J. "People Processing: Strategies of Organizational Socialization." *Organizational Dynamics,* 7 (Summer 1978), 19–36.

41. Van Maanen, J., and E. H. Schein. "Toward a Theory of Organizational Change." In *Research in Organizational Behavior,* edited by B. M. Staw, pp. 209–64. Greenwich: JAI Press, 1979.

42. Weiss, C. S. "The Development of Professional Role Commitment Among Graduate Students." *Human Relations,* 34 (1981), 13–31.

43. Wheeler, S. "The Structure of Formally Organized Socialization Settings." In *Socialization After Childhood,* edited by O. G. Brim, Jr. and S. Wheeler, pp. 53–116. New York: Wiley and Sons, 1966.

44. Zuckerman, H. A. *Scientific Elite.* New York: The Free Press, 1977.

Are Women Changing the Nature of the Academic Profession?

Without question, as labor economists Richard Layard and Jacob Mincer have observed, the tremendous rise in the number of women entering and remaining in the labor force over the last twenty years is "one of the most profound social changes of our time" [19]. Nowhere has this trend been more significant than in the traditionally male-dominated professions, such as law, medicine, and university teaching. Consider the fact that less than a quarter of a century ago about one-fifth of all university faculty members, fewer than one-tenth of all physicians, and about one-twentieth of the nation's lawyers were women. Today about one out of three college teachers, almost one out of four lawyers, and one out of five medical doctors are female.

Such trends recently provoked economist John B. Parrish [34] to ask: "Are women taking over the professions?" Professor Parrish proceeds to answer his question by summarizing the impressive gains women have made in professional and graduate school enrollments since the 1960s and especially during the 1970s. Based on his review of this primarily supply-side evidence, he concludes that there is no indica-

I would like to thank Betty Wright and Jim Neal of the United States Equal Employment Opportunity Commission, Jack Scopino of the National Science Foundation, and especially Yupin Bae of the Doctorate Records Project at the National Research Council (NRC) and Pat Mikus of the Survey of Doctorate Recipients Project at the NRC for supplying the raw data analyzed in this article. I also appreciate the helpful comments of Katharine Abraham, Arne Kalleberg, Rachel Rosenfeld, the members of the Labor Economics Workshop at the University of Maryland, College Park, and the reviewers of this journal.

Ana María Turner Lomperis is a visiting assistant professor in the Department of Economics and Business at North Carolina State University, Raleigh.

Journal of Higher Education, Vol. 61, No. 6 (November/December 1990)

tion of a slowdown in the upward movement of women into the professions [34, p. 54]. At the opposite end of the spectrum lies a consensus of opinion held by many others [5, 8] that when one examines the demand side of professional labor markets, the gains women have made are not quite as impressive. This alternative view was summarized recently by Ernst Benjamin, General Secretary of the American Association of University Professors (AAUP), at the eighth triennial conference of the International Association of University Presidents. Asked to comment on the current status of women in the academic profession, Dr. Benjamin drew on the accumulated data from the AAUP's annual academic salary surveys and observed that the increased participation of women was "disproportionately in the lower ranks and shows scant evidence of progression through the ranks." "We confront a situation," he added, "in which the manifold programs intended to improve the status of women create an appearance of privilege which offends and frightens many men and embarrasses some successful women. Yet the data unequivocally demonstrate the continuing and scarcely diminishing disadvantage suffered by women" [3, p. 76]. In short, Dr. Benjamin's analysis stands in sharp contrast to Dr. Parrish's assertion that although "only time will tell . . . the evidence to date indicates" that the movement of women into the training echelons of the "most coveted, high income employments" will translate into "high occupational achievements over occupational lifetimes" [34, p. 58].

Are women taking over the professions? If so, how? If not, could at least the *nature* of the professions be changing by virtue of the increasing presence of women in them? The purpose of this article is to address these questions by focusing on one such profession — college and university teaching. To do so, some of the major characteristics of both the supply and demand side of academic labor markets[1] in the United States and how they might have changed with respect to gender over the last fifteen to twenty years will be examined. Based on an analysis of relevant data from the National Research Council (NRC) and the United States Equal Employment Opportunity Commission (EEOC), this study concludes that though women may not necessarily be "taking over" the academic profession, their increasing presence in fields many men have abandoned, as well as in revolving door, off-track

---

[1]The reference to academic labor markets in the plural here is deliberate. For as Michael McPherson [21, p. 57] has observed "Ph.D.s are highly specialized personnel. . . . Employment conditions differ very widely among disciplines and even among subdisciplines."

positions the majority of academic men have historically avoided, has profound implications for the changing nature of the academy itself.

The Supply Side of Academic Labor Markets: Changes in Ph.D. Output with Respect to Gender since the 1970s

The primary prerequisite for obtaining, or at least retaining, a permanent faculty position at the vast majority of the nation's institutions of higher education, particularly the four-year colleges and universities, is, of course, attainment of the highest degree in one's field. In the humanities, sciences, and engineering, and increasingly in education and the professional fields, as well, the prospective job candidate on the supply side of the academic labor market must have earned or have almost completed the requirements for a doctorate degree.[2] The single most comprehensive source of data on new doctoral recipients in the United States is the National Research Council's annual census, its Survey of Earned Doctorates, begun in 1957. Although confidentiality commitments have kept the individual data files outside of the public domain, the summary statistics that are available do provide a valuable historical profile of many changes in the nature of the supply side of United States academic labor markets with respect to gender since the 1970s.

The Changing Gender Composition of Doctoral Output

The 1970s represent a critical era in the history of overall doctoral production in the United States and in female Ph.D. output, in particular. For example, 1972 was the first year in which the percentage of doctorates earned by women exceeded its peak of 15.3 percent which had been reached in the 1920s [26]. Though the roots of this trend in the "feminization" of the nation's Ph.D.'s clearly began in the 1960s, as the data in table 1 below show, the real explosion in female doctoral production occurred during the 1970s. In 1970 a total of 3,961 Ph.D. degrees were awarded to women, which represented 13.4 percent of all doctorates earned that year. By 1980 both of these figures had more than doubled to 9,406 and 30.3 percent, respectively. Throughout the 1980s, the number of doctorates awarded to women has continued to rise (to 11,344 in 1987), but at a considerably slower pace than during the previous decade. In fact, the most recent data available suggest that

[2]Throughout this study the term "doctorate" refers to all Ph.D., Ed.D, D.B.A., and other doctoral-level degrees granted by United States institutions. Excluded from this category are professional degrees such as the M.D., D.D.S., O.D., D.V.M., and J.D. In addition, for ease of exposition, the terms "doctorate" and "Ph.D." are used interchangeably when referring to all such doctoral-level degrees.

the feminization of doctoral output in the United States has reached a plateau.[3] The female share of all new Ph.D. recipients actually fell for the first time since the early 1950s from 35.4 percent in 1986 to 35.2 percent in 1987 and remained there in 1988 [30 (1970–88)].

Two key factors account for the remarkable shift in the gender composition of new doctorates in the United States from the early 1970s through the mid-1980s. First, the number of women earning Ph.D.'s each year is strikingly higher today compared with previous historical trends. Of the approximately two hundred thousand Ph.D.'s granted by United States institutions to women since 1900, 80 percent have been conferred since 1970. Secondly, the number of men earning doctorates fell continuously from 1973 to 1985. The increase in new female doctorates only partially offset this decline. Consequently, total doctoral production in the United States has leveled off, after doubling every decade prior to 1960 and tripling during the 1960s [26]. The number of new Ph.D.'s awarded by United States institutions has averaged between thirty-one and thirty-two thousand a year since the late 1970s [30 (1986, 1987)] and only very recently appears to be possibly resuming an upward, although very gradual, trend [30 (1988)].

Driving the increase in female doctoral production has been, not surprisingly, the tremendous rise in the number of women earning baccalaureate and masters degrees since the 1960s. By 1982 women were for the first time earning the majority of such degrees. An analysis of data from the National Center for Education Statistics [40, Table 166, p. 189] reveals, however, that the propensity for female college graduates to follow through with earning a doctorate has remained fairly steady since the 1960s, at a level between 2.8 and 2.9 percent. In contrast, the percentage of male college graduates who subsequently have earned Ph.D.'s fell significantly from 10.0 to 4.8 percent during the 1960s, and has gradually eroded since to about 4.2 percent in the mid-1980s.[4]

In short, these findings indicate that the feminization of Ph.D. output in the United States has been fueled by (1) the large increase in the *number* of women eligible to pursue doctoral education, *not* an increase in the *tendency* of women to do so, coupled with (2) the significant decline in the tendency of men to earn doctorates from a relatively stable pool of male college graduates eligible to do so. Men continue to earn

[3]Heath and Tuckman [17, pp. 714–15] reach a similar conclusion in their recent study of new women doctorates.
[4]The percentages of female and male college graduates who are likely to earn doctorate degrees reported here were calculated from a formula developed by the author, available upon request, which measures the ratio of doctorate to baccalaureate degrees, allowing for a time lag equal to the median number of years between such degrees.

TABLE 1

Doctorates Granted by United States Institutions for Selected Years, 1960–87 by Field and Gender

Year	EMP* Fields	Life Sciences	Broad Field Social Sciences	Human- ities	Educa- tion	Prof. Fields	Total, All Fields
1960							
Total number	2960	1729	1668	1600	1549	235	9741
Total male	2882	1576	1453	1339	1250	200	8700
Total female	78	153	215	261	299	35	1041
% female	2.6%	8.8%	12.9%	16.3%	19.3%	14.9%	10.7%
1970							
Total number	9179	4693	4566	4278	5857	888	29461
Total male	8844	4084	3829	3296	4671	776	25500
Total female	335	609	737	982	1186	112	3961
% female	3.6%	13.0%	16.1%	23.0%	20.2%	12.6%	13.4%
1974							
Total number	8215	4962	5884	5170	7241	1581	33053
Total male	7797	4056	4503	3594	5302	1361	26613
Total female	418	906	1381	1576	1939	220	6440
% female	5.1%	18.3%	23.5%	30.5%	26.8%	13.9%	19.5%
1980							
Total number	6667	5461	5856	3867	7587	1634	31072
Total male	6068	4047	3811	2335	4204	1201	21666
Total female	599	1414	2045	1532	3383	433	9406
% female	9.0%	25.9%	34.9%	39.6%	44.6%	26.5%	30.3%
1987							
Total number	8743	5742	5718	3504	6447	2063	32217
Total male	7671	3722	3269	1930	2897	1384	20873
Total female	1072	2020	2449	1574	3550	679	11344
% female	12.3%	35.2%	42.8%	44.9%	55.1%	32.9%	35.2%

SOURCE: Data compiled for 1960–80 from unpublished statistics furnished by the Doctorate Records Project of the National Research Council in Washington, D.C. to the author in February 1989. Data for 1987 from: National Research Council, Summary Report 1987: Doctorate Recipients from United States Universities (Washington, D.C.: National Research Council, 1989), appendix A, table 2.
NOTE: Includes Ph.D. recipients in known or specified fields only. The total number of Ph.D. recipients in other or unspecified fields never exceeds about 65 for the years reported.
*The EMP fields include engineering, mathematics (including computer science), and the physical sciences.

two-thirds of Ph.D.'s, however, because although fewer men than women are earning baccalaureate degrees today, such men are one and one-half times more likely to complete doctoral training than women. The higher Ph.D. output rate of men is probably also a function of the higher attrition rate of women in many Ph.D. programs (except education, for example), as other researchers have found [4].

Variations across Fields

A factor which is often cited as an important contribution to the persistent male–female earnings gap is that historically men and women have tended to pursue different fields of study [8, pp. 186–88]. Within academic labor markets, for example, it has been suggested that female academics typically earn less than men because women tend to cluster into lower-paying fields, such as English literature and foreign languages, as opposed to higher-paying fields, such as engineering and physics. Thus, the degree to which the overall supply side of academic labor markets may be changing as women earn a greater proportion of all new Ph.D.'s needs to be considered from the point of view of how the gender composition of specific disciplinary fields may be changing.

In the NRC's Survey of Earned Doctorates, respondents are asked to specify the disciplinary field of their doctoral degree from a list of about 260. The Council then uses this information to group each new cohort of doctorate candidates into six *broad* fields of study: (1) *e*ngineering, *m*athematics, and the *p*hysical sciences — including computer science (i.e., the "EMP" fields), (2) the life sciences, (3) the social sciences, (4) the humanities, (5) the professional fields, and (6) education.[5] The number of male, female, and total doctorates, as well as the female share of all doctorates earned in these six broad fields, from 1960 (selected as a base year for comparison) through 1987 (the latest year for which these data were available), are reported in the second through sixth columns of table 1. Comparing the gender composition of each of these distinct broad fields reveals some interesting patterns.

First, the EMP group, which was the "least feminine" broad field (that is, the one with the smallest proportion of doctorates awarded to women) in 1970 (only 3.6 percent female), was still the least feminine field in 1987 (12.3 percent female). Women continue to be *under*represented in the EMP fields, compared to their presence among all doctorates overall and in spite of the tripling in the number of female Ph.D. scientists and engineers over this seventeen-year span, because (1) their original numbers were so small (only 335 in 1970) and (2) the field is so large (27.1 percent of all Ph.D.'s in 1987).

Secondly, education is the only broad field today in which women earn the majority of doctorate degrees (55.1 percent in 1987 compared with 20.2 percent in 1970). This is the case because education experienced both the largest absolute increase in the number of new female doctorates between 1970 and 1987 (up by 2384), and between 1974 and 1987, the largest decrease in male doctorate recipients (down by 2435). Third, today women are even more *over*represented in the humanities and social sciences than they have been historically. The female share of all new Ph.D.'s in these two fields increased, respectively, from 23.0 and 16.1 percent in 1970 to 44.9 and 42.8 percent in 1987. Women had almost achieved parity with men in the social sciences by 1987, because the number of new female Ph.D. social scientists rose by more than

---

[5]For a complete listing of the field classification system used by the National Research Council, see [30 (1987), p. 76].

three times (up 1712) the number by which that of men fell (down 560) between 1970 and 1987. Near gender equality has come about in the humanities, however, because although the number of women doctorates graduating from the field has remained almost constant since the mid-1970s, increasing by only 592 from 1970 to 1987, the number of new male Ph.D. humanists declined by almost triple that amount (1664) between 1974 and 1987, exceeded only by the drop in the number of new male doctorates in education. Fourth, by 1987 new female Ph.D.'s were *proportionally* represented in both the life sciences and the professional fields. In other words, in 1987 one out of three of all doctorate recipients, and one out of three new Ph.D.'s in the life sciences and professional fields was a woman.

The ultimate impact of the feminization process on the supply side of academic labor markets will be largely conditioned not only by the share of all women in any particular field, but also by the extent to which men and women are segregated into different fields. The data in table 2 reveal that historically the difference between the proportion of all men and all women earning doctorates in any specific field has never been especially large, except in the EMP fields, and perhaps to some extent, in education. In fact, generally speaking, the increase in the number of female Ph.D.'s since the 1970s has been distributed across the six broad fields of study in proportion to their historical patterns. The one exception to this rule is the humanities. The overall number, as well as the proportion of men, women, and all Ph.D.'s in the humanities has been shrinking since the 1970s. Furthermore, the declining tendency of women doctorates to have studied the humanities, coupled with the rising number of female Ph.D.'s overall, has kept the size of female humanities doctorate output fairly constant. Thus, because each new humanities doctoral cohort is so small (10.9 percent of all Ph.D.'s in 1987), even if the field were to become dramatically more "feminine" in the future (for example, 75+ percent female), such a trend would have only a minor impact on the gender composition of the academic profession *en toto*.

In addition, it is apparent from table 2 that the social sciences have become considerably more feminine not only because the number of new female Ph.D.'s has been rising and that of males falling, but women doctorates have also been more likely than men to have majored in the social sciences, and increasingly so during the 1980s. The modest gains by women in the EMP fields mirror trends similar to those in the social sciences, at least through the early 1980s. Throughout the 1970s, both the number and percent of all doctorates earned in the EMP fields

TABLE 2

Broad Field Distribution by Gender for Doctorates Granted by United States Institutions for Selected Years, 1960–87

Year	EMP Fields	Life Sciences	Broad Field Social Sciences	Human-ities	Educa-tion	Prof. Fields	Total, All Fields
1960							
% of total Ph.D.'s	30.4%	17.7%	17.1%	16.4%	15.9%	2.4%	100.0%
% of male Ph.D.'s	33.1%	18.1%	16.7%	15.4%	14.4%	2.3%	100.0%
% of female Ph.D.'s	7.5%	14.7%	20.7%	25.1%	28.7%	3.4%	100.0%
1970							
% of total Ph.D.'s	31.2%	15.9%	15.5%	14.5%	19.9%	3.0%	100.0%
% of male Ph.D.'s	34.7%	16.0%	15.0%	12.9%	18.3%	3.0%	100.0%
% of female Ph.D.'s	8.5%	15.4%	18.6%	24.8%	29.9%	2.8%	100.0%
1974							
% of total Ph.D.'s	24.9%	15.0%	17.8%	15.6%	21.9%	4.8%	100.0%
% of male Ph.D.'s	29.3%	15.2%	16.9%	13.5%	19.9%	5.1%	100.0%
% of female Ph.D.'s	6.5%	14.1%	21.4%	24.5%	30.1%	3.4%	100.0%
1980							
% of total Ph.D.'s	21.5%	17.6%	18.8%	12.4%	24.4%	5.3%	100.0%
% of male Ph.D.'s	28.0%	18.7%	17.6%	10.8%	19.4%	5.5%	100.0%
% of female Ph.D.'s	6.4%	15.0%	21.7%	16.3%	36.0%	4.6%	100.0%
1987							
% of total Ph.D.'s	27.1%	17.8%	17.7%	10.9%	20.0%	6.4%	100.0%
% of male Ph.D.'s	36.8%	17.8%	15.7%	9.2%	13.9%	6.6%	100.0%
% of female Ph.D.'s	9.4%	17.8%	21.6%	13.9%	31.3%	6.0%	100.0%

SOURCE: Percentages reported here are calculated from the data reported in table 1.

by men fell. In contrast, the number of new female doctorate engineers, mathematicians, and physical scientists was increasing, although these numbers represented a shrinking share of all female Ph.D.'s. Finally, the data in table 2 help explain why new female Ph.D.'s had become proportionally represented in the life sciences and professional fields by 1987. In both cases, the share of all male doctorate recipients in these fields is virtually identical to that for females. In other words, 17.8 percent of all male and 17.8 percent of all female doctorate recipients in 1987 graduated in the life sciences. For the professional fields, the comparable figures are 6.0 and 6.6 percent. Thus, because together these two broad fields produced one-quarter of all the new Ph.D.'s in 1987 and both have been growing relatively rapidly, if these trends continue, they could signal a more pervasive movement toward a more balanced representation of men and women on the supply side of academic labor markets overall.

As in the case of occupational segregation across the full labor market, the true pattern of gender segregation across doctoral fields is masked when the data analyzed are aggregated into large categories such as the six broad fields included in tables 1 and 2. In fact, based on the data in table 2, the "index of doctoral broad field segregation" for men and women has varied little since the 1970s, from 27.1 in 1970 to 26.2 in 1980, and 28.0 in 1987. In other words, approximately one-fourth of all new male or female Ph.D.'s would have had to switch fields during this time to have been distributed identically across all fields.[6] If anything, these data indicate that there seems to be considerably less gender segregation across fields on the supply side of academic labor markets than across broad occupational categories in the full labor market.[7] As one would expect, the index increases, but not by much, when the broad field data are disaggregated into smaller units. For example, based on the data for the thirty-three "fine fields" chosen for this study and included in table 3,[8] the "index of *fine* field segregation," by gender, was 35.1 in 1970, and 34.9 in 1986.

In addition, the thirty-three fine fields in table 3 are ranked from most to least feminine for 1986. The striking pattern evident when the data are arranged in this way is (1) the *variety* of broad fields represented by the most feminine fine fields at the top of the table, (2) the clustering of EMP fields in the bottom third of the table among the least feminine (or most masculine) fine fields, and (3) the number of fine fields that have been transformed from primarily male (80.0 percent or more) to truly *gender integrated* fields since the 1970s. For example, in the top seventeen of the thirty-three fine fields ranked here (from history to health sciences), the female share of Ph.D. output varies from one-third to nearly two-thirds. In other words, for half of the fine fields in table 3, the proportion of women is at least roughly on par with the representation of females among the new Ph.D. pool overall.

That gender segregation does persist today among these fine fields, however, is clearer when one considers the relative size (not simply the female proportion) of the fine fields included in table 3. For example, among the top third "most feminine fields" are nine of the eleven fine fields that produce the largest *numbers* of female doctorates today — including (in order from largest to smallest): (1) education, non-

[6]The index of segregation (S) is often used as a measure of the degree of segregation in labor markets. It was first introduced into the literature by Duncan and Duncan [13]. The index of field segregation by gender used here is defined as follows:

$$S = 1/2 \, \Sigma \, | M_i - F_i |$$

where M_i = the percentage of males with Ph.D.'s in field "i", and F_i = the percentage of females with Ph.D.'s in field "i".

[7]For example, Blau and Ferber [8, pp. 158–59] report an index of occupational segregation by sex equal to 37.8 based on 1982 Bureau of the Census data for nine broad occupational categories.

[8]The selection of fine fields for this study is intended to strike a balance between the ability to identify characteristics that tend to vary systematically across different groups of disciplinary specialties and the desire to keep the number small enough so that the analysis remains both manageable and digestible.

TABLE 3

Female Percentage and 1970–86 Change in that Percent for Fine Fields of Doctorate Recipients from Institutions, Ranked from Most to Least Feminine in 1986

1986 Rank Fine Field	Broad Field	Total Number of Ph.D.'s		Percent Female		
		1970	1986	1970	1986	1970–86 % Change
1. Health Sciences	Life Sciences	414	772	17.1%	62.0%	44.9%
2. English & Amer. Lang. & Lit.	Humanities	1098	721	30.6%	58.4%	27.8%
3. Foreign Languages & Literature	Humanities	647	445	34.5%	57.3%	22.8%
4. Teaching, Non-Sci. Fields	Education	1326	1550	29.3%	55.9%	26.6%
5. Educ., Non-Teaching	Education	4103	4814	18.4%	54.4%	36.0%
6. Anthropology	Social Sciences	217	381	27.2%	51.7%	24.5%
7. Clincal, Couns., School Psych.	Social Sciences	707	1708	27.0%	51.2%	24.2%
8. Other Psych.	Social Sciences	1183	1363	21.4%	50.6%	29.2%
9. Other Humanities	Humanities	1084	1484	21.3%	44.1%	22.8%
10. Sociology	Social Sciences	505	492	18.4%	43.9%	25.5%
11. Oth. Prof. Fields	Prof. Fields	304	1035	32.6%	43.7%	11.1%
12. Teaching, Sci. Fields	Education	428	238	10.3%	43.3%	33.0%
13. Other Social Sci.	Social Sciences	465	546	5.8%	37.4%	31.6%
14. Microbiology & Bacteriology	Life Sciences	399	337	18.5%	35.6%	17.1%
15. Biochemistry	Life Sciences	583	571	16.6%	34.0%	17.4%
16. Other Biosci.	Life Sciences	2379	2883	14.5%	33.4%	18.9%
17. History	Humanities	1091	563	13.3%	32.7%	19.4%
18. Political Sci. & Int'l Relations	Social Sciences	636	490	9.7%	26.9%	17.2%
19. Bus., Management	Prof. Fields	584	901	2.2%	23.0%	20.8%
20. Chemistry	EMP Fields	2238	1903	8.1%	20.8%	12.7%
21. Philosophy	Humanities	358	248	13.1%	20.2%	7.1%
22. Economics & Econometrics	Social Sciences	853	861	6.1%	19.3%	13.2%
23. Earth, Atmos. & Marine Sci.	EMP Fields	510	589	3.1%	17.0%	13.9%
24. Mathematics	EMP Fields	1225	730	6.3%	16.6%	10.3%
25. Agricultural Sci.	Life Sciences	918	1157	2.5%	16.2%	13.7%
26. Industrial Eng.	EMP Fields	117	101	0.0%	13.9%	13.9%
27. Computer Sci.	EMP Fields	---	399	—	12.3%	—
28. Chemical Eng.	EMP Fields	445	476	0.4%	11.1%	10.7%
29. Physics & Astro.	EMP Fields	1655	1187	2.7%	9.2%	6.5%
30. Total other Eng.	EMP Fields	1421	1364	0.6%	7.8%	7.2%
31. Civil Eng.	EMP Fields	311	387	0.3%	4.9%	4.6%
32. Electrical, Electron. Eng.	EMP Fields	857	707	0.4%	4.7%	4.3%
33. Mechanical Eng.	EMP Fields	400	442	0.3%	3.2%	2.9%
Total, All Fields		29461	31845	13.4%	35.3%	21.9%

SOURCE: Data compiled from unpublished statistics furnished by the Doctorate Records Project of the National Research Council in Washington, D.C. to the author in February 1989.

teaching, (2) clinical, counseling, and school psychology, (3) teaching, non-science, (4) other psychology, (5) other humanities, (6) health sciences, (7) other professional fields, (8) English and American language and literature, and (9) foreign languages and literature. Moreover, these eleven most feminine fine fields also include five of the eleven fine fields which currently produce the smallest number of male doctorates, three of which are among the top third largest feminine fields — including (ordered by smallest to largest number of male Ph.D.'s): (1) anthropology, (2) foreign languages and literature, (3) sociology, (4) health sciences, and (5) English and American languages and literature. Interestingly enough, however, four of the nine fields that rank among both the most feminine *and* largest female fields are also among the top third largest male fields. These are: (1) education, non-teaching, (2) clinical, counseling and school psychology, (3) other humanities, and (4) teaching, non-science fields.

At the other end of the scale, there is almost a perfect overlap between the bottom third least feminine and smallest female fields — from earth, atmospheric, and marine sciences to mechanical engineering. The one exception is the agricultural sciences. In addition, only three of these eleven least feminine fields are also among the eleven largest male fields. Overall, the evidence, presented in tables 1, 2, and 3 indicates that with the exception of the EMP fields the increasing presence of women among new doctoral cohorts in the United States has resulted in a movement away from the virtual dominance of all Ph.D. fields by males, toward an integration of most fields with respect to gender, and not a complete feminization of any.

Finally, it should be noted that these patterns do differ somewhat from the degree of field segregation by gender at the baccalaureate level. Among undergraduate students a number of fields are clearly "female" in that 80 percent or more of their graduates are women. Obvious examples are the health professions (including nursing) and library science, in which 85.0 and 89.2 percent of the baccalaureate degrees, contrasted with only 51.3 and 56.5 percent of the doctorates conferred in 1985–86, were awarded to women [40, pp. 172–201]. In sum, although field segregation by gender at the doctorate level tends to mirror trends and changes at the baccalaureate level somewhat, the degree of gender segregation among Ph.D.'s is slightly less severe than that among college graduates.

The Changing Nature of the Academic Applicant Pool

Because this article focuses on academic labor markets, it is appropriate to ask how closely the gender characteristics of the entire pool of new Ph.D. cohorts resemble those of the subgroup who pursue academic careers, per se. Theoretically, the cumulative pool of doctorate recipients of working age can be regarded as the maximum potential supply of doctorate-trained college teachers at any point in time. In reality, today only one-half of the roughly five hundred three thousand doctorates in the sciences, engineering, and humanities employed in the United States are at four-year colleges and universities (including medical schools) [28, p. 22; 33, pp. 66–70].[9] Such institutions are those most likely to require that their faculty have doctorate degrees. Over the years the National Research Council has found that the postdoctoral plans reported by new Ph.D. recipients at the time of their graduation are fairly reliable predictors of the types of careers such individuals are likely to pursue. As an illustration, about 91 percent of the male scientists and engineers from the 1970–72 Ph.D. cohorts who were employed in the academic sector in the mid-to-late 1970s had reported plans either to enter academic employment or to pursue postdoctoral studies when they finished their degrees [24, p. 29].

Thus, a reasonable approach to measuring the number of new doctorates who are added to the academic job applicant pool each year would be to determine the number of new Ph.D.'s who plan either to enter academia immediately or to pursue postdoctoral study and are likely to seek college teaching later.[10] Accordingly, table 4 compares the postdoctoral plans of new male, female, and all Ph.D.'s for 1973 (the first year for which these data are available by gender), 1980, and 1987, by broad field for the three categories: (1) academic employment, (2) nonacademic employment, and (3) postdoctoral study. Three general patterns are apparent here. First, the percentage of new Ph.D.'s in all fields entering academia has steadily diminished since the 1970s (from 53.7 percent in 1973 to 39.8 percent in 1987). The relative decline was most dramatic for new doctorates in the social sciences (from 59.3 percent in 1973 to 35.7 percent in 1987). In the humanities, education, and the professional fields, where academic institutions (particularly the four-year colleges and universities) have been the principal employers of

---

[9]A greater share (73.0 percent) of employed humanities Ph.D.'s were at four-year colleges and universities in 1987 than was the case for doctoral scientists and engineers (50.0 percent), however [28, p. 22; 33, pp. 66–70].

[10]Because of the relatively long lead time required in applying for most academic jobs (up to one year, or even longer in the case of many senior positions), in any given year the *academic job applicant pool* tends to include many Ph.D. students who have completed all of the requirements for the degree, except for the dissertation. On the other hand, the *Ph.D. recipient cohort* for any given year includes individuals who have already contracted employment (and may actually already hold faculty positions), and therefore are technically *not* new entrants into the academic labor market the year in which they earn their degrees. For these reasons, measuring the number of doctorates who are first-time entrants into the academic marketplace is not straightforward, and the number of Ph.D. recipients in any one cohort who report plans to enter academia may be thought of as only *approximating* the number of new doctorates in the academic job applicant pool for any specific year.

Ph.D.'s, the abandonment of academic careers by new doctorates, although not as dramatic as in the social sciences, is also quite clear. Perhaps not surprisingly, the smallest percentage decline was for those in the EMP fields, who historically have been the least likely to pursue careers in the academic sector. Even when the increasing percentage of new doctorates who have taken up postdoctoral study is added in here, the overall pattern of a shrinking number of new Ph.D.'s entering academic labor markets persists.

The second major pattern evident in table 4 is that female Ph.D.'s tend to be more likely to pursue academic careers than their male counterparts. This is especially true in the short run. In 1987, for example, 46.1 percent of all new women doctorates planned to enter the academic sector immediately, while only 36.3 of all new male doctorates planned to do so. The one exception here is the social sciences. Generally, male social scientists have been slightly more likely than their female counterparts to take up academic careers, and this is still true today. Although the male-female differential diminishes somewhat when the percentage of those who plan to go on for postdoctoral study is added, this overall pattern persists.

In general, the greater tendency of female Ph.D.'s to enter academia as compared to their male peers implies that the gender composition of all new Ph.D.'s and that of the doctorate-trained, academic job applicant pool do indeed differ. For example, in 1973, 18.0 percent of all new Ph.D. recipients, compared with 20.2 percent of those planning to go directly into academic jobs, were women. The comparable figures for 1980 are 30.3 and 35.5 percent, respectively; and for 1987, 35.2 and 40.9 percent. From a longer-run perspective, however, the differences between the gender composition of all new Ph.D.'s and that of the Ph.D.-educated, academic applicant pool somewhat dissolve. If one adds the number of new doctorates who plan to pursue postdoctoral study to the number of those who plan to enter academia directly, the female proportion of this more complete "new" academic job applicant pool drops to 19.2 percent in 1973, 32.6 percent in 1980, and 36.6 percent in 1987. Still, for all three years, new Ph.D. academic job applicants are slightly more likely to be female than are the members of their respective Ph.D. cohorts.

Finally, it should be noted that at least during the 1970s, the foregoing of academic careers by many new Ph.D.'s was mirrored by their increased tendency to pursue nonacademic alternatives. Even more striking is the rise in the percentage of Ph.D.'s who have listed their postdoctoral plans as "unknown," especially during the 1980s. When

TABLE 4

Postdoctoral Plans of Ph.D. Recipients from United States Universities by Broad Field and Gender for 1973, 1980 and 1987

Postdoctoral Plans	Percent of All Ph.D.'s			Percent of Male Ph.D.'s			Percent of Female Ph.D.'s		
	1973	1980	1987	1973	1980	1987	1973	1980	1987
*Academic Employment**									
All Fields	53.7	45.3	39.8	52.2	41.9	36.3	60.3	53.1	46.1
EMP Fields	27.3	22.3	22.3	24.8	21.8	22.4	38.7	26.7	21.3
Life Sciences	32.5	23.7	20.6	32.8	23.7	18.9	31.3	23.7	23.8
Social Sciences	59.3	43.6	35.7	60.7	44.5	39.0	52.9	41.9	31.4
Humanities	77.8	65.9	65.4	78.7	64.9	64.0	73.8	67.4	67.0
Education	74.9	67.8	63.0	75.4	67.5	62.7	72.8	68.3	63.3
Professional Fields	69.1	65.6	62.2	70.1	64.9	60.3	64.5	67.4	66.3
*Nonacademic Employment***									
All Fields	20.6	26.6	23.9	22.5	29.5	25.5	12.1	19.4	20.9
EMP Fields	35.9	43.4	32.1	40.5	44.2	32.6	15.0	34.7	29.5
Life Sciences	19.4	17.7	16.8	21.6	19.4	18.3	9.2	12.4	13.8
Social Sciences	22.1	32.4	32.6	22.0	33.6	30.9	22.4	30.0	34.9
Humanities	5.1	14.6	11.4	5.2	17.1	12.9	4.6	10.6	9.5
Education	13.6	19.6	19.3	14.1	21.9	20.8	11.5	16.9	18.3
Professional Fields	20.0	24.6	19.9	20.2	26.2	20.5	19.0	10.6	18.9
Other and Unknown Employment (All Fields)	3.9	3.5	3.4	3.4	2.6	2.6	6.2	5.6	5.0
*Postdoctoral Study****									
All Fields	15.6	18.4	22.8	16.0	19.7	24.9	13.6	15.4	18.8
EMP Fields	27.4	26.7	32.9	26.3	26.2	32.6	32.3	31.3	35.1
Life Sciences	39.0	51.1	52.2	37.0	49.7	52.2	47.9	55.1	52.4
Social Sciences	8.0	11.9	14.8	7.5	10.8	13.4	10.1	14.0	16.7
Humanities	4.7	5.6	7.4	4.5	5.4	7.3	5.6	6.0	7.5
Education	2.1	2.9	4.4	1.8	2.5	4.3	3.3	3.3	4.4
Professional Fields	2.0	2.8	3.7	1.7	2.8	3.9	3.5	6.0	3.4
Status Unknown (All Fields)	6.1	6.3	10.1	5.7	6.2	10.7	7.7	6.4	9.1

SOURCE: Data compiled for the relevant survey years from: National Research Council, Summary Report 19XX: Doctorate Recipients from United States Universities (Washington, D.C.: National Academy Press, 1973, 1980 and 1989, respectively), Appendix table 2.

NOTE: Percentages in columns for each year may not exactly sum to 100.0 due to rounding.

*Includes definite and anticipated (i.e., currently seeking) employment at two-year, four-year, and foreign colleges, universities, medical schools and elementary/secondary schools. It should be noted, however, that most Ph.D.'s (90% or more) in the sciences, engineering and the humanities, at least, employed in the academic sector are at four-year colleges and universities.

**Includes definite and anticipated (i.e., currently seeking) employment in industry/business, government and non-profit organizations in the nonacademic sector.

***Includes postdoctoral fellowships, research associate positions, traineeships, as well as other types of post-doctoral study.

these percentages listed in the bottom row of table 4 are added to those for "other and unknown employment" in the middle of the table, fully 13.3 percent of all male and 14.1 percent of all female Ph.D. recipients had uncertain postdoctoral plans in 1987, compared with 8.8 percent for men and 12.0 percent for women in 1980. As one would expect, these figures vary somewhat across fields. For example, in 1987 the social sciences had the highest (16.8 percent) and the humanities the second highest (15.8 percent) share of Ph.D.'s who reported their postdoctoral plans as "unknown or other," compared with 9.6 and 13.5 percent in 1980. In contrast, new Ph.D.'s in the life sciences were the least likely to report their postdoctoral plans as "unknown or other" in 1987 (10.4 percent), and this figure was identical to that for 1980 [30 (1980, table 2, pp 30–31; 1987, appendix A, table 2)]. As a benchmark of short-term unemployment for Ph.D.'s, these figures reflect the generally deteriorating yet varying demand-side conditions in academic labor markets across different fields during the 1980s. These conditions obviously generated some important "feedback effects" on the supply side and are discussed more fully in the next section of this article. They also indicate that labor markets for new doctorates, in general, are taking longer to clear today than they have in the past.[11]

The Changing Nature of the Typical Academic

The evidence presented thus far hardly supports Professor Parrish's assertion that women are "taking over" the academic profession, at least with respect to the supply side of academic labor markets. Rather than "taking over" in the sense that would require them to "seize control" of traditional male domains, women have increased their numbers most in fields where they traditionally have been and which their male counterparts have abandoned. Although this implies that it is somewhat of an exaggeration to suggest that women are "taking over" the academic profession, a number of studies have demonstrated that the professions (college teaching included) do seem to "take over," or at least to some extent *change* the nature of, the lives of the women who enter them. It has long been well established, for example, that highly educated women in the United States, such as female doctorates, are less likely to marry, are more likely to divorce, have fewer children, and are much more likely to remain permanently childless than both the female population at large and their highly educated male counterparts [1, 9, 11, 12]. Thus it bears asking, to what extent has the increasing presence of women in academic labor markets changed the nature of the "typical academic" with regard to his or her demographic attributes?

Ideally, data would be available on these and other demographic characteristics for new Ph.D. recipients who take academic jobs, as well as for the total pool of doctorates who are employed within the academic sector, to reflect both new and existing patterns with respect to

---

[11]A related issue that warrants investigation is to what extent these figures reflect the increasing share of new Ph.D. recipients who are members of dual-career couples and thus obviously need additional time to find two suitable jobs, in the appropriate fields, in one location, in the same year.

the nature of the "typical academic." Unfortunately, the National Research Council does not cross-tabulate the demographic characteristics of new doctorates in its annual survey with these individuals' intended sector of employment. Moreover, the demographic data it does collect are quite limited. For example, the Council's categories for marital status include only "married," "not married" and "unknown." Thus one cannot tell what portion of new Ph.D.'s has never been married or is currently remarried, divorced, separated, or widowed. Nor does the National Research Council's survey include information on the fertility status of new Ph.D.'s. Consequently, pertinent analyses of the relationship between the timing of doctoral study and that of marriage, divorce, and child-rearing, for example, simply cannot be carried out with the NRC data. Unfortunately, these are important areas of investigation in the effort to understand male–female differences in the academic profession, as well as how and why these may be changing.

Nonetheless, table 5 compares three key demographic characteristics of doctorate recipients from United States institutions for 1973, 1980, and 1987, by broad field and gender. Here, three basic patterns emerge. First, in all fields except for EMP, females tend to be slightly older than their male classmates when they earn their Ph.D.'s. Although there are some important variations across fields, the gap in age between new male and female Ph.D.'s tends to be between three months to one year. Furthermore, the median age of doctorate recipients in all fields has been rising since the 1970s, from 31.3 in 1973 to 33.6 in 1987. This partly reflects the fact that women, who tend to be older than men when they receive their degrees, have been making up a larger share of all Ph.D. recipients. It also has come about because Ph.D. students are typically taking about one year longer to complete the requirements for their degrees than they did in the early 1970s [30 (1987), pp. 29–42]. The youngest of all Ph.D. recipients tend to be women in the EMP fields, of whom fifty percent were 29.7 years or younger in 1987. The oldest of all Ph.D. recipients tend to be women in education, half of whom were at least 40.3 years of age in 1987.

Second, a trend related to that of the changing gender composition of the academic profession in recent years is that of the changing citizenship status of new Ph.D. recipients in the United States. The interesting aspect of the data on citizenship status reported in table 5 is that while the share of United States citizens among all new doctorates from United States universities fell from 82.6 percent in 1973 to 70.8 percent in 1987, these changes have been much more dramatic among men than women. On average, for all fields in 1987 less than two-thirds of all

TABLE 5

Demographic Characteristics of Doctorate Recipients from United States Universities, by Broad Field and Gender for 1973, 1980, and 1987

Demographic Characteristic	EMP Fields	Life Sciences	Broad Field Social Sciences	Human-ities	Educa-tion	Prof. Fields	All Fields
All Doctorates							
Median Age at Doctorate							
1973	29.5	30.1	30.5	32.0	36.5	33.2	31.3
1980	29.6	30.0	31.6	33.4	37.0	34.5	32.2
1987	30.4	31.7	33.5	35.0	39.8	35.7	33.6
U.S. Citizenship							
1973	71.9%	78.1%	85.1%	88.7%	92.9%	81.9%	82.6%
1980	65.6%	80.4%	84.7%	87.3%	88.7%	81.0%	81.0%
1987	53.1%	73.5%	76.0%	78.0%	84.9%	68.3%	70.8%
Marital Status*							
Married							
1973	72.8%	74.7%	73.0%	68.2%	77.5%	77.4%	73.5%
1980	56.6%	61.1%	57.4%	57.9%	68.7%	67.4%	61.1%
1987	54.4%	56.7%	53.2%	54.5%	65.7%	60.4%	57.2%
Not Married							
1973	24.2%	21.9%	24.0%	28.1%	19.6%	18.2%	23.1%
1980	38.7%	35.2%	37.2%	36.4%	26.8%	27.9%	34.1%
1987	36.8%	35.4%	36.8%	36.4%	26.7%	29.3%	34.0%
Male Doctorates							
Median Age at Doctorate							
1973**	n.a.	n.a.	n.a.	n.a.	n.a.	n.a.	n.a.
1980	29.7	30.0	31.5	33.0	36.7	34.3	31.7
1987	30.5	31.6	33.4	34.8	39.4	35.4	32.8
U.S. Citizenship							
1973	71.9%	77.1%	83.9%	88.6%	92.5%	80.5%	81.3%
1980	64.7%	79.2%	82.4%	86.2%	86.4%	77.0%	77.8%
1987	51.3%	70.6%	69.4%	76.1%	81.1%	61.2%	64.6%
Marital Status*							
Married							
1973	73.5%	78.9%	76.7%	72.7%	85.8%	81.8%	77.5%
1980	57.2%	64.9%	62.1%	61.1%	78.0%	73.9%	64.8%
1987	54.9%	59.9%	57.1%	58.0%	75.8%	64.6%	59.9%
Not Married							
1973	23.4%	17.3%	20.0%	23.7%	10.9%	13.3%	18.9%
1980	38.0%	31.5%	31.9%	32.8%	17.1%	20.5%	30.2%
1987	36.1%	31.7%	32.1%	32.3%	16.6%	23.8%	30.8%
Female Doctorates							
Median Age at Doctorate							
1973	28.7	29.5	30.6	32.3	38.6	36.8	32.6
1980	28.8	30.0	31.7	34.0	37.5	35.4	33.5
1987	29.7	31.9	33.6	35.4	40.3	36.6	35.4
U.S. Citizenship							
1973	71.5%	82.0%	89.5%	88.9%	94.1%	91.0%	88.3%
1980	74.5%	84.0%	89.1%	89.1%	91.5%	91.5%	88.4%
1987	66.0%	78.8%	85.0%	80.2%	88.0%	82.9%	82.2%
Marital Status*							
Married							
1973	58.4%	53.5%	59.1%	57.1%	52.0%	49.5%	55.2%
1980	50.5%	50.0%	48.6%	53.1%	57.0%	50.7%	52.8%
1987	50.7%	50.9%	48.0%	50.1%	57.5%	52.0%	52.3%

(*continued next page*)

TABLE 5 *(Continued)*

Demographic Characteristic	EMP Fields	Life Sciences	Broad Field Social Sciences	Human- ities	Educa- tion	Prof. Fields	All Fields
Not Married							
1973	39.2%	43.9%	39.1%	38.9%	46.2%	49.0%	42.1%
1980	45.8%	46.2%	47.3%	42.0%	38.8%	46.9%	43.1%
1987	41.3%	42.2%	43.0%	41.4%	34.9%	40.6%	39.8%

SOURCE: Same as for table 4.
*The marital status of an increasing share of Ph.D. recipients has been classified as "unknown" during the period of time covered by the data in the table. For 1973 the marital status of 3.4% of all Ph.D. recipients and 2.6% of female Ph.D. recipients was unknown. For 1987 the respective percentages were 8.8% and 8.0%, as well as 9.2% for males.
**Published data on the median age of male doctorate recipients was not made available (n.a.) until 1975. Since 82.0% of all Ph.D. recipients in 1973 were male, however, it can be assumed that the median age of all doctorate recipients closely approximates that of males. In any case, whenever the median age of female doctorates is below that of all Ph.D. recipients, the median age of male doctorates is obviously above the total. Similarly, whenever the median age of female Ph.D. recipients is above that of all doctorates, the opposite is true for males.

male (64.6 percent), but more than four-fifths of all female (82.2 percent) Ph.D. recipients were United States citizens. These figures compare to those of 81.3 and 88.3 percent for men and women in 1973. Again, important variations across fields are evident from table 5. For instance, in 1987 a new male doctorate in the EMP fields was the least likely to be a United States citizen (51.3 percent). On the other hand, a new female doctorate in education was the most likely to be a United States citizen (88.0 percent). In fact, studies by the National Research Council have highlighted the importance of controlling for citizenship status when analyzing the changing gender composition of new doctorates in the United States. In 1985, for example, women made up 34.3 percent of all new Ph.D. recipients. However, when the gender composition of new doctorates who were also United States citizens is examined, the comparable figure is 39.1 percent [30 (1985), p. 15]. Since many, but increasingly not all, non-U.S. citizens return to their native countries following their doctoral studies in the United States, a careful assessment is needed on how the increasing presence of such individuals among Ph.D. recipients from United States institutions, especially during the 1980s, affects the supply side of academic labor markets in general, as well as with respect to gender, in particular. Clearly, important policy issues are involved here that warrant further investigation but are beyond the scope of the present article, which focuses on the changing gender composition of academic labor markets, per se, since the 1970s.

Third, perhaps the most interesting pattern revealed by the data in table 5 is how the typical Ph.D. recipient has changed with respect to marital status since the 1970s. Across almost all fields, women are slightly less likely to be married when they earn their Ph.D.'s today than they were in the early 1970s. Although the decline from 55.2 percent of female Ph.D. recipients who reported they were married in 1973 to 52.3 percent in 1987 is not large, it does reflect the tendency among all Americans today to delay marriage. The twin realities here that (1) at least half of all new female doctorates were 35.4 years old in 1987, and (2) the likelihood of ever marrying (or even remarrying) diminishes dramatically (for highly educated women, in particular) after the age of 30, and especially after 35 [23], lend credence to David Bloom's [9] prediction that women, such as new female doctorates who are not married when they earn their degree, are not likely to ever marry (or at least, never again) over the course of their lifetimes.

Additional support for this interpretation can be garnered from the results of the National Research Council's 1987 Survey of Doctorate Recipients, its *biennial* survey of the science, engineering, and humanities doctoral *population* in the United States (that is, as opposed to *new* Ph.D. recipients from United States institutions, in all fields).[12] At the time of the NRC's biennial survey in 1987, only 55.4 percent of female Ph.D.'s reported that they were currently married, 20.3 percent that they never had been married, and 13.1 percent that they were either separated or divorced [31]. Although these data are not strictly comparable with those reported by Centra [11] from his 1973 survey of male and female doctorates, they do suggest that female doctorates today are more likely to have been married and divorced or separated, and less likely to have never married than was true of their counterparts 15–20 years ago. Among the 1968 female Ph.D. graduates who responded to Centra's questionnaire, for example, 34.0 percent had never married and only 10.0 percent were separated or divorced [11, p. 102]. Finally, caution is needed in drawing firm conclusions regarding the marital status of the female doctorates surveyed by the National Research Council in recent years. For, the female non-response rate to the marital status question rose from 2.6 percent in 1973 to 8.0 percent in 1987 for the NRC's Survey of Earned Doctorates, and

---

[12]The National Research Council's *biennial* "Survey of Doctorate Recipients" (SDR), begun in 1973, is not to be confused with its "Survey of Earned Doctorates" (SED), begun in 1957 and referred to throughout this article. These are two separate projects, generating two independent data bases. The NRC's biennial SDR is based on a representative sampling of individuals who earned Ph.D.'s from United States institutions in the sciences, humanities, and engineering over a thirty-three-year span prior to the survey year and who were residing in the United States at the time of the survey. For example, the 1987 SDR includes doctorate recipients who earned doctorates between January 1944 and June 1986 and who were residing in the United States in the spring of 1987. On the other hand, the NRC's SED is an annual *census* of individuals who earned doctorates from United States institutions in all fields in the survey year. A primary source of new survey participants for the NRC's biennial SDR project, however, is the pool of new Ph.D.'s who respond to its SED questionnaire each year.

was 8.8 percent for its 1987 Survey of Doctorate Recipients. Because the Council has not analyzed any possible non-response bias in the demographic data it reports, it is not clear how real or significant the small change in the share of female doctorates who is married is. What seems to be safe to conclude, however, is that women doctorates who are not married today, are more likely to have been married previously and now be divorced when compared to their counterparts of the 1960s and early 1970s, who were more likely to never have been married at all.

For men, the evidence is clearer. With respect to marital status, the typical new male Ph.D. recipient has become more like the typical new female Ph.D. recipient. Whereas 77.5 percent of all new male doctorates were married in 1973, only 59.9 percent were in 1987. As in the case of women, this trend partly reflects the increased tendency of American males over the past decade or so to delay entering into marriage until their late twenties and early thirties. In addition, because the typical new male doctorate today is more likely to be both *un*married and older, it appears that a greater share of recent male Ph.D.'s is likely to remain single than has been true in the past. In fact, a comparison of the results from Centra's study with those of the National Research Council's 1987 Survey of Doctorate Recipients indicates that the likelihood of male Ph.D.'s being married at any point in time has been declining. Centra found that 87.0 percent of the men in the 1968 doctoral cohort he surveyed, were married [11, p. 102]. The comparable figure for the male doctorates who responded to the NRC's 1987 survey was only 74.7 percent [31]. As in the case of female Ph.D.'s, this trend can be partly explained by the increased tendency of male doctorates to be separated or divorced over the last fifteen to twenty years. For example, 3.9 percent of the 1968 male Ph.D. graduates in Centra's study, compared with 6.4 percent of the men in the NRC's 1987 Survey of Doctorate Recipients, were either separated or divorced at the time of the respective surveys [11, p. 102; 31].

In short, the probability of being married among new female doctorates seems to have changed little, if any at all, since the 1970s. However, because a significant portion of new male doctorates no longer tends to be married when they earn their degrees, academic men do appear to be becoming more like academic women with respect to marital status.[13] Yet differences between male and female doctorates do

---

[13]As in the case for women, the non-response rate to the marital status question for men in the NRC's Survey of Earned Doctorates rose from 3.6 percent in 1973 to 9.3 percent in 1987. However, for male Ph.D. recipients, the 17.6 percentage point drop in the share of those who reported they were married from 1973 to 1987 and the corres-

persist. Female Ph.D. recipients are more than twice as likely to be divorced or never married when compared to their male counterparts, but the differences between the percentages of male and female Ph D.'s in these marital states is narrowing.

Demand Side of Academic Labor Markets:
Changes in Academic Hiring and Faculty Characteristics
with Respect to Gender since the 1970s

To what extent have the changes in the gender composition on the supply side of academic labor markets been reflected in and contributed to changes in the nature of the academic profession on the demand side? As increasing numbers of women have acquired the qualifications needed to climb onto the academic ladder, have more of them climbed on (that is, been hired) and moved up it (that is, been tenured in)? Previous studies have indicated that academic men and women tend to *climb differently* up their respective career ladders [36, 37], or are even more likely to be on entirely *different ladders* altogether [7, 20]. Has the increased presence of women in academia affected these patterns?

The ideal complement to the first half of this study would be to analyze data that trace the patterns in hiring, the nature of employment (full-time versus part-time), tenure status, rank, and salary of male and female Ph.D.-trained college teachers in all fields at all United States institutions of higher education since the 1970s. Because the "ideal data set" does not exist, this section of the article relies on the best available alternative, data from the United States Equal Employment Opportunity Commission (EEOC), which allow at least a partial analysis of many of the important changes on the demand side of academic labor markets over the last ten to fifteen years.

Under the Equal Employment Opportunity Act of 1972, all of the nation's colleges and universities (with at least fifteen employees) are required to submit detailed records on the gender, racial, and ethnic identity of all of their employees by occupational category and salary level to the EEOC every two years. The chief advantages of the EEOC data set are that (1) its coverage of employment information from United States institutions of higher education is virtually universal, (2) its survey results are routinely reported separately by gender, and (3) because the EEOC's reporting form has remained basically unchanged since 1975, its data are comparable across time. The EEOC data do

---

ponding 11.9 percentage point rise in the portion of those who said they were not married for these years overwhelms the 5.7 percentage point rise in the non-response rate for the period.

suffer from some limitations, however, which should be borne in mind. First, confidentiality commitments have kept the EEOC's separate institutional data files out of the public domain. Secondly, the aggregated data that are available cannot be broken down by the type of institution (that is, four-year college or university, as opposed to a two-year college) from which they originate. These constraining features are important because more than 90 percent of all Ph.D.'s who are employed by academic institutions in the United States are at four-year colleges and universities alone [30 (1987), p. 22; 33, pp. 66–70]. In other words, for the purposes of this study, it would have been preferable to have been able to examine the employment patterns of Ph.D.-educated faculty at the nation's four-year colleges and universities, per se. However, the EEOC data simply do not allow this to be done.

Furthermore, the EEOC reporting form is rather limited in that it does not request any information on the educational backgrounds, fields of degree, fields of employment, teaching loads, publication records, or pertinent demographic characteristics (for example, age, citizenship, or marital status) of the academic faculty at the institutions surveyed. Therefore, the total number of faculty members in its count includes all individuals — Ph.D.'s and non-Ph.D.'s alike — who are responsible for teaching whole courses (that is, excluding graduate students who serve as teaching and research assistants) during the reporting year. Hence, the EEOC faculty pool is somewhat larger than that of only college teachers with doctorate degrees. Finally, the total number of faculty reported by the EEOC, which is based on institutional records, is likely to be slightly higher than the actual number of college teachers employed in the United States because the EEOC does not adjust its count for individuals who are employed at more than one institution of higher education at the same time.

The Changing Nature of Newly Hired Academic Faculty

One might expect that one of the first ways in which the feminization of the supply side of academic labor markets since the 1970s would have affected the demand side would be in increasing the share of women in the pool of newly hired faculty at United States colleges and universities. The data in table 6 below report the number of male, female, and total newly hired, permanent, *full*-time faculty at United States institutions of higher education for 1977 (the first year the EEOC required this information) and 1985 (the latest year for which the data are available). According to the EEOC's survey instructions, institutions are to include in their count of new hires only those persons who "were hired for full-time employment for the first time or after a break in service" between 1 July and 30 September of the reporting year [14, p. 4]. Indeed, the female share of all new faculty hired did increase for this period, by 3.6 percentage points, from 34.0 percent in 1977 to 37.6 percent in 1985. This was the case because the total number of new female faculty members hired rose slightly from 12,677 in 1977 to 13,104 in 1985, whereas the total number of new male faculty members hired declined from 24,625 to 21,724 for these same years. In contrast, however, the share of all doctorates conferred to women rose 9.5 percentage points from 24.8 percent in 1977 to 34.4 percent in 1985 [30 (1977, 1985)].[14] Ironically then, although at the aggregate level it appears that new women doctorates were overrepresented among new faculty hires for both years, the size of this seeming relative advantage of females on the demand side of academic labor markets appears to have lessened considerably as their presence on the supply side has risen.

To understand more fully the complexities regarding how women may be changing the nature of the academic profession, it is important to look beyond just the changes in the overall number and share of new faculty jobs held by women. In particular, what needs to be addressed is to what extent the typical jobs offered to academic men and women have differed and how these differences might have changed, if they have at all. Historically, academic women have tended to be disproportionately hired in nontenured, off-tenure-track positions compared to academic men [7, 36]. Thus, to be able to assess how this tendency may have changed in recent years, the data in table 6 also show the numbers and percentages of all new male, female, and total faculty who were hired in (1) tenured, (2) nontenured, but on-tenure-track, (or "tenure-track") and (3) "other" (that is, nontenured, but off-track or "nontenure-track") full-time faculty positions for 1977 and 1985. The first pattern that is evident when the data are analyzed in this way is clearly that the smallest amount of new faculty hiring occurs at the tenured level. It is important to note that the number and percentage of faculty hired at this top and most desirable level (that is, with lifetime job security) rose slightly during this period for both men (from 1159 and 4.7 percent in 1977 to 1368 and 6.3 percent in 1985) and women (from 346 and 2.7 percent in 1977 to 509 and 3.9 percent in 1985). Yet, the gap between the portion of all men and the corresponding share of all women hired at this level actually widened slightly from 2.0 to 2.4 percent for these years.

[14]In 1977 the number of female Ph.D. recipients was only 7,684, and for males, 23,858. In 1985 the corresponding figure for women was 10,699, and for men 20,502 [30 (1977, 1985)]. The sizable gap between these numbers and the number of new faculty hired by United States institutions of higher education in any given year reflects the fact that the EEOC pool of newly hired faculty includes Ph.D.'s and non-Ph.D.'s alike, as well as "job changers," rather than just new academic labor market entrants alone.

TABLE 6

Tenure Status of Newly Hired* Permanent, Full-Time Faculty at United States Institutions of Higher Education,** by Gender, 1977 and 1985

Year and Tenure Status	Total New Faculty			New Male Faculty		New Female Faculty	
	Number	% of All Faculty	% Female	Number	% of Male Faculty	Number	% of Female Faculty
1977***							
Tenured faculty	1505	4.0%	23.0%	1159	4.7%	346	2.7%
Nontenured on-track faculty	20586	55.2%	33.7%	13640	55.4%	6946	54.8%
Other faculty	15211	40.8%	35.4%	9826	39.9%	5385	42.5%
Total, all new faculty	37302	100.0%	34.0%	24625	100.0%	12677	100.0%
1985***							
Tenured faculty	1877	5.4%	27.1%	1368	6.3%	509	3.9%
Nontenured, on-track faculty	16689	47.9%	36.5%	10593	48.8%	6096	46.5%
Other faculty	16262	46.7%	40.%	9763	44.9%	6499	49.6%
Total, all new faculty	34828	100.0%	37.6%	21724	100.0%	13104	100.0%

SOURCE: Numbers of newly hired faculty by tenure status and gender from unpublished data provided by the Survey Division of the U.S. Equal Employment Opportunity Commission to the author in March 1989. Percentages reported represent calculations by the author based on these data.
*Includes all full-time faculty members hired between July 1 and September 30 of the reporting year.
**U.S. institutions of higher education which are required by law to file staff information forms biennially to the U.S. Equal Employment Opportunity Commission (EEOC) include all institutional systems, colleges and universities, including community and junior colleges, with 15 or more employees.
***The number of reporting institutions in 1977 was 3031. For 1985, the number was 2868.

The second major pattern that can be seen in table 6 is that the bulk of faculty hiring by the nation's colleges and universities occurs at the lower academic ranks, presumably at the entry level. Naturally, these are the positions for which new Ph.D. recipients wishing to pursue academic careers are most likely to compete. Of particular interest is the absolute decline in overall faculty hiring (from 37,302 in 1977 to 34,828 in 1985, or a 6.6 percent drop), especially for nontenured, but on-tenure-track slots. Obviously, this is especially significant, because full-time, tenure-track positions are considered the most desirable by new entrants into the academic marketplace. Both fewer men (22.3 percent fewer) and women (12.2 percent fewer) were hired for such jobs in 1985 compared to 1977.

Men also lost ground in the category of "other faculty," that is with respect to nontenured, off-track positions, such as one-, two-, or three-year "fixed-term" appointments. An increased *share* of all new male faculty hiring between 1977 and 1985, however, was for such off-track jobs. Still, 87 percent of the net increase in all female faculty hiring between 1977 and 1985 represents nontenured, off-track job offers, which more often than not are characterized by very limited access to job security, employment benefits, institutional research grants, summer support, and the like.

In sum, with the possible exception of the very modest improvement in the hiring picture for senior faculty, the data in table 6 reveal that the feminization of the academic marketplace has been accompanied by a general corrosion in demand conditions since the mid-1970s. The evidence indicates that junior-level males entering academic labor markets between 1977 and 1985 were most "at risk" of finding no jobs at all. Yet, even the relatively more successful experience of academic women for this period pales in significance when one realizes that the vast majority of the net increase in new jobs filled by women in between 1977 and 1985 were simply not good jobs. Finally, these data strongly suggest that the significant decline in the number and percentage of new Ph.D.'s planning to pursue academic careers since the 1970s, discussed with respect to table 4 above, can be interpreted as a rational supply-side response to worsening conditions on the demand side of academic labor markets for these years.

The Changing Nature of Academic Employment Status with Respect to Gender

The impression of shrinking employment opportunities for new permanent, full-time faculty at America's colleges and universities from the mid-1970s through at least the mid-1980s is reinforced by the data presented in table 7. Of importance here is the historical reality that in addition to being disproportionately hired in nontenured, off-track positions, academic women have also been overrepresented in part-time jobs [7, 11]. As academic labor markets have become more feminine, and if the relative employment status of academic women in general has not improved substantially, one would expect that the overall share of United States college and university faculty employed on a part-time basis would have risen since the 1970s. Table 7, which compares changes in the number and relative shares of all (that is, previously *and* newly hired) full-time *and part*-time faculty, by tenure status, for 1975 and 1985 (the first and last years such EEOC data are available), reveals that this is exactly what has taken place. Although the total number of faculty members at United States institutions of higher education actually increased by 10.1 percent from 657,819 in 1975 to 728,545 in 1985, nearly three-fourths of this increase was due to the expansion in the number of part-time faculty. Interestingly, whereas the percentage of *all* faculty in part-time positions increased little, from 32.2 percent in 1975 to 36.3 percent in 1985, the proportion of all part-time faculty who were women increased noticeably from 33.3 to 41.1 percent during the same period. Consequently, the 9.5 percent gap between the percent of all male (70.4 percent) and female faculty (60.9 percent) who were on full-time contracts in 1975 had widened by 1985 to 14.2 percent as women became even more disproportionately represented in part-time slots. In essence, although women account for almost one out of every three faculty members in academia today compared with one out of four in 1975, their relative share of full-time faculty positions is still only about one-fourth, while they comprise over 40 percent of all part-time faculty employment.

TABLE 7

Tenure Status of Faculty at United States Institutions of Higher Education* by Gender and Nature of Employment Contract, 1975 and 1985

Year and Tenure Status by Nature of Employment Contract	Total Faculty			Male Faculty			Female Faculty		
	Number	% of All Faculty	% Female	Number	% of Male Faculty		Number	% of Female Faculty	
1975**									
Full-time Faculty									
Tenured	233498	35.5%	18.1%	191269	40.1%		42229	23.4%	
Nontenured, on-track	129603	19.7%	30.5%	90038	18.9%		39565	21.9%	
Other	82933	12.6%	33.8%	54909	11.5%		28024	15.5%	
Total, full-time faculty	446034	67.8%	24.6%	336216	70.4%		109818	60.9%	
Part-time Faculty***									
Tenured	8661	1.3%	24.8%	6512	1.4%		2149	1.2%	
Nontenured, on-track	17593	2.7%	35.9%	11286	2.4%		6307	3.5%	
Other	185515	28.2%	33.5%	123412	25.8%		62102	34.4%	
Total, part-time faculty	211785	32.2%	33.3%	141225	29.6%		70560	39.1%	
Total, All Faculty									
Tenured	242159	36.8%	18.3%	197781	41.4%		44378	24.6%	
Nontenured, on-track	147196	22.4%	31.2%	101324	21.2%		45872	25.4%	
Other	268448	40.8%	33.6%	178321	37.3%		90126	50.0%	
Total, both full- and part-time faculty***	657819	100.0%	27.4%	477441	100.0%		180378	100.0%	
1985**									
Full-time Faculty									
Tenured	252778	34.7%	20.5%	201020	40.9%		51758	21.9%	
Nontenured, on-track	102469	14.1%	34.4%	67270	13.7%		35199	14.9%	
Other	108825	14.9%	37.8%	67719	13.8%		41106	17.4%	
Total, full-time faculty	464072	63.7%	27.6%	336009	68.3%		128063	54.1%	
Part-time Faculty									
Tenured	7671	1.1%	26.8%	5619	1.1%		2052	0.9%	
Nontenured, on-track	29158	4.0%	42.2%	16856	3.4%		12302	5.2%	
Other	227644	31.2%	41.5%	133250	27.1%		94394	39.9%	
Total, part-time faculty	264473	36.3%	41.1%	155725	31.7%		108748	45.9%	
Total, All Faculty									
Tenured	260449	35.7%	20.7%	206639	42.0%		53810	22.7%	
Nontenured, on-track	131627	18.1%	36.1%	84126	17.1%		47501	20.1%	
Other	336469	46.2%	40.3%	200969	40.9%		135500	57.2%	
Total, both full- and part-time faculty	728545	100.0%	32.5%	491734	100.0%		236811	100.0%	

SOURCE: Same as for table 6.
*See note "**" for table 6.
**The number of institutions reporting in 1975 was 3004. For 1985, the number was 2868.
***Totals for part-time faculty may not sum exactly due to rounding errors.

Academic institutions are shifting towards a greater reliance on part-time faculty members, and women are increasingly the ones who assume those part-time roles. To the extent that acceptance of a part-time position in lieu of a full-time one is voluntary, academia can be credited with having flexibility. But data from the NRC's biennial surveys of doctorate recipients indicate that (1) the percent of graduates working part-time and (2) the share of part-time workers seeking full-time jobs has been rising [28, p. 15; 33, table 1, pp. 21–22]. For example, among the 1981–86 humanities Ph.D. graduates in the labor force in 1987, 13.8 percent were working part-time, and two-thirds of this group was seeking full-time work. These figures compare with 8.6 percent and slightly more than one-third, respectively, for the more inclusive pool of 1944–86 humanities Ph.D. graduates in 1987 [28, pp. 15–17].[15]

Perhaps the single most revealing set of data presented in this study is the portion of table 7 that compares the tenure status for all male and female, full-time and part-time, faculty for 1975 and 1985. The female proportion of college and university faculty increased in all tenure categories between 1975 and 1985 but least in tenured (up by 2.4 percentage points from 18.3 to 20.7 percent) and most in nontenure-track (that is, "other") lines (up by 6.7 percentage points from 33.6 to 40.3 percent). In fact, an examination of the representation of women in the most desirable academic positions, that is both tenured and nontenured but on-track jobs (whether full- or part-time), reveals little improvement between 1975 and 1985. In 1975 women held 23.2 percent of such faculty jobs. Ten years later this figure had risen only by 2.6 percentage points to 25.8 percent. By contrast, the increasing presence of women in academia has been most striking in nontenure-track, part-time faculty positions. Between 1975 and 1985, the net addition of women to this category (32,292) was more than three times as large as that for men (9,838), and the share of these jobs held by women rose from 33.5 to 41.5 percent. Essentially, as Dr. Benjamin [3] of the AAUP has argued, women continue to be overrepresented in lower-status academic positions, and this situation has gotten worse as both the number and share of Ph.D.'s earned by women has risen significantly.

[15]According to the most recent comparable data from the NRC's biennial Survey of Doctorate Recipients, the problem of involuntary part-time job holding, on a relative scale, is more concentrated in the humanities. A greater number of doctorate scientists and engineers were in this job status (3,654) in 1983, however, than was true for humanities Ph.D.'s (2,103). Also, although women made up 13.2 percent of all Ph.D. scientists and engineers in the labor force in 1983, 37.1 percent of those who were working part-time but seeking full-time jobs were women [29, pp. 28-29 and 72-73].

One job category that showed relatively remarkable growth between 1975 and 1985, however, does bear special mention here. The number of nontenured, but *on-track, part-time* jobs increased by 65.7 percent during this period from 17,593 to 29,158. Even more impressive is the fact that the number of women in such positions almost doubled (up 95 percent) from 6,307 in 1975 to 12,302 in 1985. If these data reflect an increasing willingness on the part of American colleges and universities to offer an *attractive* "mommy track" (or for that matter, "daddy track") to members of their faculty, they could signal a very positive new trend in academic labor markets. How significant this trend actually is, however, is too early to tell. For every new female faculty member added in such a tenure-track, part-time slot between 1975 and 1985, six more women were added in nontenured, off-track positions — four on a part-time and two on a full-time basis.

Clearly, larger numbers of women are now on the faculties of United States institutions of higher education, but they have been disproportionately hired in positions with limited opportunity for career advancement. Fully 57.2 percent of all female faculty members compared to 40.9 percent of all male faculty members held off-track jobs in 1985. While the proportion of all faculty in such "other faculty" slots worsened for both men and women between 1975 and 1985, the corresponding diminishing share of all positions held in tenured and nontenured but on-tenure-track lines fell more dramatically for women (from 50.0 percent in 1975 to 42.8 percent in 1985) than for men (from 62.6 to 59.1 percent).[16]

The data in table 7 also quantify the relatively large loss in full-time, tenure-track positions experienced by all college and university faculty, but especially men between 1975 and 1985. There were 27,134 fewer

[16]A reasonable hypothesis here would be to propose that academic women are disproportionately concentrated in nontenured, off-track positions — that is, "bad jobs" — because female doctorates have been overrepresented in fields characterized by particularly poor labor market conditions over the last fifteen years or so, such as the humanities and social sciences. Although one cannot test this hypothesis with the EEOC data, results from the National Research Council's Survey of Doctorate Recipients Project (see note 12 above) reveal that this problem is not limited to such "soft" fields. In fact, according to the NRC data, a higher proportion of Ph.D.'s in the sciences and engineering than in the humanities held such nontenure-track slots in both 1979 and 1985. This pattern cannot be explained by an especially high percentage of doctoral *social* scientists in this tenure status, either. If anything, it is doctorates in the harder sciences (for example, astronomy, physics, chemistry, and the biological sciences) who tend to be overrepresented in nontenured, off-track positions [25, tables 1.12 and 2.12, pp. 33 and 56; 27, table 17, p. 35; 32, Appendix, tables 21 and 22, pp. 141–47].

faculty members in such positions in 1985 than in 1975, and the "lion's share" of the loss (83.9 percent or 22,768 jobs) was borne by men. While it could be expected that a number of faculty members who were pre-tenured, but on line in 1975 had been awarded tenure by 1985, the net gain in tenured positions between 1975 and 1985 (19,280) accounts for only 70.6 percent of the loss in nontenured, on-track jobs. Interestingly enough, men and women shared almost equally in the net increase in tenured slots between 1975 and 1985. Men enjoyed 50.6 percent of the net increase in tenured positions, while 49.4 percent of the increase benefited women. This implies that women actually did proportionately better in moving up the academic ladder to senior positions than did their male peers for the decade. Overall, when one compares the relative gain in tenured slots to the loss in nontenured, but on-track jobs, men on balance lost five tenure-track positions for every two tenured jobs they gained between 1975 and 1985. Women, in contrast gained slightly more than two tenured slots for every single tenure-track position they lost. In short, men suffered a net loss of 13,017 tenured plus tenure-track positions, while women enjoyed a net gain of 5,163 of such jobs.

Where did the academic job losers go between 1975 and 1985? What is evident from the data in table 7 is that the majority (57.3 percent) of the gross increase in new *full-time* faculty positions was made up of nontenured, off-track slots. Men and women about equally filled the net addition of 25,892 such new jobs (49.5 percent for men and 50.5 percent for women). In fact, the total gain of 22,561 full-time tenured and off-track faculty positions enjoyed by men almost completey offset their loss of full-time, tenure-track positions from 1975 to 1985. Although women, on balance, did considerably better than men in moving into full-time faculty positions between 1975 and 1985, 71.7 percent of their net gain of 18,245 jobs was in the off-tenure-track category.

To sum up, when one examines the overall distribution in both full-time and part-time faculty gains and losses between 1975 and 1985, the shift in the composition of academic faculty out of full-time, tenured and tenure-track slots into full-time, off-track and part-time jobs is unequivocal. In 1985 there were 7,854 fewer faculty members in full-time, tenured and on-track positions than in 1975, consisting of 13,010 fewer males, yet 5,163 more females. Virtually all the growth on the demand side of academic labor markets occurred in either (1) full-time, off-track (accounting for one-third of the increase), or (2) part-time positions (four-fifths of which were off-track slots), which together increased by 78,580.[17] While women made up 50.5 percent of the increase in full-time, off-track positions, they filled 72.5 percent of the new part-time slots and 79.8 percent of the net increase in all jobs between 1975 and 1985.

The Changing Nature of Academic Rank and Salary with Respect to Gender

One of the most frequent approaches to examining gender differences among America's college and university faculty members is to compare trends in the academic rank and salary levels of men and women. The data available from the EEOC on full-time faculty members for 1975 and 1985 reveal that women college teachers continue to be disproportionately represented in the lower academic ranks.[18] Furthermore, although their relative standing has improved somewhat, their climb up the academic ladder has not been dramatic. Indeed, while women have made modest gains among the junior ranks, the gap between the percent of all female and all male faculty who were full professors actually widened from 1975 (17.9 percent more male) to 1985 (22.3 percent more male).[19] As such, these conclusions corroborate those of others who have analyzed data from the AAUP's annual faculty salary surveys [38], the National Center for Education Statistics [8, p. 162], and the Carnegie Foundation's faculty surveys [2]. Finally, of interest is the fact that the overall distribution in the academic ranking of female and male faculty members as measured by the index of rank segregation by gender remained virtually unchanged between 1975 and 1985. For both years, either about 27 percent of all males or 27 percent of all females would have had to be in a different rank for their rank distributions to be identical.[20]

The salary data collected by the EEOC are fairly weak, especially for

[17]From the point of view of college and university faculty these trends are clearly unfavorable. Yet, it is important to note that from the perspective of the hiring academic institutions, the replacement of regular, full-time tenured and tenure-track faculty lines with temporary full-time, off-track and part-time positions can be interpreted as the rational cost-cutting response to the anticipated decline in college student enrollments, as well as the large increases in their operating costs (for example especially energy-related) beginning in the mid-1970s [15; 16, especially pp. 2–4; 35, p. 33].

[18]Unfortunately, the EEOC does not collect data on the rank and salary of part-time faculty members.

[19]These data are available from the author upon request.

[20]The indices of rank segregation reported here were calculated using the formula for the index of field segregation explained in note 6 above. The only difference is that in calculating the rank segregation index, M_i = the percentage of male faculty in *rank "i"* (that is, full professor, associate professor, and so on), and F_i = the percentage of female faculty in *rank "i"*

more recent years. The problem is that the top salary range on the EEOC's reporting form for faculty for both 1975 and 1985 was $30,000 a year and above. Still, the EEOC data indicate that, as other researchers have found, the female share of faculty across all salary ranges continues to vary inversely with the salary level.[21] Whereas only 12.5 percent of all faculty were in the annual salary range of $25,000 and above in 1975, overall earnings growth had propelled 75.7 percent of all faculty to this salary level and 56.9 percent of them to the $30,000 and above range by 1985. Academic women, however, did not move as rapidly up the earnings scale as academic men. Whereas only one-third of all full-time faculty women were earning $30,000 or more in 1985, nearly two-thirds of all faculty men were in this top earnings bracket. In contrast, in that same year 40.8 percent of all full-time, female faculty were earning less than $25,000 compared to only 18.1 percent for males.[22] In sum, today academic women tend to be twice as likely as academic men to be at the bottom, and half as likely to be at the top of the salary distribution scale.

Conclusions

Well, have women changed the nature of the academic profession? On the supply side it is clear that women are making a dent. Compared to nearly two decades ago when fewer than one out of every seven new Ph.D. recipients was female, today more than one out of three is. But trends in the gender composition of the new doctorate population since the mid-1980s indicate that the feminization process has slowed considerably and is at a plateau. Clearly, the National Center of Education Statistics' projection that by 1993–94 half the nation's doctorate degrees would be awarded to women [39, p. 84] is not likely to be realized. In fact, if the prospect of tightening labor markets and improved employment conditions in academia beckons a new generation of male scholars to pursue doctoral training, as the relatively large share of "graying" faculty in the upper ranks begins to retire and the "baby boomlet" gen-

[21]The EEOC salary data are available from the author upon request. Also, see Scott [38] for an excellent bibliography of studies that examined gender differences in academic salaries from the late-1960s through the 1970s within specific institutions, disciplines, and in general.

[22]Ideally, one needs to control salary comparisons for field, years of experience, publication record, and so on, and this cannot be done with the EEOC data. For example, in the mid-1970s Bergmann and Maxfield [6] found that female faculty earned lower salaries than their male counterparts in the same field and with the same number of years of experience.

eration reaches college age beginning in the mid-1990s, the female share of all doctorates may actually shrink in the years ahead.

The size of the dent women are making on the supply side of academic labor markets, importantly, varies by field. Today, the typical new doctorate is more likely to be female than male in the field of education. In the humanities and the social sciences, the typical new Ph.D. recipient is just about as likely to be female as male. Women are proportionally represented in the life sciences and the professional fields where they make up one out of every three new Ph.D.'s. Yet, it is still rare for a new Ph.D. in engineering, mathematics, or the physical sciences to be female. And increasingly, the typical new EMP male doctorate is likely to be a non-United States citizen. Even more distinct variations in the gender composition of new doctorates are apparent when one examines the presence of women within disciplinary fine fields.

On the demand side, what is very clear is that the nature of academic faculties has changed in many important ways since the 1970s. The typical faculty member is much more likely to be someone either in a (1) full-time, nontenured, off-track or (2) part-time position than was true a decade ago. The faculty member who is a full professor, is nine times as likely to be a male as a female. At the associate professor level, three out of four faculty members continue to be men, and at the rank of assistant professor, two out of three are men. Yet a student taking a college course from an instructor or lecturer is just as likely to have a man as a woman teaching the class.

Yes, women have *moved into* the ivy-covered halls of American higher education. Yet, they have hardly done so in positions of high prestige, rank, and salary — gains that would have been necessary for Professor Parrish's [34] claim that women are "taking over" at least the *academic* profession to have had some validity. In fact, four-fifths of the net addition of 56,433 female faculty members at United States colleges and universities between 1975 and 1985 were in positions which academic men have historically been able to avoid — that is, off-track, lower-ranked, lower-paying jobs that offer no prospect, if any, of job security or career advancement. The last ten to fifteen years in the academic marketplace have not been good for many academic men, either, especially for many younger *aspiring* academic men. In fact, the evidence presented in this study exposes the deteriorating conditions on the demand side of academic labor markets that obviously convinced many men from the mid-1970s through mid-1980s to behave rationally, in an economic sense, and not prepare for or pursue academic careers. Hence, it is hardly surprising that the Carnegie Foundation for the

Advancement of Teaching found that between its 1975 and 1984 faculty surveys the level of faculty dissatisfaction had increased. In fact, half the faculty surveyed in 1984 advised young people considering an academic career, "Don't do it . . . this is not a good time" [18, p. 1].[23]

Even though women clearly are not "taking over" the academic profession, they have joined, in large numbers, a profession whose institutions are beset with many problems. In particular, the marked increased reliance on part-time and nontenure-track faculty by American colleges and universities in fulfilling their teaching mission and the disproportionate hiring of women in such jobs, warrants a careful and thorough study of the socioeconomic costs and benefits involved as well as of the policy implications regarding our nation's quarter-of-a-century commitment to equality of opportunity and the cumulative impact of these factors on the effective quality of our system of higher education itself. In an era of increasing international competition, we simply cannot afford to underutilize our most valuable natural resource — the thousands of talented, highly educated women and men who are responsible for educating tomorrow's leaders and who hold the key to our future.

References

1. Astin, H. S. *The Woman Doctorate in America.* New York: Russell Sage Foundation, 1969.
2. Barbezat, D. A. "Communications: Salary Differentials by Sex in the Academic Labor Market." *The Journal of Human Resources,* 22 (Summer 1987), 422–28.
3. Benjamin, E. "Improving the Status of Women: A Faculty Perspective." In *International Association of University Presidents, VIII Triennial Conference Proceedings,* Guadalajara, Jalisco, Mexico, 21–27 June 1987, pp. 67–78.
4. Berg, H. M., and M. S. Ferber. "Men and Women Graduate Students: Who Succeeds and Why?" *Journal of Higher Education,* 54 (November/December 1983), 629–48.
5. Bergmann, B. R. *The Economic Emergence of Women.* New York: Basic Books, Inc., Publishers, 1986.
6. Bergmann, B. R., and M. Maxfield, Jr. "How to Analyze the Fairness of Faculty Salaries on Your Own Campus." *AAUP Bulletin,* 61 (Autumn 1975), 262–65. Cited by B. R. Bergmann, *The Economic Emergence of Women,* p. 134, New York: Basic Books, Inc., Publishers, 1986.
7. Bernard, J. *Academic Women.* University Park, Pa.: The Pennsylvania State University Press, 1964.

[23]Faculty morale has evidently improved since 1984, however. For example, only 20 percent of those responding to the Carnegie Foundation's 1989 faculty survey said, "This is a poor time to begin an academic career" [22, p. A1].

8. Blau, F. D., and M. A. Ferber. *The Economics of Women, Men and Work.* Englewood Cliffs, N.J.: Prentice-Hall, 1986.

9. Bloom, D. E. "Fertility Timing, Labor Supply Disruptions, and the Wage Profiles of American Women." *1986 Proceedings of the Social Statistics Section of the American Statistical Association,* pp. 49–63.

10. "Carnegie Foundation's Classifications of More than 3,300 Institutions of Higher Education." *Chronicle of Higher Education,* July 8, 1987, pp. 22–30.

11. Centra, J. A. *Women, Men and the Doctorate.* Princeton, N.J.: Educational Testing Service, September 1974.

12. Cooney, T. M., and P. Uhlenberg. "Family-Building Patterns of Women Professionals: A Comparison of Lawyers, Physicians, and Postsecondary Teachers." *Journal of Marriage and the Family,* 51 (August 1989), 749–58.

13. Duncan, O. D., and Duncan, B. "A Methodological Analysis of Segregation Indexes." *American Sociological Review,* 20 (1955), 210–17.

14. Equal Employment Opportunity Commission. *EEOC Form 221. Higher Education Staff Information (EEOC-6) Instruction Booklet.* Washington, D.C.: Author, April 1986.

15. Franklin, P., D. Laurence, and R. D. Denham. "When Solutions Become Problems: Taking a Stand on Part-Time Employment." *Academe,* 74 (May-June 1988) 15–19.

16. Gappa, J. M. *Part-Time Faculty: Higher Education at a Crossroads.* ASHE-ERIC Higher Education Research Report No. 3. Washingon, D.C.: Association for the Study of Higher Education (ASHE), 1984.

17. Heath, J. A., and H. P. Tuckman. "The Impact on Labor Markets of the Relative Growth of New Female Doctorates." *Journal of Higher Education,* 60 (November/December 1989), pp. 704–15.

18. Jacobson, R. L. "New Carnegie Data Show Faculty Members Uneasy about the State of Academe and Their Own Careers." *Chronicle of Higher Education,* December 18, 1985, pp. 1 and 24–28.

19. Layard, R., and J. Mincer, eds. *Journal of Labor Economics,* 3 (January 1985). Proceedings of the Conference on "Trends in Womens Work, Education, and Family Building," Chelwood Gate, Sussex, England, 31 May–3 June 1983.

20. McDowell, J. "Obsolescence of Knowledge and Career Publication Profiles: Some Evidence of Differences among Fields in Costs of Interrupted Careers." *American Economic Review,* 72 (September 1982), 752–68.

21. McPherson, M. S. "The State of Academic Labor Markets." In *The State of Graduate Education,* edited by Bruce L. R. Smith, pp. 57–83. Washington, D. C.: The Brookings Inst., 1985.

22. Mooney, C. J. "Professors Are Upbeat about Profession but Uneasy About Students, Standards." *Chronicle of Higher Education,* November 8, 1989, p. A1, A18–A20.

23. Moorman, J. E. "The History and the Future of the Relationship between Education and Marriage." Unpublished paper. U.S. Bureau of the Census, Washington, D.C., March 1987.

24. National Research Council. Commission on Human Resources. *Career Patterns of Doctoral Scientists and Engineers, 1973–1977.* An analytical study prepared for

the National Science Foundation. Washington, D.C.: National Academy of Sciences, 1979.

25. ———. Commission on Human Resources. *Science, Engineering, and Humanities Doctorates in the United States: 1979 Profile.* Washington, D.C.: National Academy of Sciences, 1980.

26. ———. Commission on Human Resources. Board on Human-Resource Data and Analysis. *A Century of Doctorates: Data Analysis of Growth and Change.* A report to the National Science Foundation, to the National Endowment for the Humanities, and to the United States Office of Education. Washington, D.C.: National Academy Press, 1978.

27. ———. Office of Scientific and Engineering Personnel. *Humanities Doctorates in the United States: 1985 Profile.* Washington, D.C.: National Academy Press, 1986.

28. ———. Office of Scientific and Engineering Personnel. *Humanities Doctorates in the United States: 1987 Profile.* Washington, D.C.: National Academy Press, 1989.

29. ———. Office of Scientific and Engineering Personnel. *Science, Engineering and Humanities Doctorates in the United States: 1983 Profile.* Washington, D.C.: National Academy of Sciences, 1985.

30. ———. Office of Scientific and Engineering Personnel. *Summary Report 19XX: Doctorate Recipients from United States Universities.* Washington, D.C.: National Academy Press, 1971–1990. (Note: Referenced in text by survey year, not publication date; 19XX designates reports from 1970 through 1988.)

31. ———. Office of Scientific and Engineering Personnel. Unpublished data from the 1987 Survey of Doctorate Recipients. Washington, D.C., March 1989.

32. National Science Foundation. *Women and Minorities in Science and Engineering.* Washington, D.C.: National Science Foundation, January 1988.

33. ———. Surveys of Science Resource Series. *Characteristics of Doctoral Scientists and Engineers in the United States: 1987.* Washington, D.C.: National Science Foundation, ca. 1989.

34. Parrish, J. B. "Are Women Taking Over the Professions?" *Challenge,* 28 (January/February 1986), 54–58.

35. Pierce, R. T. " 'Gypsy' Faculty Stirs Debate at U.S. Colleges." *Wall Street Journal,* September 25, 1986, p. 33.

36. Rosenfeld, R. "Academic Men and Women's Career Mobility." *Social Science Research,* 10 (December 1981), 337–63.

37. Rosenfeld, R., G. Marwell, and S. Spilerman. "Geographic Constraints on Women's Careers in Academia." *Science,* 205 (September 21, 1979), 1225–31.

38. Scott, E. L. *AAUP Higher Education Salary Evaluation Kit.* Prepared for the American Association of University Professors (AAUP). Washington, D.C., 1977.

39. U.S. Department of Education. Office of Educational Research and Improvement. National Center for Education Statistics. *The Condition of Education, 1985 Edition.* Washington, D.C.: U.S. Government Printing Office, 1985.

40. ———. Office of Educational Research and Improvement. National Center for Education Statistics. Information Services. *Digest of Education Statistics 1988.* Washington, D.C.: U.S. Government Printing Office, September 1988.

2   Entry into Academia: Effects of Stratification, Geography and Ecology

Robert McGinnis and J. Scott Long

Introduction

This paper has two purposes. First, it provides a brief summary of selected results of our research over the past decade into patterns of institutional stratification and their effects on the careers of scientists who are affiliated with the institutions. Our research strategy involves two distinct but interacting units of analysis: individual scientists and organizations.

Our second purpose is to present for the first time preliminary results of what may prove to be an important extension of our research. In it, we extend the concepts and measures of stratification to include those of geographic and ecological differentiation. In this way we are able to investigate the consequences of location not only in a vertical system of stratification, but also in a horizontal system that contains components such as distance, centrality, and isolation. We must emphasize the tentative and preliminary nature of the second set of results and the need for a great deal more refinement of both concepts and measures. Even so, the results seem to us to suggest a promising new line of analysis in the sociology of science.

Overview of the Academic Career

The Matthew Effect argues that unto those that have shall be given, and from those that have not shall be taken away (Merton, 1973 [1968]:445). The institutional version of the Matthew Effect argues that in systems of stratification it is easier for those who have resources to obtain additional resources than it is for those who do not (Merton, 1973 [1968]:457; Price, 1965). The application of this principle of cumulative advantage to the academic career implies that the success of a scientist in securing an initial tenure-track position may be one of the most important factors determining the success of the scientist. Obtaining a position in a prestigious university is associated with receiving three resources that are valuable for a successful research career: time, money and knowledge (Zuckerman, 1970:246).

Time is gained with lighter teaching loads and more able support staffs. Money is in effect gained with the availability of better equipment and facilities. Knowledge is gained from the availability of stimulating colleagues. To the extent that these resources can be transformed into scientific productivity, that productivity can be used to secure even more resources to facilitate further scientific productivity. The significance of departmental location, independent of other factors, on later productivity has been demonstrated by Long (1978). In short, it is found that the advantages of one's initial job placement accumulate over the career. Given the lasting impact of auspicious beginnings, it is important to understand the process by which scientists are allocated to jobs in the stratification system of science.

The process of allocating scientists to positions is also of interest for examining the normative structure of science, and in particular, the extent to which the hiring process is based on universalistic criteria. If the institutionally sanctioned goal of science is the extension of certified knowledge (Merton, 1973 [1942]:267–85), and if jobs in more prestigious institutions are a form of reward or at least a scarce resource to be sought, the allocation of Ph.D.s to positions should be based on their scientific productivity.

This would be seen in the effects of a scientist's productivity prior to obtaining a job on the success of obtaining one that is prestigious. It can also be argued that prestigious departments hire those candidates who demonstrate the most potential, where potential would be assessed on the basis of the student's training. Scientists with eminent mentors and from prestigious departments could be considered better trained, and hence potentially more productive. Alternatively, positions could be allocated on the basis of particularistic influences operating through social ties. For example, Caplow and McGee (1958:110) argue that departments often choose candidates on the basis of their social ties to the hiring department. The effects of the mentor and the Ph.D. department may then be seen not as indications of a student's potential, but of who they know who knows influential people in prestigious departments.

There is evidence that all of these factors operate in the allocation of academic positions. While it is impossible to unambiguously assign the effect of the mentor and/or Ph.D. department as a universalistic effect operating through the better training and increased potential of the student or as a particularistic effect operating through the influence of social ties, it is possible to consider the new Ph.D.'s productivity as an indicator of his or her productivity. The failure of predoctoral productivity to influence the allocation of positions relative to the influence of less clearly universalistic factors suggests the operation of particularistic factors in science. Given the importance of the initial position on later productivity, this potential inequality is likely to be magnified as the career develops.

The specific process of determining the prestige of the first position and the effects on the later career is complex. In a series of earlier papers (Long, 1978; Long, Allison and McGinnis, 1979; Long and McGinnis, 1981; McGinnis, Allison and Long, 1982; Long and McGinnis, 1985) various aspects of this process have been analyzed in detail. These will be reviewed before presenting the extensions to those analyses that are new to this paper. The first process is that determining which scientists pursue postdoctoral study, generally in the form of a fellowship. Scientists who are not in an agricultural area, who are young and unmarried upon receipt of the Ph.D., and who come from prestigious departments studying under prestigious mentors are most likely to obtain fellowships. The predoctoral productivity of the scientist has no effect on obtaining a postdoctoral fellowship position.[1] The competition for a permanent position begins after the fellowship for those seeking additional training, and immediately upon the receipt of the degree for those who do not. The allocation of scientists among the organizational contexts including faculty position in a research university (the focus of this paper), teaching positions in non-research universities, industrial research positions, non-industrial research positions and administrative positions has a lasting impact on the career of the scientist. The most interesting findings for the purposes of this paper concern the determinants of faculty positions in research universities. The two strongest effects are having a postdoctoral fellowship and obtaining a degree from a non-agricultural department. The number of pre-doctoral publications and citations does not significantly differentiate faculty in research departments from any other organizational context. For those who become faculty in research departments, the factors determining the prestige of the department are reviewed in the beginning of the results section.

Factors influencing career productivity, as measured by publications and citations to them, can be classified into three types: the reinforcing effects of prior productivity, contextual effects, and effects of training. While the prestige of the doctoral or postdoctoral department or the eminence of the mentor, which might be considered effects of training, have the most significant effect on determining the context of employment (whether among organizational contexts or to the prestige of a given department), they have only minor effects on productivity later in the career. Thus, while characteristics of the mentor and Ph.D. department are significantly correlated with later productivity, these effects disappear after controlling for organizational or departmental context and earlier productivity. Conversely, the effects of predoctoral productivity, which were negligible on determining position, are the strongest factors influencing later productivity. The best predictor of a scientist's later productivity is his productivity during graduate training.[2] Finally, organizational context and departmental prestige have strong and statistically significant effects on later productivity.

Thus, understanding the factors determining the employment of an academic scientist are important for understanding his future success. To further this understanding, we have extended our analysis of the social processes that influence entry into research universities to include geographic and ecological aspects of the process.

Effects of Geography and Ecology on Entry into Academia

We have argued that a number of factors in the educational background of biochemists strongly influenced the paths that they took into their careers. We now suggest that yet another cluster of factors, those of geography and ecology, have similar influences on their career paths. By 'geography' we refer to one's location on north–south and east–west axes at a particular point in one's career. By 'ecology' we refer to that location relative to the location of other relevant objects such as employment opportunities.

The idea that one's spatial and relative locations have a bearing on subsequent career paths is not new. Perhaps the best studied of such effects is that of physical location at a point in the career on location at a subsequent point, with the move itself being referred to as geographic mobility. It is well known that there is friction in distance. If a move is observed it is more likely to be short than long. Thus, where one ends up in a geographic move is strongly influenced by where one starts. But it is also known that both the probability of making a move and its length are positively associated with level of education (Ladinsky, 1967; Lichter, 1982).

One might extrapolate from the observed association between education and geographic mobility to conclude that, among the most highly educated – doctoral scientists in particular – such mobility should be approximately perfect, that location of destination should be nearly independent of location of origin. Such, however, is not the case. Hargens (1969), for example, in a study of career moves of a set of scientists, showed that inter-regional moves were far fewer than would have been expected under the assumption of perfect mobility. Thus, the friction of distance is a force that influences the geographic mobility of doctoral scientists as well as of most others.

For this reason, we introduce geography in the form of latitude and longitude into our analysis. The measurements are for the institutions from which our scientists received their baccalaureate or doctoral degrees, at which they did postdoctoral study, and where they were employed as faculty members. These measures permit us to derive the distance travelled in various career moves, as from the place of final professional training to that of first faculty employment. These geographic measures, in turn, permit us to examine the hypothesis that the location of the origin of a career move influences the location of its destination.

Closely related to the geography of academia is the concept of academic ecology.[3] The ideas developed here – especially those of academic centrality and competition – are rooted in the perspective of organizational ecology as developed by Hannan and Freeman (1977). For a recent statement that more fully develops the concept of organizational competition, see Hannan (1986). We must note, however, that our static analyses of academic organizations bear little resemblance to the differential equation models that characterize this perspective. Moreover, our motivation in this paper is not to examine academic organizations as a population *per se*, but rather as a set of environments in which some scientists conduct their careers. To get a better sense of this idea, consider two scientists emerging from their training and onto the job market. Suppose that one has just finished her postdoctoral training at Harvard and the other his doctoral degree at the University of Alabama in Tuscaloosa. We have argued that differences in their academic backgrounds will strongly differentiate their first steps into careers.[4] But heretofore we have not considered another difference that could be equally important: their relative distances from resources such as employment opportunities and personal contacts with potential employers. On the face of it, the one emerging from Cambridge is far more central to opportunities than is the one from Tuscaloosa. It is not difficult to imagine that this difference in centrality could differentiate their career paths quite aside from their personal and academic differences. But there is another side to this coin: coupled with the force of centrality is that of competition. Just as there are more academic employment opportunities for scientists in the Boston metropolitan area than there are in all of Alabama, there are also far more competitors for the resources. We will take account of both the concepts of centrality (which we will call 'potential' for reasons discussed in the following section) and competition in an analysis of ecological influences on entry into academia and on several aspects of academia itself.

Data and Measurement

The sample consists of 239 male biochemists who received their Ph.D.s from US universities in fiscal years 1957, 1958, 1962 and 1963 and whose first non-fellowship job was a faculty position in a department rated by Roose and Andersen (1970). Career histories were obtained from *American Men and Women of Science* (10th, 11th and 12th Editions).

The prestige of the doctoral department was measured by the complete three-digit rating of faculty quality of biochemistry departments, a partial listing of which appeared in Cartter (1966). These scores ranged from 100 for the least-prestigious to 500 for the most-prestigious. The prestige of the first job was somewhat more difficult to measure since the biochemists worked in departments in several different fields. Accordingly, a prestige score for each university was constructed based on a weighted average of the Roose and Andersen (1970) ratings of the departments of biochemistry (1/2), chemistry (1/4), physiology (1/12), microbiology/bacteriology (1/12) and pharmacology (1/12); weights in parentheses were based on approximate numbers of biochemists employed in each type of department. These scores also ranged from 100 to 500.

For all but two of the sample, the name of the mentor was obtained from *Dissertation Abstracts, Directory of Graduate Research,* or a mail survey of graduate deans. A measure of the mentor's accomplishments was obtained by counting citations to his or her first-authored publications in the 1961 *Science Citation Index*. While these counts are

347

interpreted as a measure of productivity, it should be kept in mind that they may reflect both the performance of a scientist and his or her standing in the scientific community.

Productivity of the sample members was measured using counts of both publications and citations to them. *Chemical Abstracts* (1955–1973) was used to locate the articles published by the .sample members, whether or not they were the senior author. Citations to these articles were coded from *Science Citation Index* (1961, 1964, 1966, 1968, 1970, 1972, 1974). The name of the first author on multiple-authored papers where the cohort member was not the first author was used to locate citations to junior authored papers; thus downward bias in counts for scientists who were predominantly junior authors was avoided. For a given year in the scientist's career, the publication measure reflects publications in a three-year period ending in that year. The citation measure for that year is restricted to citations to papers published in that three-year period. Since coverage of *Science Citation Index* and *Chemical Abstracts* increased during the period covered by our analyses, counts were standardized within years of the Ph.D.

In addition to these key variables, Astin's (1971) measure of selectivity of the scientist's undergraduate institution was used. This index has values ranging from one to seven, with seven being the most selective category. This measure has been interpreted by some as a crude indicator of intelligence and by others as a measure of the quality of the undergraduate education.

Geographic and ecological coding was begun by recording the latitude and longitude of each of the 383 North American academic institutions with which any biochemist was affiliated. Distances between each of the 73,000 plus pairs of institutions were computed in statutory miles.[5] The distance of each career move was derived from our distance matrix. The matrix also was essential to the operationalization of the two ecological measures of centrality to resources and competition.

To measure institutional centrality we borrowed the concept of demographic potential from quantitative geographers who, in turn, borrowed it from the Newtonian concept of gravitational potential (Hammond and McCullough, 1970). By our construction for a given institution i, its centrality to a second institution j is given by the ratio $r(j)/d(i,j)**k$, where $r(j)$ is the volume of a specified resource at j and $d(i,j)**k$ is the distance between the two raised to power k. In gravitational theory the value of k is 2, but in our case it is estimated from fitting models using different values of k. The total potential of institution i with respect to a specific resource is the sum over all other institutions of this ratio. The fundamental notion behind the concept of demographic potential is that there is friction in distance. No matter how large the resource at location j, the farther it is from location i, the less available it is to i. Moreover, the larger the value of k, the exponent of distance, the more severe the friction of distance. Although k is taken to be a positive number, assume for a moment that it is zero. Then all positive distances become identically one and resources at any location become equally available to consumers at all other locations. Consequently, distance is rendered irrelevant and centrality to resources or isolation from them become irrelevant as the measure of demographic potential becomes a constant across locations.

Several potential measures were constructed for each institution. In the analyses described below we use a variable name PHDPOT2, which measures the centrality of each US doctoral program to our set of biochemists at the time when they received a North American baccalaureate degree. It measures the relative availability of those eligible for admission to doctoral degree candidacy to each doctoral degree program. For institution i, its PHDPOT2 is the sum over all other North American baccalaureate-granting institutions j of the number of baccalaureate degrees that they grant divided by their distance from graduate program i. The number 2 in PHDPOT2 indicates that distances was raised to the power 2.

We posit the existence of a second force that may mediate between an institution's potential for acquiring a resource and its level of success in acquiring it. This second force, which we call institutional competition, was suggested by a now classic theory of geographic mobility called intervening opportunities (Stouffer, 1960). The basic idea underlying the posited second force is this: whatever advantage an institution may have from its potential, it will be mitigated to the extent that it is surrounded by successful competitors for the same resources. The measure of institutional competition that we propose is identical to that of institutional potential except that each ratio's numerator is replaced by a measure of institution j's success at acquiring the resource in question. The measure that we use in the present analysis is called PHDCOM2. It is similar to PHDPOT2, but in the numerator for each institution j it substitues the size of its graduate program as measured by the total number of doctoral degrees produced between 1957 and 1966. Thus the larger the graduate program of j and the closer its location to i, the greater is its competition to i for potential graduate students.

Since the ecological concepts that are applied below may not be familiar, let us illustrate them as in Figure 1. We create a hypothetical system consisting of three four-year undergraduate colleges that produce 100 graduates who proceed immediately into graduate training at one of three available graduate schools. The three graduate institutions, none of which produces baccalaureate degrees, are indistinguishable in all characteristics except for the size of the specific graduate program under investigation (biochemistry, in our case) and geographic location. The institutions are separated by distances given in Figure 1. Note that distances among the undergraduate institutions are not reported since they are irrelevant in our model. The purpose of the exercise is to determine how the 100 graduates become distributed among the three graduate schools that compete for them.

Assume that prior research has shown: first, the optimum exponent of distance is 1.00 for both the potential and competition measures; and second, that the estimated regression coefficients are 1.00 for potential and -0.5 for competition in a regression model in which recruitment success is the dependent variable. Note that the algebraic signs of these two coefficients are critical to the validity of the model that we posit. The potential coefficient must be positive to indicate that the greater the potential the greater the success in recruitment; the competition coefficient must be negative to indicate that the greater the competition the less the success in recruitment.

Potential measures are computed for each graduate institution by summing over undergraduate institutions A, B and C the number of graduates (the values of the potential numerator PN in Figure 1) divided by its distance to the exponent 1.00. Thus, graduate school F has a considerably larger potential measure than either of the others, due largely to its adjacency to the largest undergraduate producer C. The competition measures are computed by summing the measures of size of graduate program of the two competitors (the competition numerator CN in Figure 1) divided by distance. Because of its centrality, graduate school E is seen to be in the poorest competitive position while F, because of its relatively greater size and isolation from the other two, occupies the most favorable competitive position.

Finally, using the estimated coefficients, the 'net' potential of each graduate school is computed (to the kth power). If recruitment is linearly related to this net measure, then we see that graduate school F gets the lion's share of the entering graduate students because of its ecological position within the system. The reader may wish to verify that if elements of the system were changed then the outcomes would also change, drastically under certain different circumstances. For

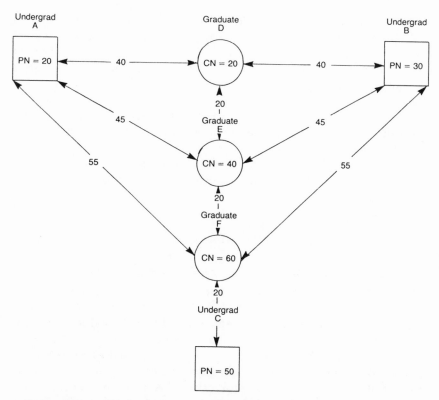

□: Undergraduate Institution (A, B, C) with PN: (Potential Numerator)
    Size of Supply—Baccalaureate Degrees Awarded in Biochemistry.
○: Graduate Institution (D, E, F) with CN: (Competition Numerator)
    Size of Competition—Doctorate Degrees Awarded in Biochemistry
← xx →: Interinstitution Distance.

Computation of Potential
Source of Supply

Consumer	A	B	C	Potential
D	20/40	30/40	50/60	2.083
E	20/40	30/45	50/60	2.361
F	20/55	30/55	50/20	3.409

Computation of Competition
Source of Competition

Competitor	D	E	F	Competition
D	0	40/20	60/40	3.50
E	20/20	0	60/20	4.00
F	20/40	40/20	0	2.50

Computation of Net Potential (= NP)
Where NP = Potential − 0.5*Competition

Net Potential Of:			Percent
D	2.083 − (.5)*(3.50)	=	0.333 11.7
E	2.361 − (.5)*(4.00)	=	0.361 12.7
F	3.409 − (.5)*(2.50)	=	2.159 75.6

Figure 1: Hypothetical System of Suppliers of Baccalaureate Scientists and Their Consumers by Graduate Program, With Computations of Potential and Competition.

instance, if the values of PN for schools A and C were reversed, the potential measures of the three graduate programs would become nearly constant.

While it is far simpler to think of these computations as resulting in unitless numbers, we argue that they have the same properties of relative units as, for example, miles per hour (MPH) or revolutions per minute (RPM). Where MPH represents units of distance per units of time, potential is just units of resources per unit of distance. Competition can be interpreted similarly, as units of competitors per unit of distance. The net competition measure is precisely what would result from a least squares estimate net of the effects of other variables entered.

Results

In our earlier papers noted above, detailed analyses were presented on the determinants of the prestige of academic positions obtained by our sample of male biochemists. The basic results are presented in Table 1. In the first equation all scientists who obtained positions in rated graduate programs either immediately upon completion of the Ph.D. or after a period of postdoctoral study are included. The prestige of the job is regressed on the prestige and size of the graduate program, the productivity of the mentor, the selectivity of the scientist's baccalaureate degree, and the scientist's predoctoral productivity as measured by their publications and citations. There are two findings of major importance.

First, predoctoral productivity has no significant effect on the prestige of the academic position. Thus, what other analyses have shown to be the most important factor predicting future productivity has no effect on the prestige of the job obtained. This finding has held up under a variety of extensions to the basic model presented in Equations 1 and 2. It could be argued that the scientists do not have enough publications for departments to assess the new Ph.D.s' work, or that students' publications are too closely linked with work of the mentor. In analyses controlling for collaboration with the mentor and examining productivity occurring during postdoctoral fellowships, it is found that the scientist's productivity at the time of applying for a faculty position still has no effect on the prestige of the job. Because the universalistic model of science posits a strong positive relation between productivity and the prestige of a position, many regression models were considered. In no instance, however, was an effect of

Table 1 Regressions Relating Pre-employment Statuses of Biochemists to Prestige of First Position[a]

	Equation 1: All Biochemists			Equation 2: Inbred Biochemists Excluded		
	B	Beta	t	B	Beta	t
INTERCEP	130.535	—	5.364	160.742	—	5.604
PHD	0.343	0.401	4.783	0.271	0.326	3.303
ENROL	−0.463	−0.165	2.151	−0.672	−0.253	2.743
MENT	4.292	0.136	1.985	2.961	0.094	1.164
SEL	7.627	0.119	1.990	8.408	0.135	1.905
PUB	−2.741	−0.026	0.328	−5.127	−0.049	0.517
CIT	4.284	0.227	1.212	4.026	0.094	0.979
R^2−F		.240	12.175		.164	5.898
df			232			180

Note: Dependent variable is the Roose-Andersen bioscience prestige score of the first academic position. Item identifications are: PHD = Ph.D. prestige, Cartter prestige of the Ph.D. department; MENT = square root of five-year citation counts for mentor; SEL = selectivity of baccalaureate institution; PUB = publication level, square root of standardized levels of three-year publication counts ending in the first year of the first job; CIT = citation level, square roots of standardized values of citations to publications in the three-year period ending in the first year of the first job; ENRL = number of biochemistry graduate students enrolled in the doctoral department in 1961.

[a] Column Beta gives standardized regression coefficients; column B gives unstandardized regression coefficients; column t gives the t− statistics (with more than 120 degrees of freedom in the regression, critical values for a two-tailed test of significance at the .10, .05 and .01 levels are: 1.645, 1.960 and 2.576, respectively; for a one-tailed test the critical values are 1.282, 1.645 and 2.326 for significance levels .10, .05 and .01, respectively).

productivity prior to the job found to have an effect on the prestige of the job.

Second, the prestige of the Ph.D. institution positively affects prestige of employment, while the size of the Ph.D. program affects it negatively. The effect of Ph.D. prestige on job prestige may be an effect of inbred scientists, those who obtain jobs at the institutions where they obtained their degrees (Hagstrom and Hargens, 1968). Equation 2 demonstrates that excluding inbred scientists does not decrease the significance of the effect of Ph.D. prestige on job prestige. It could be argued that the effect of Ph.D. prestige is spurious, that it is simply a correlate of other more fundamental variables that have been excluded from the model. A large variety of other departmental and institutional characteristics have been examined, none of which diminished the importance of departmental prestige (although see the results on geographic and ecological factors given below). Or, departmental prestige may serve as a proxy for characteristics of the student's mentor. While Table 1 includes a single measure of the mentor's productivity, there may be additional characteristics that are important.

Long and McGinnis (1985) considered a variety of such possibilities, including rank of the mentor, awards received and interactions between having collaborated with the mentor and other characteristics of the mentor. It was found that the productivity of the mentor positively affects the prestige of the student's job, if the student collaborated with the mentor. The effects of Ph.D. prestige did not, however, diminish. The only case in which the prestige of the Ph.D. department is found to have an insignificant effect on the prestige of the job is when both prestige of the Ph.D. department and prestige of the fellowship department are included in the same regression for those who took postdoctoral fellowships. In this case, the prestige of the fellowship department replaces that of the Ph.D. department in determining the prestige of the first job. In short, it appears that the prestige of training, whether in a Ph.D. program or a postdoctoral fellowship, has the strongest effect on the prestige of the first job. The reputation of past institutional affiliations, more than characteristics of one's mentor or demonstrated productivity of the student, determines the prestige of the first job.

Three interpretations of the negative effect of size of the graduate program on the prestige of the first faculty position are possible. First, large graduate programs may reflect more lenient admissions policies and thus lower average ability of graduates. Second, large enrollments may reduce the effectiveness of graduate education. Finally, large enrollments produce large graduating cohorts and the increased competition for jobs may hurt all of the graduates of the department.

Geographic and Ecological Effects

We extended the analysis reported in Table 1 to include an investigation of the geographic location of the doctoral institution and of its centrality. We first examined whether graduates in a particular region of the country might have advantages in obtaining prestigious positions, independent of the variables included in Table 1. When longitude and latitude of the doctoral institution were added to the equations reported in Table 1, their effects were not significant (regressions not shown). As a further test of the effect of geographic location, an analysis of covariance was run allowing the effects of each independent variable to differ by region of the country and for each region to have an effect. Regions were coded in a variety of ways. The effects of region on prestige were found to be insignificant (regressions not shown). Thus, there is no evidence that geographic location has an effect on job prestige independently of measures of training and productivity.

Table 2   Extension of Regressions in Table 1 to Include Two Ecological Variables

	Equation 1: All biochemists			Equation 2: Inbred Biochemists Excluded		
	B	Beta	t	B	Beta	t
INTERCEP	132.724	–	5.390	166.895	–	7.733
PHD	0.327	0.382	4.266	0.234	0.281	2.669
ENROL	−0.403	−0.144	1.708	−0.544	−0.205	2.037
MENT	4.304	0.136	1.988	2.913	0.092	1.146
SEL	7.418	0.116	1.925	7.917	0.127	1.788
PUB	−2.565	−0.024	0.306	−5.180	−0.049	−0.523
CIT	4.245	0.098	1.200	4.036	0.094	0.982
PHDCOM2	0.627	0.041	0.620	1.467	0.236	1.190
R^2−F		.241	10.463		.171	5.269
df			231			179

Note: PHDCOM2 is the competition measure of Ph.D. institution with distance squared (see text). See Table 1 for other definitions.

The ecological measure of competition for the Ph.D. institution (PHDCOM2) was then added to the model. A scientist with a large value of PHDCOM2 would come from an institution that was close to other large insititutions, while a scientist with a small value of PHDCOM2 would be from an institution that was not close to large, competing institutions. The results are presented in Table 2, where the top rows represent the same variables as those of Table 1. It was thought that graduating from an institution with large institutions nearby (i.e., having a large value of PHDCOM2) would be an advantage in that large employers would be relatively close. If this were the case, the effect of PHDCOM2 would be positive. Indeed the effect is positive, although weak and not quite significant at the .10 level for a one-tailed test. The non-significance of the effects suggests two possibilities. First, it could be argued that having large institutions nearby hurts the scientists by providing many other

Ph.D.s from those institutions competing for the same jobs, thus offsetting the advantage of having potential employers nearby. Or second, it may be that distance does not affect the job market, and consequently there is no advantage to being close to possible jobs. This leads us to consider the extent to which geographic origin affects the geographic destination of the scientist.

While geographic location was not found to have an effect on the prestige of the job obtained, this does not mean that geographic location does not have an effect on location of the first academic job. We expected to observe geographic effects to operate primarily in career moves through the hypothesized friction of distance. If the hypothesis is correct, then effects should be observed between longitudes of origin and destination and the same should be true of latitude pairs. To consider this possibility a series of regressions was run examining how location of the baccalaureate institution affected the location of the Ph.D. institution, and how the location of the baccalaureate and Ph.D. institutions affected the location of the fellowship and/or job institutions. It was consistently found that the longitude of a prior institution significantly affected the longitude of a later institution, and prior latitudes had similar, but weaker effects on later latitudes.

Table 3 Regressions Relating Location of Job Institution to Institutions of Baccalaureate, Last Fellowship and Ph.D. for Fellows Who Were Not Inbred to Fellowship Institutions

| | Equation 1: JOBLONG | | |
	B	Beta	t
INTERCEP	0.822	–	4.961
BALONG	0.041	0.050	0.444
PHDLONG	0.240	0.293	2.582
LFLONG	0.184	0.223	2.276
R^2-F		0.190	7.018
df			90
	Equation 2: JOBLAT		
	B	Beta	t
INTERCEP	0.560	–	4.853
BALAT	−0.042	−0.371	0.298
PHDLAT	−0.023	−0.019	0.142
LFLAT	0.228	0.186	1.675
R^2-F		0.032	0.979
df			90

Note: JOBLONG, JOBLAT, BALONG, BALAT, LFLONG, LFLAT, PHDLONG and PHDLAT are the longitudes and latitudes in radians of the first academic job, the baccalaureate institution, the institution of last fellowship and the doctoral institution.

Table 3 presents two regressions that represent our findings. The regressions are based on those scientists who had postdoctoral fellowships and who did not receive their first academic jobs at the institution of their fellowship. Equation 1 shows that the longitude of both the Ph.D. institution and the fellowship institution have significant effects on the longitude of the job, with nearly 20 per cent of the variance being explained. Basically, we find that obtaining a Ph.D. and/or fellowship on the east coast significantly increases the chance of obtaining a job on the east coast; and so on for the midwest, the plains and the west coast. Much weaker effects are found for latitude, with only the latitude of the fellowship having a significant influence on the latitude of the job. Thus, while those in the east tend to remain in the east, they are more likely to move from north to south.

Our findings at this point are more suggestive than definitive. Future work will refine our measures of competition by refining measures of size, experimenting with the power to which distance is taken in computing competition, and adding other demographic and ecological variables such as size of the surrounding academic and nonacademic communities.

Results for Academic Institutions

To this point our units of analysis have been individual recipients of doctoral degrees in biochemistry. However, the results reported in Tables 2 and 3 strongly suggested to us that the prestige of an institution – and quite possibly other of its salient characteristics – are determined in part by forces of geography and/or ecology. In a regression not shown here the equations in Table 2 were extended to include the competition of the job (JOBCOM2) as a factor explaining the prestige of the job. The effect was found to be large, positive and statistically significant. However, the model is not sensible at the analytic level of the individual scientist. The ecology of destination can hardly be equated with background characteristics of individual scientists. What we seem to be seeing is a consequence of the ecology of institutions on other of their characteristics. Institutional centrality/isolation may represent a force that influences other institutional characteristics.

In the remainder of this section we illustrate some of the ways in which these forces operate. We begin, naturally enough, with an analysis of the rated prestige of the 75 departments that awarded the

Ph.D. degree to at least one of our sample and that received a rating in the Cartter report. We began with a straightforward structural analysis of the hypothesis that a department's prestige is a reflection of the volume and visibility of the faculty's research. Thus, the primary analytic variables entered were the median citations received in 1961 by the members of the faculty who served as mentors of our sample and total NIH obligations to the institution obligated in FY 1964. Ownership (public versus private) was entered because of the belief that the private research universities may be more highly regarded than the publicly-owned institutions. Finally, size of faculty was included under the hypothesis that it represented both a measure of 'critical mass' and national visibility. Results of this analysis are reported in Equation 1 of Table 4. Despite the fact that only two of the four variables entered in the equation proved to be significant, the model proved to be effective, explaining nearly half of the variance in departmental prestige.

Table 4 Regressions Relating Prestige of Biochemistry at US Doctoral Institutions to Structural, Geographic and Ecological Factors

	Equation 1: Structural Factors Only			Equation 2: Geographic and Ecological Factors Added		
	B	Beta	t	B	Beta	t
INTERCEP	182.627	0.000	6.766	−57.201	0.000	−0.592
MDNMENT	0.702	0.327	3.426	0.583	0.271	2.966
NIH64	0.010	0.548	4.566	0.008	0.470	4.038
PUBPR	3.783	0.020	0.214	12.061	0.065	0.668
FAC	0.032	0.002	0.021	−0.546	−0.042	−0.367
PHDLAT				205.005	0.171	1.993
PHDLONG				60.935	0.178	1.992
PHDPOT2				2.799	0.197	2.133
R^2−F		.491	16.895		.570	12.710
df			74			74

Note: MDMENT is median citations to publications of faculty who served as mentors of the biochemists. See preceding tables for other definitions.

The two locational variables, latitude and longitude, were then added to the model along with one ecological variable, departmental centrality with respect to departments that produce B.S. degrees in biochemistry.[6] Again we reasoned that prestige may be centered in the major institutions of the midwest and east, that the north contains more highly-regarded research departments than the south and that being toward the center of activity should promote visibility and, when coupled with high levels of research, promote departmental reputations. As can be seen in Equation 2 of Table 4, each of the three added variables made at least a marginally significant addition to the model, together increasing the per cent of explained variance by eight points. The major surprise in these results was the positive sign of the coefficient estimate for longitude, suggesting that, among bio-chemistry departments, location in the west is an asset to reputation. We interpret these results to indicate that traditional structural analyses of academic stratification may be supplemented profitably by extension to less traditional geographic and ecological investigation. Once again, we must emphasize the tentative nature of this interpreta-tion. The results, especially for latitude and longitude, are only of marginal statistical significance and the measures of ecology clearly need further refinement.

Next, we present parallel evidence concerning the size of the graduate degree programs in biochemistry. We measure program size simply by using counts of the number of earned doctorate degrees that were awarded in biochemistry during the period from 1957 to 1966 by each institution. We have added the Cartter ratings of biochemistry to the other structural variables reported in Table 4. The results are reported as Equation 1 of Table 5. Two facts emerge clearly from this model: prestige rating, public ownership (as represented by the negative sign of the coefficient) and sheer size of faculty appear to be dominant factors in determining the size of graduate programs in biochemistry. Second, and surprisingly, the level of research activity in a department, as measured by size of NIH research obligations and mentors' citations have no significant bearing on the size of graduate programs.

When we turn to Equation 2 of Table 5, however, it becomes clear that Equation 1 was badly mis-specified. When geographic and ecological measures are added, the per cent of explained variance increases by nearly 22 points and the structural measures lose their statistical significance. The geographic axes turn out to be trivial, but the ecological measures of potential and competition, both of which are entered in this case (see footnote 6), are seen to be of overwhelming importance and operating exactly as hypothesized. That is, despite the fact that the two ecological variables are positively and rather highly correlated, when entered jointly in a multivariate model, they have opposite effects on program size as hypothesized. The greater a department's centrality to the supply of eligible graduates in biochemistry, the larger the graduate program. But, net of potential, the more central a department is to competing graduate programs, the smaller the number of entering graduates it recruits.

Table 5 *Regressions Relating Size of Graduate Program in Biochemistry at US Doctoral Institutions to Structural, Geographic and Ecological Factors*

	Equation 1: Structural Factors Only			Equation 2: Geographic and Ecological Factors Added		
	B	Beta	t	B	Beta	t
INTERCEP	−2.174	0.000	−0.206	−5.623	0.000	−0.216
PHD	0.112	0.406	3.077	0.061	0.220	1.831
MDNM6	−0.060	−0.101	−0.890	−0.031	−0.052	−0.547
PUBPR	−12.282	−0.036	−0.236	−0.000	−0.038	−0.298
FAC	1.388	0.389	2.954	0.362	0.101	0.847
PHDLAT				8.303	0.025	0.292
PHDLONG				−0.354	−0.004	−0.042
PHDPOT2				4.096	1.045	5.832
PHDCOM2				−4.789	−0.927	−5.504
R^2−F		.390	8.808		.606	11.124
df			74			74

Note: Size of graduate program is measured as number of Ph.D. degrees awarded by the institution between 1957 and 1966 inclusive. See preceding tables for other definitions.

Finally, we examine the process of recruiting and maintaining a faculty. We had hoped to use the numbers of our sample of biochemists recruited to colleges as the dependent variable. The distribution, however, was unsuitable since the modal number of hires by an institution was one with a small number hiring nine or ten. Thus, we turn instead to the number of biochemists that each department employed in 1963 according to American Chemical Society counts. Equation 1 of Table 6 provides a model derived from conventional wisdom in the academic community. In it we assumed that the reputation of an academic department and the resources that it brings should have a bearing on the size of faculty that the department can recruit. We also assumed that faculty size is heavily influenced by undergraduate course loads. Here our best available indicator was the number of B.S. degrees awarded to our larger sample of biochemists. The analysis produced reasonably good results with about a quarter of the variance in faculty size being explained. Somewhat surprisingly, NIH 1964 research funds and the indicator of undergraduate enrollments failed to achieve statistical significance. Better measures of research support and undergraduate teaching load might change this result.

We were troubled about whether the process of recruiting a faculty was more like that of recruiting graduate students or that of earning a reputation – whether or not competition should be taken into account. In our ignorance, we chose the former model. We had

Table 6 Regressions Relating Size of Faculty in 1962 in Biochemistry at US Doctoral Institutions to Structural, Geographic and Ecological Factors

	Equation 1: Structural Factors Only			Equation 2: Geographic and Ecological Factors Added		
	B	Beta	t	B	Beta	t
INTERCEP	0.340	0.000	0.168	2.389	0.000	0.376
PRST	0.033	0.359	4.063	0.000	0.005	0.051
NIH64	0.000	0.154	1.796	0.001	0.503	4.772
BACTOT	0.408	0.131	1.748	−0.987	−0.463	−2.688
LAT				8.301	0.089	1.075
LONG				−1.361	−0.051	−0.635
PCOM200				−1.543	−1.066	−4.008
PPOT200				1.370	1.247	4.015
R^2−F		.237	15.974		.613	15.189
df			145			74

computed measures of potential and competition at the level of employment, but problems of severe multi-collinearity forced us to fall back on the two measures at the Ph.D. level. Since these measures are available only for the institutions that produced at least one doctoral degree among our sample, we suffered a drop in degrees of freedom available. Nonetheless, the results are interesting.

When the measures of geographic and ecological location are added, as shown in Equation 2 of Table 6, some dramatic changes from the results of Equation 1 occur. Departmental prestige loses statistical significance altogether while the two remaining variables become strongly significant. The coefficient of BACTOT, the number of undergraduate degrees awarded, is reversed. Both potential and competition are highly significant and in the hypothesized directions, although geographic location plays a trivial role. The model provides a good fit, with the proportion of variance accounted for being more than double that of Equation 1. What emerges is a picture of departments that are highly active in research, avoid heavy undergraduate activities, that are central but not too close to the competition as being the departments that successfully recruit and maintain large faculties.

Conclusions

We reached our initial conclusion more than seven years ago and can find no reason to change it whether as a result of our own subsequent investigations or those of others with which we are familiar. Stratification in science is an important force that influences not only entry into careers – in other sectors as well as academia – but also subsequent outcomes, especially productivity. Our second and more important conclusion is that as stratification appears to operate in the United States it is at best independent of and at worst quite contrary to the principle of meritocracy. To over-simplify a bit, young scientists seem to be arrayed into hierarchies either in terms of pedigree, such as the prestige of doctoral institution and the visibility of mentor, or in terms of early indicators of productivity, especially predoctoral publications and citations to them. To the extent that pedigree is a poorer predictor than early productivity of later productivity – as is decisively the case in our results – then pedigree must be equated with particularism. Since, as we have shown, the rewards of prestigious academic positions are much better correlated with measures of pedigree than of productivity we conclude that the stratification system in science is out of kilter.

We hope that our third conclusion will be of some interest to our fellow researchers in the social science of science. It is that an increased emphasis on organizations that produce science in addition to that on individual scientists, with the introduction of geographic and ecological analyses may well add to our understandig of the social system of science. Although the results presented above are extremely preliminary, we think that they are of sufficient strength to support this conclusion.

Policy Implications

Our contention that the stratification system of science fails to support the principle of meritocracy may, of course, be quite wrong. Further research is needed in several areas: to determine the best early predictors of later scientific productivity, to better establish what it is about organizations that make them conducive to high levels of output, and to understand how individuals are matched – or mismatched — with appropriate organizations. Suppose such research further supports our contention, then what? Then policies should be established that improve the match between the most promising young scientists and organizations with the richest contexts for productivity. Such policies might well involve early career awards that benefit both the research of young scientists and the organizations that employ them. We recognize that any policy designed to support merit rather than equity creates political and ethical problems. These we gladly leave to the policy-makers.

Our final conclusion, if accepted, contains an obvious implication for policy-makers in agencies that support social research which, if stated, could only appear to be self-seeking. But there is a final observation to be made. If there are strong locational effects on the careers of scientists and on the organizations that train or employ them, as our evidence suggests, the fact can be of little interest to academic or science policy-makers. Location simply cannot be changed by acts of policy. There is a question, however, answers to which could be of intense interest: if centrality does indeed give an edge of advantage to individuals or organizations, what are the components that make it so? If it turns out that the advantages of Boston or Cambridge as against Tuscaloosa are merely those of prestige and extra-career delights, then little is to be done. If, however, it turns out that the advantages of centrality are made up of opportunities that can be passed on to those in more isolated locales, then the fact should be considered seriously by policy-makers. Suppose, for example, that the opportunities for intense face-to-face communication among those doing similar research proves to be an important component giving centrality its advantage. Then much could be done to provide possibly effective substitutes, such as improved electronic communication including video-networked seminars and workshops.[7] What we are suggesting is, in effect, a program of research that focuses on the friction of distance and how to eliminate it, that examines the exponent of distance in our potential and competition models and isolates the conditions by which it might be made to approach zero.

Notes

1. See Long and McGinnis (1985) for considerations of collaboration with the mentor in predoctoral productivity.
2. Throughout the remainder of this paper we will refer to scientists as males, since our results are based on a study of male scientists. A study comparing the careers of male and female scientists is currently being conducted by the junior author.
3. For a thorough discussion of organizational ecology, see Hannan and Freeman (1977) and Hannan (1986).
4. Others have shown that their gender difference is also extremely important in this regard. See Reskin (1976) and Rosenfeld and Jones (1985).

5. Latitude and longitude were coded in degrees, minutes and seconds. The measures were converted to radians and movement distances were calculated from the formula $D(P1,P2) = K \star \arcsin(((1-A)/2) \star \star .5)$, where $D(P1,P2) =$ distance between points P1 at location [lat1, long1] and P2 at [lat2, long2] on a sphere; $K =$ diameter of the sphere (7900 miles for the earth); and, $A = \cos(long1-long2) \star \cos(lat1) \star \cos(lat2) + \sin(lat1) \star \sin(lat2)$.
6. We did not enter PCOM2 in this equation because we would not be able to interpret how the two centrality measures would operate differentially in influencing the rated prestige of a graduate program. Unlike competition for limited resources, the establishment of a reputation does not appear to represent a zero-sum game.
7. We note in this regard that this paper was written by two co-authors who were separated by about 2000 miles. Despite the distance, the paper was the result of frequent and intense interaction between the authors by means of an international network that links the two computers on which we work.

References

Astin, A.W. (1971) *Predicting Academic Performance in College*, New York: The Free Press.

Caplow, T. and McGee, R. (1958) *The Academic Marketplace*, Garden City: Doubleday.

Cartter, A.M. (1966) *An Assessment of Quality in Graduate Education*, Washington: American Council on Education.

Hagstrom, W.O. and Lowell L. (1968) *Mobility theory in the sociology of science*, paper presented at the Cornell Conference on Human Mobility, Ithaca, NY, October 31, 1968.

Hammond, R. and McCullagh, P. (1970) *Quantitative Techniques in Geography*, Oxford: Clarendon Press.

Hannan, M.T. (1986) *A Model of Competitive and Institutional Processes in Organizational Ecology*, Technical Report 86-13, Dept. of Sociology, Cornell University.

Hannan, M.T. and Freeman, J.H. (1979) 'The Population Ecology of Organizations', *American Journal of Sociology*: 82, 929–964.

Hargens, L.L. (1969) 'Patterns of mobility of new Ph.D.s among American academic institutions', *Sociology of Education* 42: 247–256.

Ladinsky, J. (1967) 'Sources of geographic mobility among professional workers: A multivariate analysis', *Demography* 4: 293–309.

Lichter, D.T. (1982) 'The migration of dual-worker families: Does the wife's job matter?', *Social Science Quarterly* 63: 48–57.

Long, J.S. (1978) 'Productivity and academic position in the scientific career', *American Sociological Review* 43: 889–908.

Long, J.S. and McGinnis, R. (1981) 'Organizational context and scientific productivity', *American Sociological Review* 1981, Vol. 46 (August: 422–442).

Long, J.S. and McGinnis, R. (1985) 'Effects of the mentor on the academic career', *Scientometrics*, Vol. 7, Nos. 3–6, pg 255–280.

Long, J.S. Allison, P.D. and McGinnis, R. (1979) 'Entrance into the academic career', reprinted from *American Sociological Review*, Vol. 44, No. 5, Oct 1979.

McGinnis, R., Allison, P.D. and Long, J.S. (1982) 'Postdoctoral training in bioscience: Allocation and outcomes', *Social Forces*, Vol. 60: No. 3 March.

Merton, R.K. (1968) 'The Matthew effect in science', *Science* 159 (No. 3810): 56–63. Reprinted in *The Sociology of Science*, Ch. 20, pp. 439–459.

Merton, R.K. [1942] (1973) 'Science and technology in a democratic order', *Journal of Legal and Political Sociology* 1: 115–126. Reprinted in *The Sociology of Science*, Ch. 13, pp. 267–278.

Price, D.K. (1965) *The Scientific Estate*, Cambridge: Belknap.

Reskin, B.F. (1976) 'Sex and status attainment in science', *American Sociological Review* 41: 597–612.

Reskin, B.F. (1977) 'Scientific productivity and the reward structure of science', *American Sociological Review* 42: 491–504.

Roose, K.D. and Andersen, C.J. (1970) *A Rating of Graduate Programs*, Washington: American Council on Education.

Rosenfeld, R.A. and Jones, J.A. (1985) 'Patterns and effects of geographic mobility for academic women and men', *Journal of Higher Education*, Vol. 58, No. 5, 493–515.

Stouffer, S.A. (1960) 'Intervening Opportunities and Competing Migrants', *Journal of Regional Science*, Vol. 2, No. 1, Spring 1960, pp. 1–26.

Zuckerman, H. (1970) 'Stratification in American science', pp. 235–257 in Laumann, E.O. (Ed.), *Social Stratification*, Indianapolis: Bobbs-Merrill.

Charting the Changes in Junior Faculty

Relationships among Socialization, Acculturation, and Gender

> I think just the sheer amount of pressure that is indigenous to being an assistant professor at a good school, you are going to change. You're going to have to change, or you're gonna leave, before you get fired or promoted. (Jeff)

As Jeff indicates, the beginning years in the academic environment are a time of change. But not all junior faculty go through the same kinds of changes. In this article I use case studies to illustrate some of the changes junior faculty experience as they interact with their departments and institution in the years prior to the tenure decision. The cases of Greta and Jeff illustrate how professors learn to adjust to a new department when their views of social interdependence closely resemble those of the existing departmental culture. The cases of Nancy, Steve, and Cathy demonstrate how beginning professors cope in an environment where their views of social interdependence differ from that of the existing culture. The article concludes with a discussion of the relationships among socialization, acculturation, and gender.

Theoretical Underpinnings

Although socialization and acculturation are often used interchangeably, they are theoretically distinct constructs. Socialization, or enculturation as it is commonly referred to in anthropology [22], refers to the process by which an individual acquires the norms, values, and behaviors of the group [10, 23, 24, 32]. In other words, socialization is the de-

Anne Reynolds is a research scientist at Educational Testing Service in Princeton, N.J.

Journal of Higher Education, Vol. 63, No. 6 (November/December 1992)

velopment of an initial world view. World view comprises seven logically and structurally integrated cognitive categories — self, other, relationship of self to other, time, space, causality, and classification [27] — as well as the ethos of a people, the "tone, character, and quality of their life, its moral and aesthetic style and mood . . . the underlying attitude toward themselves and their world that life reflects" [16, pp. 126–27]. Once initial socialization takes place, as in the rearing of a child, succeeding socialization experiences assume a *congruence* between the individual's world view and that of the new group. Acculturation, in contrast, is a process that assumes initial *differences* in world view between the individual and the group. Originally, acculturation was seen as a process of forced assimilation of a cultural world view [36]. Now it encompasses the strategies used by individuals who must cope with minority status in a new culture [37].

To understand the socialization and acculturation processes, we have to analyze the newcomer's experiences with others in the culture [24]. This means making sense of the individual's views in three of the world view categories: self, other, and relationship to other. The combination of these three categories is what I call "social interdependence" in this article. Unfortunately, there is a paucity of empirical research on the socialization and/or acculturation experiences of beginning professors from their own vantage points. We must turn to findings from studies in four major areas to gather pieces of the puzzle. The four areas of literature are: problems beginning professors face [29, 30, 33]; faculty career development [1, 2, 7, 14]; women in academia [6, 9, 25, 35]; and socialization outside of academia [3, 5, 13, 21].

From these studies we see that: (1) Junior faculty may find the new culture difficult to understand due to different norms, expectations, and practices; (2) They often feel unprepared for the various roles they must play (teacher, colleague, lone academic); (3) They are passing through a critical period for learning the job and forming attitudes about it, most notably, commitment to the academic way of life; (4) They may move from liberal, idealistic perspectives to more conventional, bureaucratic ones; (5) They are strongly influenced by significant others (peers, superiors) and highly regard their feedback and expectations; and (6) Women and men may experience different things during the early years, such as others' expectations concerning how they should allocate time to work and family life.

In light of current theories regarding socialization and acculturation, this last finding about gendered experiences is intriguing. If women and men have different experiences during their early years, is it due to gendered differences in world view, especially in views of social interdependence? If so, can we assume that all junior faculty go through a process of socialization [9, 11]? Or do some beginning professors, especially women [25], experience acculturation? Such questions lead to an examination of the literature on the development of gendered views of social interdependence.

Males and females go through early "genderization" that encourages their views of social interdependence to be more cooperative, competitive, or individualistic, or some combination of the three [8, 15, 17, 34]. Competitive social interdependence means that individuals are linked to others in a way that as one succeeds, the other fails [26]. Individualism signifies no interdependence; one works alone to attain predesignated criteria of success [26]. In such an environment, the "Separate Self" experiences relationships in terms of fairness and reciprocity between separate individuals and grounds itself in roles that are based on obligations and duties [17, 28]. Cooperation is characterized by positive interdependence, where individuals are connected with others in a way that one cannot succeed without the other [26]. The "Connected Self" experiences relationships as a response to others in their terms and maintains caring and connection with others [17, 28]. This cooperative, connected way of interacting with others is frequently posited as the hallmark of women's ways of knowing [4, 17, 28].

The incompatibility between women's ostensible cooperative view of social interdependence and the more competitive and individualistic views found in research-oriented faculty cultures [7, 14] prompted me to design a study in which I could examine more closely the changes junior faculty experienced. I turned a special eye toward possible gender differences in views of social interdependence that might result in acculturation rather than socialization. Specifically, I wanted to know:

1. Do women and men interpret differently their experiences as beginning faculty in a research university? If so, in what ways?
2. Do these interpretations reflect gender differences in views of social interdependence?
3. What happens to these views over time?

In the remainder of the article I describe this qualitative study of junior faculty, and then, in five case studies, I illustrate the differences I uncovered between and among the socialization and acculturation experiences. The case studies are not means to represent *all* possible experiences junior faculty may have; rather, they are offered as frames through which to view possible differences between socialization and acculturation.

Methodology

Despite a seemingly shared culture, humans give different meanings to actions that, on the surface, look identical. Therefore, to understand causal links among actions, we must uncover the meanings individuals give to their actions. This uncovering is the aim of interpretive research [12]. The research reported in this article is an interpretive study of the meanings junior faculty give to their experiences; thus, it utilizes qualitative data collection and analysis methods.

Nineteen faculty members formed the nucleus of the study. These key informants were criterion-base selected according to willingness to participate and representativeness of three areas of possible comparison/contrast in world view: gender (9 women, 10 men), status (11 pre-tenure, 8 tenured), and discipline (7 natural sciences, 8 social sciences, 4 humanities). Eight of the informants (3 men, 5 women) were married, and seven (5 men, 2 women) had children. Age-wise, three men were in their early 50s to mid-60s; the other informants split evenly above and below the mid-30s (3 men/5 women and 4 men/4 women, respectively). All but one informant grew up in the United States: six (2 men, 4 women) were raised in the Midwest; six (4 men, 2 women) were raised in the East; one woman was raised in the South; and five (3 men, 2 women) were raised in the West. One male informant was raised outside of the United States. All had attended well-respected schools, such as Harvard and Berkeley, for their undergraduate work and top research universities, such as Stanford and MIT, for their graduate work. All but seven informants began their academic careers at the West Coast research-oriented university where my research took place. Of those who started elsewhere, only one came to the present university after more than five years at other schools.

Over the course of a year, I collected data through four semi-structured, tape-recorded interviews with each informant. The interviews were designed to elicit information about the informants' experiences as beginning professors, their feelings about life in the academy, their underlying values, and their professional duties as academics. I transcribed all of the interviews verbatim and returned them to the informants for any deletions, additions, or "off-the-record" comments. Informal conversations and observations of other faculty at faculty gatherings, such as an American Association of University Professors session on tenure, supplemented the interviews. Participant observation at talks given by faculty members and written documents and records from individuals and university archives, such as curricula vitae, job offer letters, and letters from professional associates rounded out the data collection efforts.

The conceptual framework I developed to structure both data collection and analysis was based on work by Kearney [27] and Geertz [16]. I coupled Kearney's world view universals, which define world view in cognitive terms, with Geertz's definition of world view, which focuses more on the individual's emotional interpretation of the world. The resulting framework comprised seven categories: *Self* refers to the perceptions and expectations junior faculty had of and for themselves prior to becoming professors and into their first years in the university. *Other* consists of the perceptions and expectations informants had of and for other people (colleagues, students, staff, and so on) and their subject matter as they began their careers in academia. *Relationship of Self to Other* refers to the perceptions and expectations informants thought others had of and for them during their early years as professors. *Time* refers to informants' ideas about where their "year" began and ended, and what they considered "free" time and what was "work" time, how they spent their time in their professional lives (and personal lives where there was overlap or conflict with their professional lives), and so forth. *Causality* refers to the professors' sense of agency, that is, when did they see themselves as acting and when as being acted upon? *Classification* refers to the meanings professors gave to terms that describe and divide the academic world (for example, "good" versus "poor" scholarship, teacher/researcher). Conceptions of *Space* were reflected in the ways professors talked about and divided up their material world (for example, offices, labs) and their social world (for example, who were colleagues, who were not). Four other conceptual categories emerged during the data analysis: problems during the early years of a professorship, career influences, stories, and passages significant for a methodological appendix [38]. I used this conceptual framework to analyze the data inductively through qualitative methods, such as memoing and narrative text displays [31], the constant comparative method [18], and simple descriptive statistics.

For purposes of this discussion of junior faculty socialization and acculturation, I concentrate on three of the world view categories: "self," "other," and "relationship of self to other." These categories illuminate junior faculty perceptions about themselves in their interactions with others within the new social setting. I use the words "social interdependence" as a shorthand for these three categories in the remainder of the article.

Changes during the Early Years of the Professorship

Though all informants in the study spoke of changes in themselves during their years in the institution, the five case studies that follow demonstrate the contrast between socialization and acculturation. Jeff's and

371

Greta's cases are interwoven to show the similarities between the sexes when both undergo a socialization experience. Nancy, Steve, and Cathy experienced acculturation; their cases represent three different acculturative strategies described by Spindler [37]. Nancy's case illustrates a cultural synthesis of conflicting cultural elements. Steve's case protrays a managed identity. And Cathy's case depicts a reaffirmation of traditional values and behavior patterns. Throughout each of the case studies, I focus on the individual's view of social interdependence and how it changed during the experiences of the early years.

Jeff and Greta: Learning the Ropes through Socialization

The first years in the university were difficult for Jeff and Greta. The scientific side of work went well, but Jeff and Greta had problems interacting with students and other faculty members. As Jeff related, "It's no longer you against the scientific problem anymore. It's no longer that. It's *you* and graduate students, *you* and fellow assistant professors, fellow associate professors, senior faculty, post docs, *you* and bureaucrats, *you* and other people, *you* and contract officers, *you* and granting agencies, *you* and reviewers — I mean, it's just wild — It's hard —not because of the science — if it was just that, I'd just skate right through it. It's hard because it's demanding in a number of other areas that are close to my Achilles heel." To Jeff, the department was a "fiefdom system" where there was "no collegiality" and "no shared interest." He found it hard to talk science with his colleagues because of the constant need to speak in a politically acceptable way. He summed up his feelings in this way: "I do not have a single senior colleague in this department that I trust at the level of being able to talk to. Not one."

Interactions with junior colleagues were much better, but still there was a self-imposed barrier between them. Jeff commented:

> Everybody's kinda living with that thing that some of us are going to make it, some of us aren't; none of us really know . . . who is and who isn't. So you try to be cooperative and help out one another as best you can, but there's a desire to maintain some distance on my part. I don't want to emotionally have to deal with that person's failure or that person's success. . . . You see, if they change when they're promoted, you don't know what they're going to do relative to what you've been open with them about. Essentially, I don't trust anybody in this department, and that is a statement not so much of paranoia as it is a practical way of operating.

While Jeff wanted to sequester himself in his laboratory to do science "at the bench," Greta sought interaction with other people and took on "more administrative duties than anybody had a right to expect," such as being the chairwoman of the graduate committee during her second year. She was vocal about getting students graduated and about professors pulling their weight in terms of advising students. She sent vitriolic memos to colleagues about these two issues, which angered students and a few faculty members. As Greta said, "I alienated a few faculty members when I called a spade a spade about a lot of their students, and just the way they were supervising their students." Greta also took on more graduate students than she could effectively handle, and her style of advising, modeled after her graduate advisor's directive style, antagonized them. Greta spoke of her experience this way: "What I didn't realize, and this was my big mistake, was that there are certain things you can pull off as a 6'5" sixty-year-old male that you can't pull off as a female that's only a few years older than most of the graduate students. That was really what I didn't understand, and that really was the source of all the problem. It was because there was a lot of resentment."

Over time, Greta learned that memos with negative comments about students and faculty only ostracized her from the very people with whom she had to interact. She also learned that diplomacy and tact, as they were defined by the departmental culture, were less alienating than her forthright style. She said, "These are all things that I think that I would back off from now, and I would have never done the way I did. I just would have been a little more diplomatic, a little more tactful. I think that if somebody had advised me, they might have suggested ways that I could have accomplished most of the same things but not with so much alienation of people." Unfortunately, Greta felt her colleagues left her to "sink or swim," though she remembered that one male colleague was instrumental in helping her through her early years.

The changes Greta and Jeff saw themselves going through centered mainly around becoming more politically wise. As Jeff said:

> When I came here, I had no political adroitness. Now I have pretty good savvy. I'm not nearly as good as I should be. I don't kiss as much ass as I ought to, and I don't pay homage to people's neuroses and paranoias as well as I should. But I'm significantly better than I was. I don't get as upset anymore. I don't know if I'm successful or not. There are some people that think I'm successful, and they welcome my opinions and I'd like to give them my opinions, but I have to stay in the position where I'll be able to give them my opinions, so — you either bend or you break, and if there's anything to this game, the amount you bend boggles the mind, and you cannot afford to be particularly bothered by it.

And Greta recalled, "I did change my behavior in the last year before tenure, in the sense that I kept my mouth shut a few times because I didn't want to antagonize people who I knew I'd already antagonized, and I thought I'd better back off." At the end of our talks, Greta had become the second woman in the department to be tenured and promoted to associate professor; Jeff was nearing tenure review.

The bending and breaking Jeff and Greta experienced are characteristic of both socialization and acculturation. However, in these cases, it is the socialization process that is at work. Jeff's and Greta's competitive and individualistic views of social interdependence were quite similar to what they believed their respective departmental cultures to be like, but the greatest difference between their views and that of their colleagues was brutal honesty with their students. Even though Greta interpreted her students' and colleagues' discontent to mean that her style was not appropriate for a young recently appointed woman professor, this style of interaction was also frowned upon by Jeff's colleagues. To reflect the expectations of their colleagues and students, both Greta and Jeff changed their behavior. However, as Greta's next comment suggests, in her case this behavioral change was largely a political move. She mused, "I think I'm probably more relaxed in terms of my interactions with my colleagues because of the tenure business being over. I'm much more willing to say what I think. Not that I've been all that shy about it, but it just makes things — it used to be that I could never stop myself from saying things, in fact, that was one of my big regrets. Then I did it, and I know it was wrong. Now I do it, and I don't care! That's the big difference." Given Jeff's pre-tenure position, he continued to bow to what he perceived to be departmental expectations, but it is likely that with tenure his comments would mirror Greta's.

Steve, Nancy, and Cathy: Coping through Acculturation

Before their dissertations were finished, Nancy, Steve, and Cathy took academic positions. Cathy moved directly into the university where she now works, and Nancy and Steve moved to teaching-oriented institutions. Nancy welcomed the opportunity to return to an environment similar to her undergraduate institution. She thoroughly enjoyed the work and, until she received an offer to apply for her current position, considered remaining there for the rest of her life. Steve took a job in another state due to financial straits at the university, which precluded fourth-year graduate support. The lack of time for research and writing, the heavy course load, and the unambitious students dissatisfied Steve. Within two years, both Steve and Nancy had received offers to work at their current university.

While Steve eagerly anticipated time to do research in this new position, both Cathy and Nancy felt ambivalent about working in a prestigious university. Cathy wanted to see if she would enjoy the rigorous academic environment where she could do research without a large teaching load. Yet, at the same time, she wondered if she were really committed to such a lifestyle: "I had a very 'look and see' attitude about academic work at this place. And maybe that's significant in terms of the ambivalence I've had of sort of committing myself to the long work hours one has to do. The free time commitment of an academic is sort of assumed." Nancy also had mixed emotions about leaving her teaching-oriented college: "I think I was and continue to be very ambivalent about whether what I want is a small college and community and interactions with undergraduates — that whole thing, or whether what I really want is the research and the prestige and to be part of the action."

Like Jeff and Greta, Cathy, Steve, and Nancy experienced an intensive workload during their first years. Instead of spending most of their time just doing research, they were swamped with teaching and advising responsibilities for both undergraduate and graduate students and from people outside the university for talks and interviews about their work. Other faculty members expected Nancy, Steve, and Cathy to participate on departmental committees, as well as to continue to be top-notch researchers. The intense workload was especially difficult on Steve and Cathy, who had small children at home. Steve shared primary childcare responsibilities with his wife and felt pulls from two directions. He remarked, "And it's torture for me to go home and have dinner and say I'm gonna put in a couple more hours. I can't do that now because when I go home, I'm a family person." Shadowing all of Steve, Cathy, and Nancy's activities was the question of how everything either led to or away from a favorable tenure decision.

All three beginning professors found the intellectual stimulation at the university satisfying, but they bemoaned the lack of substantive interaction with their colleagues. As Nancy lamented, "People don't seem to talk very much about their research to each other, which I find sort of odd. Everything's very formalized. One doesn't know what people in the department are doing most of the time. . . . I found that very difficult last year. It made me extremely unhappy, because this is a place where you could sit in your office for weeks, literally, and no one would ever come by for any reason. . . . " Steve, too, had little substantive interaction with his colleagues beyond department meetings. In his first three years, no one shared papers they'd written, and no one asked to read papers Steve had written. A few colleagues talked to him about what he would need for tenure, though the advice wasn't always wise, for example, "write a textbook," which Steve knew to be lethal. In Steve's third year, two new assistant professors joined the department, and Steve felt happier. He finally had "someone to be an assistant professor with." Also Steve moved his office closer to his doctoral students, which gave him more interaction with them and with his assistant professor colleagues. Cathy thought of her co-workers as colleagues, but she complained that "collegiality is not high, and it's not high because people don't have or don't take time to practice their colleagueship. Even the collaborative research model here tends to be a collection more than a collaboration — a collection of researchers where one meets together to share research, but not to be collaborative."

Over time, Steve, Cathy, and Nancy felt themselves changing as a result of interactions with the institution. Steve's change was slight. As he said, "I'm comfortable with who I was before I got here, or uncomfortable. I'm still me." Yet he did see some changes, such as going from feeling like an imposter (that is, someone whose word was given legitimacy because he was at the elite university and not at the local community college) to someone who was truly part of the university faculty. A second change was Steve's perception of the "big names" at the university — people who had written texts Steve had used — which changed from awe to distanced respect as Steve grew to see himself as an intellectual equal. A third change was in learning to say no to requests from others, in order to do the things that were important for tenure, such as publishing.

The changes Nancy saw herself going through were more dramatic. She lowered her expectations for interactions with her colleagues: "And what I find is that my norms have changed so that I no longer, if I walk by somebody's office and their door's open, it no longer occurs to me to stop and say hello. We have a new faculty member across the hall, and I used to think, how could somebody possibly be just a few steps away and not be constantly going [over there] — and now it never occurs to me to go over there and say hello. . . . So, clearly my behavior and my sense of what you do has changed a lot in the last year." To counterbalance this tendency towards isolation, Nancy tried to initiate contact with her colleagues by asking them to read her work and by participating in a lunchtime discussion group. She even vented her frustrations at faculty meetings, but found that "people who had been here for awhile didn't really understand your complaints. It was total noncomprehension. You'd say, 'People never talk to each other.' And they'd say, 'What do you mean, we have these seminars once a month.' They didn't understand that what I was talking about was informal interaction, or they believed that informal interaction was impossible because people were so busy. It was very hard for us who were new to talk to the people who were old about this thing because we were clearly thinking in different ways about it." Despite her attempts to change the cultural norms, Nancy felt herself becoming more and more like the typical colleague in the department. She remembered, "I kept thinking, I don't want to become like them, but it's become more clear to me that I've become much more like them. It's a lot easier for me, because it doesn't make me so unhappy because I'm used to it now." Nancy thought optimistically about the changes in herself and explained, "I think it's mostly a matter of sort of realizing that there are trade-offs and finding ways to deal with them. I mean, I guess finding ways to deal with them, coming to terms with them — those changes are for the good even if the world isn't always the way I'd like it to be."

Cathy also saw changes in herself. As tenure drew near, Cathy realized that she did not belong in this type of university. She stated, "It was more the second and third years that I began to really worry about my productivity and certainly the conflict I felt right away between what I enjoyed in my job, which was working with students and also participating in intellectually stimulating things, and doing my own private work." Though she *could* meet the publication standards, Cathy was unwilling to put in the time and effort needed. Her expectations for herself as far as publications went were different from those of the institution and her colleagues: "I decided that I would do my job the way it was comfortable for me. . . . For me, if I do one good paper a year I'm perfectly satisfied with that. I don't see why that isn't sufficient. I mean, it is sufficient for me. It's just not for [this university]. [I] recognized that it was a misfit for me to be in a high pressure research-oriented university." Other factors were involved in Cathy's decision to leave, such as the desire to spend more time with her new husband and child and the desire not to ask her colleagues to vote on her tenure when she thought her work was not up to their standards. But Cathy's decision was largely based on the disparity between her own expectations for herself and those the university culture had for her.

After a sabbatical year away from the campus, Cathy announced her resignation. She continued to perform her duties as an assistant professor, but she investigated other job possibilities for a full-time research position outside of academia. When her resignation became effective, she took on a new administrative position in the university.

In each of these cases, a different acculturative strategy was used to cope with the new culture. While Nancy's view of social interdependence accentuated cooperation and interaction among people, she believed her department prized individualism. Nancy was forced to find a way to minimize her discomfort in the environment: she began to view the departmental interaction patterns as normal and to interact with others in an individualistic manner. She did not like interacting this way, but she wanted to fit into the culture, so she changed her behavior. Yet she didn't totally give up the behavior she was comfortable with. She found ways to remain in contact with other colleagues, for instance, during lunchtime meetings. In sum, Nancy coped with the discordant elements of her immediate culture by adopting some new behaviors while retaining the old. In acculturative strategy terms, Nancy's case depicts a cultural synthesis of conflicting cultural elements [37] .

Steve's case offers a view of a managed identity [37]. He wanted the opportunity to research, write and teach in a cooperative environment. To some extent, he found this opportunity in his department. The departmental culture valued individualism with some collegial interaction. Yet, Steve also wanted to provide primary childcare to his two small children. This was not part of the work culture. In fact, Steve thought that the departmental expectations for a junior faculty member made outside activities almost impossible. Thus, Steve was forced to cope by being two people: the industrious beginning professor at work and the committed family member at home. The strain of such a double-identity was hard on him, and Steve thought seriously about leaving the culture for one in which he would be less stressed.

Though Cathy's view was in some ways similar to what she believed the departmental culture to be like, a very important aspect was quite different. As in Steve's case, this was the expectation that junior colleagues would be devoted to the academic values, norms, and behaviors as they existed. Cathy couldn't accept the standards, so she chose to leave the culture for one that was more compatible with her own view. In this choice, Cathy demonstrated the acculturative strategy of a reaffirmation of traditional values and behavior patterns.

Relationships among Gender, Socialiation, and Acculturation

As the case studies in this article suggest, the changes junior faculty go through are not all the same. What appears to govern the changes that the individual experiences is the view of social interdependence with which the newcomer enters and the interaction of that view with the newcomer's perception of the view held by members of his or her department. If a beginning professor enters the department with a view of social interdependence that is different from what he or she perceives to be the department's view, for example, a view that is more cooperative than competitive or individualistic, then it's likely that the professor will undergo acculturation rather than socialization. We saw this in the case of Nancy. Or the professor may contemplate or actually leave the university in order not to change, as the cases of Steve and Cathy illustrate. On the other hand, if a professor enters the department with a view of social interdependence that is similar to what he or she believes is the existing departmental view, then it's likely that the professor will go through socialization. Jeff and Greta are cases in point.

The cases also suggest that it is not the sex of the assistant professor that is the major influence on the changes she or he will go through during the early years in the professorship. Nevertheless, the sex of the beginning professor may play a role in shaping the newcomer's experiences. In light of current descriptions of research faculty culture, it is not surprising to find women's experiences in the research university (or any competitive, individualistic culture, for that matter) reflective of acculturation more often than socialization. The reverse may hold for men's experiences. However, it is important to stress that even though genderization influences how one views social interdependence, both males and females can undergo either socialization or acculturation.

By itself, a discussion of whether junior faculty members undergo socialization or acculturation is pedantic. More important is the effect such changes have on the individual's research and teaching and, by extension, on society. Faculty members in universities construct knowledge through their research efforts. This knowledge is legitimized by members of similar thought collectives. The knowledge is then disseminated to the public via teaching, writing, and oral presentations. Given this situation, it seems critical to ask whether or not the acculturation process is encouraging a homogenized way of knowing and of sharing knowledge with others. Research by Gumport [19, 20] suggests that some individuals are able to resist the acculturative forces and find ways to maintain views of social interdependence that do not coincide with the dominant one while remaining in the institution. Such findings are encouraging, yet they do not diminish the importance of asking questions that challenge the status quo: should we not be concerned about the prevalence in research universities of individualistic and competitive views of social interdependence? About the exodus of people with divergent views from these universities? About the changes we see junior faculty undergoing — changes from cooperative views of social interdependence to those of individualism and competition? What kind of an effect do individualistic and competitive views of social interdependence have on the knowledge that is produced? On the methods used to disseminate that knowledge? On student learning?

As Jeff commented at the beginning of the paper, the junior faculty years are fraught with great change. It is important for us to examine critically the nature of these changes and their impact on the academy, for as Nancy explains, "I think coming here . . . wasn't just a change of jobs. It was a real choice of values, and I think it is likely to affect what I am as a human being, and part of my ambivalence about coming here is because I think the environment you put yourself in does affect the kind of person you become. I think I will become — I probably aready am — a different person than I would have been had I stayed at [my former college]."

References

1. Baldwin, R. "Adult and Career Development: What Are the Implications for Faculty?" *Current Issues in Higher Education,* 2 (1979), 13–20.

2. Baldwin, R. G., and R. T. Blackburn. "The Academic Career as a Developmental Process: Implications for Higher Education." *Journal of Higher Education,* 52 (November/December 1981), 598–614.

3. Becker, H. S., et al. *Boys in White. Student Culture in Medical School.* Chicago: The University of Chicago Press, 1961.

4. Belenky, M. F., et al. *Women's Ways of Knowing. The Development of Self, Voice, and Mind.* New York: Basic Books, Inc., 1987.

5. Berlew, D. E., and D. T. Hall. "The Socialization of Managers: Effects of Expectations on Performance." *Administrative Science Quarterly,* 11 (September 1966), 207–23.

6. Bernard, J. *Academic Women.* University Park: Pennsylvania State University Press, 1964.

7. Brown, J. W., and R. C. Shukraft. "Personal Development and Professional Practice in College and University Professors." Ph.D. dissertation, University of California — Berkeley Graduate Theological Union, 1974.

8. Chodorow, N. "Feminism and Difference: Gender Relation and Difference in Psychoanalytic Perspective." *Socialist Review,* 46 (1979), 42–64.

9. Clark, S. M., and M. Corcoran. "Perspectives on the Professional Socialization of Women Faculty: A Case of Accumulative Disadvantage?" *Journal of Higher Education,* 57 (January/February 1986), 20–43.

10. Clausen, J. A. "Introduction." In *Socialization and Society,* edited by J. A. Clausen, pp. 1–17. Boston: Little, Brown, 1968.

11. Connolly, J. J. "Viewing Faculty Orientation as a Socialization Process." ERIC 031 226, 1969.

12. Erickson, F. "Qualitative Methods in Research on Teaching." In *Handbook of Research on Teaching, Third Edition,* edited by M. C. Wittrock, pp. 119–61. New York: Macmillan Publishing Company, 1986.

13. Erlanger, H. S., and D. A. Klegon. *Socialization Effects of Professional School: The Law School Experience and Student Orientation to Public Interest Concerns.* Discussion Paper No. 434-77. Madison: University of Wisconsin, Institute for Research on Poverty, 1977.

14. Freedman, M. B., and J. W. Brown. *Academic Culture and Faculty Development.* Berkeley, Calif.: Montaigne, Inc., 1979.

15. Gardiner, J. K. "Self Psychology as Feminist Theory." *Signs: Journal of Women in Culture and Society,* 12 (Summer 1987), 761–80.

16. Geertz, C. *The Interpretation of Cultures.* New York: Basic Books, Inc., 1973.

17. Gilligan, C. *In a Different Voice.* Cambridge, Mass.: Harvard University Press, 1982.

18. Glaser, B. G. "The Constant Comparative Method of Qualitative Analysis." In *Issues in Participant Observation: A Text and Reader,* edited by G. J. McCall and J. L. Simmons, pp. 216–27. Reading, Mass.: Addison-Wesley Publishing Company, 1969.

19. Gumport, P. "The Social Construction of Knowledge: Individual and Institutional Commitments to Feminist Scholarship." Ph.D. dissertation, Stanford University, 1987.

20. ———. "Curricula as Signposts of Cultural Change." *Review of Higher Education,* 12 (Fall 1988), 49–62.

21. Hall, D. T., and B. Schneider. *Organizational Climates and Careers. The Work Lives of Priests.* New York: Seminar Press, 1973.

22. Herskovits, M. J. *Man and His Works.* New York: Alfred A. Knopf, 1948.

23. Homans, G. C. *The Human Group.* New York: Harcourt, Brace & World, 1950.

24. Hurrelmann, K. *Social Structure and Personality Development.* New York: Cambridge University Press, 1988.

25. Jensen, K. "Women's Work and Academic Culture: Adaptations and Confrontations." *Higher Education,* 11 (January 1982), 67–83.

26. Johnson, D. W., and R. T. Johnson. *Cooperation and Competition. Theory and Research.* Edina, Minn.: Interaction Book Company, 1989.

27. Kearney, M. *World View.* Novato, Calif.: Chandler & Sharp, Publisher, 1984.

28. Lyons, N. P. "Two Perspectives: On Self, Relationships, and Morality." *Harvard Educational Review,* 53 (May 1983), 125–45.

29. Mager, G. M., and B. Myers. "If First Impressions Count: New Professors' Insights and Problems." *Peabody Journal of Education,* 59 (January 1982), 100–106.

30. ———. "Developing a Career in the Academy: New Professors in Education." ERIC 236 127. Portland, Oreg.: Portland State University, 1983.

31. Miles, M. B., and A. M. Huberman. *Qualitative Data Analysis. A Sourcebook of New Methods.* Beverly Hills, Calif.: Sage Publications, 1984.

32. Mortimer, J. T., and R. G. Simmons. "Adult Socialization." In *Annual Review of Sociology,* edited by R. H. Turner, J. Coleman, and R. C. Fox, pp. 421–54. Palo Alto, Calif.: Annual Reviews, 1978.

33. Reynolds, A. "Making and Giving the Grade: Experiences of Beginning Professors at a Research University." Paper presented to the American Educational Research Association, New Orleans, La., 1988.

34. Rossi, A. S. "The Biosocial Side of Parenting." *Human Nature,* 1 (June 1978), 72–79.

35. Simeone, A. *Academic Women. Working Towards Equality.* South Hadley, Mass.: Bergin & Garvey Publishers, 1987.

36. Spicer, E. H. "Acculturation." In *International Encyclopedia of the Social Sciences. Volume 1,* edited by D. L. Sills, pp. 21–27. U.S.: Crowell, Collier, and Macmillan, 1968.

37. Spindler, L. *Culture Change and Modernization: Mini-Models and Case Studies.* Prospect Heights, Ill.: Waveland Press, 1977.

38. Whyte, W. F. *Street Corner Society: The Social Structure of an Italian Slum.* Chicago: University of Chicago Press, 1943.

Acknowledgments

Altbach, Philip G. "Problems and Possibilities: The U.S. Academic Profession." *Studies in Higher Education* 20 (1995): 27–44. Reprinted with the permission of Carfax Publishing Company.

Finkelstein, Martin J. "The Emergence of the Modern Academic Role." In *The American Academic Profession: A Synthesis of Social Scientific Inquiry Since World War II* (Columbus: Ohio State University Press, 1984): 7–31. Reprinted with the permission of Ohio State University Press.

Baldwin, Roger G. and Robert T. Blackburn. "The Academic Career as a Developmental Process: Implications for Higher Education." *Journal of Higher Education* 52 (1981): 598–614. Reprinted with the permission of Ohio State University Press.

Gappa, Judith M. and David W. Leslie. "Employment Profiles of Part-Timers." In *The Invisible Faculty: Improving the Status of Part-Timers in Higher Education.* (San Francisco: Josey-Bass, 1993): 45–64. Reprinted with the permission of Jossey-Bass Publishers Inc.

Altbach, Philip G. and Lionel S. Lewis. "Professorial Attitudes—An International Survey." *Change* 27:6 (1995): 51–57. Reprinted with the permission of the Helen Dwight Reid Education Foundation. Copyright 1995. Published by Heldref Publications.

Clark, Burton R. "The Ties of Association." In *The Academic Life: Small Worlds, Different Worlds* (Princeton, N.J.: Carnegie Foundation for the Advancement of Teaching, 1987): 233–54. Reprinted with the permission of the Carnegie Foundation for the Advancement of Teaching.

Tierney, William G. and Robert A. Rhoads. "Conceptualizing Faculty Socialization." In *Faculty Socialization as a Cultural Process: A Mirror of Institutional Commitment*, ASHE-ERIC Higher Education Report No. 93-6 (Washington, D.C.: George Washington University, School of Education and Human Development, 1994): 21–31. Reprinted with the permission of the George Washington University Graduate School of Education and Human Development. Please call the ERIC Clearinghouse on Higher Education at 1-800-773-3742 for a complementary Publication Catalog of other titles available in the ASHE-ERIC Higher Education Report Series.

Van Alstyne, William. "Tenure: A Summary, Explanation, and 'Defense.'" *AAUP Bulletin* 57 (1971): 328–33. Reprinted with the permission of the American Association of University Professors.

Bowen, Howard R. and Jack H. Schuster. "The Flow of Faculty to and from Academe." In *American Professors: A National Resource Imperiled* (New York: Oxford University Press, 1986): 165–87. Reprinted with the permission of Oxford University Press.

Burke, Dolores L. "Change in the Academic Marketplace: Faculty Mobility in the 1980s." *The Review of Higher Education* 11 (1988): 311–17. Reprinted with the permission of *The Review of Higher Education*.

Fairweather, James S. "The Value of Teaching, Research, and Service." In *NEA 1994 Almanac of Higher Education* (Washington, D.C.: National Education Association, 1994): 39–58. Reprinted with the permission of the National Education Association.

Boice, Robert. "New Faculty as Teachers." *Journal of Higher Education* 62 (1991): 150–73. Reprinted with the permission of Ohio State University Press.

Blackburn, Robert T. and Janet H. Lawrence. "Faculty Research." In *Faculty at Work: Motivation, Expectation, Satisfaction* (Baltimore: Johns Hopkins University Press, 1995): 115–76. Reprinted with the permission of Johns Hopkins University Press.

Clark, Shirley M. and Mary Corcoran. "Perspectives on the Professional Socialization of Women Faculty: A Case of Accumulative Disadvantage." *Journal of Higher Education* 57 (1986): 20–43. Reprinted with the permission of Ohio State University Press.

Lomperis, Ana María Turner. "Are Women Changing the Nature of the Academic Profession?" *Journal of Higher Education* 61 (1990): 643–77. Reprinted with the permission of Ohio State University Press.

McGinnis, Robert and J. Scott Long. "Entry into Academia: Effects of Stratification, Geography and Ecology." In *Academic Labor Markets and Careers*. Edited by David W. Breneman and Ted I.K. Youn (Philadelphia: Falmer Press, 1988): 28–51. Reprinted with the permission of Falmer Press.

Reynolds, Anne. "Charting the Changes in Junior Faculty: Relationships among Socialization, Acculturation, and Gender." *Journal of Higher Education* 63 (1992): 637–52. Reprinted with the permission of Ohio State University Press.